Concurrent and Real-time Programming

Manuel I. Capel

Concurrent and Real-time Programming

Principles and Applications

Manuel I. Capel
Department of Computer Languages and Systems
University of Granada
Granada, Spain

ISBN 978-3-031-85232-9   ISBN 978-3-031-85233-6   (eBook)
https://doi.org/10.1007/978-3-031-85233-6

This book is an enlarged version of the original Spanish edition: "Programación Concurrente y en Tiempo Real" by Manuel I. Capel, © Ibergarceta Publicaciones, Madrid, Spain 2022.

© The Editor(s) (if applicable) and The Author(s), under exclusive license to Springer Nature Switzerland AG 2026

This work is subject to copyright. All rights are solely and exclusively licensed by the Publisher, whether the whole or part of the material is concerned, specifically the rights of reprinting, reuse of illustrations, recitation, broadcasting, reproduction on microfilms or in any other physical way, and transmission or information storage and retrieval, electronic adaptation, computer software, or by similar or dissimilar methodology now known or hereafter developed.
The use of general descriptive names, registered names, trademarks, service marks, etc. in this publication does not imply, even in the absence of a specific statement, that such names are exempt from the relevant protective laws and regulations and therefore free for general use.
The publisher, the authors and the editors are safe to assume that the advice and information in this book are believed to be true and accurate at the date of publication. Neither the publisher nor the authors or the editors give a warranty, expressed or implied, with respect to the material contained herein or for any errors or omissions that may have been made. The publisher remains neutral with regard to jurisdictional claims in published maps and institutional affiliations.

This Springer imprint is published by the registered company Springer Nature Switzerland AG
The registered company address is: Gewerbestrasse 11, 6330 Cham, Switzerland

If disposing of this product, please recycle the paper.

*I give this gift to my children, Ruth Matilde and Manuel,
as a thank you for the time I spent away from them
because of work.
It shows that we can achieve anything if we try.*

Preface

This book provides a comprehensive exploration of the principles of concurrent programming, focusing on both theoretical foundations and practical implementation techniques. Written for students, educators and professionals, the book covers essential concurrency concepts, including process synchronisation, communication and distributed systems.

Content Overview

The book is divided into four chapters, each building on the fundamental aspects of concurrent and parallel programming. Topics range from basic concepts such as thread creation and process management to more advanced topics such as interprocess communication, synchronisation mechanisms and memory management.

Chapter 1 introduces concurrent programming, which involves executing multiple processes simultaneously, in contrast to the linear sequence of instructions in sequential programming. It explains key concepts such as:

- Processes: Independent execution units that perform tasks concurrently.
- Concurrency Benefits: Improves efficiency, especially for tasks with frequent input/output operations, and allows parallelism even with limited processor cores.
- Concurrency Model: Describes how concurrent programs handle synchronization, communication and execution order using techniques like mutual exclusion and synchronization primitives.
- Process Creation: Covers methods like fork/join and POSIX threads, which enable dynamic process creation and concurrent task execution.

The chapter highlights how concurrent programs better reflect real-world systems where multiple activities happen simultaneously, enhancing program efficiency and responsiveness.

Chapter 2 explores key process synchronization mechanisms in concurrent programming, focusing on both mutual exclusion problems and the use of monitors as a high-level solution for managing shared resources, such as the following:

- Mutual Exclusion: The chapter begins by addressing the classical problem of ensuring that multiple processes do not access critical sections simultaneously, introducing solutions like busy waiting and software algorithms like Dekker's and Peterson's algorithms, which ensure that processes enter critical sections safely and without conflicts.
- Monitors: A significant portion of the chapter focuses on monitors, a powerful abstraction that simplifies synchronization in concurrent systems. Monitors encapsulate shared resources and provide built-in mechanisms for ensuring that only one process at a time can be executed within a critical section, thus preventing race conditions.
- Java Monitors: The chapter also highlights how Java implements monitors through synchronized methods and blocks, using constructs like `wait()`, `notify()` and synchronized. Java's approach to concurrency makes it easier to ensure thread safety and manage access to critical sections in multi-threaded programs.

This chapter combines foundational algorithms for process synchronization with advanced programming constructs like monitors, emphasizing how they provide efficient, structured solutions to concurrency challenges in modern programming.

Chapter 3 focuses on message passing systems as a fundamental approach for communication and synchronization in distributed systems, where processes cannot share memory. Key concepts of this chapter include:

- Message Passing: Processes communicate by sending and receiving messages instead of using shared memory. This is essential in distributed systems where processes are located on different machines or cores.
- Rendezvous: This is a form of synchronous communication where both the sending and receiving processes must be ready at the same time to exchange messages.
- Communicating Sequential Processes (CSP): CSP is a formal model for designing distributed systems. It uses guarded commands and selective wait constructs to allow non-deterministic communication between processes. The CSP model emphasizes that processes interact strictly through message passing, avoiding shared variables and synchronizing only through defined communication events.
- Remote Method Invocation (RMI): RMI allows objects in different processes (even on different machines) to interact through method calls as if they were in the same memory space.

The chapter illustrates the importance of message passing for efficient distributed computing, especially in systems without shared memory, and provides models like CSP and technologies like RMI to facilitate structured, reliable communication between processes.

Chapter 4 dives into the scheduling mechanisms of Real-Time Systems (RTS), focusing on how tasks are prioritized and scheduled to meet strict timing constraints. Key topics in this chapter include:

- Rate Monotonic Scheduling (RMS): RMS is widely used for periodic tasks, ensuring schedulability by maintaining a processor utilization threshold based on the number of tasks. The chapter discusses how RMS provides sufficient but not always necessary condition for task scheduling.
- Priority Inversion: The chapter explores strategies to mitigate priority inversion, such as the Priority Inheritance Protocol, where a lower-priority task temporarily inherits the higher priority of the blocked task, reducing blocking time and improving system responsiveness.
- Sporadic and Aperiodic Tasks: Unlike periodic tasks, sporadic tasks occur irregularly but with a guaranteed minimum interval between activations. Aperiodic tasks, on the other hand, have flexible deadlines. The chapter introduces sporadic servers and aperiodic servers, which handle these tasks by reserving processor time, ensuring that they do not interfere with the critical timing of periodic tasks.

The chapter emphasizes the importance of using scheduling techniques, such as RMS, and advanced protocols like Priority Inheritance to optimize system performance, manage sporadic and aperiodic tasks and prevent issues like priority inversion in real-time systems.

The book also includes detailed case studies and exercises that allow the reader to practice and consolidate their understanding of the theoretical concepts discussed.

Classroom Use

This book is designed to be used as a primary or supplementary textbook for undergraduate and graduate courses in concurrent programming, operating systems and distributed systems. Its well-structured layout, comprehensive case studies and real-world examples make it an ideal teaching resource.

Introductory courses: For beginning students, instructors can focus on the foundational chapters that introduce the fundamentals of concurrency, allowing students to gain a solid understanding of thread management and basic synchronisation techniques.

Advanced courses: More advanced courses can explore the later chapters on distributed systems and message-passing libraries (MPI). Students can work on larger projects that involve solving concurrent problems and implementing algorithms that optimise parallel execution.

Lecturers are encouraged to use the many examples in the book as classroom exercises. Each example is carefully designed to illustrate critical concepts in concurrent programming. In addition, the exercises at the end of each chapter provide a solid foundation for class discussions, assignments and exams. The code examples provided in Java and C make the book highly relevant to computer science students working with these widely used programming languages.

Acknowledgements

I would like to express my gratitude to Computer Science and Mathematics degree students at the *ETS de Ingenierías Informática y Telecomunicación* of the University of Granada. Without the experience gained in classes over many years and the opportunity to apply the material presented here, this work would never have been published.

Granada, Spain Manuel I. Capel
October 2024

Contents

1 Introduction to Concurrent Programming 1
   1.1 Basic Concepts and Motivation for the Study of Concurrent
        Programming 1
   1.2 Concurrent Programming Abstract Model 3
        1.2.1 The Abstract Model of Concurrency 4
        1.2.2 Hardware Considerations 7
   1.3 Mutual Exclusion and Synchronisation 8
        1.3.1 Synchronisation 9
        1.3.2 Process Creation 10
   1.4 Low-Level Synchronisation Mechanisms in Shared Memory 16
        1.4.1 Disable Interruptions 17
        1.4.2 Locks 17
        1.4.3 Semaphores 24
   1.5 Properties of Concurrent Systems 32
        1.5.1 Safety Properties 32
        1.5.2 Liveness Properties 33
        1.5.3 Fairness Properties 34
   1.6 Hoare's Program Logic and Concurrent Programs Verification 35
        1.6.1 Options Available for Testing Concurrent Software 36
        1.6.2 Program Verification Based on the Axiomatic Semantics
                of a Programming Language 37
        1.6.3 Verification of Concurrent and Synchronisation Statements 42
        1.6.4 Verifying Concurrent Programs Using Global Invariants 45
   1.7 Exercises 49
        1.7.1 Solved Exercises 49
        1.7.2 Proposed Exercises 62

2 Algorithms and Process Synchronisation Mechanisms Based on Shared Memory ... 69
2.1 Introduction to the Two-Process Mutual Exclusion Problem ... 69
2.1.1 How to Solve the Mutual Exclusion Problem ... 70
2.1.2 Verification of Dekker's Algorithm Correction Properties ... 76
2.2 A Simple Solution to the Mutual Exclusion Problem: The Peterson Algorithm ... 77
2.2.1 Solution for Two Processes ... 77
2.2.2 Solution for N Processes ... 79
2.3 Monitors as a High-Level Concurrent Programming Mechanism ... 83
2.3.1 The Definition and Characteristics of a Monitor ... 83
2.3.2 Synchronisation Operations and Monitor Signals ... 86
2.3.3 Semantics of Monitor Signalling Mechanism ... 88
2.3.4 Priority Condition Variables ... 91
2.4 Programming Languages with Monitors ... 92
2.4.1 Concurrent Programming in Java ... 93
2.4.2 Programming with Java Monitors ... 97
2.5 Implementation of Monitors ... 103
2.5.1 Implementation of the SX Signals ... 103
2.5.2 Implementation of SU Signals ... 105
2.5.3 Equivalence of the Different Types of Monitor Signals for Implementation ... 107
2.6 The Problem of Nesting Monitor Calls ... 111
2.7 Verification of Monitors ... 113
2.7.1 Axioms and Inference Rules for Monitors ... 113
2.7.2 Rules for Verification of SC Signals ... 116
2.8 Exercises ... 117
2.8.1 Solved Exercises ... 117
2.8.2 Proposed Exercises ... 154

3 Message Passing Based Systems ... 161
3.1 Introduction to Distributed Programming ... 161
3.1.1 Multiprocessors and Multiprocessing ... 162
3.1.2 Implementation of the Multiprocessing Models ... 165
3.2 Basic Mechanisms in Message-Passing Systems ... 168
3.2.1 Blocking Message-Passing Operations ... 171
3.2.2 Non-blocking Message-Passing Operations ... 174
3.3 Distributed Programming Models and Languages ... 176
3.3.1 Selective Wait with Guarded Commands ... 177
3.3.2 The CSP Model of Distributed Programming ... 180
3.4 Verification of Distributed Programs with Communicating Processes ... 190
3.4.1 Axioms, Interference Rules and Satisfiability Proofs ... 191
3.4.2 Communication Axioms ... 192

   3.4.3 Satisfaction Rule for the Synchronous Communication
     Between the Processes.................................... 192
   3.4.4 Communication Orders with Guarded Commands 194
   3.4.5 Demonstration of Non-interference........................ 196
 3.5 Message-Passing Libraries.. 199
   3.5.1 Functions of MPI.. 201
 3.6 High-Level Mechanisms for Programming Distributed Systems 211
   3.6.1 The Remote Call Operation................................ 212
   3.6.2 Remote Procedure/Method Call............................ 213
   3.6.3 Model Based on Synchronisation with Rendezvous 217
 3.7 Exercises 221
   3.7.1 Solved Exercises 222
   3.7.2 Proposed Exercises 255

4 Real-Time Systems 261
 4.1 Introduction to Real-Time Systems 261
   4.1.1 Classification of RTS..................................... 263
   4.1.2 Measurement of Time 264
   4.1.3 Timers and Delays....................................... 266
   4.1.4 Waiting Time Limits 268
 4.2 Simple Real-Time Task Model 269
   4.2.1 Simple Task Model Characteristics 269
   4.2.2 Temporal Attributes Associated with a Task 270
 4.3 Periodic Task Scheduling with Prioritisation........................ 272
   4.3.1 Rate Monotonic Scheduling............................... 273
   4.3.2 Test of Schedulability 274
   4.3.3 Schedulability Tests for EDF Based on Processor Utilisation..... 278
 4.4 General Models of Real-Time Tasks 279
   4.4.1 Maximum Response Times Shorter Than the Task Period 280
   4.4.2 Interactions Between Real-Time Tasks 281
   4.4.3 Non-preemptive Critical Section 283
   4.4.4 Priority Inheritance Protocol 285
   4.4.5 Priority Ceiling Protocol 287
 4.5 Scheduling Analysis of Aperiodic and Sporadic Tasks 289
   4.5.1 Background Server....................................... 290
   4.5.2 Aperiodic Polling Server 291
   4.5.3 Deferred Server Approach for Efficient Aperiodic
     Task Handling 292
   4.5.4 Scheduling Analysis..................................... 293
 4.6 Exercises 296
   4.6.1 Solved Exercises 296
   4.6.2 Proposed Exercises 301

Bibliography 307

Introduction to Concurrent Programming

1.1 Basic Concepts and Motivation for the Study of Concurrent Programming

A sequential program is a set of data definitions and instructions executed in a single sequence, linear sequence. In contrast, a concurrent program is written in a high-level programming language that specifies two or more independent execution units, which we will call processes. These units cooperate to perform useful work, which is essential for the progress of the program's computations, which is their main task.

A process should be understood as an abstract, dynamic and active software entity. It executes instructions and transitions through different states[1]. It is important to note that a set of instructions by itself cannot be considered a process. Therefore, the older definition of a concurrent process as "a sequential program in execution", found in some old operating system texts, is misleading.

For a computer processor to manage a process, it must have access to the process's state at any given time. A process is not only the independent execution of a sequence of instructions, it also includes its current state and its capacity to interact with the environment of the program. The state of a process integrates a set of values that define it at each point during execution. These values are stored in the processor's registers and in system memory.

To manage a process, the processor needs to know the values of certain processor's registers: the program counter (PC), the stack pointer (SP), and the heap memory (Heap). It also must handle data related to devices accessed by the process, such as files and any

---

[1] For now, we will understand the concept of program state as the set of values of visible and invisible variables: program counter (PC), stack pointer (SP) at each differentiated moment of our program execution.

other resources it owns. These values must be protected from competitive or uncontrolled access by other concurrent processes.

> In a concurrent program, there may be many instruction execution sequences with, at least, one independent control flow or execution *thread* for each of the processes running in it.

From the point of view of the operating system, a process is characterised by a memory area divided into several zones (Fig. 1.1). These zones include the sequence of instructions to be executed, a fixed-size data area used by global or static variables, the stack (a variable-size area for local variables of procedure parameters) and a dynamic area called heap memory, which holds non-statically allocated variables (i.e., variables created, allocated and destroyed before the process terminates).

> In programs containing many IO-bound or message-receiving instructions, exception handling, signal processing, …, the processor time utilisation of any concurrent program containing such instructions is much better than of an equivalent sequential program, i.e., one that would have been programmed to perform the same tasks or achieve the same results, but with a single execution sequence of instructions.

If the execution platform where the program runs has fewer cores or independent processing units than the number of processes in the program, the control flows of multiple processes are interleaved and form an execution sequence for each core. This interleaving maintains the logical parallelism of the program, regardless of how many processors are executing the code concurrently. As a result, concurrent programs are more efficient than sequential ones because they allow the advancement of multiple threads of control to progress simultaneously. This setup also prevents processes with frequent input and output operations from slowing down other processes that require more computation. In general, the existence of concurrent processes in programs avoids delays in processor execution by

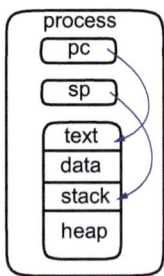

Fig. 1.1 Model of concurrent process

allowing computations to continue while other processes wait for data from the program's environment.

Furthermore, concurrent programs are fundamental for simulation applications. The concurrent programming paradigm represents real-world systems more accurately than sequential programming. Physical systems typically consist of multiple activities running in parallel, and each activity can be simulated more naturally with an independent concurrent process. In contrast, a sequential program, which follows a one-dimensional cycle of polling signals or messages sent by the program's environment, is less representative of real-world systems.

Hence, we use terms like "concurrent" and "concurrency" to describe the potential for parallel execution in any program written in modern programming languages. Concurrency refers to the potential for parallelism within certain code units, algorithms, application or systems—logically independent of the number of processors or cores provided by the system's hardware.

> We can define concurrent programming as the set of programming notations and techniques used to express the potential parallelism of programs and, consequently, to be able to solve the synchronisation and communication problems of the processes that make up such programs.

1.2 Concurrent Programming Abstract Model

Concurrent programming is not just a programming paradigm or model but primarily an abstract model of computation. It expresses the potential parallelism of computer programs at an appropriate level of abstraction[2], independent of how that parallelism is implemented at the architectural level of a computer system.

Good concurrent languages should provide useful primitives to address synchronisation and communication between concurrent processes, allowing the same code to run on different computer architectures. While this is an ideal goal, the abstract model of concurrency we will introduce represents significant progress towards the achievement of this maximal objective. It provides a set of tools that help conceptualise and design concurrent programs, allowing us to reason about solutions to synchronisation and communication problems. This model simplifies programming by enabling the use of high-level instructions for communication and synchronisation, without relying on system calls or machine-level code. In addition, this abstraction ensures that programs will be portable between

---

[2] A level of abstraction that allows solving problems that are of interest to us in the field of concurrency, without getting bogged down in the details of the implementation of parallelism at the microprocessor level.

Fig. 1.2 Interleaving sequences of two-process atomic instructions

P_1	P_2	possible sequences
I_{11}	I_{21}	$I_{11}\ I_{11}\ I_{11}\ \ldots$
I_{12}	I_{22}	$I_{21}\ I_{12}\ I_{21}\ \ldots$
I_{13}	I_{23}	$I_{12}\ I_{21}\ I_{22}\ \ldots$
I_{14}	I_{24}	$I_{22}\ I_{13}\ I_{23}\ \ldots$
$\ldots$	$\ldots$	$I_{13}\ I_{22}\ I_{12}\ \ldots$
$\ldots$	$\ldots$	$\ldots\ \ldots\ \ldots.$

architectures. The only requirement is that the appropriate compiler for the concurrent programming language exists for the platform being used.

1.2.1 The Abstract Model of Concurrency

The abstract model of concurrent programming is based on five key principles or axioms:

1. Atomicity and Instruction Interleaving
2. Ensuring Consistency of Program Data After Concurrent Access
3. Unrepeatability of Any Sequence of Atomic Instructions
4. Independence of Relative Speeds of Processes During Program Execution
5. Processes Finite Progress Hypothesis

1.2.1.1 Atomicity and Instruction Interleaving

From a concurrent program written in a compiled programming language, it is possible to derive a corresponding set of instructions at the assembly level, as shown in Fig. 1.2.

This instruction level typically corresponds to the machine or assembly language instruction set. Each instruction is executed atomically, meaning that once it starts, it runs to completion without being interrupted by a context switch or any system-level call. This indivisibility guarantees that concurrent execution, whether achieved through real parallelism[3] or logical parallelism (using time-sharing), does not affect the results of the program; only the performance or speed is impacted.

Figure 1.2 illustrates a possible sequence of instructions generated by a concurrent program P scheduling two processes. Each process's atomic instructions are represented as $\{I_{1x}\}$ and $\{I_{2x}\}$. The set of all possible interleaved sequences of these atomic instructions defines the observable behaviour of the program P. Each execution of P results in one of these sequences that define its behavior[4], but which specific sequence occurs cannot be

---

[3] True parallelism means simultaneous execution of instructions by a different processor or multiprocessor cores.
[4] The set of all interleaving sequences of atomic instructions that are generated from the program processes

1.2 Concurrent Programming Abstract Model

predicted or influenced directly. This fundamental characteristic is often referred to as nondeterminism in concurrent programs.

This model of concurrent program execution describes parallelism at the logical level, independent of the specific hardware architecture on which the program code was ultimately executed.

1.2.1.2 Ensuring Consistency of Program Data After Concurrent Access

The concurrent execution of two single atomic instructions accessing the same memory address must produce the same results, whether both instructions are executed in real parallelism or logical parallelism, where they are executed sequentially, one after the other, but in an arbitrary and unpredictable order. Consistency in data access means that after both processes have completed their operations, the memory representation of the data must remain in a state consistent with the data type to which they belong. Figure 1.3 illustrates that the result could be 1 or 2 (without predicting which), but the value will remain consistent with the variable's definition and its allowed values, as specified in the program.

In Fig. 1.3, since instructions I_1 and I_2 access the location of the processor's accumulator registers sequentially, the final value of variable x is not predetermined. However, it will coincide with the last value assigned, as x is assigned twice by different processes during code execution in an unpredictable order. If the shared variable's memory location were accessed simultaneously without the contention managed by the memory bus arbiter, data could become corrupted, leading to incorrect values in x.

This hypothesis of the abstract model assumes that concurrent memory access will not corrupt data, which is supported by the memory access control hardware in real computer systems. This consistency in data values after simultaneous access to the same address is guaranteed by the memory controller's bus arbiter in computers.

1.2.1.3 Unrepeatability of Any Sequence of Atomic Instructions

The number of possible interleaved sequences of atomic instructions in a concurrent program is extremely large, making it quite unlikely that two successive executions of the program will follow the exact same sequence of atomic instructions. This unpredictability makes debugging and verifying the correctness of concurrent programs very difficult, leading to the emergence of transient errors (errors that occur in some execution sequences but not in others). These errors are difficult to detect and fix in the program code.

```
P₁                      P₂                          interleaving sequences
I₁:x: = 1               I₂:x: = 2                   I₁:<store x,1>   I₂:<store x,2>
I₁:<store x,1>          I₂:<store x,2>              I₂:<store x,2>   I₁:<store x,1>
...                     ...                         {x=2}            {x=1}
```

Fig. 1.3 Sequentialisation of the execution of concurrent processes in accessing shared variables by the order imposed by the hardware memory bus controller

To address the tendency of transient errors to arise in concurrent software, more robust methods are required. As we will discuss later, formal methods, with the rigour of mathematical logic, are essential for verifying the correctness of concurrent programs and for identifying and eliminating transient errors that may surreptitiously appear during the execution.

1.2.1.4 Independence of Relative Speeds of Processes During Program Execution

The correctness of concurrent programs must not depend on the relative execution speed of one process compared to others. If this requirement were not met, the following issues could arise when running a concurrent program on different computing platforms:

- Lack of portability, if assumptions about the process execution speed are made, the program may be not portable across platforms. The program might fail to function correctly on platforms with different processor characteristics.
- Race conditions occurrence, erroneous results may occur if processes concurrently access shared variables or code sections. If the correctness of a program depended on process speed, countless transient errors may occur even with slight changes in process context.

Figure 1.4 shows two processes, P_1 and P_2; both access and modify a shared variable `data` (initially 0). Depending on the order and speed of execution, data could end up as either value: +1, 0, -1, with no way to predict the final result. If one of these outcomes is incorrect according to the program's specification, we identify this as a race condition between the two processes.

An exception to this model exists in real-time applications, where timing and execution order are critical. In these cases, processes have different priority levels and privileges, which influence their execution speed. These programs, used in safety-critical systems, deviate from the typical abstract model of concurrency.

Lastly, the abstract model of concurrent programming assumes that all processes will complete in finite time. Without this assumption, correctness properties like process liveness cannot be guaranteed, as they would then depend on the execution platform.

1.2.1.5 Processes Finite Progress Hypothesis

To verify the correctness of concurrent programs, all processes must be able to execute and continuously make progress in their computations. This progress can be understood at two levels:

Fig. 1.4 Example of race condition between two processes

```
Process P1:      Process P2:
  a:= data;        b:= data;
  a:= a+1;         b:= b-1;
  data:= a;        data:= b;
```

1.2 Concurrent Programming Abstract Model

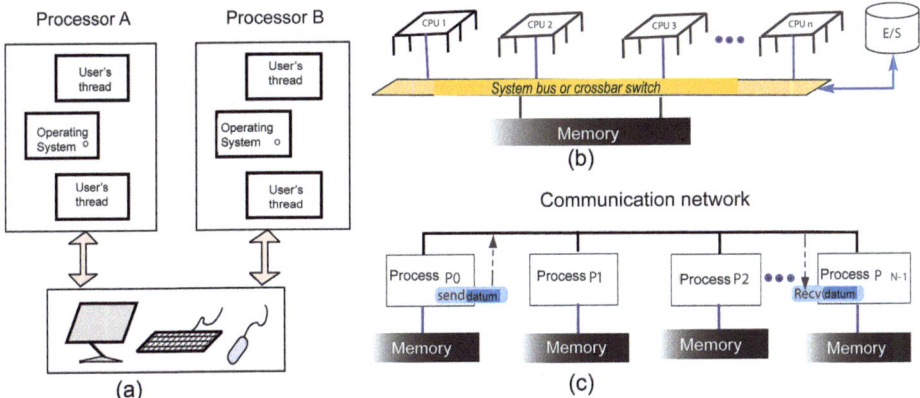

Fig. 1.5 System architectures with different degrees of parallelism: (**a**) multi-core processor (**b**) multiprocessor (**c**) multi-computer

1. Global progress: if at least one process is ready to execute, it must be allowed to run, provided the program has not entered a deadlock situation. In other words, eventually[5], some process will be allowed to execute in a correct concurrent program.
2. Local progress: any process that starts executing a section of code must eventually complete that section.

In summary, we can say that the finite progress hypothesis is defined as follows: there should be no situation during a program's execution where a process arbitrarily stops for an indefinite amount of time. In other words, no hidden condition (such as counters, registers, etc.) should cause a process to halt its progress indefinitely along any sequence of states in the program's execution.

1.2.2 Hardware Considerations

Depending on their computer architecture, computer systems currently implement concurrency according to three general models, which can also be hybridised, as shown in Fig. 1.5.

General multiprocessors capable of parallel computing can be classified according to the number of processors and their distribution: (a) multi-core processors represent a type of architecture in which there are usually many more processes than cores (independent physical execution units) and parallelism has to be modelled by interleaving multiple threads of execution; this model can be understood as a category of systems in which concurrency in the execution of processes can be achieved with or without real parallelism; (b) multiprocessors will always provide real parallelism, and this type of multiprocessor is usually designed to be programmed with languages or libraries that have specific

---
[5] That is, at some point in the future that cannot be postponed for a long time

instructions that efficiently translate into parallel instructions for a particular multiprocessor architecture, i.e., the program code will execute several elementary instructions simultaneously in different processors, and there will be a common memory through which the processes can communicate which each other at high speed. That is, the program code will simultaneously execute several elementary instructions in different processors. (c) Multicomputers are distributed multiprocessors in which each processor or physical execution unit has an independent memory that is not shared with the others, so that to communicate processes located in different processors, it is necessary to use a network or high-speed interconnection that allows a high level of scalability[6], and they usually have a more complicated programming notation than any of the previously introduced systems.

1.3 Mutual Exclusion and Synchronisation

Mutual exclusion ensures that a set of statements in a process's code, shared with other processes in the program, is executed in an indivisible or atomic manner. In other words, no more than one process in the program is allowed to execute a block of these statements at the same time[7]. A block (or section) of instructions that can only be executed by a single process is called a *critical section*.

Using the appropriate language programming primitives, if two or more processes attempt to execute a critical section, only one will succeed at a time, while the other must wait until that process finishes before trying again.

An example of mutual exclusion access is resource allocation such as file backups, plotters, printers, etc. managed by an operating system for various client processes. Mutual exclusive access to these resources is necessary because if the jobs from different user processes were mixed, the output produced by the shared device would become unusable.

The acquisition and restitution protocols are instruction blocks designed to ensure that the mutual exclusion condition is met whenever a process accesses a critical section. The acquisition protocol decides, in case of contention between multiple processes, which one enters the critical section first; the others must wait until the process that entered first has finished executing CS instructions. The restitution protocol allows a new process, which may have been waiting, to enter the critical section once it becomes free again. The typical structure of a process containing a critical section is as follows.

> Rest of instructions
> Acquisition protocol
> <Sentences in Critical Section (CS)>
> Restitution protocol.

---

[6] Integration of many new cores/processors depending on the computational power required to execute an algorithm, without loss of performance.

[7] It may not match a program block, as understood in most programming languages.

1.3.1 Synchronisation

In concurrent programs, processes need to communicate during execution to work collaborating on a common task. As mentioned earlier, communication between processes can occur via shared variables or messages, depending on the type of parallelism supported by the platform running the concurrent program. This inter-process communication creates the need for synchronisation between processes during execution.

There are two basic scenarios of synchronisation between processes: (a) Conditional synchronisation, which involves pausing the execution of a process until a specific condition is met. At a lower system level, this means the process cannot be allowed to change its state—i.e., it cannot execute the next instruction—until the condition, which is usually evaluated from the program's variable values, is satisfied. (b) Mutual exclusion, a special synchronisation condition, is crucial when a process must wait to enter a critical section until it becomes available. This prevents simultaneous access to a shared resource, avoiding potential conflicts.

The bounded circular buffer model shown in Fig. 1.6 is a classic example illustrating the difference between the two forms of synchronisation commonly used in concurrent programs. In this model, producer processes insert data into the circular buffer, and consumer processes remove data from it. The circular buffer is designed to decouple the execution of producer and consumer processes, allowing them to run independently without worrying about buffer overflows or trying to retrieve data from an empty buffer.

For example, if several producer processes run first without any consumer process ready to retrieve the data, the produced data is temporarily stored in the buffer, waiting to be consumed when a consumer process executes. In this bounded circular buffer implementation, mutual exclusion synchronisation ensures that no producer and consumer

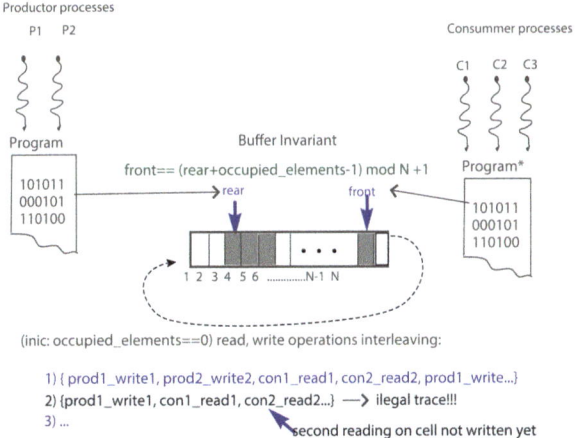

Fig. 1.6 Circular buffer of N elements in the concurrent producer-consumer program example

access the buffer at the same time, preventing race conditions that could occur if multiple processes try to access the same buffer element simultaneously[8].

Conditional synchronisation in this scenario ensures that a message inserted into the buffer is not overwritten before being extracted and that data are not inserted into a full buffer or extracted from an empty one. These are examples of transient errors that could occur, such as a consumer process attempting to retrieve data twice after a producer has inserted only one element into an empty buffer, as shown in the sequence labelled "illegal" in Fig. 1.6.

From the point of view of the abstract model of concurrent programming, the role of synchronisation is to limit the possible execution sequences to only those that are considered correct, ensuring the fulfilment of the concurrency properties required by the program.

1.3.2 Process Creation

Early notations in imperative programming languages for expressing the execution of concurrent processes in a program did not include independent process creation and synchronisation primitives. Instead, process creation operation itself implicitly synchronised the program with the termination of processes being created. Modern languages and systems with concurrent programming facilities separate the two concepts and impose a structure to the program and their processes.

The first step in separating process creation was the introduction of a process declaration primitive as a distinct program block within a program. This allowed developers to explicitly declare routines to be executed concurrently, while synchronisation between processes could later be handled explicitly with specific primitives in the rest of the program code.

Process declaration in concurrent programming can be categorised based on their duration during program execution: (a) static process declaration, when a fixed number of processes are declared at the beginning of the program and are activated when the program starts; (b) dynamic process declaration, when a variable number of processes can be declared and activated at any point during program's execution. In this case, it is also possible to eliminate processes that are no longer needed, to save memory and other resources.

The following are examples of programming languages that use one of the above mechanisms, MPI (Message Passing Interface) [42], which defines groups of connected processes within each session[9]. Occam [28] for transputer programming and Concurrent Pascal [8] and Modula [47] use static process creation. The most widely used language that supports dynamic process creation is Ada [5].

---

[8] If such a race condition were to occur with a buffer containing complex elements, a partially written message could be read from the buffer.

[9] Each communicator in MPI provides each process in the declared group with an independent identifier that identifies it within an ordered connection topology.

1.3 Mutual Exclusion and Synchronisation

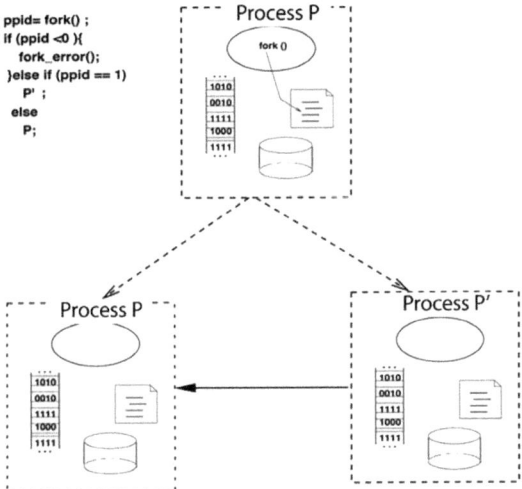

Fig. 1.7 Result of executing one `fork()` operation in UNIX

1.3.2.1 Process Creation by Branching

UNIX operating systems and their variants use an unstructured from of process creation that relies on two basic instructions: `fork()` and `join()`.

The `fork()` command creates a new process by duplicating the calling process's control flow. This results in the execution of a new, concurrent process, running independently of the original program. As shown in Fig. 1.7, when `fork()` is called, a second copy of the program (P′) is created, which is completely independent of the original program (P) that initiated the execution. Both processes (P and P′) continue to run concurrently, with their instructions interleaved.

The `join()` command, on the other hand, allows a process P to wait for another process (P′) to complete its execution before proceeding. In this case, P is the process calling the `join()` operation, and P′ is the target process. Once the `join()` call finishes, we can be certain that the target process has safely terminated.

The semantics of the `join()` operation establishes that it is a null operation if the target process (P′) has already completed when the `join()` is called. This means no unnecessary processor cycles are consumed and no context switches occur in such cases. The advantage of the fork/join mechanism, which branches off a control flow and later waits for it to finish, is that the process calling `join()` is suspended and does not consume CPU cycles until the target process (P′) finishes. This is in contrast to a busy wait loop, where the process would consume cycles unnecessarily while waiting for P′ to finish.

The main advantages of process creation by branching over other mechanisms are that this form is practical and powerful, allowing dynamic, unstructured and very flexible creation of concurrent processes. However, the main drawback is that this unstructured approach can make programs harder to understand. Since `fork()` and `join()` can appear in loops, conditionals or recursive functions, the resulting code can become difficult to debug and verify.

1.3.2.2 Structured Process Creation

The pair of process creation instructions, `cobegin`, `coend`, found in some concurrent languages is considered a structured statement because it clearly defines the start and end of concurrent execution. The `cobegin` instruction initiates the concurrent execution of the following instructions, functions, processes, etc. The block concludes with the `coend` instruction, which ensures that all concurrent operations within the block have completed before proceeding to the next statement in the program.

The statement following the `coend` statement in the previous program fragment will not be executed until all the component statements ($S_1;S_2;...S_n$), which interleave their instructions in an indeterminate command, have completed execution. Thus, the block of code initiated by `cobegin` has a single termination point, where all the concurrent control flows are merged back into one, resuming the control flow that existed before the `cobegin` instruction.

$$\text{cobegin } S_1;S_2;...S_n \text{ coend}$$

The block of code defined between `cobegin` and `coend` is part of the overall program execution and depends on the completion of all concurrent statements within it. As a result, this construct ensures that the code block behaves like a traditional structured block, with a single entry and exit point, thereby maintaining the structure and clarity of the program.

1.3.2.3 POSIX Threads Creation

The independence between the memory areas of processes in UNIX provides implicit protection in the access to program variables, but it is not very flexible when we need to use it to define synchronisation mechanisms in cooperative interactions due to the following drawbacks: (a) the time cost and resource consumption required to perform context switching between multiple UNIX processes is high, (b) the system scheduler can only efficiently manage up to a certain number of processes, (c) the system operations associated with this type of process creation are too slow to use shared synchronisation variables (locks, semaphores, etc.) (d) in addition, the `fork()` statement is an unstructured process creation mechanism, which usually leads to programming errors, as it is sometimes not clear which instance or realisation of the original process is being executed at any given time[10].

---

[10] To distinguish between the instances of the same process, the `fork()` function returns the value 0 if the code being executed at that moment is that of the parent process (the one started the "branching").

1.3 Mutual Exclusion and Synchronisation

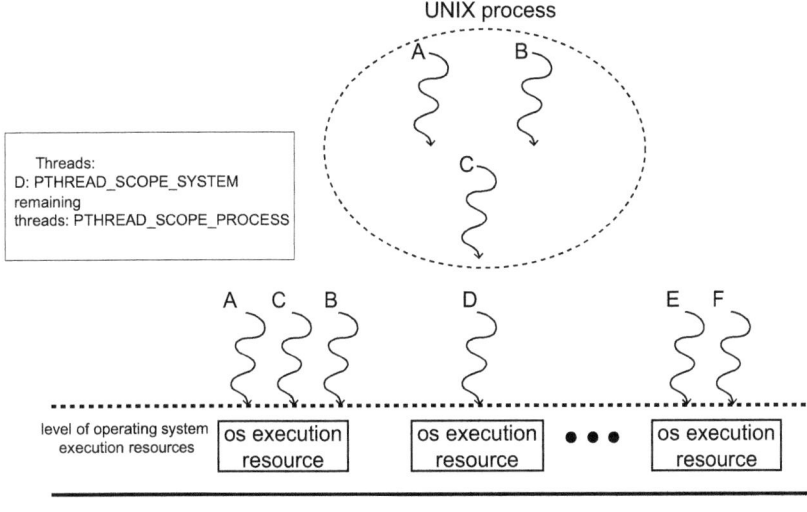

Fig. 1.8 Representation of POSIX 1003.1c thread scheduling (part of POSIX thread package)

One possible solution would be to abandon the protection afforded by the separate address spaces assumed when programming directly with UNIX processes. This leads to the concept of a separate control thread within a process as a scheduling unit. POSIX 1003.1c compliant operating systems—such as Linux—schedule processes and threads (see Fig. 1.8). A process can now contain one or more threads. We can therefore think of a thread as a control flow that shares the text of the process to which it belongs with other threads. Each thread has its own stack, which is initially empty, where it stores its local variables, and shares with other threads the data area, where the global variables and the process heap are located.

1.3.2.4 POSIX Threads Creation Function

Each process has a text or program associated with it, which initially exists as a single thread executing the main() function in C/C++ programming languages. As the program progresses, the thread that originally executed main() can create one or more POSIX threads associated with the same process. A thread that creates another thread specifies a function f() for the latter to execute and continues its own execution after the new thread is started. The latter will run concurrently with the rest of the program threads until the program terminates itself or one of the thread termination conditions included in the POSIX specification is met. Using the POSIX 1003.1c interface, the function that creates and initiates a new thread is as follows.

```
int pthr_create(pthread_t *new_thread, const pthread_attr_t *atr,
                void *(*function_name)(void *), void *args);
```

The parameters of the above function, in order of appearance from left to right, are as follows:

(a) `pthread_t` is an opaque type that acts as a handle to the new thread, i.e., this handle will be used as a reference when the standard operations of the newly created thread need to be called.
(b) `pthread_attr_t` is a creation attribute that is associated with specific functions that modify the internal data structure that stores the initial creation characteristics, including the size of the stack to store thread variables, the policy with which it is scheduled (real time, shared time), whether another thread can wait for it to finish by calling `pthread_join()` or whether it is a system (independent) thread (see Table 1.1).
(c) `void*(*function_name)(void*)` must be replaced with the name of the function to be executed by the thread.
(d) `void *args` is a pointer to the beginning of the list of arguments of the function to be executed by the thread and can be replaced with NULL if it has no arguments.

The causes of termination of a created thread include (a) in the case of threads other than the initial one, when the function specified as the third argument to `pthread_create()` finishes its execution; (b) the created thread calls `pthread_exit()` in its code; (c) its execution is terminated by another thread of the program, which calls `pthread_cancel()`, specifying its identifier; (d) the same UNIX process in whose scope the thread was created terminates by calling `exit()`; and (e) the thread associated with the `main()` function terminates its execution without calling `pthread_exit()`, which would cause it to terminate as another thread of the program.

Example 1.1 As an example of POSIX thread creation, we will implement a simple program that functions as an alarm scheduler, which users of the system can use as a basic agenda. The user interface in this example is minimal, supporting only textual input. The functionality of the program can be summarised as follows:

1. User requests are continuously accepted in a loop.
2. A full line of text is entered for each such request, until either an error is detected or the end of the file is reached in `stdin`.
3. Each input line starts with a number that specifies the number of seconds to wait before displaying the warning message.
4. The rest of the line (up to 64 characters) contains the warning message.

1.3 Mutual Exclusion and Synchronisation

The program is structured into several sections or phases. In the first phase, the following declarations are made:

- Importing necessary libraries
- Declaring a global data type (`control_package`) to store the suspension time (in seconds) and the warning message
- Declaring resources, such as the file pointer (`fp`) where warnings will be logged

```
#include <stdio.h>
#include <errno.h>
#include <pthread.h>

typedef struct control_package{
  int seconds;
  char message[64];
  } control_package_t;

FILE *fp;
```

The `warning()` function contains the code common to all the threads in the program. Each thread calling this function independently suspends itself for the number of seconds specified in its control packet. Once it resumes, the thread prints the string with the user's warning message. The `warning()` function, executed by each thread to handle a warning request, will be programmed as follows:

```
void *warning(void *arg){
        control_package *pct= (control_package_t *) arg;
        int status;
        status= pthread_detach(pthread_self());
        if (status != 0)
            fprintf(stderr, "warning thread\n"), exit(0);
        sleep(pct->seconds);
        fprintf(fp, "(%d)%s\n", pct->seconds, pct->message);
        free(pct);
        return NULL;
}
```

Each thread passes its argument as a pointer to a `control_package_t` structure. By calling `pthread_detach()`, the thread becomes independent of the main thread—meaning, it can use resources independently and continue running even after the main thread terminates. However, the UNIX process containing the thread cannot exit or abort while the thread is active. The `sleep()` function suspends the thread for the number of seconds specified by the user. Once the thread resumes, it logs the suspension time and the warning message to the `fp` file. Afterwards, it releases the dynamically allocated memory for the `control_package` structure.

```
while (1) {
  printf("Warning demand> ");
  if (fgets(line, sizeof(line), stdin) == NULL)
    exit(0);
  if (strlen(line) <= 1) continue;
  int seconds;
  char message[65];
  if (sscanf(line, "%d%64[^\n]", &seconds, message) < 2) {
    if (seconds == -1)
      break;
    else {
      fprintf(stderr, "Bogus input\n");
      continue;
    }
  }
  control_package_t* pcontrol = malloc(sizeof(control_package_t));
  if (pcontrol == NULL) {
    fprintf(stderr, "assign memory to pcontrol\n");
    exit(0);
  }
  pcontrol->seconds = seconds;
  strcpy(pcontrol->message, message);
  status = pthread_create(&thread, NULL, warning, pcontrol);
  if (status != 0) {
    fprintf(stderr, "thread creation warning\n");
    exit(0);
  }
}
```

All the threads created in this program share the same memory address space as the UNIX process running them. The `malloc()` function call creates a dynamic structure of type `control_package_t` containing the values of the timeout and warning message associated with each new user request. A pointer to such a structure is passed as the fourth parameter in the call to `pthread_create()` within the `main()` function. Since the program does not need the main thread to wait for all the warning threads to finish, the threads are created with the detached (non-joinable) thread option. This ensures that the resources used by each thread are automatically returned to the system once the program terminates.

The main thread serves as the execution backbone of the program and runs the `main()` function, which includes the `pthread_create()` call to start the execution of an independent thread in each iteration of an infinite loop. The loop continues until the user enters a blank line or specifies '−1' as the suspension time, which is interpreted as the command to terminate the program. An empty line causes the program to exit by calling `exit(0)`, without waiting for the termination of a warning thread.

1.4 Low-Level Synchronisation Mechanisms in Shared Memory

However, to implement synchronisation mechanisms, some high-level concurrent programming languages use very-low-level instructions that exploit the synchronous nature of the hardware. These mechanisms basically consist of making a concurrent process non-interruptible by using an assembler instruction or by exploiting the fact that the memory hardware can only serve one request at a time, thus sequencing access to certain program

1.4 Low-Level Synchronisation Mechanisms in Shared Memory

variables, which could lead to race conditions between concurrent processes, which are generally undesirable.

1.4.1 Disable Interruptions

In this case, a machine instruction will be used to disable system interrupts[11]. New interrupts are delayed until the active process executes an instruction that re-enables them. If a process succeeds in disabling interrupts before executing a critical section, then it is safe to execute its instructions in a fully exclusive manner. However, other processes that may be critical to the proper functioning of the system would stop executing until interrupts are re-enabled.

The only advantage of this method is that it is very fast, since only one machine-level instruction is needed to turn it on. However, it has the following disadvantages, some of which are unacceptable in system programming:

(a) Once interrupts are disallowed, real-time events cannot be handled, e.g., hardware devices that require a lot of service and update their state with high temporal frequency; long critical sections make it very difficult to achieve good performance in concurrent scheduling if we use this method.
(b) It excludes non-conflicting activities from interleaving their instructions.
(c) When critical sections are executed, interrupts are prohibited.
(d) If critical sections are executed without interrupts, then no clock-dependent instructions or tasks can be scheduled within them.
(e) It has problems of violating the concurrent safety property if nesting of such critical sections were allowed.
(f) Deadlocks can occur if the instruction to re-enable interrupts on exiting a critical section is not scheduled.

1.4.2 Locks

They are based on an explicit memory synchronisation instruction called `test_and_set(TST)`. This function performs two operations as a single atomic operation, i.e., it cannot be interrupted by interleaving instructions until it is finished: First,

---

[11] Obviously, we are mainly referring to the interruption caused by the rescheduling of concurrent processes, for example, by round-robin, since hardware interrupts cannot be inhibited without stopping the computer from running.

reads the value of the synchronisation variable. Then, it sets a value for this variable. Then it gives you the value that it read in the first operation it did on the synchronisation variable.

Therefore, since it is not allowed, during the execution of the atomic function `test_and_set()`, to execute any instruction of another process in the middle of the execution of the two previous operations, a process can read and modify the value of a synchronisation variable which would force the rest of the processes to perform busy waiting[12] until it returns to its initial value.

The use of locks in concurrent programs prevents the occurrence of race conditions between processes accessing shared data, although they can cause an indefinite busy wait for threads waiting to read a particular value of the synchronisation variable, which is favourable for them to continue executing the rest of their instructions.

In order to use the locks in synchronisation efficiently and safely, the `test_and_set()` operation must be an operation belonging to the repertoire of low-level instructions of the platform on which the program is executed. However, for didactic purposes, to solve synchronisation problems, without going into unnecessary detail, we could write it as a function of any algorithmic programming language:

```
atomic function test_and_set(var c:boolean): boolean;
  begin
    test_and_set:= c;
    c:= true;
  end;
```

The variables of type Lock take only two values, so in the simulation that we are doing with a high-level function, it is practical to declare them of type Boolean. The use of the mechanism that provides us with the synchronisation variables associated with the locks to solve the problem of access in mutual exclusion of a group of concurrent processes to a critical part of the program requires the programming of two protocols of acquisition and restitution, respectively:

---

[12] Iterating in an empty loop until the value of the variable changes. It is called busy waiting because it consumes cycles by iterating until the condition of the loop changes.

1.4 Low-Level Synchronisation Mechanisms in Shared Memory

```
type sync_variable= boolean;
var c: sync_variable:= false;
...
-- Adquisition
procedure SectionBegins(var c: sync_variable);
 begin
   while test_and_set(c) do null;
 end;
-- Critical section of the program to be protected
-- Restitution
procedure SectionEnds(var c: sync_variable);
 begin
   c:= false;
 end;
```

Since each critical section contains a set of shared variables that need to be protected, an independent synchronisation variable is associated with each of these groups. In this way, groups of processes acquiring different locks can interleave their instructions without having to wait for each other.

1.4.2.1 POSIX Locks 1003

If the POSIX interface is used, locks are usually allocated memory either statically as in C programming language:

```
pthread_mutex_t lock;
...
```

Either dynamically by calling the function `malloc()`:

```
pthread_mutex_t *mp;
...
mp=(pthread_mutex_t*)malloc(sizeof(pthread_mutex_t));
    ...
```

Two methods are also used for its initialisation. The first one consists of using an initialiser, which in old POSIX versions only guarantees its operation with statically assigned variables. This restriction has been removed in the latest version of the POSIX standard and can now also be used when the variable is an automatic variable defined in the body of a function:

```
pthread_mutex_t lock= PTHREAD_MUTEX_INITIALIZER;
```

The NULL value will initialise the lock with the default values of its attributes, and the initialisation of this type of variable must be unique for each execution of a program. The second method uses an `init()` function from the `pthread` library:

```
pthread_mutex_init(&lock, &atr);
```

and is used when we need special features of the mutex construction, such as being able to use it recursively or being able to share it between different processes, not just between threads.

The static variant is usually preferable if the conditions of the program allow it; it allows us to write sections of code that are executed at the start of our program much more easily. It is also true that if we enter program's code during its execution that uses `mutex_init()`, we can be sure that the mutex has always been initialised; this is a very useful safety mechanism in a multi-threaded context.

1.4.2.2 Properties of Programs That Use Locks

Locks are an easy mechanism to implement and allow easy verification of programs written with them. It is a synchronisation mechanism that can be used on multiprocessors with shared memory. Unlike disabling the interrupt mechanism, lock operations do not prevent processes from accessing critical unrelated sections at the same time. This means that using this synchronisation primitive in the case of single processors, processes accessing different critical sections can freely interleave their instructions unless other synchronisation instructions, such as semaphore operations, are explicitly programmed in their code. If there are several critical sections in a program, a lock is declared for each of them, in an attempt to encourage as many interleaving as possible and thus optimise the concurrency of the processes' execution.

The most important drawback of locks is that some of the concurrent processes of the program may be marginalised or *starved*, which fail to execute useful instructions because they never manage to read a value of the synchronisation variable that is favourable to them in order to advance in the execution of their calculations and have to do busy wait for an indefinite time, as they might be continuously waiting to acquire the lock. If there are several processes waiting for the synchronisation variable of the lock to change value, it is not possible to know which of them gets access and acquires the lock first.

1.4 Low-Level Synchronisation Mechanisms in Shared Memory

In summary, scheduling concurrent programs with multiple processes using locks will not be very efficient due to the waiting time wasted by processes that do not yet have the lock that will allow them to progress in their computations. In addition, if multiple locks are needed in a program, they would have to be acquired and released in reverse hierarchical order; otherwise, deadlocks may occur.

Example 1.2 As an example of programming with POSIX locks, we will introduce an improvement of the program in the previous Example 1.1, which created a prompt thread for each user request, containing a timeout and the label of the prompt to write to a file. In this new, more efficient version of the program, a single server thread is used to extract the first item from the list of requests. The main thread, whose operation is obtained from the main() function of the program, inserts new requests into the above list, but sorted by the shortest time remaining until the prompt is printed. The request list must be protected by a list_mutex lock, and the server thread will pause for at least 1 s in each iteration to ensure that the main thread has a chance to acquire the lock and insert a new request from the client into the request list. Unlike the first declaration section in Example 1.1, the control_package structure now contains time_t, whose value is the absolute time in seconds since the start of the UNIX epoch at which each request occurs. This allows requests to be ordered globally according to a single timescale. The seconds member of the control_package structure only stores the warning suspension time from the time the user's request occurred.

```
#include <stdio.h>
#include <errno.h>
#include <pthread.h>
#include <time.h>

Typedef struct control_package{
   struct control_package* link;
   time_t time;
   int seconds;
   char message[64];
   } control_package_t;

pthread_mutex_t list_mutex= PTHREAD_MUTEX_INITIALIZER;
control_package_t *list_pet = NULL;

FILE *fp;
```

It would not be sufficient to obtain a complete ordering of the warning requests to store only the seconds until the warning expires, since the server thread would not be able to determine how long each request has remained in the list, and therefore the warnings would not occur in a timely manner according to the stored request.

The behaviour of the specialised server thread is determined by the code of the following function:

```
void *server(void *arg){
  control_package_t *pcontrol;
  int sleep_time;
  int status;
  time_t now;
  while (1) {
    status= pthread_mutex_lock(&list_mutex);
    if (status !=0)
      fprintf(stderr,"Error when locking list_mutex\n"),exit(0);
    pcontrol = (control_package_t*)list_pet;
    if (pcontrol==NULL) sleep_time = 1;
      else{
        list_pet= pcontrol->link;
        now= time(NULL);
        if (pcontrol->time<= now) sleep_time=0;
           else sleep_time = pcontrol->time-now;
      }
    status= pthread_mutex_unlock(&list_mutex);
    if (status !=0)
      fprintf(stderr, "error at unlocking mutex"),exit(0);
    if (sleep_time >0) sleep (sleep_time);
      else sched_yield();
    if (pcontrol != NULL){
      fprintf(fp,"(%d)%s{%ld}\n",pcontrol->seconds, pcontrol->message,
      pcontrol->time);
      free(pcontrol);
    }
  }
}
```

If the list of requests accessed by the `pcontrol` reference is not empty, the server thread extracts its first element and determines the time remaining for the warning to expire. If the warning time has expired, i.e., the expression `pcontrol->time<= now` evaluates to true, then `sleep_time` is set to 0; otherwise, the number of seconds the current warning must wait before being printed must be calculated, and this value is also set to `sleep_time`.

The purpose of calling the `sched_yield()` function of the POSIX thread interface when `sleep_time` is 0 is to give the main thread an opportunity to run and check if it has a pending user entry to add to the list. On the other hand, if `sleep_time` is positive, i.e., the warning time has not yet expired, then the server thread is suspended for the time remaining until that moment. Finally, note that the server thread releases the `list_mutex` lock by calling the function `pthread_mutex_unlock(&list_mutex)`, before suspending.

In order for the main thread to correctly add a new user request to the list, it must have mutually exclusive access to the list of requests, which is guaranteed by having previously acquired the lock by executing

```
pthread_mutex_lock (&list_mutex)
```

The main code of the alarm program with the order list by shorter times is the following:

1.4 Low-Level Synchronisation Mechanisms in Shared Memory

```
int main (int argc, char *argv[]){
  int status; char line[128];
  control_package_t*pcontrol,**ult,*sig;
  pthread_t thread;
  if ((fp= fopen("outputs", "w"))==NULL)
    fprintf(stderr,"Error in the outputfile\n"),exit(0);
  status=pthread_create(&thread,NULL,server,NULL);
  if (status != 0)
    fprintf(stderr,"Error at thread creation"),exit(0);
  while (1){
    printf("Warning petition> ");
    if(fgets(line,sizeof(line),stdin)==NULL) exit (0);
    if (strlen(line) <= 1) continue;
    pcontrol=(control_package_t*)malloc(sizeof(control_package_t));
    if(pcontrol== NULL)
      fprintf(stderr,"by assigning memory to control packet"), exit(0);
    if(sscanf(line,"%d%64[^\n]", &pcontrol->seconds, pcontrol->message)<2){
      if (pcontrol->seconds==-1) break;
         else{printf(stderr,"Bogus input\n");
      free(pcontrol);}
    }
    else{
      pthread_mutex_lock(&list_mutex);
      if (status !=0)
        fprintf(stderr,"Error at lockin mutex"),exit(0);
      pcontrol->time=time(NULL)+pcontrol->seconds;
      ult=  &list_pet;
      sig= *ult;
      while (sig != NULL){
         if (sig->time >= pcontrol->time){
           pcontrol->link = sig; *ult = pcontrol;
         }
         ult = &sig->link;
         sig= sig->link;
      }
      if (sig == NULL) {
        *ult= pcontrol; pcontrol->link= NULL;}
      status= pthread_mutex_unlock(&list_mutex);
      if (status != 0)
        fprintf(stderr,"Error unlocking mutex"),exit(0);
      }
    }
  }
}
```

The above code corresponds to the main thread whose task, in addition to creating the server thread by calling the function pthread_create(...), is to calculate the absolute time at which the warning will be printed by obtaining the current UNIX epoch time with the time(NULL) function and updating the value stored in the time member of the structure control package and then to insert a new pcontrol structure in the request list with the user's request data before the first element of list_pet that has a warning time not shorter than that of this new request. If the entire request list is traversed and no element with a warning time that satisfies the above condition is found, then it is inserted at the last position in the list. Finally, the main thread releases the lock providing mutually exclusive access to the request list.

1.4.3 Semaphores

The semaphore is an abstract data type proposed by Edsger Dijkstra in 1968 for the structured development of multi-user operating systems. Since then, it has been used in concurrent programming as a powerful process synchronisation primitive. Semaphores are usually system primitives designed to synchronise processes through shared memory and are usable in certain high-level programming languages; consequently, if several semaphores are needed in a program, an equivalent number of variables of type semaphore must be declared.

Since mutual exclusion access to a critical section is a special case of synchronisation between processes, semaphore variables can be used both to define critical sections in the programs and to synchronise the concurrent processes that we may have defined. In addition, semaphores introduce only the synchronisation strictly necessary to achieve the maximum interleaving[13] of atomic instructions of a concurrent program; for example, processes using different semaphores can run in parallel, since there would be no synchronisation constraint between these processes at all. Critical sections can therefore be easily nested by simply using different semaphores to access them one after the other. There should also be no possibility of blocking if care is taken not to create permutations when programming the calls to the semaphore operations of the critical sections nested in this code.

1.4.3.1 Definition and Operations on a Semaphore

From an algorithmic perspective, semaphores can also be understood as an abstract data type (ADT), which has only non-negative values defined and for which only three operations are defined:

> *initialisation*:
>   To be executed only once at the beginning of the program; values must be non-negative.
> `wait(s)` or *P(s)*:
> If $s > 0$, then $s := s - 1$
>   Otherwise, exclusively block the process in a queue associated to the semaphore variable s.
> `signal(s)` or *V(s)*:
>   Check if there are blocked processes.
>   If there are, then resume one (not necessarily the one that has been blocked the longest) otherwise assign the semaphore variable: $s := s + 1$

---

[13] That is, they exclude the smallest possible number of interleaving sequences of atomic instructions from the processes; only those that violate the synchronisation condition expressed by the semaphore invariant, which must always be met, are excluded.

There are no further operations defined on semaphore variables, for example, it is not legal to check the value of the semaphore's protected variable. Semaphore operations are usually implemented in the operating system kernel and are provided as other low-level system calls. Unnecessary execution of semaphore operations should be avoided, e.g., executing the operation `signal(s)` when the queue of the semaphore variable s is empty, since like any other operating system call, it will cause a processor context switch, which has a cost in terms of performance and final program execution time.

```
void* p1(void *arg){                void* p2(void *arg){
  while (1){                          int s0;
    wait(s1);                         while (1){
    s= s+1;                             wait(N);
    if (s mod 5==0)                     wait(s2);
      signal(s2)                        sum= sum + s;
    else signal(s1)                     s0= s;
  }                                     signal(s1);
}                                       write(s0);
                                      }
                                      write(sum);
                                    }
```

```
int main (int argc, char *argv[]){
  Semaphore s1, s2, N;
  int s, sum, status;
  pthread_t h1,h2;
  s=0;
  sum= 0;
  init(s1, 1); init(s2, 0); init(N,10);
  pthread_create(&h1,NULL,p1,NULL);
  pthread_create(&h2,NULL,p2,NULL);
}
```

In the earlier example, we want to calculate the series of the cumulative sums of the first ten multiples of 5, for which two operations are used: the first calculates the sequence of the natural numbers, and the second writes the multiples of 5 and writes the sum of the multiples found so far. It stops at the tenth multiple of 5.

1.4.3.2 Atomicity of Operations and Types of Semaphores

The operations on the synchronisation variable are performed atomically, because if the instructions of several operations on the same semaphore variable were allowed to interleave, the final value of the protected variable s would be unpredictable, and neither the safety properties nor the liveliness properties of the program using them would be guaranteed.

The semaphore variables used in concurrent programs are classified according to the set of values that the non-negative[14] variable of synchronisation s can take, thus obtaining two types of semaphore, depending on the data they can take. Each type of semaphore has different characteristics and is chosen according to what it is used for in the program code. Therefore, according to the range of values that the synchronisation variable of the semaphore can take, we will have (a) binary semaphores, where the synchronisation variable will only take the values 0 and 1, and (b) general semaphores: in this case, the synchronisation variable can take any non-negative integer value.

Another way of obtaining the same classification of types of scheduling semaphores would have been to classify them according to their use:

(a) Mutual exclusion: they are so-called because they are generally used to ensure that a section of program code is executed as a critical section; this type is equivalent to binary semaphores, the synchronisation variable is initialised to the value 1 and the second process that tries to execute the wait(s) operation will be blocked, because it will find the protected variable s with the value 0.
(b) General synchronisation: the semaphore variable s is usually initialised to the value 0, the first process attempting to execute the wait(s) operation is blocked and the value of the variable s could reach arbitrarily large non-negative values if the signal(s) operation is executed many times.

1.4.3.3 Properties of Programs That Use Semaphores as a Synchronisation Primitives for Concurrent Processes

Semaphores prevent processes from performing busy waiting by locking processes in a queue separate from the queue of processes subject to scheduling by the processor and therefore do not consume processor cycles while they are suspended. If multiple processes are waiting for a particular condition to occur during program execution, they are blocked until the program state changes and the condition is satisfied. The processes check for the satisfaction of such a synchronisation condition, and if it is not satisfied, they would execute the wait(s) operation of the synchronisation semaphore "s", declared as a global variable, to block and enter the queue of such a semaphore.

With the above informal semantics of the semaphores, it can be understood that nothing prevents the processes of a concurrent program from simultaneously executing operations of different semaphores. However, if several semaphores are declared in a concurrent program, they must be used hierarchically, i.e., following the same order of resource acquisition (wait(s) operation) and resource release (signal(s) operation); otherwise, deadlocks may occur, as in the following example.

---

[14] "Non-negative" means that the protected variable s of a semaphore is of type integer and can never take negative values.

1.4 Low-Level Synchronisation Mechanisms in Shared Memory

```
void* p1(void *arg){              void* p2(void *arg){
wait(s1);                         wait(s2);
 wait(s2);                        wait(s1);
-- rest of instructions           -- rest of instructions
}                                 }

void* p3(void *arg){              void* p4(void *arg){
wait(s);                          wait(s);
-- rest of instructions           wait(s1);
}                                 -- rest of instructions
                                  }
Main program
int main (int argc, char *argv[]){
  Semaphore s1, s2, s;
  pthread_t h1, h2; srand (time(NULL));
  if (rand()%2){
    init(s1, 1); init(s2, 1);
    pthread_create(&h1,NULL,p1,NULL);
    pthread_create(&h2,NULL,p2,NULL);
    --program in deadlock if processes p1 and p2 are executed as corrutines
  }
  else{
    init(s1, 0);init(s, 1);
    pthread_create(&h1,NULL,p3,NULL);
    pthread_create(&h2,NULL,p4,NULL);
    --program in deadlock if p4 starts before p3
  }
}
```

The main disadvantage of using semaphores as synchronisation primitives in concurrent programming languages is that they are difficult to program correctly because, being global objects of the programs, the execution of operations can affect the value of the semaphore protected variable s in other blocks of the program, thus causing unforeseen locks in concurrent processes.

Programming with semaphores generally does not follow the modern principles of structured programming. Moreover, their indiscriminate use can lead to process starvation, since the `signal(s)` operation does not ensure which process in the s queue will be released first, since the queue associated with each semaphore need not have a FIFO queue structure.

1.4.3.4 Semaphores POSIX 1003

Semaphores are an optional synchronisation facility in the POSIX thread programming interface. Not all implementations of the thread interface for concurrent programming will offer the ability to program with semaphores. To verify this, just check whether the `_POSIX_SEMAPHORES` constant is defined in the `<unistd.h>` file of your Linux distribution. The semaphores belong to the old P1003.b standard, rather than the new P1003.1c which defines pthreads, so their programming interface has a slightly different style than the other POSIX synchronisation variables.

The semaphores defined in the POSIX standard can be of two types: (a) unnamed, which are like other thread-like synchronisation variables, and (b) named, which are associated with a globally known string in the system that is similar to a UNIX path name. Unnamed semaphores are stored directly in memory, while named semaphores are accessed using string identifiers and, are allocated memory within the address space of a process and must be initialised with a specific operation.

They could be used by more than one process, but this would have to be indicated by assigning certain values to the arguments of the initialisation operation. Named semaphores are always shared by multiple processes, have an identifier known to the applications using them, a group identifier, and UNIX permission-based protection, just like regular system files. To be portable between POSIX-compliant systems, the name of a semaphore must begin with a slash (/), contain no other slashes, and may include letters, digits, and underscores. Note that since the namespace is shared by all processes in the system, if a number of processes use the same name, then we will get the same semaphore. Both types of semaphore (unnamed and named) are represented by the type `sem_t`, and all operations and other semaphore entities are defined in the header file `<semaphore.h>`.

1.4.3.5 Initialisation Operations of POSIX Semaphores

Unnamed semaphores are initialised by the operation:

```
int sem_init(sem_t*semaphore,int pshared,
             unsigned int counter)
```

The initial value of the semaphore is assigned to `counter`. If `pshared` is non-zero, then the semaphore can be used by threads residing in different processes; otherwise, it can only be used by threads within the address space of a single process. An unnamed semaphore can be destroyed by the operation:

```
int sem_destroy(sem_t* semaphore)
```

To be properly destroyed, the semaphore must have been explicitly initialised with the `sem_init(...)` operation before being used in the code. The operation `sem_destroy(...)` should not be used with named semaphores. This operation returns an error if the implementation detects that the semaphore is being used by other locked threads that have called the operation `sem_wait(...)` on the semaphore variable in question.

With regard to the initialisation operation defined on named semaphores, the first thing to do would be to establish a connection between the semaphore and the calling process in order to be able to perform operations on that semaphore.

```
sem_t* sem_open(const char* name,
         int oflag [, unsigned long mode, unsigned int value])
```

The semaphore remains usable until it is closed. The `sem_open()` operation returns the address of the semaphore to the calling process. The `name` parameter points to a string naming the semaphore object. If there is an error condition, it returns "−1" and assigns `errno` to indicate the error condition. The operation `sem_open()` is idempotent, i.e., if a process makes several calls to the operation with the same name value, the same semaphore address will always be returned. The `oflag` flag determines whether the semaphore is created or accessed by the `sem_open()` operation call. Valid values of `oflag` are: `'0'`, `O_CREAT`, `O_EXCL`. If '0', it means to open an existing semaphore; if `O_CREAT`, a semaphore will be created if it does not already exist; or `O_CREAT|O_EXCL` can be specified which will fail if the semaphore already exists. After a semaphore has been created with the `O_CREAT` flag and given a name, other processes can connect to this semaphore by calling `sem_open()` and using the value of the semaphore name, but without setting bits in `oflag`. Moreover, if the `oflag` flag is used, two more arguments must be given: the mode (third argument), which sets the permissions of the semaphore after clearing all the bits assigned in the process file creation mask, and the value (fourth argument) to create the semaphore with an initial value that must be less than or equal to `SEM_VALUE_MAX`. On the other hand, the operation `int sem_close(sem_t* semaphore)` is used to close the connection to a named semaphore and must not be used on unnamed semaphores (Fig. 1.9).

1.4.3.6 POSIX Semaphore Synchronisation Operations

For each type of semaphore, application threads will call the function `int sem_wait(sem_t* s)`, passing it a semaphore identifier initialised with the value '0', to use it as a general synchronisation semaphore that immediately blocks the thread, or if the value is other than '0', then s is decremented by one and does not block the thread.

The opposite operation to the previous one is `int sem_post(sem_t* s)` and serves to signal blocked threads in a semaphore queue and make one of them ready to execute. If there are no blocked threads in this semaphore, then the execution of this operation simply increments the value of the protected variable s. It should be noted, to use this operation correctly, that there is no unlock order defined if there are multiple threads waiting in the semaphore queue, since the system-level implementation of the `sem_post(...)` operation assumes that the scheduler can choose to unlock any of the

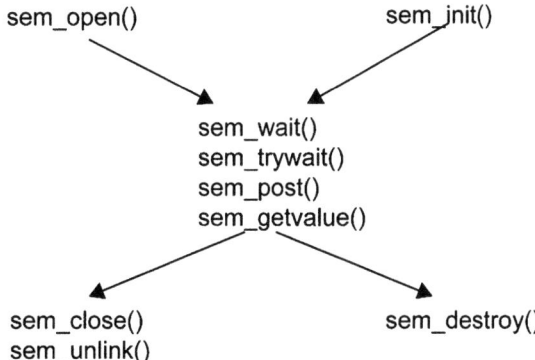

Fig. 1.9 Representation of the correct order of use of library functions Semaphore

suspended threads without such a choice affecting the safety property of the program. In particular, the following scenario could occur, another running thread could decrement the value of the semaphore pointed to by the `sem_post(...)` operation before any thread is unlocked from the semaphore queue and the awakened thread would then be re-blocked.

The two functions explained above may return errors if the semaphore is not correctly initialised before either of them is executed. The internal implementation of the previous operations is asynchronously safe, which means that if a signal fired by a program thread interrupts an operation that is being executed in another thread, while the latter has exclusive access to the semaphore variable, the semaphore will not remain in an inaccessible state for other operations on it that may be performed later by that thread or by others, i.e., there is atomicity of the semaphore operations that are executed concurrently by the threads of an application against asynchronous signals external to the thread.

On the other part, sometimes, it is convenient to avoid the blocking caused by calling the `sem_wait(...)` operation when the value of s is '0'. As an alternative to the latter, we can use another POSIX semaphore function: `int sem_trywait(sem_t* s)`, which atomically decrements the value of s only if it is positive; otherwise, it returns the error value '−1'. In addition, the following function `int sem_getvalue(sem_t* s, int *valuep)` is used to get the current value of the semaphore variable s. After it has been fully executed, it will store this value in `valuep`.

Example 1.3 The following example shows two threads, one writing to the global variable `protected_data` and the other reading from this variable. Each thread performs 10,000 iterations of a loop in which the threads repeatedly write or read the value of the shared variable. Two unnamed semaphores, called `write_ok` and `read_ok`, are declared and initialised in the program to write and read the value of the variable, respectively. Initially, only the write thread can act, so the value '1' is passed in the third argument of `sem_init(...)` for the `write_ok` semaphore, and the same is done for the mutex semaphore. Similarly, if the shared variable cannot be read initially because nothing has been written to it, the value '0' is passed in the third argument of the `sem_init(...)` function for the semaphore `read_ok`. The purpose of the mutex semaphore is to ensure that no errors occur in the screen output, since access to this resource could cause a race condition between the two program threads.

```
#include <pthread.h>
#include <iostream>
#include <semaphore.h>
  sem_t write_ok, read_ok, mutex;
  unsigned long protected_data;
  const unsigned long num_iter = 10000;
  sem_t write_ok, -- must be initialized to 1
  read_ok, -- must be initialized to 0
  mutex ; -- must be initialized to 1
```

1.4 Low-Level Synchronisation Mechanisms in Shared Memory

Normally, we need to specify the compilation directive '-l' to link with the `pthread` library and, optionally, 'rt' (if we need to use the librt real-time library in our program). Note that the include `<pthread.h>` allows us to use the pthread functions in the program, but unlike the functions declared in the other written includes, such as `studio.h`, the actual code of the functions in `pthread.h` is not linked by default when we compile our program with gcc. Consequently, if we use functions from the POSIX thread library and do not specify the `-lpthread` option when compiling, the linking phase with the pthread library will fail because it will not be able to find the functions it needs, such as `pthread_create(...)`.

```
--Code of the writer thread
void* write( void* p ){
  unsigned long counter=0;
  for( unsigned long i= 0; i< num_iter; i++ )
  {
    counter= counter + 1;
--generates one new value
    sem_wait( &write_ok );
    protected_data = counter;
-- write the value
    sem_post( &read_ok );
    sem_wait( &mutex );
    cout << "written data == " << counter << endl << flush;
    sem_post( &mutex );
  }
  return NULL;
}

--Code of the reader thread
void* read( void* p ){
  unsigned long read_value;
  for( unsigned long i= 0; i< num_iter; i++ )
  {
    sem_wait( &read_ok );
    read_value= protected_data;
-- read the protected value
    sem_post( &write_ok);
    sem_wait( &mutex );
    cout << " read value == " << read_value << endl;
    sem_post( &mutex );
  }
  return NULL ;
}
```

Finally, we just need to initialise the unnamed semaphores that we are going to use in the `main()` function, create the threads that will support the concurrent processes of our program and compile with the correct directives, and that's it!

```
Main Program
 int main(){
   pthread_t writer, reader;
   sem_init( &mutex, 0, 1 ) ;
   sem_init( &write_ok, 0, 1);
   sem_init( &read_ok, 0, 0);
   pthread_create( &writer, NULL, write, NULL );
   pthread_create( &reader, NULL, read, NULL );
   pthread_join( writer, NULL ) ;
   pthread_join( reader, NULL );
   sem_destroy(&write_ok); sem_destroy(&read_ok ); sem_destroy(&mutex);
 }
```

1.5 Properties of Concurrent Systems

In concurrent systems[15], a property is understood as a correctness attribute that must be satisfied in every execution of the system. The set of all possible executions, whose correctness we need to verify, define the concept of system's behaviour. Any property of a concurrent system, however complex it may be, can be formulated as a combination of two fundamental types of properties: (1) safety[16], or the certainty that the behaviour of the system will never enter a situation where all its processes are deadlocked, and (2) the property[17] ensuring that the system will eventually[18] reach a desired state, for example, that all its processes will eventually reach the critical section. To verify this property, it must be shown that no execution of the system indefinitely delays reaching this desired state, even if it is not possible to set a specific time limit for when it will be achieved.

1.5.1 Safety Properties

Safety properties define conditions[19] that must be upheld throughout the execution of a program. These often include mutual exclusion conditions, precedence relations between instructions or processes and the absence of deadlock. A practical rule for distinguishing safety properties from other properties is to check whether the property would always be

---

[15] We will understand the term "system" as a set of active components that interact, through communication and synchronisation. It would include concurrent and real-time programs and applications; but not only that, hardware devices controlled by the software are also considered part of it.

[16] The property states that no execution included in the system behaviour can enter a forbidden state.

[17] This concurrent property is called "liveness".

[18] The term "eventually" indicates that the system must reach a desired state within a time frame that is in principle indefinite, but not arbitrarily long.

[19] They usually coincide with requirements that must always be met by the system, which are also called static system specifications, i.e., they are always met regardless of the concrete execution that the system may dynamically follow.

1.5 Properties of Concurrent Systems

satisfied if the software were implemented as a sequential program. For example, the impossibility of reaching a deadlock—where processes cannot proceed—is a critical safety property that must be verified. In a sequential version of the software, deadlocks will not occur because processes would sequentially obtain all the resources needed to complete their tasks. As a result, the second of Coffman's conditions[20] for deadlock would not be met.

There are several practical examples of safety properties in concurrent systems, which are common in solving well-known concurrent programming problems:

- Mutual exclusion problem: the condition that two program processes can never simultaneously execute the instructions belonging to a critical section is a safety property.
- Producer-consumer problem: similarly, a safety property ensures that the consumer process cannot extract data from an empty buffer and the producer process cannot insert data into a full buffer.
- Deadlock situation: this represents the most serious violation of safety properties. A deadlock occurs when none of the processes in a system release their resources while all are trying to access memory, causing memory to fill up and preventing any process continuing.

1.5.2 Liveness Properties

Liveness properties express that a system will reach certain desired states within a finite amount of time. This means there must be executions in the system's behaviour that reach these "good states", identifying correctness attributes, and that this happens often. Liveness properties also ensure that the system's execution conditions do not lead to certain processes being starved[21], i.e., processes are not indefinitely delayed or prevented from making progress. There are several practical examples that help illustrate liveness properties, such as the following scenarios that occur in the paradigmatic examples mentioned earlier:

- Mutual exclusion: if a process wants to enter a critical section, the protocol must guarantee that no process is locked in a busy waiting state indefinitely, leading to starvation. To satisfy the liveness property, it must be proven that every process will eventually be able to enter the critical section.
- Producer-consumer: a process that wants to insert or remove data from the buffer must be able to do so within a finite amount of time. This result must be provable based only on the values of the shared variables involved in the buffer access protocol.

---

[20] In operating systems, it is studied that four conditions must be met for a mutual deadlock or interlock to occur between processes in a concurrent program, known as the "Coffman conditions".

[21] Processes suffer starvation when they are systematically overtaken by others and fail to make progress in the execution of useful instructions.

The most serious violation of the liveness property results in the starvation of one or more processes in the concurrent system under test. While this is less severe than a complete system deadlock, since other processes can still perform some useful work, allowing any process to starve is unacceptable. Starvation indicates that the system contains inoperative code, meaning it does not adhere to the principles of concurrent programming and would be considered incorrect.

1.5.3 Fairness Properties

In addition to the liveness property in a concurrent system, it is essential to ensure that when a process is ready to run, it can do so with justice compared to other concurrent processes. This property requires the system to meet more stringent conditions than those needed to demonstrate the liveness. Whether or not fairness can be guaranteed often depends on the implementation of the process scheduler on the specific execution platform.

A classic example where the fairness property is not typically satisfied is in real-time systems, where different priorities are assigned to application processes. In such cases, the "unfairness" is intentional and necessary because not all the processes have the same criticality in terms of reliability or timeliness. Ensuring that higher-priority processes receive more CPU time is essential for the system to function properly in these scenarios.

Example 1.4 Five philosophers dedicate their lives to two activities: thinking and eating. Both activities take an unknown but limited amount of time. These philosophers share a round table with five chairs, each one belonging to one philosopher. On the table, there are five plates of slippery spaghetti and five chopsticks (instead of forks, to better fit the analogy). As shown in Fig. 1.10, philosophers require two chopsticks to eat their spaghetti.

When a philosopher is not trying to sit at the table, he is assumed to be thinking, a task to which the philosophers devote most of their time. From time to time, a philosopher feels

Fig. 1.10 The five philosophers at the table with *chopsticks* between them

hungry, approaches the table and attempts to grab the two chopsticks closest to him. Once in possession of the chopsticks, the philosopher can eat from the plate and will not release the chopsticks until he has finished eating and is ready to return to thinking.

However, philosophers are very stubborn: if one manages to grab one chopstick, he will never release it, even if he is unable to acquire the second chopstick. Similarly, no philosopher will allow another to take the chopstick he already holds while he waits for the second one. To solve this problem, a protocol must be invented that ensures each philosopher can eventually eat while maintaining the safety and liveness properties of the concurrent philosopher processes.

The most serious violation of the safety property would occur if each philosopher indefinitely held onto one chopstick without being able to acquire the second, leading to a situation where no philosopher can eat. In the above scenario, none of the philosophers would release their chopstick, and all would starve.

A less severe, but still problematic, violation scenario of the liveness property could occur if two philosophers conspired to starve the philosopher sitting between them. In this scenario, when one of the two conspiring philosophers finished eating and releases the chopsticks, the other immediately takes them, leaving the philosopher between them perpetually short of either the left or right chopstick. This would result in the starvation of the middle philosopher, demonstrating that the liveness property is not satisfied, as at least one process-philosopher would be prevented from making progress.

According to Coffman's second condition for deadlock (where processes hold onto resources while waiting indefinitely for additional resources), if each philosopher attempts to acquire one chopstick at a time, the system inevitably reaches a deadlock state where no philosopher can proceed, leading to starvation for all.

One possible solution to this problem is to introduce an additional butler process. If philosophers cannot acquire all the resources at once, the butler could limit the number of philosophers allowed to sit at the table to a maximum of four at any given time. This ensures that at least one philosopher will always be able to acquire two chopsticks and eat. Starvation of the philosophers can also be prevented by the butler by ensuring that no philosopher is permanently excluded for sitting at the table.

> The most general definition of software correctness that we can give, and that can be applied to both sequential and concurrent systems, is the following: a system is correct if it always satisfies its predefined properties, during any of its executions.

1.6 Hoare's Program Logic and Concurrent Programs Verification

A program is said to be partially correct if, given that the program terminates, the results obtained after its execution are as expected. In addition, a program is said to be completely correct if it is partially correct and its termination can always be proved. However, the above concepts are tied to proving the correctness of sequential programs and, therefore, cannot be considered adequate to define the correctness of concurrent systems or applications, since we will not normally be able to assume a termination state in our proofs, as concurrent systems are implemented to be in perpetual execution. In fact, their termination is usually associated with the occurrence of an error condition, followed by an abort, or the occurrence of an exception or a forced system restart. Operating systems, real-time control systems, ATM software, flight control and reservation software, etc. are classic examples of systems that are designed to run continuously and are concurrent systems by nature.

1.6.1 Options Available for Testing Concurrent Software

In order to demonstrate that a code written in any programming language is correct, i.e., to carry out the activity called "software verification", we could consider that different software testing methods (not necessarily concurrent) can be used, such as the following:

- *Code debugging*[22], which consists of exploring some of the possible executions of a code generated by a concurrent program and verifying that these executions are acceptable because they satisfy the initially specified properties. The problem is that it is not useful for verifying concurrent systems, because it will never be possible to prove the absence of transient errors that may occur in the execution of a concurrent program due to the occurrence of race conditions in unexplored execution sequences.
- *Operational point of view*—this method of software testing could be understood as performing an exhaustive case analysis, i.e., exploring all possible execution sequences of a given code, considering all possible interleavings of the atomic instructions that its processes will generate. However, this is not feasible for concurrent systems due to the astronomical number of interleaved instruction sequences that even a short piece of software with a few threads of execution can produce.
- *Assertive reasoning* is a formal analysis based on predicate logic that allows an abstract representation of the concrete states that a program reaches during its execution. Recall that a state of a program is defined by the values that the program variables have at a given moment of its execution. Therefore, if the initial state is an assertion that satisfies the input data or initial conditions and the final state is satisfied by the expected results of the program, we will have a demonstration in which the number of states to be checked is equal to the number of instructions in the code.

---

[22] Debugging or testing is the name for this activity in the texts.

1.6.2 Program Verification Based on the Axiomatic Semantics of a Programming Language

It is based on the use of assertive reasoning, i.e., based on assertions or propositions that are evaluated as true or false, thanks to a formal logic system (FLS) that facilitates the elaboration of certain assertions, with a precise logical-mathematical basis. This semantics interprets the constructs of a programming language based on the states of a program that uses them and on the evolution of these states during execution. More specifically, the mathematical definition of an FLS is as follows:

$$FLS = \{\text{symbols, formulas, axioms, inference rules}\}$$

1.6.2.1 Symbols: {Programming Language Sentences, Propositional Variables, Operators of Logic, etc.}

The *Formulas* are well-formed sequences of symbols *Rules of inference* indicate how to derive true formulas from axioms (formulas that we know to be true) and from other formulas that we have earlier proved to be true.

The inference rules have the following meaning: if all the hypotheses are true, then the conclusion C is also true: $(\textit{rule name}) \dfrac{H_1, H_2, \ldots, H_n}{C}$

Both the hypotheses and the conclusion of the inference rules must be syntactically well-formed formulas or a schematic representation of them.

Additional concepts for verifying code using this method are the definition of theorems and the way in which they can be proved. A logic theorem, or proposition, is a formula that makes a certain statement about facts that belong to the domain of discourse. In our case, facts can be understood as the values of the states reached by the execution of a program and their relation to the fulfilment of the previously specified properties that the program must satisfy. From a technical point of view, the asserts of our FLS, which we will define precisely, correspond to the logical lines or sentences in which the proof of a program is structured. A proof of the correctness of a program is a sequence of asserts such that each one can be derived from the previous ones by applying an inference rule of the FLS.

For an FLS to be formally acceptable, and for the proofs we make using it to be reliable, such an FLS must satisfy the abstract properties called *soundness* and *completeness*, for whose definition we will need to introduce the concept of interpreting formulas.

- *Interpretation*: In order to know whether a well-constructed FLS assertion is true, it is necessary to provide an evaluation of the certainty of the formulas which is mathematically well defined, such as the following correspondence: *Interpretation* → *Logic Constants*: $\{F, V\}$. This means that every formula constructed with our logic must be evaluated to determine whether it is true (V) or false (F).

- *Soundness*: the FLS we define is certain with respect to a given interpretation if all the asserts that can be derived with this system are true facts of the domain of discourse. Therefore, if we define the set facts = {certainties expressed as formulas} and the set asserts = {demonstrable formulas}, then the FLS has the property named soundness if the following inclusion relation is satisfied: $asserts \subseteq facts$.
- *Completeness*: this property is satisfied if every true assertion of the FLS is provable, i.e., the following inclusion relation must be satisfied: $facts \subseteq asserts$. We will interpret that every fact in the domain of discourse is provable with the FLS we propose, using for this the axioms and the derivation rules of the FLS.

1.6.2.2 Propositional Logic

This is a clear example of an FLS that can be used to formalise what we normally call common sense reasoning. The formulas of this logic are called propositions, and their symbols are the following:

- *Propositional constants*: $\{V, F\}$
- *Propositional variables*: $\{p, q, r, \ldots\}$
- *Logical operators or connectors*: $\{\neg, \wedge, \vee, \rightarrow, \leftarrow \ldots\}$
- *Expressions using constants, variables, and operators*

As for the interpretation of a propositional formula, we can understand this concept in the context of the propositional logic by the evaluation we obtain from the formulas after substituting the values of the variables in each state of the program, for example, $\{X = a\}$ evaluates as true if indeed in the current state of the program it is satisfied that the value of the variable is identically equal to 'a'. We can formally define the concept as follows: given a state s of a program, described by the formula P, in which we replace each propositional variable by its value in that state and then use the truth table of logical connectors $\{\neg, \wedge, \vee, \rightarrow, \leftarrow \ldots\}$ to obtain the result, the propositional formula interpretation coincides with its overall truth value of P.

Moreover, the certainty of a formula P will depend on the state at a given point of the program's execution, according to the following definitions:

- One formula is satisfied in one state s if and only if it has a true interpretation in that state.
- One formula will be satisfiable in a program p if and only if there exists some state of p in which the formula can be satisfied.
- One formula is valid if and only if it can be satisfied in any state of p.

Valid propositions are called tautologies in the Logic. In a propositional logic, the soundness property of an FLS is always fulfilled. This is because it can be shown that all axioms are tautologies, since every axiom must always be valid.

1.6.2.3 Tautologies or Propositional Equivalence Laws

These laws can be understood as equivalences that allow the substitution of a proposition by its equivalent, thus simplifying complex formulas in demonstrations:

1. Law of negation: $P = \neg(\neg P)$
2. Excluded media law: $P \vee \neg P \rightarrow V$
3. Contradiction law: $P \wedge \neg P = F$
4. Law of implication: $P \Rightarrow Q \equiv \neg P \vee Q$
5. Equality Law: $(P \rightarrow Q) \wedge (Q \rightarrow P) \equiv P \Leftrightarrow Q$
6. Or-Simplification laws:

    $P \vee P = P$
    $P \vee V = V$
    $P \vee (P \wedge Q) = P$
    $P \vee F = P$

7. And-Simplification laws:

    $P \wedge V = P$
    $P \wedge P = P$
    $P \wedge F = F$
    $P \wedge (P \vee Q) = P$

8. Commutative laws:

    $(P \wedge Q) = (Q \wedge P)$
    $(P \vee Q) = (Q \vee P)$
    $(P = Q) = (Q = P)$

9. Associative laws:

    $P \wedge (Q \wedge R) = (P \wedge Q) \wedge R$
    $P \vee (Q \vee R) = (P \vee Q) \vee R$

10. Distributive laws:

    $P \wedge (Q \vee R) = (P \wedge Q) \vee (P \wedge R)$
    $P \vee (Q \wedge R) = (P \vee Q) \wedge (P \vee R)$

11. Morgan's laws:

    $\neg(P \wedge Q) = \neg P \vee \neg Q$
    $\neg(P \vee Q) = \neg P \wedge \neg Q$

12. And-deletion: $(P \wedge Q) \rightarrow P$
13. Or-deletion: $P \rightarrow (P \vee Q)$

Rule 12 can be explained by saying that the set of states satisfying P trivially includes the set of states satisfying $(P \wedge Q)$; proposition P is said to be weaker and is therefore implied by the stricter expression $(P \wedge Q)$. According to the above, the constant F (or false) is the strongest proposition, since it implies every other proposition of the Logic, and the constant V (or true) is the weakest proposition since it would be implied by every proposition of the logic.

1.6.2.4 Program Logic

It is an FLS that allows precise statements to be made about the execution of a program. Program Logic (PL) symbols include the statements of a programming language and the logical formulae, which are called triples, are of the form $\{P\} \, S \, \{Q\}$, where P and Q are asserts and S is a simple or structured statement of a programming language. The free variables of P and Q belong to the program or are logical variables. The latter act as containers for the values of the common variables of the program and cannot be assigned more than once, i.e., they always keep the value to which they were assigned the first time. They only appear in asserts, not in statements, and are usually represented in uppercase to distinguish them from program variables, which appear in lowercase.

Triples $\{P\} \, S \, \{Q\}$ are interpreted theorems of PL, i.e., we say that a triple is true or the logical formula it represents evaluates to true if the execution of the instruction S starts in a state of the program that satisfies the assert P (or precondition) and that the final state must satisfy the assert Q (or postcondition), after any interleaving of atomic instructions as a result of the execution of S. Note that an assert characterises an acceptable state of the system, i.e., a state that can be reached by the program if its variables take certain values. Each state of the program must satisfy its associated assert for the interpretation of the triple to have the value V (true).

The assert $\{V\}$, the logical constant V, will represent all the possible states of the program, since this assert is satisfied in every state of the program independently of the values taken by the variables at any state, i.e., $\{P\} \rightarrow V$ is a valid formula. On the other hand, an assertion equivalent to the logical constant F is not true in any state of the program, i.e., $F \rightarrow \{P\}$ is also a valid formula.

The axioms and rules of inference of PL are defined in the following list:

1. *Axiom of the null instruction*: $\{P\}null\{P\}$: if the assertion is true before the execution of the null sentence, it remains true after the execution.
2. *Textual substitution*: $\{P_e^x\}$ is the result of substituting the expression e in any free occurrence of the variable x in P. The names of the free variables of the expression e must not conflict with bound variables that exist in P; and, therefore, any relation of the program state that has to do with the variable x and that is true after the assignment must also have been true before the assignment.

1.6 Hoare's Program Logic and Concurrent Programs Verification

3. *Axiom of assignment*: $\{P_e^x\} x := e \{P\}$: this sentence of the programming language assigns a value e to a variable x and thus, in general, modifies the state of the program. An assignment changes only the value of the target variable; all other variables keep the same value as before the execution of the assignment sentence. For example, the triple $\{V\} x := 5 \{x = 5\}$ is a true assert, because the textual substitution of 5 in the variable x always is tautologic $\{x = 5\}_5^x \equiv V$. In PL, there are inference rules for each of the statements that affect the flow of control in a structured sequential program, plus three additional inference rules for connecting triples in program demonstrations.

4. *Rule of consequence* (1): $\dfrac{\{P\} S \{Q\}, \{Q\} \to \{R\}}{\{P\} S \{R\}}$ The interpretation of this rule is that it is always possible to make the postcondition weaker, i.e., to replace the postcondition of a triple by a weaker assert and that its interpretation is preserved, in which case the triple with postcondition $\{R\}$ remains true.

5. *Rule of consequence* (2): $\dfrac{\{R\} \to \{P\}, \{P\} S \{Q\}}{\{R\} S \{Q\}}$ The meaning of this rule is that the precondition of a triple can always be made stricter and that its interpretation is preserved, i.e., the triple with precondition $\{R\}$ remains true, given that the original triple does.

6. *Composition rule*: $\dfrac{\{P\} S_1 \{Q\}, \{Q\} S_2 \{R\}}{\{P\} S_1; S_2 \{R\}}$ allows to obtain the composition of postcondition and precondition of two sentences together, from the precondition of the first one and the postcondition of the second one, if the postcondition of the first one coincides with the precondition of the second one.

7. *If rule*:

$$\dfrac{\{P\} \wedge \{B\} S_1 \{Q\}, \{P\} \wedge \{\neg B\} S_2 \{Q\}}{\{P\} \text{ if } B \text{ then } S_1 \text{ else } S_2 \text{ fi } \{Q\}}$$

Suppose that the precondition of the if statement to be proved is $\{P\}$ and the postcondition to be reached is $\{Q\}$; then, to prove the certainty of $\{Q\}$, we need only prove that the two branches of the if statement make the same postcondition $\{Q\}$ true.

8. *Iteration rule*: $\dfrac{\{I \wedge B\} S \{I\}}{\{I\} \text{ while } B \text{ do } S \text{ enddo} \{I \wedge \neg B\}}$ A while statement can be iterated an arbitrary number of times, including 0, without affecting the certainty of the invariant I. For this reason, the rule of iterative inference is based on this loop invariant, i.e., an assert $\{I\}$ that is satisfied before and after each iteration of the loop. The final postcondition of the while complete statement is identically equal to the conjunction of the invariant and the negation of the loop iteration condition.

1.6.3 Verification of Concurrent and Synchronisation Statements

The verification of concurrent programs is affected by a problem known as interference between assertions and statements running on another thread. When such interference occurs, the individual process assertions made with the PL are invalidated, i.e., the inference rules are no longer sound. This is because another concurrent process can execute an atomic instruction that makes the precondition (or postcondition) of a statement within the first demonstration false. If this were to happen, the soundness property would no longer be satisfied in the PL system, and PL would not be useful for verifying concurrent programs. The following program is an example of interference between processes of a concurrent program. Depending on which register is loaded (load y) and incremented (add z)[23] before, after or at the same time as the two right assignment operations ($y := 1$ and $z := 2$), the execution of this program results in a value of $x \in \{0, 1, 2, 3\}$, but we cannot determine which one.

$$y := 0; \ z := 0;$$
$$\texttt{cobegin} \ x := y + z \ \| \ y := 1; \ z := 2 \ \texttt{coend};$$

A peculiarity of the above program is that it can produce the final value of $x = 2$ although $y + z = 2$ does not correspond to any valid state of this program.

We must bear in mind that not all nested sequences of process instructions are acceptable, and race conditions can occur, leaving variables shared by the processes with incorrect values. Therefore, if we make good use of synchronisation statements in our programs, such interference between concurrent processes can be avoided.

Variants of the synchronisation constructs are often used in different programming languages to avoid inter-process race conditions and transient errors in execution sequences:

- Critical sections: programmed as instruction blocks in the process code, which must be executed respecting the property of mutual exclusion when accessing the instructions they contain. In this way, simple atomic instructions are combined into structured atomic actions that are executed indivisibly by the program processes.
- Conditional synchronisation: delays the execution of a process until an assert is satisfied, indicating that the program has reached a certain desired state, and then allows the delayed process to continue without unwanted interference with other running processes. An example of this type of instruction would be the use of semaphore operations `sem_post()` and `sem_wait()` in simple concurrent programs (without the use of monitors, actors, etc.) or programming with condition variables used in monitor procedures.

---

[23] $x := y + z$, interpreted as load y; add z; store x

1.6.3.1 Elemental Atomic Action and Concurrent Composition Inference Rule

The abstract statement marked "<Sentence>" is used to express the atomicity of the code between brackets and has different realisations in concurrent programming languages, such as synchronised blocks, critical regions, monitor procedures, etc. In sequential programs, assignments are always atomic actions, since there is no intermediate state visible to the rest of the processes; however, this situation does not occur in concurrent programs, since an instruction containing the assignment statement is often equivalent to a sequence of elementary atomic operations:

> An elementary atomic action, no matter how many instructions it contains, performs an indivisible transformation of the program state.

$\{x=0\}$
$x := x+1;$
$\{x=1\}$
the assignment to variable x is
compiled into the next atomic
instructions:
<load x, 0>
<add, 1>
<store, x>
and finally the postcondition is $\{x=1\}$

The effect of declaring an elementary atomic action in the text of a process is that any intermediate state that might exist during the execution of that statement would not be visible to the rest of the processes in the program, and therefore, transient errors in the program execution sequences would be avoided.

The process P_1 "sees" only two possible states of this program, before and after the atomic action <x := x+2>, i.e., the precondition $\{x = 0\}$ and the postcondition $\{x = 2\}$ of the atomic action contained in the process P_2. Something completely equivalent happens to the process with respect to the atomic action <x := x+1> seen by the other process. As a consequence, the precondition and postcondition of both processes now become disjunctions if we assume that both processes are executed simultaneously, for the purpose of performing a test to prove the non-interference of both atomic propositions:

$P_1 :: \{x = 0 \vee x = 2\} <x := x+1>; \{x = 1 \vee x = 3\}$
$P_2 :: \{x = 0 \vee x = 1\} <x := x+2>; \{x = 2 \vee x = 3\}$

and now we can apply the inference rule of concurrent composition.

More formally, the atomic assignment action a does not interfere with the critical assertion $\{C\}$ if the triple $\{C \wedge pre(a)\}\, a\, \{C\}$ can be proven as a theorem of PL. This triple is interpreted to mean that the execution of a does not change the truth value of $\{C\}$. In other words, the certainty of the assertion $\{C\}$ remains invariant with respect to the atomic action a executed by another process, which must start in one state that satisfies the precondition $\{pre(a)\}$.

To correctly demonstrate non-interference between an atomic action and a critical program assertion, it may be necessary to rename the local variables of $\{C\}$. This avoids potential conflicts between the local variables in $\{C\}$, the instruction a and the precondition $\{pre(a)\}$.

> A set of processes is said to be free of interference if there is no atomic action in any of these processes that interferes with any critical assertion contained in the demonstration of any other process.

This statement is the antecedent of the following new PL inference rule:

9. *Rule of safe composition of concurrent processes*:

$$\frac{\{P_i\}\,S_i\,\{Q_i\} \text{ are non interferring triples}, 1 \leq i \leq n}{\{P_1 \wedge P_2 \wedge \ldots \wedge P_n\}\, \texttt{cobegin}\, S_1 \,\|\, S_2 \,\|\ldots\|\, S_n \,\texttt{coend}\,\{Q_1 \wedge Q_2 \wedge \ldots \wedge Q_n\}}$$

The interpretation of the above rule is as follows: if we can prove that the set of concurrent processes S_i is interference free, then their concurrent composition transforms the conjunction of the preconditions of the processes $\{P_1 \wedge P_2 \ldots \wedge P_n\}$ of the state before the `cobegin` statement into the conjunction $\{Q_1 \wedge Q_2 \ldots \wedge Q_n\}$ of their postconditions satisfied in the state after the `coend` statement, i.e., the demonstrations of the individual processes S_i as sequential programs are valid even though these processes run concurrently, and no additional demonstration is required to ensure that such code satisfies the safe concurrent composition of these processes.

1.6 Hoare's Program Logic and Concurrent Programs Verification

$$\{x=0\}$$
$$cobegin$$
$$\{x=0\}\ P_1::<x:=x+1;>\{x=1\}\ \|\ \{x=0\}\ P_2::<x:=x+2>\{x=2\}$$
$$coend$$
$$\{x=3\}$$

$$\{x=0\}$$
$$cobegin$$
$$\{x=0\ \lor\ x=2\}\quad\{x=0\ \lor\ x=1\}$$
$$x:=x+1;\quad\|\quad x:=x+2$$
$$\{x=1\ \lor\ x=3\}\quad\{x=2\ \lor\ x=3\}$$
$$coend$$
$$\{x=3\}$$

Fig. 1.11 Two processes with elementary atomic actions and the correctness demostration of the program with the two processes

Thus, applying the rule of safe concurrent process composition, to demonstrate the correctness of the example shown in Fig. 1.11, and since it can be shown that the processes P_1 and P_2 do not interfere with each other, the demonstration written schematically as the second block of code in the figure is valid.

1.6.4 Verifying Concurrent Programs Using Global Invariants

Global invariants (GIs) are predicates in programming logic (PL) used to prove the safety properties of concurrent programs in a straightforward way. This avoid the need to apply the concurrency rule, which can be tedious in complex systems with many processes (S_i:1...N). In such systems, proving noninterference between N atomic instructions and N critical assertions would require N^2 non-interference demonstrations.

The GIs are expressions defined from the global variables of a program and are typically formulated as predicates in PL that capture the relationships between the variables shared by the processes. They are preferred over non-interference proofs because GIs eliminate the need to prove all non-interference theorems between the critical assertions $\{C\}$ and atomic actions a in individual process demonstrations.

If any critical assertion $\{C\}$ in the individual demonstrations of a concurrent process $\{P_i\}S\{Q_i\}$ can be written as a conjunction of the form $\{GI \land L\}$, where GI is a global invariant of the program and $\{L\}$ is a predicate involving only local process variables or function parameters, then it becomes unnecessary to perform the non-interference demonstrations required by the rule 9 of PL, named of safe composition of concurrent processes. This GI-based rule can be applied directly to the set of processes to prove the desired result: $\{\wedge_{i=1}^{n} P_i\}\{\|_{i=1}^{n} S_i\}\{\wedge_{i=1}^{n} Q_i\}$.

However, an additional check is required for a predicate {I}, defined from the shared variables among the processes of a concurrent program, to be considered a valid global invariant. The following conditions must be satisfied:

1. The proposed predicate {I} must be valid for the initial values of the variables involved.
2. {I} must remain true after the execution of each atomic action a, concurrently executed by other processes. In other words, the following triple[24] must be proven for every action a included in the system:

$$\{I \wedge pre(a)\}a\{I\}$$

Put differently, it must demonstrate that there is no interference between the predicate {I} and any elementary atomic process action a performed by the concurrent processes of the program.

Example 1.5a As an example of verifying the safety property of a concurrent program using *GI*, we will present a concurrent program scheme to perform secure transfers between two accounts of the same bank as a transaction[25], as this operation is understood in DBMS. We will therefore have to program the minimum critical sections necessary for a customer to make a safe withdrawal from one account and deposit into another, i.e., without at any time missing money from the total sum of the balances of all the bank's accounts. In addition, the banking system's software will iteratively execute code in parallel with other transfers to verify that the sum of the bank's account balances always remains constant. The necessary synchronisation operations must be included in the solution, trying to optimise the overall concurrency of the program. The elementary atomic action represents the transaction consisting of two operations, (1) withdrawal and (2) deposit, from the ordering account to the beneficiary account.

Solution Let us consider two processes: the first process P_1, performs a transaction consisting of two operations: decreasing the balance of account x by K units and increasing the balance of account y by the same amount, K. It is important that the intermediate state (where the balance of account x has been decreased but the balance of account y has not yet been increased) remains invisible to the second process P_2. This ensures that, from the perspective P_2, the total sum of the balances across all accounts always appears constant.

P_2 periodically checks that the sum of the all the account balances, represented by the array $c[i]$, remains unchanged. The global invariant {*GI*} that must be satisfied throughout the execution of the program is expressed by the assertion: *Total* = $c[1] + ...c[n]$ = *constant*.

To verify the safety property, the proof for process P_1 can be written by proving the following triple:

---

[24] The triple demonstration is the proof of non-interference between the atomic action a and the global invariant *GI*.

[25] A unit of work performed within a system against a database or repository and handled in a consistent and reliable manner so that it does not interfere with other transactions. A transaction is generally used to make any change to a database while maintaining data consistency.

1.6 Hoare's Program Logic and Concurrent Programs Verification

$var\ c:array[1..n]\ of\ int;$

$P_1::$

$\{A_1::c[x]=X \land c[y]=Y\} \land \{GI\}$

$S_1: <c[x]:=c[x]-K; c[y]:=c[y]+K>$

$\{A_2::c[x]=X-K \land c[y]=Y+K\} \land \{GI\}$

on the other hand, for P_2 we will have to carry out the proof given by

$P_2::$

$var\ Sum:=0;$

$i:=1;$

$\{Sum = \sum_{x=1}^{i-1} c[x]\}$

$while(i \le n)\ do$

    $begin$

        $\{B_1\} = \{Sum = \sum_{x=1}^{i-1} c[x] \land i \le n\}$

        $S_2: Sum:=Sum+c[i];$

        $\{B_2\} = \{Sum = (\sum_{x=1}^{i-1} c[x] + c[i]) \land i \le n\} \to \{Sum = \sum_{x=1}^{i} c[x] \land i \le n\}$

        $S_3: i:=i+1;$

        $\{B_3\} = \{Sum = \sum_{x=1}^{i-1} c[x] \land i \le n+1\}$

    end

    $enddo$

$\{B_4\} = \{Sum = \sum_{i=1}^{n} c[i]\} \to \{GI\}$

For process P_2 we must perform the demonstration using the sequence of triples described earlier. It is important to note that the P_1's assertions $\{A_1\}$, $\{A_2\}$ are not critical because the process instructions of P_2 only read the values of the elements in the array $c[i]$ without modifying them. Therefore, evaluating the logical value of these assertions cannot interfere with the execution of the program fragment in the demonstration of P_2.

However, the assertions B_1, B_2 are critical because their interpretation can be interfered by the assignment of array elements, which is programmed as an elementary atomic action S_1 in process P_1. This action will be executed concurrently with the atomic actions of P_2 in an order that is not predetermined. For instance, the values of the elements $c[x]$ or $c[y]$ in the array c could be modified while the process P_2 is summing these values in the execution of S_2.

To ensure the correctness of the global concurrent program, the instructions in P_2 must be preceded or *guarded* by a synchronisation mechanism. This synchronisation would prevent P_2 from accessing the same array elements at the same time as P_1. An example of such a synchronisation instruction could be:

$$S_1 : \langle wait((x < i \land y < i) \lor (x > i \land y > i)) \to c[x] = c[x] - K; c[y] = c[y] + K \rangle.$$

To prove safety properties of concurrent systems, it is often convenient to formulate them as the negation of predicates that characterise certain system states that cannot be reached by more than one process simultaneously. For instance, in the mutual exclusion problem, the safety property can be expressed by stating that the preconditions for access to the critical sections of processes P_1 and P_2 can never be true at the same time.

Let's define *NOTSAFE* as a predicate that characterises a program state where conflicting conditions can be true simultaneously. In other words, {*NOTSAFE* = P_1 at CS ∧ P_2 at CS}. To prove that program P satisfies the mutual exclusion property, it is sufficient to show that the system can never reach this unsafe state. This can be done by proving the validity of the formula P_1 at CS ∧ P_2 at CS = *False* throughout the entire execution of the program P.

More formally, let *NOTSAFE* be a predicate that characterises an undesirable state of the program. Suppose that we can prove the triple {P} S {Q}, where the assertion {P} characterises the initial state of the program. If we define {*GI*}, a global invariant of the proof, then S satisfies the safety property specified by ¬ (*NOTSAFE*) for any execution if we can prove the validity of the formula: {*GI*} →¬ (*NOTSAFE*). This can be considered an alternative definition of the safety property for the concurrent program under consideration. Therefore, in the example above, *NOTSAFE* ≡ ($x \geq i \lor y \geq i$) ∧ ($x \leq i \lor y \leq i$).

Example 1.5b In the case of bank transfers between accounts within the same bank, it can be shown that S_1 (transfer between accounts) and S_2 (constant balance calculation) are executed concurrently but always under mutual exclusion.

To demonstrate this, we use the invariant {*GI*} ≡ {*Total* = $c[1] + c[2]$ ... $c[n]$ = *Sum* = *constant*}, which states that the sum of the elements in the array c remains constant throughout the execution. The predicate

$$NOTSAFE = pre(S_1) \land pre(S_2) \equiv \{A_1 : c[x] = X + \epsilon \land c[y] = Y + \delta\}$$
$$\land \{B_1 : Sum = \sum_{x=1}^{i-1} c[x] \land i \leq n\}$$

represents a program state where the sum of the array values is no longer constant, and such a state could be visible in the total balance calculation.

In order to verify the safety property of the program, we must show that it is impossible for the preconditions of both S_1 and S_2, represented by their respective predicates A_1 and B_1, to be true simultaneously. It can be trivially verified that {*GI*} →¬ (*NOTSAFE*) is a valid formula. By the very definition of {*GI*} and *NOTSAFE*, this formula can be interpreted as "the maintenance of {*GI*} throughout any execution guarantees that the program will never reach the unsafe state represented by *NOTSAFE*".

1.7 Exercises

A series of exercises, whose solutions can be derived from the theory presented in this chapter, are included to facilitate the acquisition of working techniques and mental aids to face the problems of synchronisation and communication that arise when programming algorithms and applications with several concurrent processes. Various paradigmatic examples of concurrent programming will be used: "Dining Philosophers' Problem", "Multiple Rendezvous", "Mutual Exclusion", etc. The correct approach to find the correct solution to these problems usually consists in considering what can be the demonstration of the processes in which the program is structured according to the axioms and verification rules of PL, extended with the rules of non-interference and concurrency previously introduced.

1.7.1 Solved Exercises

Exercise 1.1 Build the concurrent programs that correspond to the precedence graphs in Fig. 1.12 (1) using the concurrent instructions (cobegin, coend) and (2) with the process branching instructions (fork, join).

Solution

1. Each of the instructions S_i that can be executed concurrently using structured process creation (cobegin, coend) have been represented as a node of the precedence graphs, and the synchronisation dependencies between these instructions have been represented as directed arcs (arrows).

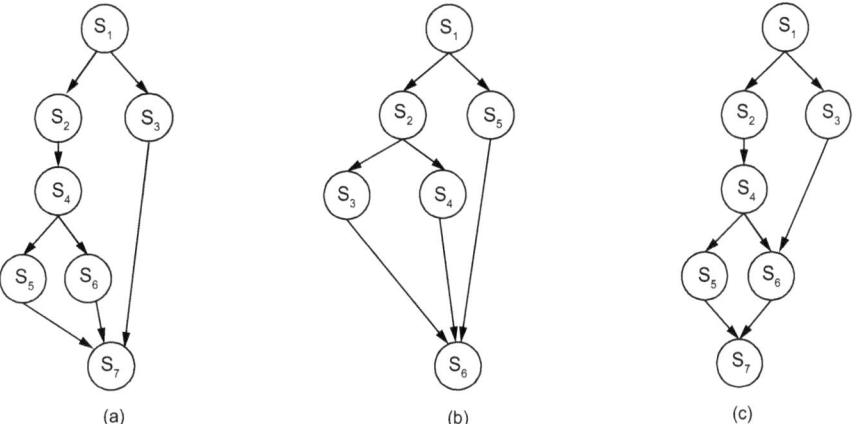

Fig. 1.12 Precedence graphs

```
a)                      b) S1;                   c) S1;
S1;                        cobegin                  cobegin
cobegin                       begin                    S3;
   S3;                           S2;                   begin
   begin                         cobegin                  S2;
      S2;                           S3;                   S4;
      S4;                           S4;                end;
      cobegin                    coend;             coend;
         S5;                   end;
         S6;                                        cobegin
      coend;                   S5;                     S5;
   end;                        coend;                  S6;
coend;                         S6;                  coend;
S7;
                                                    S7;
```

(c) In the synchronisation graph, there is no precedence relationship between the instructions S_3 and S_5; therefore, we must assume that S_5 wait for the completion of S_3, as a possible implementation of graph (c), to maintain the block structure of the program.

2. The creation of processes by branching (fork, join) is independent of the block structure of the program; therefore, it can be understood as the main control line is split when executing a fork instruction S_j, which will then meet with the instruction join(Sj), which does not have to be executed in the same program block of the first instruction. In this way, the synchronisation graph (c) can now be solved in a simple way, without the need to make additional assumptions, as in the case of its resolution with cobegin, coend.

```
a)                              b)                              c)
S1;                             S1;                             S1;
fork S3; --S3 runs in           fork S5;                        fork S3;
         --parallel             S2; --S3,S4 depend on S2        S2;
S2; --main thread               fork S3;                        S4;
    --continues                 fork S4;                        fork S5; --after S4
S4;                             join S3; --waits for S3         join S3; --waits for S3
fork S5; --after S4                      --to complete                   --to complete
fork S6;                        join S4; --waits for S4         S6; --depends on S3
join S6; --waits for S6                  --to complete          join S5;--waits for S5
         --to complete          join S5; --waits for S5                 --to complete
join S5; --waits for S5                  --to complete          S7; --depends on S5
         --to complete          S6; --runs after S3,S4,S5           -- and S6
join S3; --waits for
         --S3 to complete
S7; --runs after all joins
```

Exercise 1.2 Given the following code fragment with two nested structured process creation statements, obtain their corresponding precedence graph.

```
S0;
cobegin
   S1;
   begin
      S2;
      cobegin S3; S4 coend;
      S5;
   end;
   S6;
coend
S7
```

1.7 Exercises

Fig. 1.13 Precedence graph representing a program with two nested cobegin/coend instructions

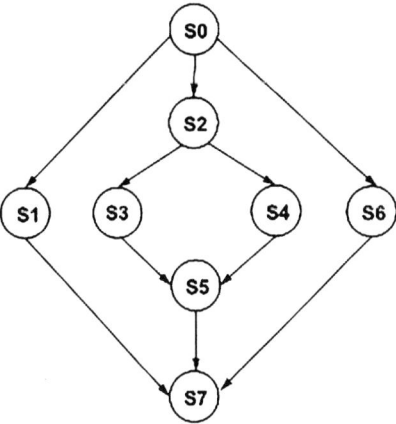

Solution The key observation in solving this problem consists in realising that, while ensuring the precedence relationships between instructions appearing in the code are respected, each of the interleaving sequences that may be formed globally does not consider the level of nesting of the instructions with respect to their appearance within a hierarchy of nested (cobegin, coend) statements (Fig. 1.13).

Exercise 1.3 Consider the following program fragment for two processes P_1 y P_2. The two processes can run at any speed. What are the possible resulting values for the variable x? Assume that x must be loaded into a register to increment and that each process uses a different register to perform the increment.

```
process A()
begin
  for (int i:=0 ; i<2; i++)
    x:= x+1;
end;

process B()
begin
  for (int i:=0 ; i<2; i++)
    x:= x+1;
end;
```

```
Program main()
begin
  x:=0;
  cobegin A(); B(); coend;
end;
```

Solution The possible values of the variable x are $\{2,3,4\}$ since each of the two processes P_1 y P_2 make two reads, $\{L_{11}, L_{12}, L_{21}, L_{22}\}$, and two writes, $\{E_{11}, E_{12}, E_{21}, E_{22}\}$. If each process independently increments two times the variable x, starting from 0, the final value will comply with $x \geq 2$. If the two processes write the value of the register before its content is updated with the value of the local variable of each one, it is possible to register the four increments of x without losing any of them:

x	P_1	P_2	x	P_1	P_2	x	P_1	P_2
0	L_{11}	–	0	L_{11}	–	0	L_{11}	–
0	–	L_{21}	0	–	L_{21}	1	E_{11}	–
1	E_{11}	–	1	E_{11}	–	1	–	L_{21}
1	–	E_{21}	1	–	E_{21}	2	–	E_{21}
1	L_{12}	–	1	L_{12}	–	2	L_{12}	–
1	–	L_{22}	2	E_{12}	–	3	E_{12}	–
2	E_{12}	–	2	–	L_{22}	3	–	L_{22}
2	–	E_{22}	3	–	E_{22}	4	–	E_{22}

Exercise 1.4 Build a program that takes full advantage of concurrency to copy a sequential access file f to another file g using the cobegin/coend instruction for creating concurrent processes.

Solution

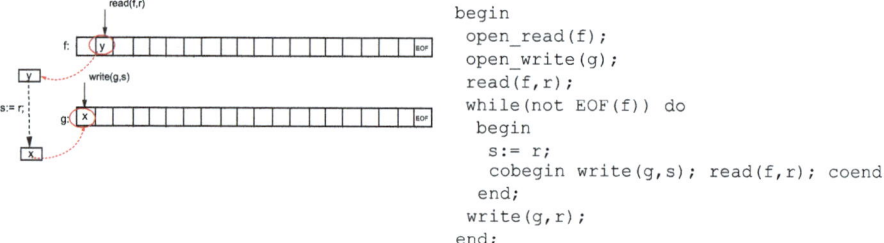

```
begin
  open_read(f);
  open_write(g);
  read(f,r);
  while(not EOF(f)) do
    begin
      s:= r;
      cobegin write(g,s); read(f,r); coend
    end;
  write(g,r);
end;
```

Exercise 1.5 Calculation of the execution time of two concurrent instances of a vector sorting procedure. Suppose a concurrent program in which there are, in shared memory, two vectors a and b of integers and with even size, declared as follows:

$$\text{var } a, b : \text{array } [1...2 \cdot n] \text{ of integer}; \;\; -- \; n \text{ is predefined constant}$$

We want to write a program to obtain in array b a sorted copy of the contents of the array a (we don't care what state a is in after obtaining b). For this we have the function sort(s,t) that sorts a section of a (between the entries s and t, both included). We also have the function copy(o,s,t), which copies a section of a (from s to t) in b (from o).

```
procedure sort(s,t: integer)        procedure copy(o,s,t: integer)
  var i,j: integer;                   var d: integer;
  begin                               begin
    for(i:= s to t-1)                   for(d:=0 to (t-s-1))
      for(j:= s+1 to t)                   b[o+d]:= a[s+d];
        if(a[i] < a[j]) then          end;
          swap(a[i],a[j]);
end;
```

1.7 Exercises

The program for sorting can be implemented in two ways: (a) Sort the entire vector *a*, sequentially with the `sort(s,t)` function, and then copy each entry of *a* into *b*, with `copy(o,s,t)` function; (b) sort the two halves of *a* concurrently, and then mix those two halves into a second vector *b* (for mixing we use a `merge` procedure).

```
procedure sequential();         procedure concurrent();
  var i: integer;                 begin
begin                               cobegin
  sort(1,2n);                         sort(1,n);sort(n+1,2n)
  copy(1,2n);--copy a               coend;
end;                                merge(1, n+1, 2n);
                                  end;
```

Solution The code of `merge(o,s,t)` is in charge of reading the two halves of *a*, at each step, selecting the smallest element of the next two to be read (one in each half) and writing that smallest element in the next half of the mixed vector *b* The code is as follows:

```
procedure merge(lower, middle, upper: integer)
  --next position to write in b
  var write: integer:= 1;
  --next position to read in the first half a
  -- next position to read in the second half of a
  var read1:integer:= lower;
  var read2:integer:= middle;
  begin
    --as long as one half is not finished
    while read1 < middle and read2 <= upper do
      begin
        if(a[lread1]<a[read2])
          begin --minimum in the first half
            b[write]:= a[read1];
            read1:= read1 + 1;
          end
          else --minimum in the second half
            begin
              b[write]:= a[read2];
              read2:= read2 + 1;
            end;
        write:= write + 1;
      end;
    --one of the halves has been copied, copy what
    --is left on the other half
    if(read2 > upper)
       -- copy first
       copy(write, read1, middle-1);
       --copy second
        else copy(write, read2, upper);
  end;
```

We call $T_s(k)$ to the time taken by the `sort(s,t)` procedure when acting on one segment of the vector with `k` entries. We assume that the time taken (on average) for each iteration of the inner loop in `sort()` is the unit (by definition). It is obvious that this loop must perform $k(k-1)/2$ iterations; therefore, $T_s(k) = k(k-1)/2 = 1/2\,k^2 - 1/2k$. The time taken by the sequential version on $2n$ elements will be $T_s(2n) = 1/2\,(2n)^2 - 1/2(2n) = 2n^2 - n$.

With these definitions, we will calculate the time the parallel version will take, in two cases:

(a) P_1: the two concurrent instances of `sort(s,t)` are executed on one processor.
(b) P_2: each instance of `sort(s,t)` is executed on a different processor.

Finally, we write a qualitative comparison of the three times (T_s, P_1, P_2). For this, we must assume that when the `merge(o,s,t)` procedure acts on a vector with p entries, it takes p units of time to execute, which is reasonable considering that in these circumstances, `merge(o,s,t)` copies p values from vector a to vector b. If we call this time $T_m(p)$, we can write $T_m(p) = p$.

(a) In case the `sort` procedure is executed on 1 processor for $2n$ elements: $P_1 = 2T_s(n) + T_m(2n) = (n^2 - n) + 2n = n^2 + n$. The execution time of the fully sequential version required to order the same elements is $2n^2 - n$.
(b) If each instance of sort is executed on a different processor, then the total execution time will be reduced according to the following equation: $P_2 = T_s(n) + T_m(2n) = (1/2n^2 - 1/2n) + 2n = 1/2n^2 + 3/2n$.

Exercise 1.6 Program a correct synchronisation to the concurrent five philosophers' dining problem, for which simulate the performance of each philosopher as a different concurrent process, and synchronise the access and release of the holding resources (chopsticks and chair) using semaphore operations.

1.7 Exercises

Solution

```
semaphore_t chopstick[5];
semaphore_t chair;
sem_init(chair, 4);
for (i = 0; i < 5; i++)
    sem_init(chopstick[i], 1);
process philosopher(int i)
  begin
    while (true) do
      begin
        think();
        sem_wait(chair);
        sem_wait(chopstick[i]);
        sem_wait(chopstick[(i + 1) mod 5]);
        eat();
        sem_post(chopstick[i]);
        sem_post(chopstick[(i + 1) mod 5]);
        sem_post(chair);
      end
    enddo;
  end
```

Exercise 1.7 Two types of processes (type A and type B), simulating two distinct groups of people entering a room, are to be scheduled with semaphores to implement multiple appointments with different numbers of participants. According to the analogy of people entering and leaving a room in teams, a person of type A cannot leave the room until there are 10 people of type B inside, and, similarly, a person of type B cannot leave the room until there are at least one person of type A and nine people of type B in the room.

Solution

```
sem_init(s, 1);
sem_init(presentA, 0);
sem_init(presentB, 0);
int nA:= 0;
int nB:= 0;
bool initiated_exit:= false;
```

```
process A()                                     process B()
 begin                                           begin
  sem_wait(s);                                    sem_wait(s);
  while (true) do begin                           while(true) do begin
    if (not initiated_exit)                        if (not initiated_exit)
     then begin                                     then begin
      nA:= nA + 1;                                   nB:= nB + 1;
      while(nB < 10) do                              while (nA = 0 OR nB < 10)do
       begin                                          begin
        sem_post(s);                                   sem_post(s);
        sem_wait(presentB);                            sem_wait(presentA);
        sem_wait(s);                                   sem_wait(s);
       end                                            end
      enddo;                                         enddo;
      if (not initiated_exit)                        if (nA >= 1 and nB= 10)
       then begin                                     then sem_post(presenA);
        initiated_exit:= true;                       if (not initiated_exit)
        sem_post(presentA);                           then begin
        sem_post(s);                                   initiated_exit:= true;
        break;                                         sem_post(presentB);
       end                                            sem_post(s);
     end;                                             break;
    sem_wait(s);                                    end
     if (initiated_exit)                          end;
      then begin                                  sem_wait(s);
       nA:= nA - 1;                                if (initiated_exit) then
       nB:= nB - 10;                                begin
       initiated_exit:= false;                      nA:= nA - 1;
      end;                                          nB:= nB - 10;
    sem_post(s);                                    initiated_exit:= false;
   end                                            end;
  enddo                                          sem_post(s);
 end;                                            end
                                                enddo;
                                               end;
```

Exercise 1.8 Use semaphores to program two processes that read data from a file. For each data they read, they check if the data is in a table (they read directly from the table), and if it is, they mark it (it is written to the table); otherwise, they finish reading and do nothing. Note that a process finishes when it reaches the end of the file, that access to the file is by mutual exclusion and that two processes can read in the table at the same time; but if one of the processes is writing, the other cannot work on the table, neither reading nor writing. Nor can it be the case that when one process is reading, the other can start writing.

1.7 Exercises

Solution

```
int nl,                   --number readers reading
    ne,                   --number of writers writing
semaphore_t read, write, s;
int num_readers= 2;
sem_init(write,1);
sem_init(read, num_readers);
sem_init(s,1);

procedure start_reading()              procedure end_reading()
begin                                  begin
 sem_wait(read);                        sem_wait(s);
 sem_wait(s);                           nl:= nl - 1;
 nl:= nl + 1;                           if (nl = 0) then
 if (nl= 1) then                         sem_post(write);
   sem_wait(write);                     sem_post(s);
 sem_post(s);                          end;
 sem_post(read);
end;

procedure start_writing()              procedure end_writing()
begin                                  begin
 sem_wait(read);                        sem_post(write);
 sem_wait(write);                       sem_post(read);
end;                                   end;

process Pi(i: 1..2)       --generic process
 begin
 open_read(f);
 sem_wait(s);
 read(f,datum);
 sem_post(s);
 while(!EOF(f)) do
  begin
    start_reading();
     if(datum in table)then
      begin
        end_reading();
        start_writing();
        write(mark_datum);
        end_writing()
      end
      else end_reading();
      sem_wait(s);
      read(f,datum);
      sem_post(s);
  end
  enddo;
```

Exercise 1.9 Prove that the following statement has the postcondition: $s\{x \geq 0, x^2 = a^2\}$.
`if a > 0, then x:=a else x:=-a.`

Solution We will use the notation of triples to demonstrate this, with textual substitution and based on the rule of inference of the conditional *if* statement, which states:

1. $$\frac{\{a>0 \wedge V\} \Rightarrow \{a \geq 0 \wedge V\} \; x := a \{x \geq 0 \wedge x^2 = a^2\}, \{a \leq 0\} \; x := -a \{x \geq 0 \wedge x^2 = a^2\}}{\{V\} \; if \; a>0 \; then \; x := a \; else \; x := -a \{x \geq 0 \wedge x^2 = a^2\}}$$

With this inference rule, we demonstrate the triples:

$$\{V \wedge a > 0\} \; x := a \{x \geq 0, \; x^2 = a^2\}$$

$$\{V \wedge a \leq 0\} \; x := -a \{x \geq 0, \; x^2 = a^2\}$$

2. We will have proved the triple that proves what is requested in the exercise, since it would coincide with the "denominator" of the if rule. Indeed, (1) or the direct branch of if is proved by the application of the axiom of textual substitution and applying the rule of consequence (strengthening of the precondition):

$$\{x \geq 0, \; x^2 = a^2\}_a^x \equiv \{a \geq 0 \wedge a^2 = a^2\} \equiv \{a \geq 0 \wedge V\}$$

By strengthening the precondition, it is also true:

$$\{a > 0 \wedge V\} \Rightarrow \{a \geq 0 \wedge V\}$$

It is also true (2), the inverse branch of if since it can be demonstrated simply by applying textual substitution:

$$\{x \geq 0, \; x^2 = a^2\}_{-a}^x \equiv \{-a \geq 0 \wedge (-a)^2 = a^2\} \equiv \{a \leq 0 \wedge V\}.$$

The demonstration of triples (1) and (2) makes the antecedent of the if rule true and, therefore, demonstrates the objective of the exercise.

Exercise 1.10 Prove the partial correctness of the following program fragment:

```
{V}
sum:= 0; j:= 1;
while (j<c) do
begin
  sum:= sum+j; j:= j+1;
end;
{sum = c*(c-1)/2}
```

1.7 Exercises

Solution We will assume that the constant c is a positive natural number, whose value indicates the number of terms of the arithmetic progression of constant ratio 1 to be added plus one.

Based on PL, we will apply the inference rule of the iteration statement structure (while) which states, according to the conditions of the program, the following:

$$\left\{sum = j \cdot \frac{(j-1)}{2} \wedge j \neq c\right\} \text{while } j \neq c \text{ do begin } sum := sum + j;$$

$$j := j+1; end \left\{sum = j \cdot \frac{(j-1)}{2} \wedge j = c\right\}$$

By the above inference rule, if we prove the triple of the upper part of the iteration rule, we will have proved the triple of the lower part, or in other words, we will have proved the partial correctness of the proposed program fragment. Indeed, the triple of the upper part is first proved by textual chain substitution in the following way.

Applying now the rule of composition and the axiom of textual substitution:

$$\left\{sum = (j+1) \cdot \frac{j}{2}\right\}^{sum}_{sum+j} \equiv \left\{sum + j = (j+1) \cdot \frac{j}{2}\right\} \equiv \left\{sum = j \cdot \frac{(j-1)}{2}\right\}$$

$$sum := sum + j; j := j+1;$$

$$\left\{sum = j \cdot \frac{(j-1)}{2}\right\}$$

Thus, proving the triple:

$$\left\{sum = j \cdot \frac{(j-1)}{2} \wedge j \neq c\right\} \Rightarrow \left\{sum = j \cdot \frac{(j-1)}{2}\right\}$$

$$sum := sum + j; j := j+1; \left\{sum = j \cdot \frac{(j-1)}{2}\right\}$$

Can be done by considering the rule of consequence (strengthening of the precondition) and applying it to the previously demonstrated triple:

$$\left\{sum = j \cdot \frac{(j-1)}{2}\right\}^{j}_{j+1} \equiv \left\{sum = (j+1) \cdot \frac{((j+1)-1)}{2}\right\} \equiv \left\{sum = (j+1) \cdot \frac{j}{2}\right\}$$

from where we can conclude the verification and demonstration of the partial correctness of the program fragment of this exercise.

Exercise 1.11 Find the precondition and prove the correctness of the triple:

$$\{P\}\ a[i] := b; \{a[i] = 2 \cdot a[i]\}.$$

Solution Applying the textual substitution axiom:

$\{a[j] = 2 \cdot a[i]\}_{b}^{a[i]} \equiv \{a[j] = 2 \cdot b\}$
-- i is renamed to j, to avoid variable's *capture* by assignment
$\{a[j] = 2 \cdot b\}\ a[i] := b\ \{a[j] = 2 \cdot a[i]\}$
$\{P\} \equiv \{a[j] = 2 \cdot b\}$
-- and $i = j$

Exercise 1.12 Prove the termination of the program given by the following code. What condition must be imposed in order to perform the demonstration?

```
max:= a[0]; i:= 0;
while (i <> n +1) do
begin
   if (a[i] >= max) then
      max:= a[i]; i:= i+1;
end;
```

$\wedge_{i=1}^{n} \{\max \geq a[i]\} \Leftrightarrow$ *final postcondition after loop*

Solution The termination of this program is studied in relation to the behaviour of the loop on which it is based. Therefore, the evolution of the program must be studied for each iteration of the variables involved in the exit condition of the loop. Only when the exit condition is reached (in this case it would be $i = n + 1$, since the loop continues as long as i is different from $n + 1$), the loop ends after a finite number of iterations and the program terminates.

Since the loop counter variable i is initialised to 0 and incremented by one unit in each iteration, the exit condition $i = n + 1$ is satisfied for some i, which must be at least the initial value of i (the smallest value of i). Therefore, the termination of the program is proved if we add the precondition $\{0 <= n + 1\}$ or equivalent $\{n >= -1\}$. More precisely:

1. If $n < -1$, i would always be different from $n + 1$ and the loop would never end because it would increase by 1 unit indefinitely after each iteration.
2. If $n = -1$, the exit condition is checked only once before entering the loop, so that the program terminates.
3. If $n > -1$, the exit condition is checked after $n + 1$ iterations (a finite number), so that the program will also terminate in this case.

1.7 Exercises

Exercise 1.13 Suppose we have a program with three arrays (a, b and c) of floating values declared as global variables. The sequential multiplication of a and b (storing the result in c) can be done by means of a procedure MultiplicationSec, declared as shown here:

```
var a, b, c : array[1..3,1..3] of real ;
procedure MultiplicationSec;
 var i,j,k : integer ;
begin
 for i := 1 to 3 do
   for j := 1 to 3 do
     begin
       c[i,j] := 0 ;
       for k := 1 to 3 do
         c[i,j] := c[i,j] + a[i,k]*b[k,j] ;
     end
end
```

Write a program for the same purpose but using three concurrent processes. Assume that the elements of the arrays a and b can be read simultaneously, as well as that elements other than c can be written simultaneously.

Solution Parallelise the product matrix c by calculating independently its rows or its columns. To parallelise the calculation of the rows of the result matrix, use three concurrent processes CalculateRow(i:1..3) to do this:

```
var a, b, c : array [1..3,1..3] of real ;
Process CalculateRow[i:1..3];
var j, k : integer ;
begin
  for j := 1 to 3 do
  begin
    c[i,j] := 0 ;
    for k := 1 to 3 do
      c[i,j] := c[i,j] + a[i,k]*b[k,j] ;
  end
end
cobegin
   CalculateRow[1] ;
   CalculateRow[2] ;
   CalculateRow[3]
coend;
```

Exercise 1.14 A piece of program executes nine routines or activities (P_1, P_2, ..., P_9), repeatedly, concurrently with cobegin/coend (see code snippet), but requiring synchronisation according to a certain graph (see figure).

```
while true do
  cobegin
    P1;P2;P3;
    P4;P5;P6;
    P7;P8;P9;
  coend
enddo;
```

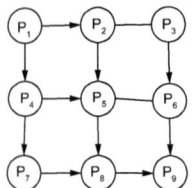

Solution A vector of logical values will be used. This vector has to be initialised only once before the next iteration of the loops, and at the end of process 9, this vector will be re-initialised.

```
--Shared among all
--processes: {P1, P2,...P9}
var finished: array[1..9] of
boolean:= (false,..,false);

procedure WaitFor(i:integer)
begin
  while not finished[i] do
    begin ; --busy waiting
    end
  enddo
end

procedure P1;
begin
  --do P1 work
  Finish(1);
end;

procedure P2;
begin
  WaitFor(1);
  -- do P2 work
  Finish(2);
end;

procedure Finish(i: integer)
var j: integer;
begin
  if i < 9 then
    finished[i]:=true;
  else
    for j := 1 to 9 do
      finished[j] := false ;
    enddo;
  endif;
end

... procedure P8;
begin
  WaitFor(5);
  WaitFor(7);
  -- do P8 work
  Finish(8);
end;

procedure P9;
begin
  WaitFor(6);
  WaitFor(8);
  -- do P9 work
  Finish(9);
end;
```

1.7.2 Proposed Exercises

Exercise 1.15 When developing programs and applications for single-processor systems, what exactly is the advantage of concurrency?

Exercise 1.16 What is meant by transient errors in concurrent program execution sequences?

Exercise 1.17 What is a race condition between concurrent processes?

1.7 Exercises

Exercise 1.18 What are the differences between concurrent, parallel and distributed programming?

Exercise 1.19 Suppose we have an electricity meter that generates pulses every time it consumes 1 kW of energy, and we want to implement a system that counts the number of pulses generated in 1 h. Each pulse increases the number of kW consumed up to that moment. To do this, the system will consist of two processes: (1) An accumulator process that keeps track of the pulses received. (2) A writing process that prints to the printer. The pulses are counted in a variable (n). Assuming that the system is in a state corresponding to the value of the variable ($n = N$) and that, under these conditions, a new impulse and the end of the 1-h period occur simultaneously, obtain the possible sequences of execution of the processes, and which of them are correct and why.

Exercise 1.20 The following program is expected to print due to its execution: 110 or 50. Is the following code correct?

```
var x: integer;                     program main;
                                    begin
process P1;                           x:= 100;
 begin                                cobegin P1;P2 coend
   x:= x + 10;                      end;
 end;
Process P2;
 begin
   if x>100 then
      write(x)
      else write (x - 50);
 end;
```

Exercise 1.21 Suppose two concurrent processes, P_1 and P_2, are trying to use the same I/O device. More specifically, suppose that P_1 is trying to read from block 20 of the device, while P_2 is trying to write to block 88. If the operations of reading and writing a block can be considered atomic, the execution of P_1 and P_2 would not cause any race condition problems, but if these operations could be decomposed into the basic operations of jumping to the corresponding block and reading or writing, as shown below, transient errors could occur in both processes. Which of the possible execution sequences that can be generated by processes P_1 and P_2 is correct, and which is not? Explain your answer.

$$read(20) \Leftrightarrow jump-to(20); read(\ ); \quad write(88) \Leftrightarrow jump-to(88); write(\ );$$

Exercise 1.22 Suppose a multiprocessor system has an instruction called Test_and_Set() (T&S()), such that the concurrent execution of T&S(x=1) by any program's process would give the same result as the execution of the following two statements: <x:= read(c); c:=1> atomically (indivisible), where x is a local variable and c is a global variable of the system. Using the T&S(·) instruction, construct the protocols of acquisition, restitution and initialisation of variables to give a solution to the problem of access in mutual exclusion to a critical section shared by two processes of a concurrent program.

Exercise 1.23 Let be a sequence of numbers in which each term is the sum of the previous two: $a(1) = 0$; $a(2) = 1$; ...$a(i) = a(i-1) + a(i-2)$. To calculate the partial sums of the odd terms of this sequence, we will have two processes: sequence and sum. The first one calculates the terms of the sequence, and the second one calculates the partial sums of the odd terms. Implement the previous concurrent algorithm, including in its code only operations on semaphores, which must be correctly created and initialised to obtain the above terms and partial sums.

Exercise 1.24 If you want to pass a semaphore as a parameter to a procedure, how should you pass it, by value or by reference, or is there no difference between the two cases? What would happen if you chose the wrong option?

Exercise 1.25 How can you know in a concurrent program how many processes are blocked in one semaphore?

Exercise 1.26 Program 2 functions, `genwait()` and `gensignal()`, to simulate general semaphores using only binary semaphores.

Exercise 1.27 Demonstrate that if the `sem_wait()` and `sem_post()` semaphore operations are not executed atomically, the mutual exclusion provided by the concurrent programming mechanism called semaphore would not be verified.

Exercise 1.28 Add a semaphore to the following program to always write 40.

```
int n;                          Program Main();
Process Inc();                  begin
  begin                           n:= 0;
    int i;                        cobegin
    for i:=1 to 20 do               Inc(); Inc();
      n:=n+1;                     coend;
    enddo;                        write(n);
  end;                          end;
```

Exercise 1.29 Suppose that smoking a cigarette requires three ingredients: (a) tobacco, (b) paper and (c) matches. Suppose also that there are three smokers sitting around a table, each of whom has an unlimited supply of one of the ingredients: one smoker always has tobacco, another always has paper and the third always has matches. Suppose that there is also a referee who is not a smoker and allows each smoker to roll cigarettes. The referee arbitrarily (not deterministically) chooses two smokers, takes from them one of the ingredients they each have and places it on the table. The referee then informs the third smoker that the two ingredients he needs to roll are already on the table. That smoker picks up the ingredients and uses them along with his own to roll a cigarette, which takes a while to smoke. Meanwhile, the referee, waits until the table is empty again, chooses two smokers again at random and takes one ingredient from each and places it on the table. This process is repeated. Bearing in mind that a smoker cannot start rolling another cigarette until he has finished smoking the last one he has prepared and that smokers cannot reserve ingredients that appear on the table, i.e., if the referee placed tobacco and paper while the match smoker was smoking, the tobacco and paper will remain on the table until the match smoker finishes his cigarette and picks up these ingredients from the table to roll and smoke the next cigarette. The correct synchronisation between the referee and the smokers must be programmed using semaphores.

Exercise 1.30 Suppose we are in a discotheque, and it turns out that the girls' toilet is out of order and everyone has to share the boys' toilet. The aim is to establish a protocol for entering the cloakroom using semaphores that ensures that the following restrictions are respected: (a) restrictions for girls, only one can be in the cloakroom; (b) restrictions for boys, more than one can enter, but a maximum of five will be allowed inside the cloakroom.

1. Male chauvinist version of protocol: Boys have priority over girls. This means that if a girl is waiting to go into the toilet and a boy arrives, he can pass, and she continues to wait. Even if the boy who arrived cannot enter immediately because there are already five boys inside the toilet, he will pass before the girl when a boy leaves the toilet.
2. Feminist version of protocol: Girls have priority over boys. This means that if a boy is waiting and a girl arrives, the girl must pass in front of the boy. Even if the girl who has arrived cannot enter the toilet immediately because there is already a girl inside, she will pass in front of the boy when the girl inside comes out.

You are asked to implement the two versions of the above protocol using POSIX semaphores.

Exercise 1.31 Construct a synchronisation network that establishes a priority between the S_i processes so that the following code (sequential program) can be executed by the processes concurrently and without interference problems. A state S_0 of initialisation of the variables can be assumed. To solve it correctly, it is necessary to find interleavable instruction sets that do not cause race conditions when the processes access the variables. This would give us the processes that can be started simultaneously in `cobegin/coend` pairs:

```
S1:: cuad = x*x;              S4:: z= m1+m2;
S2:: m1= a*cuad;              S5:: y= z+c;
S3:: m2= b*x;
```

Exercise 1.32 What does it mean to have a correct concurrent program?

Exercise 1.33 Doesn't the fact that the processes of a concurrent program can starve contradict the requirement that the processes must necessarily progress in the execution of their instructions (finite progress hypothesis)? Explain your answer.

Exercise 1.34 For each of the following code fragments, find the corresponding postcondition:

```
a) {i<10} i:= 2*i+1; { }          d) { F } a:= a+7; { }
b) {i>0}  i:= i - 1; { }          e) {     } i:=3; j:= 2*i; { }
c) {i>j}  i:= i+1;j:= j+1;{ }     f) {     } c:=a+b;c:=c/2; { }
```

Exercise 1.35 Explain the differences between the following three conditions on the degree of fairness in the allocation of the processor to the processes of a concurrent program (assuming time-sharing scheduling):

1. Unconditional equity: ensures that an active process gets to see its instructions executed very often.
2. Weak equity or fairness: ensures that a process whose code has programmed instructions that depend on the truth value of conditions will execute those instructions very often if the truth value of those conditions remains true.
3. Strong fairness: if the conditions on which the execution of certain instructions depends are met very often, then these instructions will be executed frequently.

Exercise 1.36 State the type of fairness with which a process scheduler would ensure that the next program of two concurrent processes would always finish in a not arbitrarily large amount of time:

```
bool cont = true;
sem_t try;
sem_init(&try, 0, 1);
sem_wait(&try);
cobegin
S1:: while (cont) {
        sem_post(&try);
        if (cont)
            sem_wait(&try);
     }
S2:: sem_wait(&try);
     cont = false;
coend;
```

1.7 Exercises

Exercise 1.37 Given the concurrent program:

```
int x = 5;
int y = 2;
cobegin < x = x + y > || < y = x * y > coend;
```

1. What can x and y be?
2. What would be the possible values of x and y if brackets were suppressed and each assignment order was implemented using three atomic instructions: read from memory, add or multiply and write from register to memory.

Exercise 1.38 Check to see if $\{x \geq 2\} < x = x - 2 >$ causes interference with each of the following triples:

(a) $\{x \geq 0\} < x := x + 3 > \{x \geq 3\}$	(d) $\{y \geq 0\} < y := y + 3 > \{y \geq 3\}$
(b) $\{x \geq 0\} < x := x + 3 > \{x \geq 0\}$	(e) $\{x \text{ is odd}\} < y := x + 3 > \{y \text{ is even}\}$
(c) $\{x \geq 7\} < x := x + 3 > \{x \geq 10\}$	

Exercise 1.39 Investigate the final values of the variables x and y after the execution of the following program. Insert asserts between the braces before and after each statement to create a demonstration trace of the program:

1. `int x:= C1;`
2. `int y:= C2;`
3. `x:= x+y;`
4. `y:= x*y;`
5. `x:= x - y.`

Exercise 1.40 Prove that the following triple is true:

```
{x= 0}
cobegin
<x:= x + 1> || <x:= x + 2> || <x:= x + 4>
coend
{x=7}
```

Exercise 1.41 Show that the triple $\{x = y\}\ P\ \{x = y\}$ is true, given the following concurrent composition construction:

```
P::
cobegin
<x:= x - 1>;<x:= x + 1> || <y:= y - 1>;<y:= y + 1>
coend
```

Exercise 1.42 Apply the property at most once[26] to the evaluation of statements such as x:= expression, which are evaluated by the following concurrent processes. Which of the following evaluations can be considered to be atomic (<x:= expression>) (assuming that the initial values of the variables are equal to 0 and that a and b are constants)?

(a) P_1: : cobegin $x := y + a$ || $y := x + b$ coend
(b) P_2: : cobegin $x := y + a$ || $y := f(x) + b$ coend
(c) P_3: : cobegin $x := y + a$ || $y := a + b$ coend
(d) P_4: : cobegin $x := x/y$ || $y := a + b$ coend

Exercise 1.43 The following triple is indemonstrable unless one of the following conditions is met (select the condition that applies):

$$\{x = 0 \wedge y = 0 \wedge z = -1\}$$
$$<x := z + a> \| <y := x + b>$$
$$\{x = a \wedge y = b \vee y = a + b \wedge z = -1\}$$

1. It must be satisfied whenever $a = 1$.
2. It must be satisfied whenever $a = 1$ and $b = 0$.
3. It must be satisfied whenever $b = 0$.
4. The values of the variables a and b are non-negative.

---

[26] An assignment statement of $x := x + y$ can be considered to be executed atomically if only one process can simultaneously read or write any of the shared global variables, i.e., there is no problem in that one process P_1 reads the value of variable x from the above expression and another P_2 writes it, but P_1 and P_2 cannot simultaneously read or write x or $x + y$.

2 Algorithms and Process Synchronisation Mechanisms Based on Shared Memory

2.1 Introduction to the Two-Process Mutual Exclusion Problem

There have always been low-level solutions to solve the problem of accessing a critical section in mutual exclusion, for example, locks or instructions for reading and atomic allocation of a variable in memory ($TST(m)$) however, since 1965, a series of software solutions have been studied to solve it. These solutions are intended to be independent of the instructions of a specific machine and make it possible to ensure that the processes comply with all the properties required of a concurrent program. Essentially, the aim is to achieve solutions that provide equal access of processes to a critical section of the program. We are only going to consider, for now, solutions to the problem of mutual exclusion in the access to critical sections by concurrent processes using the basic instructions of reading or writing the value of a variable in memory.

The algorithms that will be introduced below represent a selected sample of the many that have been published [15, 16, 29, 37], trying to respect the chronological order of appearance of the proposed solutions and have an unquestionable pedagogical value for the understanding of basic concepts of concurrent programming.

Algorithms for solving the mutual exclusion problem are usually categorised into two groups:

- Centralised: those that use variables shared between processes, which express the state of the processes. These variables are usually accessed in separate sections of the processes' code, called acquisition and restitution protocols, which must be executed by the concurrent processes before and after the critical section appears in the program.

- Distributed: they do not use shared variables between processes. They typically use only message-passing instructions to stop processes when the critical section is busy or to inform them that it is free again.

2.1.1 How to Solve the Mutual Exclusion Problem

The most basic mechanism for synchronisation between processes competing for access to a critical section is to program a loop that iterates and forces the process to wait, which continuously checks the value of a condition. This solution is called *busy waiting* because the processes iterate through an empty loop, i.e., whose component block contains only a null instruction, such as the ';' of some languages, before entering the critical section and until such entry is safe. This type of implementation of the protocol to be followed by processes accessing the critical section consumes system resources, such as processor time in single-processor systems or memory access cycles in multiprocessor systems, without the process under busy-waiting to make any significant progress in the execution of the useful instructions or scheduled computations.

Busy waiting can be considered an acceptable solution to the problem of mutually exclusive access to a critical section as long as the system does not have many processes. Solutions using busy waiting loops and shared variable values between processes resulted in many proposals that were not easy to evaluate for compliance with concurrent correctness properties.

Edsger Dijkstra [15] established a systematic method for obtaining an algorithm that allows finding a solution to the problem and proving that it satisfies the conditions which should fulfil to be accepted as such. Dijkstra's conditions are as follows:

(1) Make no assumptions about the instructions or number of processes supported by the computing platform: we can only use the basic instructions, such as read, write or check a memory location to solve the problem. The above instructions are executed without interruption, atomically, i.e., in case two or more instructions are likely to be executed simultaneously by the processes of the program, the result of such execution is non-deterministic or, equivalently, the execution of such instructions is performed sequentially, but in an unpredictable order.
(2) Make no assumptions about the speed of execution of the processes other than it is non-zero.
(3) A process cannot prevent another process from entering the critical section if it is not executing within the critical section.
(4) The critical section will eventually be reached by one of the processes trying to enter it. This condition always ensures the safety property known as reachability of the critical section by the processes. This property, if it is always satisfied, excludes the possibility that, during the execution of the program, a process deadlock could occur, i.e., no process would ever manage to enter the critical section, but it does not ensure that

2.1 Introduction to the Two-Process Mutual Exclusion Problem

all the processes of the protocol will ever manage to enter the critical section (absence of process starvation), let alone that they will manage to do so in an equal way (fairness).

2.1.1.1 Method of Successive Refinement

In addition to the conditions that an algorithm must fulfil to be considered a solution to the mutual exclusion problem, Dijkstra proposes a method to obtain the algorithm to solve it in four steps or modifications from an initial scheme. First, it is assumed that the processes alternate their entry into the critical section according to the value of a global variable *turn* shared between them. Each of the following modifications to the first stage is considered as a new stage in the process of finding the acceptable solution to the mutual exclusion problem. This is finally obtained in the fifth stage, and this solution is the so-called Dekker algorithm.

First stage. A *turn* variable is used that contains the identifier of the process that, at each moment of execution, can enter the critical section. This variable can have a value of 1 or 2; initially, we assume that its value is 1.

```
var
  turn: integer;
--initially = 1 or 2

procedure Process1;
begin
  while true do
    begin
      Remainder;  -- outside CS
      while (turn <> 1) do
        begin
          null;  --busy wait
        end
      enddo;
      Critical_Section;
      turn:= 2;
    end;
  enddo;
end;
```

```
procedure Process2;
begin
  while true do
    begin
      Remainder;  -- outside CS
      while (turn <> 2) do
        begin
          null;  --busy wait
        end;
      enddo;
      Critical_Section;
      turn:= 1;
    end;
  enddo;
end;
```

Second stage. The strict alternation in the access to the critical section that occurred in the first stage was because, in order to decide which process entered the critical section, global information on the state of the program had to be stored in a *turn* variable that was only changed by a process when it exited the critical section. To avoid this, the idea now is to associate with each process its state information in a key variable that indicates whether that process is in a critical section or not at that instant of the algorithm execution.

Consequently, according to this scheme, each process now reads the key of the other but cannot modify it.

```
var
  c1, c2: integer;
--both initially set to 1

procedure Process1;
begin
  while true do
    begin
      Remainder;
      while (c2 = 0) do
        begin
          null; --busy wait
        end
      enddo;
      c1 := 0;   --enters CS
      Critical_Section;
      c1 := 1;   --exited CS
    end;
  enddo;
end;
```

```
procedure Process2;
begin
  while true do
    begin
      Remainder;
      while (c1 = 0) do
        begin
          null; --busy wait
        end;
      enddo;
      c2 := 0;   --enters CS
      Critical_Section;
      c2 := 1;   --exited CS
    end;
  enddo;
end;
```

In this case, the safety property fails because, if both processes are running at the same speed, they check that the other process still has its key at 1, i.e., its state is not observed as entering the critical section, then both could enter the critical section, thus violating the safety property of the algorithm. The explanation for this error scenario is simple: when one process sets its key to 0, it is too late for the other to detect it, as the latter has already managed to pass the busy waiting loop.

Since the solution proposed by this second stage would only work depending on the relative execution speed between the processes, it is said to be unacceptable because it does not fulfil Dijkstra's second condition.

Third stage. The issue with the previous solution is that one process could be checking the state of the other process at the same time as this is modifying it, and thus the final value is not detected. This occurs because the exit from the inner busy-waiting loop and the assignment of its key to '0' are not performed as a single atomic operation. The scenario is that one process could be pre-empted after exiting its busy wait loop, allowing the other process to advance to the critical section before the first process changes the value of its key. This leaves the program in an unsafe value. The second process could then become active without detecting the new value of the key, still seeing it as '1', and exits its busy-wait loop as well, potentially leading to both processes entering the critical section simultaneously.

2.1 Introduction to the Two-Process Mutual Exclusion Problem

```
var
  c1, c2: integer;
--both initially set to 1

Procedure Process1;
begin
  while true do
    begin
      Remainder;
      c1:= 0;  --intends CS
      while (c2 = 0) do
        begin
          null; --busy wait
        end
      enddo;
      Critical_Section;
      c1 := 1;   --exited CS
    end;
  enddo;
end;
```

```
procedure Process2;
begin
  while true do
    begin
      Remainder;
      c2:= 0;  --intends CS
      while (c1 = 0) do
        begin
          null; --busy wait
        end;
      enddo;
      Critical_Section;
      c2 := 1;   --exited CS
    end;
  enddo;
end;
```

This solution ensures mutual exclusion, as only one process can enter the critical section at a time. However, it is not considered correct because it introduces the possibility of deadlock. If both processes set their respective variables ($c1$ and $c2$) to 0 at the same time, they will continuously wait for the other process to change its variable back to 1. This results in both processes being stuck in their busy waiting loops indefinitely, leading to a deadlock.

This protocol violates Dijkstra's fourth condition, which requires that progress is guaranteed, meaning that at least one process should be able to proceed when both are competing for the critical section. In this case, no progress is made, and the protocol is therefore unacceptable.

Fourth stage. The problem in the third stage was that when a process modifies the value of its key, it cannot be certain whether the other process is doing the same at the same time, which could lead to deadlock. In the fourth stage, the proposed solution is to allow a process to recheck and possibly change its key back to '1' if, after setting its key to '0', it detects that the other process has also set its key to '0'.

```
var                                     procedure Process2;
   c1, c2: integer;                     begin
--both initially set to 1                  while true do
                                              begin
Procedure Process1;                              Remainder;
begin                                            c2:= 0;  --intends CS
   while true do                                 while (c1 = 0) do
      begin                                         begin
         Remainder;                                    c2:= 1;
         c1:= 0;  --intends CS                         while (c1 = 0) do
         while (c2 = 0) do                                begin
            begin                                            null; --busy wait
               c1:= 1;                                    end;
               while (c2 = 0) do                       enddo;
                  begin                                c2:= 0;
                     null; --busy wait              end;
                  end;                            enddo;
               enddo;                             Critical_Section;
               c1:= 0;                            c2 := 1;   --exited CS
            end;                                end;
         enddo;                                enddo;
         Critical_Section;                  end;
         c1 := 1;   --exited CS
      end;
   enddo;
end;
```

However, the modified algorithm still has potential issues. If both processes were running at the same speed, a deadlock between them could still occur in this fourth stage. This happens because both processes could set their keys to 0 and 1 in succession, and keep waiting for each other in the outer loop, just like in the third stage. Although the likelihood of deadlock is reduced in this version, it is still possible, making the solution unacceptable.

The algorithm does not satisfy Dijkstra's second condition (processes velocity independence) as a process could potentially wait indefinitely even when the other process is also in a waiting state. It also fails to meet Dijkstra's fourth condition (progress), since both processes may continue iterating in their respective outer loops without making any progress actual towards entering the critical section.

To solve the problem, it is necessary to establish a predetermined order for entering the critical section when a conflict arises between processes at a given point during the execution of the algorithm. This order can be enforced using a *turn* variable. Without such a mechanism, the processes may enter a state of livelock, continuously updating their keys without ever observing a favourable value in the other process's key, thereby preventing them from advancing into the critical section.

2.1.1.2 Dekker's Algorithm

This solution can be seen as the fifth stage in the method of successive refinement, and it represents a solution that satisfies the safety properties. Dekker's algorithm is based on the concepts introduced in the first and fourth stages of Dijkstra's method. In the first stage, a safe solution was produced, but the use of a global *turn* variable introduced the issue of strict alternation. This meant that a process could not enter the critical section if it was not its turn, even if the other process was passive, violating Dijkstra's third condition. The fourth stage introduced separate keys (c_1, c_2), which are modified by one process and read by the other. These keys represent each process's intention to enter the critical section. However, the solution still failed to meet Dijkstra's fourth condition (progress), as it could lead to situations where both processes indefinitely gave way to each other. Dekker's algorithm addresses these issues by introducing the *turn* variable and using it only when both processes are trying to enter the critical section at the same time.

```
var
   c1, c2: integer;
--both initially set to 1 and turn to either of the 2 processes
```

```
Procedure Process1;
begin
  while true do
    begin
      Remainder; --outside CS
      c1:= 0; --intends CS
      while (c2 = 0) do
       if (turn =2) then
         begin
           c1:= 1; --yield to P2
           while (turn = 2) do
             begin
               null; --busy wait
             end;
           enddo;
           c1:= 0;
          end;
        endif;
      enddo;
      Critical_Section;
      turn:= 2; --change turn
      c1 := 1;   --exited CS
    end;
  enddo;
end;
```

```
procedure Process2;
begin
  while true do
    begin
      Remainder; --outside CS
      c2:= 0; --intends CS
      while (c1 = 0) do
        if (turn =1) then
          begin
            c2:= 1; --yield to P1
            while (turn = 1) do
              begin
                null; --busy wait
              end;
            enddo;
            c2:= 0;
          end;
        endif;
      enddo;
      Critical_Section;
      turn:= 1; --change turn
      c2 := 1;  --exited CS
    end;
  enddo;
end;
```

```
Main Program
cobegin
  Process1; Process2
coend;
```

The key idea of Dekker's algorithm is to use the `turn` variable only when both processes attempt to enter the critical section simultaneously. When a process sets its `c1` or `c2` to 0 to indicate its intent to enter the CS, it checks the key of the other process. If the other process has also set its key to 0, it checks the value of the `turn` variable. If the turn is not in its favour, the process resets its key to 1 and waits until the turn changes. This prevents livelock, and once the turn changes, the process proceeds. This approach solves the problem while also ensuring that the processes do not deadlock or starve each other, fulfilling Dijkstra's conditions.

2.1.2 Verification of Dekker's Algorithm Correction Properties

2.1.2.1 Safety

We must prove that the mutually exclusive access to the critical section and the critical section reachability property are always satisfied.

Mutual Exclusion A process P_i enters the critical section only if the other process maintains its key $cj = 1$. Since a process can only modify its own key and checks the other's key (cj) only after setting $ci = 0$ to signal its intent, this ensures that when P_i enters the critical section, the condition $cj = 1$ holds throughout its execution within the critical section.

If we examine the acquisition protocol of the algorithm, the condition expressed by the values of these variables necessarily implies that only one process can access the critical section at any given time. Each time a process P_i enters, the condition $ci = 0$ and $cj = 1$ is fulfilled, and similarly, when the other process P_j enters, it is also fulfilled $ci = 1$ and $cj = 0$.

Critical Section Reachability To demonstrate this property, we use a proof by reductio ad absurdum (proof by contradiction):

1. Assume that the process P_i tries to enter the critical section alone, it will find the key of the other process P_j with the value $cj = 1$. Therefore, P_i can enter the critical section, as shown earlier in the safety property proof.
2. Now, if both processes P_i and P_j attempt to enter the critical section and $turn = i$, the following sub-scenarios may occur:

   (a) P_j finds the key $ci = 1$, allowing it to enter the critical section.
   (b) P_j finds the key $ci = 0$ and $turn = i$, so it waits in its innermost busy-wait loop and assigns $cj = 1$, a value that remains as long as the $turn = i$.
   (c) P_i finds the key $cj = 0$, so it continues iterating in the outermost busy waiting loop with $ci = 0$. It will eventually read $cj = 1$, which happens as described in scenario (b), and P_i will enter the critical section, while P_j cannot.

2.1.2.2 Liveness

Depending on the memory access control hardware, Dekker's algorithm could potentially starve one of the two processes. For example, if P_i is a very fast and repetitive process, there is a possibility that it could repeatedly enter the critical section, preventing the other process, P_j, from doing so.

A problematic scenario could occur if P_j exits its inner loop but fails to update the value of its key cj to 0. This may happen because P_i continuously reads cj when evaluating the state of its outermost busy-wait loop. If read operations are prioritized over writes, P_j may be prevented from updating its key. However, once P_j successfully assigns its key cj, the risk of starvation is resolved, and P_j can enter the critical section. Ultimately, whether a process can be indefinitely delayed depends on the fairness of low-level mechanisms that handle concurrent memory access.

2.1.2.3 Protocol Fairness

The fairness of the Dekker algorithm ultimately relies on the fairness of the underlying hardware. If two processes simultaneously request access to the same memory location—one attempting to read and the other to write—and the hardware always resolves the conflict by prioritising the read request, Dekker's algorithm cannot guarantee fairness. This could potentially lead to the starvation scenario for one of the processes, as described earlier.

2.2 A Simple Solution to the Mutual Exclusion Problem: The Peterson Algorithm

Gary L. Peterson [37] proposed a simple way of solving the mutual exclusion problem for two processes, which has since been considered the canonical solution to this problem. This solution also allows an easy generalisation to the case of *N-processes*, maintaining the structure of the protocol for the case $N = 2$ processes.

2.2.1 Solution for Two Processes

The shared variables for the processes are:

```
var c: array [0..1] of boolean; turn: 0..1;
```

The *array* c is initialised to *false* and indicates whether or not the process P_i is trying to enter the critical section. The variable `turn` is used to resolve conflicts when both processes attempt to enter the critical section simultaneously. Assuming $i = 0$ and $j = 1$ correspond to the process identifiers P_i and P_j, respectively, the code for the process P_i is as follows:

```
process Pᵢ();
begin
 while(true) do
   begin
     c[i]:= true;
     turn:= i;
     while(c[j] = true and turn = i) do
       null;
     enddo;
     CriticalSection;
     c[i]:= false;
   end
 enddo
end;
```

2.2.1.1 Safety

Mutual Exclusion To prove that the algorithm satisfies this property, we use the proof by contradiction method. Suppose that both processes P_i and P_j are in their critical sections simultaneously. This would imply that both `c[i]` and `c[j]`, are true. However, this is not possible because the busy-wait conditions of both processes could not have been satisfied at the same time. The shared variable `turn` must have been set to either *i* or *j* before either process entered its busy-wait loop. Since it is impossible for both `turn` = *i* and `turn` = *j* to hold simultaneously, we reach a contradiction. Therefore, only one of the processes could have entered the critical section. The process that tried to enter last would have set the final value of the `turn` variable, and so the other process did not have to wait.

Now, assume that the process that proceeds is P_i, since it has found `turn` = *j*. Thus, it could not have entered the critical section simultaneously with P_j since P_j would have needed to find `turn` = *i* to proceed. However, once P_i sets `turn` = *i*, it must wait if P_j is still attempting to enter, thereby ensuring mutual exclusion.

Reachability of the Critical Section Assume that P_i is continuously delayed, waiting to enter its critical section. Now, suppose either that P_j is passive and not attempting to enter or P_j is also constantly waiting to enter the critical section.

- The first case, where P_j is passive and `c[j]` = *false*, allows P_i to enter its critical section.
- The second case, where both processes are waiting, the situation is impossible. This is because the shared variable `turn` must hold either the value *i* or *j*, which will ensure that the busy-wait condition of at least one of the processes evaluates to false. This allows the corresponding process to enter the critical section.

2.2 A Simple Solution to the Mutual Exclusion Problem: The Peterson Algorithm

Therefore, it would be a contradiction to assume that both processes could be in a deadlock state indefinitely.

2.2.1.2 Fairness

Not only does this protocol satisfies the liveness property, but it also ensures fairness in the execution of both processes at all times. To demonstrate this, assume that P_i is blocked while waiting to enter the critical section, and P_j repeatedly enters the critical section, monopolising access. This leads to a contradiction: for P_j to enter the critical section again, it must assign `turn:= j`, which would allow P_i to falsify its waiting condition and enter the critical section immediately. This contradicts the assumption that P_i is permanently blocked and denied fair access to the critical section.

2.2.2 Solution for *N* Processes

The generalisation of Peterson's algorithm is straightforward: repeatedly apply the two-process solution (up to $n - 1$ times) to progressively eliminate at least one process at each stage until only one process remains to enter the critical section. We will also show that the safety property (mutual exclusion) is maintained for this process inside the critical section. The shared variables between the processes are:

```
var c: array [0..n-1] of -1..n-2;
--values of c[i] represent the stages each process will go through
--before entering critical section

turn: array[0..n-2] of 0..n-1;
--represents the identifier of the process that performs busy
--waiting in each stage, as it owns the turn of that stage
--and thus resolves possible conflicts
```

The initial values of the `c` and `turn` arrays are -1 and 0, respectively. The value `c[i] = -1` means that the process is passive and has not yet attempted to enter the critical section. The value `c[i]= j` indicates that the process has reached the j-th stage of the protocol.

To better understand this, think of the algorithm as implementing a queue with $n - 1$ positions that the processes must pass through to enter the critical section. It should be noted that moving on to the next stage creates a competition between the processes, and a process blocked at one stage may be overtaken by other processes in subsequent stages as they leave the critical section and restart the protocol. The following code belongs to the process P_i. The local variables, `i`, `j`, and `k` are used, and the numbers or identifiers of the n processes are taken in the range `i: 0..n-1`.

```
process P_i();
begin
while true do
  begin
    Rest of the instructions;--non-critical section code
    (1) for j=0 to n-2 do
    (2)   begin
    (3)     c[i]:= j;
    (4)     turn[j]:= i;
    (5)     for k:=0 to n-1 do
    (6)       begin
    (7)         if (k=i) then continue;
    (8)         while(c[k]>=j and turn[j]=i) do
    (9)           null; --busy waiting at stage j
    (10)        enddo;
    (11)      end;
    (12)   end;
    (13) c[i]:= n-1; --meta-instruction
    (14) <critical section>.
    (15) c[i]:= -1
  end
enddo;
end;
```

2.2.2.1 Formal Verification of Algorithm Properties

We say that the process P_i precedes the process P_j if and only if the former process has reached a more advanced stage than the latter, i.e., if their respective key values satisfy the strict inequality $c[i] > c[j]$. The verification that Peterson's algorithm satisfies the properties desirable for a fully correct concurrent solution, at least safety and liveness properties, and that it also ensures a fair access of all processes to the critical section is carried out by proving the following four lemmas.

Lemma 1 A process that precedes all others can advance at least one stage. Let P_i be a process in the protocol. When this process evaluates its busy-wait condition of the *while* sentence at (8), it finds that $c[i] > c[j]$, $\forall j \neq i$, as it precedes all other processes. Therefore, condition in (8) for continuing the wait is not satisfied, and P_i can advance to stage $j + 1$. Since this condition is not checked atomically it may happen that during the evaluation, one or more processes reach the same stage as P_i. However, as soon as the first of these processes (P_k) updates the variable `turn[j]`, with its own identifier (k), process P_i can continue, i.e., to advance to next stage, because it is no longer the last process to assign the stage *j*'s turn. It could, however, be overtaken in the next stage if multiple processes reach and progress through stage *j* of the algorithm.

Lemma 2 When a process moves from stage *j* to stage *j* + 1, one of the following conditions must be verified:

1. It precedes all others, or
2. it is not alone in stage *j*.

2.2 A Simple Solution to the Mutual Exclusion Problem: The Peterson Algorithm

Assuming that P_i is about to advance to the next stage. The condition of Lemma 1 holds if (1) is satisfied. Otherwise, for P_i to advance, it must observe that `turn[j]` $\neq$ `i`, in which case the process P_i must be accompanied by at least one other process in stage j and has not been the last process to assign the *turn* value for that stage. Regardless of the number of processes that have modified `turn[j]` after P_i, there will be a process P_r that was the last to update it. This process does not satisfy the condition for exiting the wait, since `turn[j]` = `r` will be satisfied and P_r remains at stage j. Therefore, P_r's presence ensures that condition (2) of the lemma is satisfied. It can also happen that the process P_i proceeds to the next stage because it has found that condition (1) is true, and meanwhile another process reaches the same stage, making condition (1) temporarily invalid. However, in this case, condition (2) would become true, and the process P_i would proceed to the next stage anyway.

Lemma 3 If there are at least two processes in stage j, then there must be at least one process in each of the previous stages. The proof is by induction on variable j.

1. For ($j = 0$). The statement is vacuously true, as there are no preceding stages.
2. To prove the case ($j = 1$), Lemma 2 above is used. If we suppose that there is a process at stage $j = 1$, then if another process (or more than one) joins it, then at least one process must have been in stage 0. This process, which has remained at stage $j = 0$, cannot progress as long as it is alone at that stage.
3. Now suppose that Lemma 2 holds for stage $j - 1$. If there are two or more processes in stage j, then, when the last of these processes left stage $j - 1$, at least one other process must have been present at that stage. By the induction hypothesis, all stages prior to stage j must be occupied. Furthermore, Lemma 2 ensures that none of these stages could have been left empty at the time the process advanced from stage $j - 1$ to j.

Lemma 4 The maximum number of processes that can be in stage j will be $n - j$, given that $0 \leq j \leq n - 2$. Applying Lemma 3, if each of the preceding stages $0...j - 1$ must have at least one process, then stage j can contain at most $n-j$ processes. If any of the earlier stages becomes empty, which would happen if a process progresses ahead of the others and consistently advances, then by Lemma 3, at most one process can reach stage j. An important corollary of this lemma, is that at most two processes can be in stage $n - 2$.

2.2.2.2 Safety
Mutual Exclusion Suppose there is one process at stage $n - 2$ of the algorithm and another process at stage $n - 1$ (which is the meta-stage that coincides with the critical section itself). According to Lemma 2, the process at stage $n - 2$ cannot advance to the critical section because it does not precede all other processes and it is the only at stage $n - 2$. When the process at stage $n - 1$ exits the critical section, the condition that the process at stage $n - 2$ must precede others is then satisfied, allowing it to proceed to stage $n - 1$.

Now, suppose there are two processes at stage $n - 2$. In this case, only one of them can advance, because if the first one moves forward, the second one would no longer satisfy the condition of Lemma 2 to proceed to the next stage.

Thus, in both of these scenarios, only one process can enter the critical section (i.e., the stage $n–1$). Once a process reaches the critical section, the remaining processes are unable to advance to the next stage until the current process in exits the critical section.

Reachability of the Critical Section The contradictory hypothesis for this proof is that processes could become blocked at a stage of the acquisition protocol and fail to progress to the next stage. This hypothesis leads to a contradiction in both possible scenarios:

Scenario (1):
If we assume that one process precedes all others, then by Lemma 1, it cannot get blocked at any stage and will continue to progress until the *stage* $(n - 1)$.
Scenario (2):
If there are processes that precede the given process, and it reaches a stage where are other processes already present, then those processes at that stage will be able to proceed to the next stage.
In both cases, one process will eventually reach the critical section, contradicting the assumption that processes could become blocked and not progress any further.

Fairness in Accessing the Critical Section Suppose all processes are attempting to enter the critical section and process P_i, which was the last to assign `turn[0]`, becomes blocked at stage 0. In the worst case, this process is overtaken by the remaining $n - 1$ processes, which may enter the critical section before P_i and return to the entry protocol. Let P_k the last process to assign `turn[0]`, meaning that `turn[0]= k`. The assignment will satisfy the condition, as stated in Lemma 2, which allows process P_i to exit its waiting state. As a result, P_i will be unblocked and move to stage 1. The same situation will hold for the remaining $n - 1$ processes.

We can conclude that the maximum number of rounds any process might have to wait during the execution of the algorithm, even in the worst scheduling scenario, is finite and equal to $d(n) = n - 1 + d(n-1) = \dfrac{n \cdot (n-1)}{2}$ turns.

Thus, the maximum wait time for any active process to enter the critical section is bounded and depends on the number of processes, which is a known, and fixed value before execution begins.

2.3 Monitors as a High-Level Concurrent Programming Mechanism

Monitors, understood as a *class* that supports structured programming by implementing data abstractions and defining global invariants, have as a remote antecedent an early practice in operating system programming, specifically, the construction of *a monolithic module*. These modules[1] were used by programmers to ensure the safe execution of code in the system's address space, which was accessed concurrently by multiple processes that could modify shared resources or data structures. Such monitors were programmed as modules that ran in a privileged or protected mode from other system programs or from the execution of user processes.

When code belonging to a monolithic monitor is executed by operating systems, we say that the system "enters the monitor". During such execution, interrupts are usually forbidden as mutual exclusion in access to the resources to be protected must be guaranteed. It is also common practice in monitor-based programming that programs are only allowed to access certain areas of system memory or execute selected input and output instructions when the code of the procedures contained in a monitor is executed.

Modern programming languages implement exclusive access to critical monitor resources, which avoids race conditions between processes, by encapsulating those resources in a decentralised version of the original monolithic monitor module[2]. This encapsulated form resembles a Java package or a C module, but differs in important ways: nested import of monitors are generally forbidden, and monitors can only be instantiated by a generalisation or parameterisation mechanisms, not through inheritance-based entity polymorphism. The monitor serves requests from concurrent processes on a one-to-one basis, always leaving the resources it protects in a consistent state before serving the next request. Figure 2.1 shows that only one process (P_1, in the example) may execute any of the monitor's procedures at a given time. This enforced entry mechanism ensures that no more than one procedure from the same monitor can be active at once during program execution. Alternatively, we could say that admitting one process to a monitor precludes adding another process until the first has exited.

2.3.1 The Definition and Characteristics of a Monitor

Monitors are used in the context of concurrent processes in multiprocessor system programs with memory shared by individual processors. Monitors are modules of programming languages that are not a suitable construct for distributed computing systems. These

---

[1] Module is a software *entity* that groups related procedures and data.
[2] Each monitor will now be in charge of a specific functionality of the application and will therefore contain its own privileged data and instructions, which differentiates it from the process code and the main program procedure.

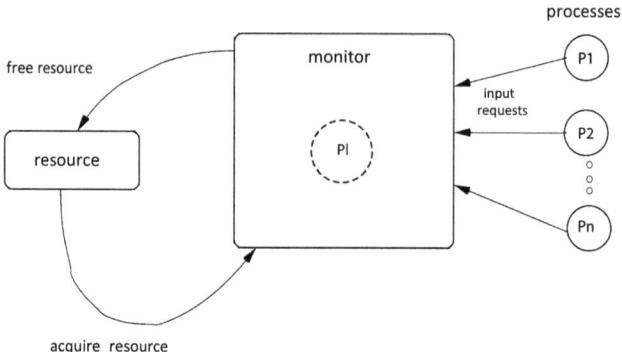

Fig. 2.1 Graphical representation of the elements associated with a monitor module

systems are characterised by a decentralised computing environment. Consequently, a concurrent program will comprise two distinct types of constructs: the processes or active software entities of the program and the monitors, which possess a passive entity character. Unlike processes, monitors do not initiate any computation by themselves; rather, they offer their procedures to be called by the program processes, which are the entities that actually initiate any computation or processing. Furthermore, processes can only interact or communicate[3] by invoking the procedures provided by the monitors declared in the program.

2.3.1.1 Critical Services Centralisation

The design of different monitors allows for the protection of different resources from concurrent access by processes within the same program. This results in an overall enhancement in program efficiency, as the procedural code of unrelated monitors can be interleaved concurrently without interference between processes and global invariants. Compliance with these invariants ensures secure access to the dataset protected by each monitor. Moreover, the use of monitors would enhance the overall robustness of the global program. In the event of an error or exception occurring during the access of a program process to a variable of monitor *M1*, this would not affect the variables of another monitor, like *M2*.

2.3.1.2 Structuring Access to Monitor Data

A monitor is also an ADT (*Abstract Data Type*)[4] whose procedures can be executed by a set of concurrent processes that take turns at the input to the monitor. Conversely, the encapsulation of data provided by a monitor precludes processes from accessing the

---

[3] Although in today's concurrent languages there is nothing to prevent declaring global variables to the program that can serve as a means of communication between processes or program threads, this should be considered a bad practice if the programming model with monitors is followed.

[4] A monitor = ADT + protection of the data it contains to ensure its secure concurrent access by the program processes.

2.3 Monitors as a High-Level Concurrent Programming Mechanism

internal representation of the data, thereby circumventing the potential for interference in concurrent access and, consequently, race conditions that could yield inconsistent values in monitor variables.

The standard syntax of monitors as outlined by Brinch-Hansen [8] and Lampson [30] incorporates a form of polymorphism based on the parameterisation of the monitor module. This allows for the declaration of distinct copies or instances of the same monitor within a concurrent program. However, it is important to note that this form of polymorphism is distinct from the inheritance mechanism proposed by object-oriented programming languages. Each instance of a monitor represents a copy of the *permanent* variables[5] declared in the monitor, the data structures used in its implementation and the *signals* used for the internal synchronisation of the monitor's procedures (Fig. 2.2).

Each monitor defines a principal procedure, which is a sequence of instructions (the block between the initial and final instructions) that are automatically executed when the program in which the monitor is declared begins. The body of the monitors is utilised to provide initial values for permanent variables. Permanent variables are exclusively accessible by the monitor's procedures and their scope and lifetime correspond to those of the monitor itself, in contrast to the parameters and local variables of the procedures whose scope and lifetime coincide with those of the procedures. The appropriate syntax for calling a monitor procedure typically encompasses the name of the monitor procedure and the name of the procedure to be executed, separated by a dot:

```
monitorname.procedurename(...current parameters...);
```

In order to prevent the permanent variables from reaching unsafe values, given that they are modified concurrently by the processes, it is not permissible to utilise a global variable

```
Monitor name [(<parameters>)]    -- To create instances.
var ...              -- Declaration of permanent variables.
Procedure P1[(<parameterss>)]  -- The parameters of the
begin            -- procedures constitute the interface
end;   -- with the processes of the concurrent program.
...
Procedure Pn[(<parameters>)]
begin
...
end;
begin                           -- Monitor body starts.
...           -- Initialisation of the monitor variables.
end;
<parameters>::= [var]<statement>{;[var]<statement>}
```

Fig. 2.2 Basic syntactic notation for monitors instances

---

[5] Those whose values persist after one operation of the monitor is executed, and before the next operation is executed, that would change those values.

of the concurrent program within the text of the procedures. This is because such a variable would be declared outside the scope of the monitor and its final value may depend on the interleaving of the elementary actions of the processes of the program. Consequently, communication between the processes of the same concurrent program can only occur via the parameters of the monitor procedures, which, upon execution, will alter the values of the permanent variables, potentially affecting the state of another process when subsequently executing the appropriate procedure of the same monitor.

2.3.2 Synchronisation Operations and Monitor Signals

The processes of a concurrent program with monitors are not required to include synchronisation operations in their code, as they only need to call the monitor procedures, which already include the necessary synchronisation operations for the correct cooperative interaction between these processes, as well as ensuring that the data is left in a consistent state when their execution is finished. In accordance with this model, monitor procedures may be interrupted on multiple occasions during their execution. Consequently, the code of a monitor procedure must possess the *re-entrancy* property[6].

As previously stated, synchronisation must be explicitly programmed within the monitor procedures using a novel data type, namely, condition variables or signals. These are employed within the monitor procedures to facilitate the separation of processes that must delay their execution until the monitor state satisfies a specific condition. This is reflected in the nomenclature, with these variables being designated as condition variables.

The conditions that must be met for processes to be synchronised are defined as expressions, included in conditional sentences, which are evaluated from the values of the permanent variables of the monitor during the execution of the procedures.

The type of monitor synchronisation variables defines two fundamental operations and one operation to ascertain whether there are blocked processes awaiting the condition to become true. One of these operations is employed to suspend processes until the required synchronisation condition is satisfied, while the other is utilised to resume the execution of a blocked process upon the condition's fulfilment.

The declaration of condition variables is conducted within the permanent variable declaration section of the monitor, as *cond-type* objects. It is not necessary to initialise them, as they are not expected to have any associated value, in contrast to what occurs with semaphore type variables. As illustrated in Fig. 2.3, processes are only required to wait if the single resource protected by the monitor is being accessed by the process inside the monitor. A single condition variable will therefore be needed to correctly synchronise the processes calling the two procedures of this resource monitor.

---

[6] Code shared by several processes that can run part of it, be interrupted and run again where they left off, without any loss of information

2.3 Monitors as a High-Level Concurrent Programming Mechanism

```
Monitor resource (r: integer);
  var busy: boolean;
  not_busy: cond;--variable condition
procedure acquire_resource();          Procedure release_resource();
  begin                                  begin
    if busy                                busy:= false;
      then not_busy.wait();                not_busy.signal();
    busy:= true;                         end;
  end;
begin
  busy:= false;
end;
```

Fig. 2.3 Resource access operations scheduled as single-monitor procedures

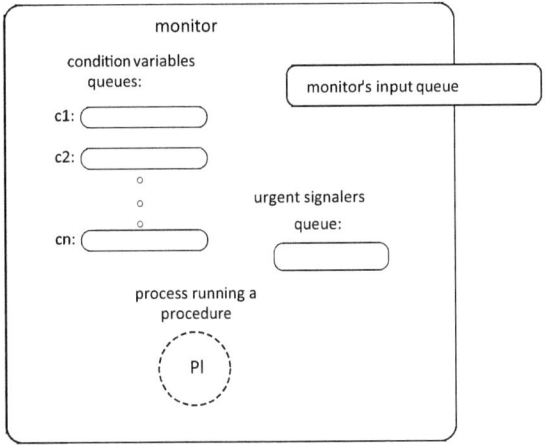

Fig. 2.4 Graphical representation of the queues in the implementation of the monitors

It is therefore possible, thanks to the condition variables, to have more than one process suspended in the monitor, waiting to resume in the queue corresponding to the relevant condition. However, only one process can be active at any given time, executing the instructions of one of its procedures within the monitor. Consequently, the waiting state of the processes is represented internally in the monitors, resulting in their blocking in the process queue associated with a condition variable until the condition becomes true. The internal representation of these queues, as illustrated in Fig. 2.4, is not accessible to application processes utilising the monitor[7], which may invoke their procedures at a designated point in their execution.

---

[7]A programmer using a monitor in his/her program cannot inspect the contents of the queue associated with a condition variable, nor can selectively order a blocked process to be unblocked from the queue, etc.

It is recommended that, in order to ensure optimal use of monitors, programmers should associate a condition variable with each logical condition that may result in the waiting of program processes until it is evaluated as true. This may be done either explicitly in the monitor or implicitly, depending on the programming language with monitors available. It is imperative that, when programming monitor procedures, the condition is verified to be satisfied prior to the programming of the corresponding signalling operation.

The standard monitor syntax includes a pair of operations, `wait()` and `signal()`, which are used to block or reactivate processes blocked in the condition variable queues. These operations are similar in name to the semaphore operations, but they have entirely different semantics. In contrast to semaphore variables, condition variables do not keep any internal protected values that, like semaphores, indicate the number of times processes may invoke the `wait()` operation without blocking:

`c.wait()`: The `c.wait()` operation causes the invoking process to block and enter the queue of blocked processes associated with the condition variable `c`, waiting for the condition to become true. The unblocking of the processes is scheduled according to a first-in, first-out (FIFO) order.

`c.signal()`: In the event that the queue of condition variable `c` is not empty, the invocation of `c.signal()` will result in the unblocking of the first process that is currently awaiting within that queue. In the absence of a blocked process in the queue, the operation is null, that is to say, it has no effect on the state of the monitor or the program.

It is crucial to consider that when the `c.wait()` operation is executed, the monitor must be available to allow another process to enter. Otherwise, the monitor procedures would be inaccessible to other processes, as the monitor would be occupied with a blocked process for an unpredictable duration. Ultimately, this could result in the entire program becoming unresponsive.

2.3.3 Semantics of Monitor Signalling Mechanism

The classical definition of monitor signals assumes that the process sending the signal (the signaller) must give access to the monitor[8] to the signalled process (by unblocking it in the queue of the corresponding condition), thus preventing other processes waiting in the input queue to the monitor from jumping ahead and postponing the resumption of the signalled process. This effect is known as *signal stealing* and should be avoided in good monitor programming practice, as the intruding process could change the logical value of the condition, possibly causing the permanent variables to reach inconsistent values when the initially signalled process finally manages to enter the monitor.

---

[8] This signal semantics is known as preemptive.

2.3 Monitors as a High-Level Concurrent Programming Mechanism

Signals with preemptive semantics imply an immediate resumption of the signalled process and prevent it from being subject to signal stealing by an intruding process. However, such preemptive semantics is not the only semantics employed by programming languages for the implementation of synchronisation with conditions on monitors. To illustrate, one might consider an implementation of signals in which a process executing the `c.signal()` operation would not immediately exit the monitor, and the signalled process would remain blocked until the signaller completes the procedure or exits the monitor after executing a `c.wait()` operation. The semantics of the latter type of signals will primarily affect the specific behaviour of the signalling process and must ensure that, in any case, only a maximum of one process can exist within the monitor during the entire execution of the program.

Concurrent languages with monitors employ five distinct mechanisms within the code of their monitor procedures to send signals to blocked processes in a condition queue. The semantics of each of these signalling mechanisms are presented in Table 2.1.

AS is a mechanism for sending signals implicitly, i.e., the signals are included by the compiler itself when the program code is generated. Therefore, the programmer need only include, in the text of the monitor procedures, the `c.wait()` statements required to stop the processes until a condition is verified that depends on the permanent variables of the monitor at each execution instant. On the other hand, the programming language runtime system is responsible for resuming execution of blocked processes when the program reaches a state in which the condition becomes true.

The signals SC, SX, SW and SU assume that the `c.signal()` operation is to be explicitly programmed into the monitor procedures, and then the programmer must include sufficient signals when writing the text of the monitor procedures such that when the synchronisation conditions become true, the blocked processes in the condition queues are notified. If it did not, then processes using the monitor could remain blocked indefinitely.

SC signals have a non-preemptive semantics, i.e., the process executing the `c.signal()` operation continues to execute and is therefore not preempted by the processor, as is the case with other signal semantics. Since the signalling process does not immediately leaves the monitor, it must be assumed that it continues to execute until the

Table 2.1 Different signalling mechanism of the monitors

Acronym	Name of the type of signal	Description of behaviour and characteristics of use and internal implementation
AS	Automatic signals	Implicit signal
SC	Signal and continue	Explicit, non-preemptive signal
SX	Signal and exit	Explicit, preemptive signal; the process has to exit the monitor after executing the signal operation
SW	Signal and wait	Signal explicit, preemptive; signalling process waits in the input queue at the monitor after exiting
SU	Urgent signals	Signal explicit, preemptive; signalling process waits in a queue of urgent processes

procedure terminates or itself blocks because subsequently executes, after signalling, a `c.wait()` operation in the same procedure.

The signals SX, SW and SU are preemptive, i.e., any process executing the operation `c.signal()` is obliged to yield the processor to the first blocked process, according to a FIFO order, in the condition queue associated to the condition variable c; if such a process does not exist, the signalling process would continue to execute, and the mentioned operation `c.signal()` would have no effect on the monitor state. The process' unblocking-condition associated with sending the signal must be true when this operation is executed and, thanks to its preemptive semantics, remains true when the signaled process starts its execution. It should be noted that if a different semantics is assumed, as is the case with SC signals, this assumption cannot be made, since another process could enter the monitor because of a signal steal before the signalled process resumes.

On the other hand, the following three types of signals cause a different behaviour of the signalling process after the `c.signal()` operation has been executed. SX signals force the process to leave the monitor, so with this type of signal semantics, the `c.signal()` operation must always be programmed as the last instruction of the monitor procedure in which it appears, or it must be followed by a `c.wait()` instruction. If the signal semantics is SW, the signalling process is blocked in the monitor input queue. With SU signals, the process is made to wait in a queue of urgent processes (see Fig. 2.4). This queue contains processes that have priority to resume and re-enter the monitor over other processes that may be attempting to enter the monitor and will be blocked in the entry queue.

2.3.3.1 Good Programming Practices with Signals

In our programs, we need to ensure that processes are only blocked when necessary. It is therefore the responsibility of the programmer to include enough `c.signal()` operations in the text of the monitor procedures to unlock, one by one, the set of processes in the c queue. This happens when the program reaches states in which it can be assumed that the unlock condition has been met.

Therefore, if some processes remain blocked indefinitely in a monitor's condition queue, then such a program can not be considered correct. If there is an execution scenario where no further processes can make progress, violating the safety property, or where certain processes are perpetually unable to execute; in the latter case, the liveness property will not be satisfied.

On the other hand, a program using monitors will always run more efficiently if the `c.signal()` operation is executed only when necessary, since the execution of this operation causes a context switch in the execution of the entire concurrent program. It is good programming practice with monitors to only use `c.signal()` within the monitor procedure code when there are blocked processes waiting for the condition associated with the condition variable c to become true. To avoid such unnecessary context switches, we can use the `c.queue()` operation, which returns true if there are blocked processes waiting for the condition and false if there are not.

2.3 Monitors as a High-Level Concurrent Programming Mechanism

Some programming languages that support monitors also include the `c.signal_all()` operation, which causes all processes in the queue of the condition variable c to be unblocked. The effect of this operation on the state of the monitor's condition variable queues is equivalent to executing the following loop:

```
while (c.queue()) do
  c.signal()
end
enddo
```

The above loop should never be used in procedures that rely on monitors with preemptive signalling semantics, as executing such a loop would cause all processes in the queue to be unconditionally unblocked. This may lead to race conditions if some of those processes do not satisfy the condition for proceeding upon reentering the queue.

2.3.4 Priority Condition Variables

In certain types of applications, it may be necessary to use condition variables that schedule the unlocking of processes according to a priority order, instead of following the order in which the processes were blocked. This differs from the standard synchronization operations of monitors, which typically assume a FIFO queue without priority.

In order to obtain an order to unlock the processes according to their priority, a new operation defined for the condition variables is introduced, called *priority wait*, whose definition is as follows:

`c.wait(priority)`: blocks the processes in the queue *c* but orders them automatically according to the value that its priority argument has when this operation is called. `priority:` non-negative number indicating the higher importance of the process for smaller values.

In Fig. 2.5, it is shown an example of a monitor that implements an alarm clock in a program that allows a simple timer to trigger an alarm at different times based on the requests previously made by its user processes. The alarm clock monitor records the requested times and responds to each of the requests at the specified moment. It has been programmed by creating a process[9] for each of the requests. When the time is reached, the monitor signals the corresponding process or several processes if several share the same time in their request, thereby initiating a specific activity of the application, such as a bell starts ringing, a log file is written and so on. The processes are blocked in the queue of

---

[9] It would be better to create a thread for each alarm clock request, if the programming language allows it.

Monitor module definition

```
Monitor AlarmClock;
Var
  now: integer;
  wake: cond; --priority
```

Monitor's procedures definition

```
Procedure wake_me_up(n: integer);
  var alarm: integer;
  begin
    alarm:= now + n; --Set alarm to current time + wait duration
    while (now < alarm) do
      wake.wait(alarm);
    end do;
    wake.signal();    --  Signal the next process
                      --waiting with the same alarm time
  end;

--Init procedure of the monitor
begin
  now:= 0;
end;
```

```
Procedure tick();
begin
  now:= now +1;
  wake.signal();
end
```

Fig. 2.5 Monitor implementing an alarm programmed with a priority signal

the prioritising condition variable `wake` after the `wake_me_up(this_time)` procedure has been called. The `tick()` procedure is assumed to be triggered with the system clock interrupt of the computer running the application that uses the following monitor.

While it is possible to simulate condition variables with priority using FIFO condition variables this approach will inevitably result in reduced efficiency compared to an internal implementation by the programming language itself.

2.4 Programming Languages with Monitors

The development of the concept of concurrent programming, as exemplified by monitors, has its immediate antecedents in the concepts of class, objects, subclassing and inheritance, as well as coroutines, and virtual procedures. These concepts first emerged in the history of computer science in a language called SIMULA-67, which was proposed by Ole-Johan Dahl [14] and Kristen Nygaard at the end of the 1960s. Subsequently, the concept of associating data encapsulation with mutual exclusion in the access to a shared resource, which forms the basis of the monitor construction, was developed by Edsger W. Dijkstra [16], Per Brinch-Hansen [9] and C.A.R. Hoare [23]. As a consequence of the ideas of these and other researchers, monitors were incorporated into the first generation of concurrent programming languages, most of which emerged during the 1970s, as synchronisation constructs that allow processes to mutually exclude access to resources and coordinate under certain conditions. The language called Concurrent Pascal of P. Brinch-Hansen [8] was the first to offer monitors as a useful syntactic construct for systems

2.4 Programming Languages with Monitors

programming. Later concurrent languages with monitors were Modula, Modula-2 by N. Wirth [47], Modula-3 [35], Mesa [30], Pascal Plus [46], Concurrent Euclid [25] and Turing Plus [26]. These are all relevant examples of programming languages from that era that sought to address the problem of nested monitor calls first identified by Andrew Lister [32] and later surpassed by an even more complex issue known as the inheritance anomaly identified by Yonezaba [49] in concurrent object-oriented programming languages. The incompatibilities first discovered in the 1990s, problems arising from the interaction between the classification mechanisms, inheritance and concurrency, have contributed to hinder the adoption of monitors or classes with concurrently invocable methods in today's programming languages.

Recently, however, the concepts of monitors has inspired the design of concurrent programming constructs in several widely used programming languages, such as Java (with the `wait/notify` methods), Python (via the `threading.Condition` class) and C++ (through `std:thread`). In the context of system programming, it is also worth noting the emergence of several libraries that enable the construction of monitor-like structures in languages that, in principle, do not consider them as their own primitives. One such library is `Pthreads`. Normally, when using function calls from these libraries, it is left to the programmer to mark the start and end of the code to be executed in mutual exclusion by the threads.

The Java programming language has significantly influenced how monitors and their associated programming primitives (condition variables, synchronisation operations, etc.) are understood and implemented nowadays. By introducing such concepts into one of the most widely used object-oriented programming languages, Java has become the most prominent example of a mainstream programming language that has used the monitor concept to develop concurrent multi-threaded programs.

2.4.1 Concurrent Programming in Java

The Java programming language contains a number of constructs and classes specific to concurrent programming. The most important of these are:

- `java.Lang.Thread`, used for thread initiation and control (Fig. 2.6).
- `java.Lang.Object`, which includes the `wait()` statement and *notifications* with their specific operations: `wait()`, `notify()` and `notifyAll()`.

Java programming language also introduces a set of qualifiers to indicate to the code generator and the Java Virtual Machine (JVM) the need to protect code that can be executed concurrently by threads, to avoid race conditions and to define the execution duration of these "critical sections" of the program, such as the *synchronised* and *volatile* decorations.

The correct programming of concurrent elements in our applications, with the creation of threads, is fundamental to the implementation of good code in Java, as it allows us to obtain applet animations and efficient network server programming, for example.

Fig. 2.6 *Thread*'s status within the Java class hierarchy

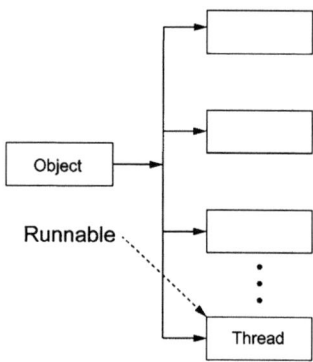

Fig. 2.7 Creating a thread class as an extension of *Thread*

```
class A extends Thread{
    public A(String name) {super(name);}
    public void run(){
        System.out.println(``name= ``+ getName());
    }
}
class B{
    public static void main(String[] args){
        A a= new A(``My thread'');
        a.start();
    }
}
```

The Java programming environment imposes on applications the obligation to implement the `Runnable` interface and therefore to call *run ()* on the main method programmed within a class that we want to make a thread. There are several alternatives for creating thread classes in Java, which we present below:

1. Extend the `Thread` class and redefine the public method *run ()* (Fig. 2.7).
2. Implement the `Runnable` interface in a class with the public method *run ()* (Fig. 2.8).

The second way of creating threads is better because Java does not allow simultaneous inheritance of multiple classes (or multiple inheritance) of other object-oriented programming languages. If, in order to create a new thread class, we were to extend the `Thread` class of the Java class hierarchy (Fig. 2.6), we would lose the possibility of inheriting from any other class, which might be of interest to facilitate the implementation of our application. Moreover, from the point of view of ease of programming, the creation of the thread object can be included in the constructor method of the class (Fig. 2.9); this way, we get a better encapsulation, since the constructor would reflect the fact that calling it would also create a thread that supports each new instance of this class, which will then have the duality of being a thread and an object.

2.4 Programming Languages with Monitors

```
class A extends OtherClass implements Runnable{
-- class that we wish to convert into a thread
public void run(){
  System.out.println(``name= `` + Thread.currentThread.getName());
  }
}
class B{
public static void main(String[] args){
  A a= new A();
  Thread t= new Thread(a, "A");
  t.start();

}
}
```

Fig. 2.8 Creating a Java thread in two steps

```
class A extends AnotherClass implements Runnable{
  private Thread t = null;
  public A(){
    t = new Thread(this, "A");
    t.start();
  }
  public void run(){
  ... }
}
```

Fig. 2.9 Creation of the new thread within the Java class constructor

In addition, the Thread class has four constructors that take as an argument any object (or group) that conforms to the *Runnable* interface and return a reference to an object of the *Thread* or *ThreadGroup* class:

- *public Thread(Runnable object)*
- *public Thread(Runnable object, String name)*
- *public Thread(ThreadGroup group, Runnable object)*
- *public Thread(ThreadGroup group, Runnable object, String name)*

2.4.1.1 States of a Thread

When the Thread object is created in a Java program with the statement *Thread t=new Thread(o);* from a reference to an object 'o' of a class that implements the *Runnable* interface, we obtain a skeleton of a potentially executable thread, which would initially be in a passive state, which we call new thread (see Fig. 2.10). Then, when the *t.start()* method is called, a reference (thread identifier) becomes visible to the system's thread scheduler, and we say that the new thread has passed to the runnable state. When the corresponding thread's *run()* method finally starts executing on any processor, we say that it has reached the running state.

Fig. 2.10 Thread states in Java

In addition to the thread creation methods introduced above, the `Thread` class supports the execution of a number of class methods; among the most commonly used are the following:

- `Thread.sleep(int);`—time in milliseconds.
- `Thread.yield();`—the executing thread yields the processor.

When a thread executing on any processor calls the `yield()` method, it leaves the processor and enters the runnable state. A thread enters the blocked state when it calls the `sleep()` method and returns to the runnable state when the call to this method returns, and the correct use of this method is:

$$\texttt{Thread.sleep(time\_milliseconds)}.$$

The Thread class, as shown in the state diagram in Fig. 2.10, supports calls to the following most commonly used instance methods:

- `start()`
- `join()`
- `stop()`
- `suspend()`, `resume()`
- `setPriority(int)`, `getPriority()`
- `setDaemon(true)`
- `getName()`

A thread in the runnable state enters the suspended state when its `suspend()` method is called. The thread returns to the running state when its `resume()` method is called by another thread.

Threads are *blocked* when they call the `wait()` method within a block or a *synchronised* method and return to the runnable state when another thread calls `notify()` or `notifyAll()`. They are also blocked when they call the `join()` method to synchronise with the termination of another thread that has not yet finished its execution. Blocking can also occur during I/O operations that involve synchronous data transfers, such as reading from disk. A thread is in the *blocked-suspended* state if the thread that is being blocked is also being suspended by another thread. When the blocking operation is finished, the thread goes into the suspended state. If another thread calls the `resume()` method while the thread is still in the suspended state, the thread returns to the *blocked* state. When the execution of a thread's `run()` is finished, or when its `stop()` method is called, the thread enters the `dead` state.

2.4.2 Programming with Java Monitors

Monitors, as defined in C.A.R. Hoare's classic article, "Monitor and operating system structuring concept" [23], differ in a number of important respects with respect to how they are programmed to achieve a similar construction in Java. In Hoare's original proposal, condition variables and their associated queues are explicitly declared, and a monitor may contain multiple such condition variables.

Programming with *Hoare monitors* contrasts with Java monitors, as this programming language only allows a single implicit condition queue[10] where all program threads that cause the execution of the `wait()` operation are blocked.

In Hoare-style monitors, separating threads into distinct queues based on different condition variables reduces unnecessary context switching and reactivation of threads during execution. However, in what follows, we will focus only on programming with Java monitors.

In Java, the `notify()` operation does not define which thread exactly is being notified. As a result, the thread that actually receives the notification may vary depending on a number of factors, including the JVM implementation, thread scheduling and program execution timing. Consequently, it is not possible to predict, even on a single-processor platform, which of the program's threads receives the notification. As with the `notify()` operation, the `notifyAll()` method does not allow control over which thread receives the notification and resumes execution, since all blocked threads are notified. By waking up all threads, we can design programs in which the threads themselves determine which one should proceed next.

> An example of the usefulness of `notifyAll()` can be found in a *producer-consumer* scenario of Java notifications: when producers generate data that may satisfy more than one consumer, it is often difficult to determine how many consumers can be triggered with the notification to consume. In such cases, one option is calling `notifyAll()` as a practical solution: it awakens all waiting consumers, allowing them to coordinate among themselves and determine which one will proceed to consume the data.

---

[10] That is, it is not necessary to declare any condition variable associated with this single queue in the program.

Since in Java a synchronised instruction block can only be executed by one thread at a time. When the `notifyAll()` method is called, all waiting threads are awakened but they must still reacquire the lock on the synchronized block. These threads do not run in parallel; each must wait for the lock to be released before it can proceed. Therefore, even if all waiting threads are notified, only one can be executed and only after the thread that called `notifyAll()` releases the lock.

The `wait()` method is tightly integrated with the synchronised block safety mechanism, and no race conditions can occur between threads. The synchronised block lock is not actually released until a thread waiting to acquire it is in a state where it can execute instructions. The Java runtime system thus prevents race conditions from occurring during the period of time when the `wait()` method releases (or reacquires) the block lock.

The designers of the Java language [31] argued that the apparent inefficiency of the mechanism of *anonymous* notifications to monitor threads was not such because, in practical concurrent programming with Java, threads waiting for evaluation of different conditions usually do so at different times in the program execution, and, therefore, the extra cost due to the reactivation of threads that will later block is eliminated. Even if this were to happen, they argued that the cost of extra thread rescheduling does not usually cause a major problem with respect to application efficiency.

2.4.2.1 Synchronised Code and Methods

The `synchronised` qualifier is used to make a block of code or a method protected by the internal object lock, i.e., to prevent access to it by more than one thread concurrently. Therefore, threads must acquire the lock on a Java object *(obj)* before executing any synchronised code:

```
synchronized (obj) {
  -- synchronised code block
}
```

If all critical sections that need to be accessed are within the code of a single object, we can use `this` to reference that object and do not need to name it or run its constructor:

```
synchronized (this) {
 -- synchronised code block
}
```

In addition, the entire main block of a method could also be synchronised code:

```
method type (...) {
synchronized (this) {
--synchronised method code
   }
  }
```

Or use the following construction directly, which would be equivalent to the previous one:

```
synchronized method type (...) {
  --synchronised method code
}
```

Therefore, declaring a Java class with all its methods synchronised, capable of being executed concurrently, is the way to create a monitor-like Java primitive construct.

Figure 2.11 shows the code of a counter monitor, which serves to protect the operations of incrementing and decrementing the value of an integer variable in a *thread-safe* way, i.e., to be accessed by a set of threads that satisfy the safety concurrent property.

2.4.2.2 Semantics of Notifications

A key distinction between Java monitors and Hoare's original definition lies in the semantics of the notification mechanism used to manage waiting threads. As outlined in Sect. 2.3.3, Hoare-style monitors use explicit condition variables and well-defined signaling semantics, such as signal-and-continue (SC), which allow more precise control over which threads are unblocked and when.

In Java, however, notifications rely on implicit condition queues and are handled through the `wait()`, `notify()`, and `notifyAll()` methods. These notifications approximate SC semantics in that they require notified threads to re-evaluate their waiting conditions upon waking. This makes it possible to simulate similar behavior to monitors with SC signals.

However, Java does not support declaring multiple condition variables to manage different categories of waiting threads. As a result, all threads—regardless of their roles, such as producers or consumers—are placed in a single, shared queue. This lack of separation can lead to less efficient synchronization, especially in scenarios where fine-grained control over thread blocking and unblocking would be beneficial.

Monitor module definition
```
class Counter{
   private int current;
```
Monitor's procedures definition
```
public Counter (int initial){              --Class runnable in the main program
   current = initial;                      class User extends Thread {
}                                             private Counter cnt;
public synchronized void dec (){              public User(String nom,Counter cnt){
   current--;                                    super (nom);
}                                                this.cnt = cnt;
                                              }
public synchronized void inc (){              public void run () {
   current++;                                    for (int i=0; i<1000; i++) {
}                                                   cnt.inc ();
public synchronized int value(){                    System.out.println ("Hi, I'm " + this.getName()+",
   return current;                           my counter is "+cnt.value());
   }                                             }
 }                                            }
}                                           }
```

Fig. 2.11 Program with a Java monitor to implement a *thread-safe* counter

In Java, the notified thread has no priority to immediately enter the monitor; therefore, it will move from the blocked state to the runnable state (see Fig. 2.10), joining the queue of threads ready to be selected by the system scheduler at runtime at some future time. In addition, the thread invoking the `notify()` operation is not obliged to release the monitor and may continue executing. The conditions for which threads wait must always be re-evaluated in Java before they can acquire the monitor lock, since the condition may have been invalidated in the time since they were notified. The `notify()`, `notifyAll()` and `wait()` methods have been implemented in the language as final methods of the `Object` class; therefore, they are available in all classes and can only be used within `synchronized` contexts that keep the lock on the object granting *thread-safe* access.

Unlike Java's notification semantics, Hoare's signal-and-wait, preemptive, semantics grant the notified thread immediate priority to re-enter the monitor without rechecking its condition, thereby avoiding unnecessary condition evaluations. This mechanism ensures deterministic handoff and can lead to more predictable scheduling behavior. However, implementing Hoare-style signaling is more complex and incurs additional overhead due to the need for strict control of thread transitions and monitor ownership. In contrast, Java's simpler notification model—though less precise—offers practical advantages. Its design reduces implementation complexity and may yield better overall performance in many applications by avoiding the cost of context switching or managing multiple condition queues, especially when re-evaluations are unlikely.

2.4.2.3 Java Utility Classes: Useful in Concurrent Monitor-Based Programming

So far, we have focused on final methods of the `Object` class, such as `notify()`, `notifyAll()` and `wait()`, which have been part of Java distributions since its earliest versions. Such methods are adequate to perform very basic tasks in concurrent programming, and if we needed higher-level syntactic constructs (monitors, barriers, reader-writer latches, etc.), we would have to program the utility classes ourselves.

Java 5 introduced a new Java package to the Java platform, the *java.util.concurrent* package, which contains a set of classes and interfaces designed to facilitate the development of concurrent applications in Java. This package is particularly useful when building complex concurrent applications that better exploit the possibilities of today's multiprocessor and *multicore* systems. In this subsection, we will study some of the high-level concurrency primitives that were introduced in Java version 1.5, all of which have been retained and extended in subsequent versions. Most of these primitives have been implemented in the interfaces and classes of the `java.util.concurrent` package. Also useful for concurrency are the new data structures that appear in Java *Collections*.

Java 5 and later versions provides several advanced concurrency tools that simplify the development of multi-threaded applications, especially compared to traditional synchronized blocks. Key features include:

2.4 Programming Languages with Monitors

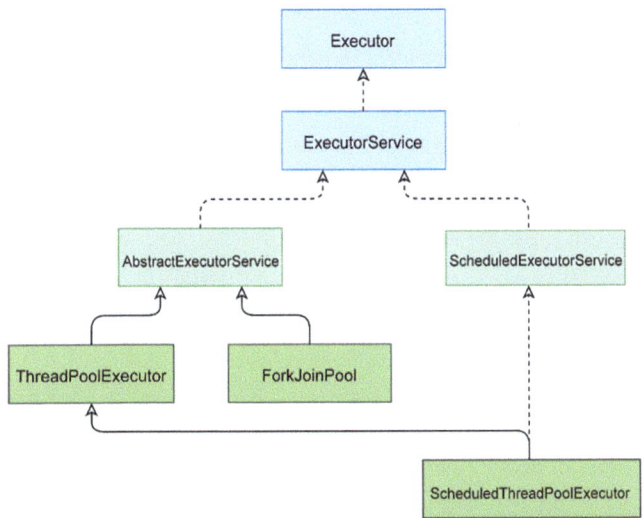

Fig. 2.12 `Executor` framework for executing concurrent tasks

- `lock()` and `unlock()` methods can be invoked from different methods enabling more modular designs, unlike synchronised blocks which have to be included in the code of a single method. `lock()` instances support features such as fair queuing (preserving thread order), optional timeouts, and greater flexibility.
- *Executors* that define a framework for launching and managing threads. Implementations of the `Executor` type (Fig. 2.12) provided by the `java.util.concurrent` package offer thread pool management suitable for large-scale application programming.
- *Concurrent collections*, these data structures simplify the handling of shared data and reduce the need for explicit synchronization, improving performance and code clarity.
- *Atomic variables*, these variables support lock-free, thread-safe operations and help prevent memory consistency errors with minimal synchronization overhead.
- `ThreadLocalRandom` introduced in Java 7 (version 1.7), provides efficient pseudo-random number generation in a multi-threaded execution context by eliminating contention through per-thread random number generators.

2.4.2.4 The `Lock` and `Condition` Interfaces

The `lock()` method of the `java.util.concurrent.locks.Lock` class causes the calling thread to wait uninterruptibly, if the critical section is already occupied. The thread remains blocked until another thread calls the `unlock()` method. The `LockInterruptibly()` method behaves in a manner analogous to the `lock()` operation, except that the first thread's wait may be interrupted by another thread or by the system. The interface (Fig. 2.13) also provides the `TryLock()` method, which attempts to acquire the lock and returns *true* if the `lock` is available. This method can

```
Java package definition
package java.util.concurrent.locks;
Package interfaces definitions
public interface Lock {                         public interface Condition {
  public void lock();                             public void await() throws InterruptedException;
  public void lockInterruptibly(                  public Boolean await(long time,TimeUnit unit)
  throws InterruptedException;                    throws InterruptedException;
  public Condition newCondition();                public long awaitNanos(long nanosTimeout)
  public boolean tryLock();                       throws InterruptedException;
  public boolean                                  public void awaitUninterruptible();
  tryLock(long time,TimeUnit unit)                public Boolean awaitUntil(java.util.Date deadl)
  throws InterruptedException;                    throws InterruptedException;
  public void unlock();                           public void signal();
                                                  public void signalAll();
}
```

Fig. 2.13 Java 5 interfaces for *locks* and *condition* variables

be used with a timeout and a time unit to specify how long the thread should wait. If the lock becomes available within the specified duration, *true* is returned; otherwise, it returns *false*. The `unlock()` method releases the lock, so that it can be acquired by another thread and does not have to be invoked by the same thread that called the corresponding `lock()` method.

The `java.util.concurrent.locks.Condition` interface allows threads to suspend their execution until a given condition is true. A `Condition` object is necessarily bound to a `Lock` and must be created via the `newCondition()` method. In this context, we refer to these as condition variables, following the terminology of classical monitor-based concurrent programming. Condition variables provide the `await()` method and their variants to suspend execution of a thread until another thread signals that the awaited condition may now be satisfied. When a thread calls `await()`, it releases the associated lock and suspends itself—analogous to calling `Object.wait()` in the classic Java synchronization model.

Consider a bounded buffer example (Fig. 2.14), where threads interact with `put()` and `take()` methods to insert and remove elements. If a thread calls `take()` when the buffer is empty, it must wait until an element is inserted. Similarly, if a thread calls `put()` when the buffer is full, it must wait until space is available. To manage these situations efficiently, two separate condition variables—`notFull` and `notEmpty`—can be declared and used by the respective methods. The methods in Fig. 2.14 include calls to the `await()` method of the initially declared condition variables: `noFull` and `noEmpty`, which causes the thread to lock and the associated `lock` to be released atomically and makes the thread wait until:

- Another thread calls the `signal()` method and the thread is selected to resume.
- Another thread calls the `signalAll()` method, causing all waiting threads to be signalled.
- The thread is interrupted by another thread.
- The first thread is spuriously or unexpectedly unlocked.

2.5 Implementation of Monitors

Monitor definition in Java
```
class BuferLimited{ --permanent monitor's variables definition
    final Lock lock= new ReentrantLock();
    final Condition notFull= lock.newCondition();
    final Condition notEmpty = lock.newCondition();
    final Object[]items= new Object[100];
    int putptr, takeptr, count;
```

Monitor's procedures
```
    public void put(Object x) throws InterruptedException{
      lock.lock();
      try {
        while (count==items.length)
          notFull.await();
        items[putptr]= x;
        if (++putptr == items.length)
          putptr= 0;
        ++count;
        notEmpty.signal();
      }
      finally { lock.unlock();}
    }
    public Object take() throws InterruptedException {
      lock.lock();
      try {
        while (count == 0)
          notEmpty.await();
        Object x = items[takeptr];
        if (++takeptr == items.length)
          takeptr = 0;
        --count;
        notFull.signal();
        return x;
      }
      finally {lock.unlock();}
    }
} --ends monitor definition
```

Fig. 2.14 Constrained *buffer* monitor implemented with condition variables

When the `await()` method returns, it is guaranteed that the thread that called it will immediately reacquire the `lock` associated with that condition variable.

2.5 Implementation of Monitors

Each of the signalling mechanisms we have studied requires a different implementation, using an inter-process synchronisation mechanism at the operating system level.

2.5.1 Implementation of the SX Signals

SX signals (Sect. 2.3.3) have the advantage that they can be used directly in a concurrent programming language, without the need to use other system-level synchronisation primitives, such as semaphores. However, studying a possible semaphore implementation of the SX signalling mechanism for monitors, although not strictly necessary, helps better understand the semantics of this type of signals.

A possible implementation with semaphores of the SX signals would be the one shown below, in which we assume the declaration of an independent semaphore `sem_cond` for each condition variable `c` that we need in the programming of the monitor:

Input operation:

```
wait(s);              --Monitor lock acquired.
```

Operation c.wait():

```
-- Count the threads waiting on the queue.
count_cond:= count_cond + 1;
  -- Release monitor lock, before blocking.
signal(s);
-- Block the thread in the semaphore queue.
wait(sem_cond);
            -- One less locked thread in queue.
count_cond:= count_cond -1;
```

Operation c.signal():

```
if count_cond > 0 then
    -- Resumption of first thread waiting.
  signal(sem_cond)
  else    --As there is no process waiting,
            --monitor lock is released.
  signal(s);
```

Variables definition and initialisation:

```
var
  Semaphore s, sem_cond;
int count_cond= 0;
init(s, 1);
init(sem_cond, 0);
```

Because of the semantics associated with this type of signals, we have restricted the appearance of the operation `c.signal()` to be the last instruction of the monitor. This allows it to be combined within a single control structure (`if count_cond > 0 then...`) with the monitor entry lock being released via the `else` branch (`signal(s)`), thereby enabling other threads to enter the monitor if there is no thread waiting in the condition. If `count_cond > 0`, then these threads are signalled with priority over those waiting to enter the monitor. Threads waiting to enter the monitor are in the queue of the semaphore `s`, initialised to the value 1, which serves to simulate the monitor lock. The state transitions of the threads triggered by the calls to the previous operations can be seen in Fig. 2.15. When a thread calls `c.wait()`, it enters a blocked state, and the monitor becomes available to

2.5 Implementation of Monitors

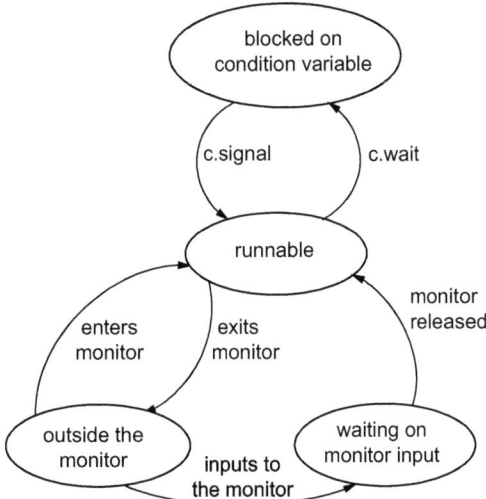

Fig. 2.15 States of threads calling synchronised procedures of a monitor

another thread waiting at its entry. The execution of the `c.signal()` causes a thread that is blocked on the condition (if one exists) to resume and transition to the runnable state. In both cases, the signaling thread exits the monitor and transitions from the runnable state to the outside monitor state.

As a result of executing a monitor procedure, the incoming process must call `wait(s)`, which grants exclusive access to the monitor. When a signaled process eventually resumes, it inherits the mutual exclusion held by the signaling process prior to its exit from the monitor. This ensures that there is no signal stealing by another process in the input queue, simulated by semaphore `s`, of the monitor.

2.5.2 Implementation of SU Signals

With this approach, signaling threads are no longer required to immediately terminate the execution of the procedure and exit the monitor (SX semantics). Instead, they are temporarily blocked in the queue named *urgent* in Fig. 2.4 of the highest priority, among all those defined for the implementation of monitors (see Fig. 2.17). When a thread that was previously resumed from a condition queue by a signalling thread releases the monitor, either by completing its procedure or by executing `c.wait()`, then the signaling thread that initially unblocked it has priority to re-enter the monitor over any new processes waiting in the monitor's input queue. It may also happen that the thread resumed by a signalling process signals in turn and may then enter the *urgent* queue, behind the previously signalling thread.

The priorisation of blocked signalling threads in the *urgent* queue, which is represented in the implementation in Fig. 2.16 by the `usem` semaphore, is achieved by ensuring that a process executing either a monitor exit operation or the `c.wait()` operation transfers control of the monitor to the first thread waiting in the $usem$ queue. The transfer occurs before giving way to processes waiting in the monitor entry queue, which is associated with the semaphore s queue (Fig. 2.17).

```
Input operation:
   wait(s);                          -- Monitor lock acquired.
Exit operation:
   if urgent >0 then     -- There are signaller threads suspended,
      signal(usem)                   -- resume one signaller.
   signal(s);                        -- Release the monitor lock.
Operation c.wait():
   count_cond:= count_cond+1;  -- Count threads waiting blocked.
   if urgent > 0 then
      signal(usem)
   else
      signal(s);                     -- Release the monitor lock.
   wait(sem_cond);   -- Block the thread in the semaphore queue.
   count_cond:= count_cond -1;       -- One less blocked thread.
Operation c.signal():
   urgent:= urgent + 1;   --One more signaller thread will wait.
   if count_cond > 0 then
     begin
       signal(sem_cond);     --Immediate resumption of one process
                                 -- waiting on the sem_cond queue.
       wait(usem);       -- The signaler thread becomes blocked.
     end;
   urgent:= urgent -1;   -- One suspended signaller thread less.
Variables definition and initialisation:
Var
   Semaphore s, sem_cond, usem;
int count_cond:= 0;
int urgent:= 0;
init(s, 1);
init(sem_cond, 0);
init(usem, 0);
```

Fig. 2.16 Semaphore implementation of *SU* semantics signals

2.5 Implementation of Monitors

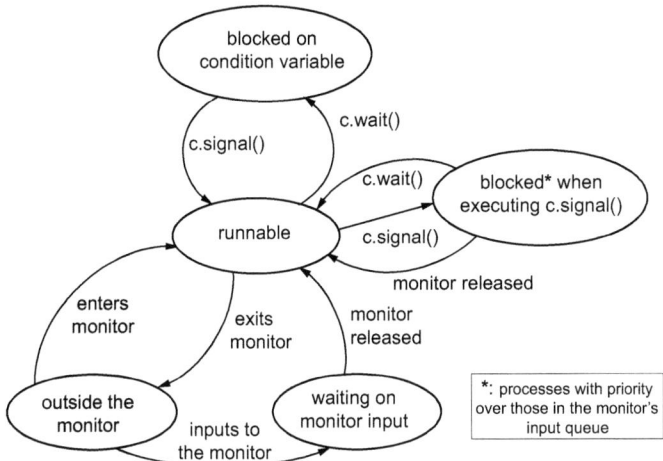

Fig. 2.17 Thread states of a monitor with SU signal semantics

2.5.3 Equivalence of the Different Types of Monitor Signals for Implementation

Since the different types of signals can simulate each other, they have the same ability to solve synchronisation problems between processes in a concurrent program. The difference between the different signalling mechanisms is that some signal types allow a solution to a given synchronisation problem to be expressed more easily than others.

If certain conditions are met, the different types of signals can be interchanged without requiring changes to the text of the monitor's procedures. In these cases, the monitor would still have the same safety properties, with only the order of execution of the processes and perhaps the fairness property of the concurrent program being affected. Of course, to be sure that two signalling mechanisms are interchangeable, their equivalence must be proved, i.e., that any program using either of them maintains the same concurrency properties, which is demonstrated by the following constructive method.

1. **Equivalence Between SC and AS signals**
   To prove that SC simulates AS, it would be necessary to consider the possibility of defining, for each condition B, a condition queue associated with the variable condition C_B, in which the processes[11] accessing the monitor must wait. Accordingly, the `await(B)` operation of the automatic signals could be simulated with a loop that performs a wait operation with the semantics of the SC signal until condition B is true:

---

[11] The process of identifying blocking conditions can be quite laborious when the dependent variable, B, is defined locally within the parameters and variables of the various processes occurring concurrently in a program. Nevertheless, it is a task that can be completed.

```
Pi:                              Pj::
...                              ...
await(B)                         while not B do
                                     C_B.wait();
                                 enddo;
```

Given that SC signals constitute an explicit signalling mechanism, it is necessary for the language runtime system to include a call to the relevant operation at those points in the text of the monitor procedures where condition B is evaluated to be true. This ensures that processes which are blocked in the condition queue will eventually be resumed.

Conversely, it can be argued that automatic signals are capable of simulating SC signals. In order to simulate SC signals from AS signals, it is necessary to declare an array of Booleans, called `blocked[i]`, for each condition variable with SC semantics declared in the monitor. The index i is used to traverse the identifiers of the n processes. This approach replaces the declaration of a condition variable with SC signal semantics and the calls to the synchronisation methods of this variable:

```
var                   Pi::                Pj::
C_B  : cond;          ...                 ...
                      C_B wait();         C_B signal();
```

They can be simulated with AS signals according to the following scheme:

```
Pi::                                    Pj::
...                                     ...
--Insert the process identifier i       if not empty(queue C_B) then
--at the end of the queue C_B               begin
blocked[i]:= true;                           k:= first(queue C_B);
await(not blocked[i]);                       blocked[k]:= false;
                                            end
                                        endif
```

2. **Equivalence Between *SW* and *AS* signals**

   SW signals are capable of emulating automatic signals (AS), in a manner analogous to the simulation conducted previously with SC signals. The `await(B)` operation inherent to automatic signals is transformed into a loop utilising SW signals and the `wait()` operation.

```
                    while not B do
                        C_B .wait();
                    enddo;
```

It is sufficient to require the fulfilment of the monitor invariant (MI) as a postcondition of the operation $C_B.wait()$, given that the unlocking condition B must be satisfied in order to exit the previous loop. Furthermore, in order to ensure that the liveness property of the processes is not violated, additional operations must be included at the points in the monitor procedures where condition B is evaluated as true and the IM is true. This is due to the fact that the SW signals have a $c.signal()$ operation with preemptive semantics, which will immediately cause a process to return from

2.5 Implementation of Monitors

`c.wait()` and execute the next instruction upon execution. Incorporating an adequate number of `c.signal` operations within the designated monitor procedures will prevent the undue blocking of processes in the program, which is solely attributable to the simulation of the `await(B)` operation. This will ensure the satisfaction of the concurrent liveness property.

Conversely, SW signals can be emulated with the automatic signals, in a manner analogous to the aforementioned simulation of SC signals. However, in this case, it is necessary to ensure that the process unblocked by sending the signal is executed immediately, given that the semantics of SW signals is preemptive. Furthermore, to ensure the correct implementation of the `c.signal()` operation, it is essential that the processes attempting to enter the monitor prior to executing the code of the invoked procedure first execute the `await(not signal_pending)` operation. This simulates the insertion of the call into the monitor entry queue[12], preventing signal stealing, which could otherwise occur if a process were to directly enter the monitor ahead of another process that has just been signalled (Fig. 2.18).

3. **Equivalence Between *SC* and *SW* signals**

   The two types of signals are equally capable of representing the necessary information for synchronisation mechanisms and of resolving synchronisation issues between processes in a concurrent program. Indeed, it is straightforward to demonstrate that both types of signals can simulate each other, given that they are equivalent to automatic signals (SA), as previously shown. This then allows us to prove that the following equivalence relations are satisfied:

   (a) SC simulates SA simulates SW
   (b) SW simulates SA simulates SC

In many cases, SC and SW signals are directly interchangeable, as a monitor using either type can maintain identical syntax and safety properties. The key distinction lies in broadcast signaling: it is defined for SC signals but not for SW signals due to their preemptive semantics. With preemptive signals, it is not possible to be certain that the next loop

Initial values of the global variables for the simulation
```
pending_signal: boolean:=false;
blocked: array[1..n] of boolean:= false;
```

```
Operation c.wait():
  --insert process identifier i at the end of queue C_c
  blocked[i]:= true;
  await(not blocked[i]);
  pending_signal:= false;
```

```
Operation c.signal():
  if not empty(queue C_c)
  then begin
    k:= first(queue C_c);
    pending_signal:= true;
    blocked[k]:= false;
    await(not pending_signal);
  end
  endif;
```

Fig. 2.18 Simulation of operations with *SW* signal semantics with those of *SA* signals

---

[12] For SW signals, processes must also be blocked in this queue after sending a signal.

```
while C_B.queue() do
    C_B.signal();
enddo;
```

does not degenerate into an infinite waiting. This happens because, under SW semantics, signaling threads must exit the monitor, and there is no guarantee that the signaled process will not immediately execute the signal operation again. If this pattern repeats, the condition queue may never empty, causing the loop to run indefinitely.

2.5.3.1 Conditions for Exchanging *SC* and *SW* Signals

The conditions depicted in Fig. 2.19 must be satisfied in order to enable the interchange of SW and SC signal operations without the necessity of additional modifications to the monitor code. These conditions may be regarded as a programming discipline when developing monitor procedures, whereby adherence to this discipline ensures the direct portability of their code between monitor languages with different signal semantics.

It is essential that the MI holds true prior to the execution of any `c.signal()` operation within a monitor procedure. Furthermore, the monitor's permanent variables do not require a stronger condition as a postcondition of the `c.wait()` operation beyond the invariant MI itself. This ensures that the same safety properties of the program are preserved, regardless of whether SC or SW signals are used. Consequently, no modifications are required to the monitor procedures, as the verification rules of the `c.wait()` operation for SC and SW signals are identical for both signal types. To comply with SW signal semantics, any call to `c.signal()` with SC signals must either occur before a `c.wait()` call or be the final instruction within a monitor procedure. Moreover, `c.signal()` operations must not be followed by assignment statements that alter permanent monitor variables. This constraint ensures that, even when SC signals are used, the truth value of a predicate at the time of signaling remains valid until the signaled process resumes, mimicking the behavior of SW signals. Since SC signals do not enforce this automatically, prohibiting changes to permanent variables after signaling maintains logical consistency.

In order to maintain equivalence between the two signals, it is not possible to use the operation of broadcasting a signal `c.signal_all()` to all processes that are blocked in a condition queue, since, as discussed above, this operation does not have well-defined semantics for preemptive signals.

i) Only the MI has to be fulfilled as the postcondition of the `c.wait()` operation.
ii) After a call to the `c.signal()` operation the process must exit the monitor.
iii) The `c.signal_all()` operation cannot be used: sending a signal to a process group is forbidden.

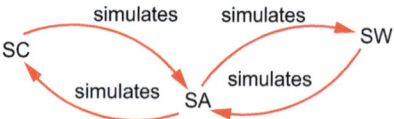

Fig. 2.19 Exchange conditions of synchronisation operations for the different signals

```
--Case (a)                              --Case (b)
Monitor Semaphore_FIFO1;                Monitor Semaphore_FIFO2;
{MI: s >= 0}                            {MI: s >= 0}
  var                                     var
    s: integer;                             s: integer;
    c: cond;                                c: condition;
  procedure P;                            procedure P;
  { s >= 0 }                              { s >= 0 }
  begin                                   begin
    if s = 0 then                           while s = 0 do
      c.wait();{ s > 0 }                      c.wait();
    s:= s - 1;                                { s >= 0 }
    { s >= 0 }                              enddo;
  end;                                      s := s - 1;
                                            { s >= 0 }
  procedure V;                            end;
  { s >= 0 }                              procedure V;
  begin                                   { s >= 0 }
    s := s + 1;                           begin
    { s > 0 }                               c.signal();     -- wake one
    c.signal();                                       -- order not guaranteed
    -- wake one waiter                      s := s + 1;
    { s >= 0 }                              { s >= 0 }
  end;                                    end;

  begin      --initialization block
    s := 0;         -- or any desired
    {MI: s >= 0 } -- initial count
  end;
```

Fig. 2.20 Alternative implementation of two FIFO semaphores with monitors

Figures 2.20(a) and 2.20(b) illustrate these concepts: case (a) works correctly with SW signals but fails with SC signals due to possible negative values in s, since SC signals do not prevent signal stealing by another process, which is not notified; case (b), on the other hand, works with SC signals but may lead to deadlock under SW semantics.

2.6 The Problem of Nesting Monitor Calls

Acquiring and releasing mutual exclusion is a non-trivial problem if calls to monitors are allowed to be nested. For example, suppose that the procedure *proc1()* of monitor *mon1* calls the procedure *proc2()* of monitor *mon2*, then if *proc2* contains a *c.wait()* operation, there will be a choice between two options:

(a) Release exclusion only in *mon2*.
(b) Release the exclusion on both monitors: *mon1* and *mon2*.

If we first consider option (a), the consequence is that all monitors that have been called before `mon2` become inaccessible to the rest of the program processes. The effect of this situation is a loss of application efficiency; it could even lead to a deadlock situation if the resumption of the process that called `c.wait()` depends on another process that only resumes after performing the same sequence of monitor calls before calling the `c.signal()` operation.

Option (b), i.e., releasing mutual exclusion of all monitors being accessed in the above sequence of calls, would need to implement a way to remember which monitors the process that called `c.wait()` had already entered. Implementing a stack that stores the calls seems to be the most obvious solution. However, getting the blocked process on the last monitor to recover the mutual exclusion of all previous monitors is very difficult to implement, since other processes may now exist on those monitors. An additional implication of this option is that the invariant of `mon1` has to be restored before the call of `mon2` occurs, which is not easy to implement, in general.

The analysis of the monitor calls nesting problem, as previously discussed, demonstrates that the two proposed solutions have significant drawbacks. It is evident that a more straightforward and radical approach would be to implement a unified global exclusion mechanism for all monitors, as opposed to implementing a local mutual exclusion mechanism for its permanent variables separately for each monitor. However, the utilisation of a global mutual exclusion mechanism effectively eliminates the issue of nested calls. It should be noted that the gain in simplicity of this solution is not without cost, as the degree of potential parallelism of the system is artificially reduced. An alternative approach to addressing the issue of nested monitor calls would be to prohibit them entirely. However, this would impose a significant limitation on monitor programming, which would be untenable in any hierarchically structured system.

A solution to the nested monitor calls problem was implemented in P. Brinch-Hansen's Concurrent Pascal programming language [9], whereby a local exclusion mechanism was defined for each monitor, in accordance with option (b) above.

In conclusion, the proposal by Parnas [36] posits that the nesting of calls to monitor procedures should not be subject to a single, universal rule applicable to all programming languages. This is because the nesting of calls to monitor procedures can be used as a structuring tool for shared resources that are subject to concurrent access and there is no need for a single rule to be established for all languages. In such cases, the procedures of a monitor can be executed concurrently without adverse effects, or the invariant of the monitor can be established more easily, even before a nested call is made. Consequently, there would be no problem in releasing the mutual exclusion of that monitor. Parnas' proposal, which eventually prevailed, defines monitors as a structuring primitive for concurrent programming, thereby allowing the specification that certain procedures can be executed concurrently and that the monitor's mutual exclusion is released for certain calls, but not for others. All these concepts have been implemented in the Mesa programming language [30].

2.7 Verification of Monitors

In concurrent programs using monitors, the partial correctness of processes and monitors must first be proved. Then the concurrency rule is applied to show that sequential processes cooperate without interfering with each other and that monitor invariants are maintained throughout the execution of the program.

The proof of the correctness of the monitor procedures is mainly done by defining global invariants for the data (permanent variables, structures and registers, parameters) protected by each monitor. In the following, we will focus on proving the validity of the invariants of the monitors, assuming that the sequential processes of the program are individually well programmed and therefore correct, using the FLS developed in Sect. 1.3. We will also assume that there is no interference between processes or in the parameters of monitor procedure calls made by the application processes, because, aside from the permanent variables of the monitors which are not visible to the processes, only locally declared variables are used within each process.

2.7.1 Axioms and Inference Rules for Monitors

It is not possible for the programmer of a monitor to know in advance the order in which the monitor procedures will be called. Consequently, the demonstration of partial correctness of the monitor procedures must be based on the verification of a relationship that is maintained throughout the lifetime of the monitor, called the monitor invariant (MI). The MI serves to establish a constant (invariant) relationship between the allowed values of the monitor's permanent variables. It is imperative that the MI holds before the execution of procedures and when the monitor becomes accessible to other processes. This occurs either upon the termination of the execution of a monitor procedure or prior to the execution of the `c.wait()` synchronisation operation.

2.7.1.1 Axiom of Monitor Variable Initialisation
The initialisation of variables must be conducted in accordance with the following axiom. The code which initiates the monitor scope must be programmed as a distinguished procedure, separated from the other procedures of the monitor, which is referred to as the monitor body. This procedure must include the assignment of all variables which are to be the permanent variables of the monitor, prior to the first instance of the monitor's procedures being called by concurrent processes. Once the initialisation process has been completed, the MI must be established before a process is permitted to access the monitor.

$$\{V\}\,initialisation(\,);\{MI\}$$

2.7.1.2 Axiom of the `c.wait()` Operation for Preemptive Signals

The axioms governing the `c.wait()` and `c.signal()` operations pertain solely to the observable[13] states of the program, as reflected by the values assumed by the permanent monitor variables and the values of any auxiliary variables defined within the monitor procedures. These axioms do not account for the order in which processes are unblocked when the `c.signal()` operation is executed. The execution of the `c.wait()` operation, irrespective of the signal type programmed into the procedures, results in handing over the mutual exclusion of the monitor[14]. Therefore, it is essential to ensure that the MI is true prior to executing such an operation.

A `c.wait()` call is correctly programmed within a monitor procedure if the following axiom, expressed as a triple of the FLS, is satisfied:

$$\{MI \wedge L\} \; c.wait(); \; \{C \wedge L\}$$

All signals with preemptive semantics have a defined operation `c.signal()` that immediately resumes the signalled process, which is waiting blocked in the queue of the condition variable c since the operation `c.wait()` was executed. Good monitor programming practice also associates a predicate C with each condition variable c, representing the condition under which suspended processes should be unblocked. For example, in the case of programming a synchronised buffered monitor used for concurrent reads and writes, the unblocking condition for producer and consumer processes would be that the buffer is not full or not empty, respectively.

```
Monitor's procedures
procedure take(var x: message_type);         procedure insert(m: message_type);
    if (not_full.queue() and (n ≠ N))             if (not_empty.queue() and (n ≠ 0))
        then                                          then
            not_full.signal;  -- the condition of         not_empty.signal  -- the condition of
                              --unblocking is satisfied:                   -- unblocking is satisfied
                              --it must be signaled to   ;                 -- it must be signaled to
                              -- the producers waiting                     -- consumers waiting
    ...                                           ...
```

The monitor maintains the same state from the time a process signals that condition C is satisfied until the signalled process resumes execution. Therefore, C is part of the postcondition of `c.wait()`. The predicate $\{L\}$ indicates an invariant defined only in terms of the local variables of the procedure.

2.7.1.3 Axiom of the `c.signal()` Operation for Preemptive Signals

The `c.signal()` operation immediately resumes a process blocked in the queue associated with condition variable c, following a FIFO order of unblocking. Therefore, any condition defined from the monitor variables that holds true before the execution of `c.signal()` will remain true when the signalled process resumes. This is because the mutual exclusion of the monitor is transferred directly from the signalling process to the

---

[13] Non-visible or hidden states of the program, such as the execution order of processes calling procedures, the state of monitor queues, etc., are excluded.

[14] That is, to allow another process to enter the monitor

2.7 Verification of Monitors

signalled process, preventing any third process from stealing the signal. The predicate $\{C\}$ in the precondition of the following inference rule, which coincides with the predicate of the postcondition of `c.wait()`, represents such an unblocking condition:

$$\{ \neg\ empty\ (c)\ \wedge L \wedge C\}\ \texttt{c.signal();}\ \{MI \wedge L\}$$

Since the process will be unblocked from queue c, it may subsequently cause the predicate $\{C\}$ to become false for the remainder of the execution of the monitor procedure[15]. Therefore, the only condition that can be assumed to hold after the operation `c.signal()` returns is that only the MI is satisfied. It is evident that this scenario can only occur when the monitor becomes free again. Whether the signalling process resumes execution after the signalled process exits the monitor depends on the specific semantics of the preemptive signals used (SX, SW or SU) and the state of the monitor's internal queues at that particular point in time.

The operation `c.signal_all()` unblocks all processes that are currently blocked in the queue of the variable condition c. However, only one of these processes will resume execution immediately; the others must wait until the monitor is free again and there are no processes waiting in a higher priority queue, such as the queue of processes that have previously signalled if SU class of preemptive signals were used. This operation is axiomatically equivalent to the `c.signal()` operation.

The inclusion of signals in the programming of monitors introduces the risk of unresponsiveness. If the program reaches a state where a condition becomes true but the programmer has not written a corresponding `c.signal()` operation within the monitor's procedure, blocked processes may remain indefinitely suspended. To address this, one might envision a mechanism where the programming language automatically[16] includes signal operations upon detecting that a condition has become true. Such automation could reduce programmer error and prevent incorrect blocking. However, this approach is rarely adopted in practice, as implementing automatic condition signalling is generally inefficient at the compiler or library level.

Additionally, the improper programming of the `c.wait()` operation within the context of monitor procedures could potentially lead to security concerns, as it is possible that a programmer's misuse of a `c.wait()` operation could result in a program process becoming indefinitely blocked.

It follows that assertion-based verification methods, such as our FLS and its extension to monitors, cannot, on their own, guarantee the absence of deadlocks caused by programming mistakes, such as those discussed above. This is because termination of program instructions must always be assumed for axioms and inference rules to be safely applicable. Therefore, it is the programmer's responsibility to ensure correct synchronisation, avoid faulty scheduling in monitor procedures, and design for liveness to prevent deadlocks during program execution.

---

[15] Or until it executes another wait operation

[16] For example, if the compiler were to use automatic signal semantics

2.7.2 Rules for Verification of SC Signals

The semantics of this type of signal dictate that executing the operation `c.wait()` causes the running process to yield the mutual exclusion of the monitor and then block on the queue associated with the condition variable `c`. This implies that the monitor must be released so that other processes can enter and execute their procedures. It is therefore essential to ensure that the monitor invariant (MI) holds immediately before invoking `c.wait()` in any monitor procedure that uses SC semantics. Once the process that executed the `c.wait()` operation resumes and before it re-enters the monitor, the invariant must again be assumed to be true. This is because, for the mutual exclusion of the monitor to be released, the rest of the processes must again be executing outside the monitor or waiting in the input queue or blocked in a condition queue. Although the values of some permanent monitor variables may have changed while the process was suspended, it is assumed that, upon resumption, the new state still satisfies the invariant. Based on this reasoning, the following axiom can be proposed for the `c.wait()` operation under SC semantics:

$$\{MI \wedge L\} \; c.wait(); \; \{MI \wedge L\}$$

The distinction between the prioritarian `wait()` and the other operations lies in the sequence in which the processes are arranged in the queue of the condition variable c. This order determines the sequence in which they are unblocked upon receiving a signal. The semantics of the priority signals may impact the liveness properties of the concurrent program, potentially leading to starvation of some processes. However, this does not compromise the soundness[17] of the verification rule used to prove safety properties.

Unblocking processes from a condition queue is achieved through the execution of the `c.signal()`[18] and `c.signall_all()` operations. Under SC semantics, the signalling process retains control of the monitor after executing signal operations. Consequently, since the signalling process does not yield the monitor, no permanent monitor variable changes value due to the signal itself. Therefore, these operations can be considered to have the same axiom as the null statement of any programming language:

$$\{P\} \; c.signal() \; \{P\}$$

The `c.signal_all()` operation broadcasts the signal to all processes blocked on condition c, unblocking the entire queue. As with the `c.signal()` operation, since the signalling process keeps the monitor lock, the value of any permanent monitor variable remains unaltered; thus, the axiom for both operations is identical.

---

[17] That is, any demonstration performed assuming FIFO-scheduled signals is equally valid for priority signals and vice versa.

[18] The Java programming language, which defines an anonymous signalling mechanism, calls these operations `notify()` and `notifyAll()`.

2.8 Exercises

Related to the synchronisation and communication problems presented by the programming of algorithms and applications with several concurrent processes. Different paradigmatic examples of concurrent programming will be used: "the dining philosophers problem", "multiple rendezvous", "mutual exclusion", etc. The appropriate approach to find the correct solution to these problems is usually to consider how to demonstrate the processes in which the program is structured according to the axioms and verification rules of our FLS extended with the rules of *non-interference* and *concurrency*.

2.8.1 Solved Exercises

Exercise 2.1 An algorithm for which we could only show that it satisfies Dijkstra's four conditions, what kind of concurrent properties would it satisfy?

(a) Safety
(b) Liveness
(c) Fairness

Justify answers.

Solution

(a) *Safety*: for an algorithm of this class to fulfil this property, there cannot be a scenario in which an execution leads to the deadlock of all processes or more than one process be in critical section at the same time. Knowing that the algorithm in question fulfils Dijkstra's four conditions, we can be sure that there will be no deadlock (Dijkstra's fourth condition) and that it will never get more than one process into critical section at the same time. We can therefore conclude that the algorithm is safe, i.e., it always satisfies the concurrent safety property.
(b) *Liveness*: Dijkstra's four conditions guarantee mutual exclusion in the access to the critical section by the processes and ensure the critical section is reachable (no deadlock situation can occur). However, these conditions do not prevent the possibility of starvation. For example, although Dekker's algorithm satisfies all four conditions, starvation may still occur: one process could be repeatedly and rapidly checking the other's key without giving it the opportunity to update its own key to indicate that it is no longer passive.In such a scenario, the slower process may be indefinitely delayed. Consequently, while the four conditions are necessary for correctness, they are not sufficient to guarantee the liveness property in concurrent programs, as starvation cannot be entirely ruled out.
(c) *Fairness*: for the fairness property of an algorithm to be fulfilled, all the processes that execute it concurrently must do so while managing to advance in the execution of their

```
(1) process Pi;
(2) begin
(3) repeat
(4)   turn:=i;
(5)   while turn ≠ i do; enddo;
(6)     (*Critical Section*)
(7)   turn:=j;
(8) forever
(9) end;
```

Fig. 2.21 Alternative implementation of one of the two processes of Dekker's algorithm

instructions in a fair manner. In case of starvation, this property is not fulfilled, as a process may never reach the critical section if the other processes always overtake it.

Exercise 2.2 What would happen if Dekker's algorithm had been programmed as shown in (Fig. 2.21)?

Solution This algorithm violates the safety property — mutual exclusion in access to the critical section (*CS*) — as well as the liveness property, since a process may experience starvation.

Breach of the safety property of the algorithm: If the process P_i assigns the variable `turn:= i` in line 4, then it can directly enter the *CS* because the waiting condition of the loop in line 5 is not fulfilled, but the other process P_j also requests access to the *CS* by assigning `turn:= j` in the same line 4 of its code. In the same way as the previous process P_j would access, and then 2 processes could be in *CS* at the same time.

Starvation of one of the processes: Suppose process P_i requests access to *CS* by assigning `turn:= i`. If the other process P_j is very fast and repetitive, it could allocate `turn:= j` on line 4 before process P_i can check the loop condition on line 5, and then P_j will always enter *SC*, with P_i waiting in the busy waiting loop indefinitely. The algorithm violates the liveness property.

Exercise 2.3 The following algorithm is known as Hyman's solution to the mutual exclusion problem (it was published as a correct solution to the mutual exclusion problem in an impact journal in 1966[19]). Is this solution correct?

```
var c0: integer:= 1;
cl: integer:= 1;
turn: integer:= 1;
```

Shared variables and initial values (Fig. 2.22)

---

[19] Harris Hyman, "Comments on a problem in concurrent programming control", Communications of the ACM, v.9 n.1, p.45, 1966

2.8 Exercises

```
(1) process P0;                        (1) process P1;
(2)   begin                            (2)   begin
(3)     while true do begin            (3)     while true do begin
(4)       c0:= 0;                      (4)       c1:= 0;
(5)       while turn!= 0 do begin      (5)       while turn!= 1 do begin
(6)         while c1 = 0 do begin end; (6)         while c0 = 0 do begin end;
(7)         turn:= 0;                  (7)         turn:= 1;
(8)       end;                         (8)       end;
(9)       CS:--critical section        (9)       CS:--critical section
(10)      c0:= 1;                      (10)      c1:= 1;
(11)      RS:--remainder of sentences  (11)      RS:--remainder of sentences
(12)    end                            (12)    end
(13) end                               (13) end
```

Fig. 2.22 Hyman's solution to the mutual exclusion problem for two processes

Solution This algorithm was published by Hyman in 1966, in the belief that it was correct and a simplification of Dijkstra's algorithm. It later turned out that this was not the case. In particular, neither mutual exclusion nor the limited waiting of processes in accessing the critical section is fulfilled.

Breach of the safety property of the algorithm: There is a unsafe sequence that allows both processes to be in the critical section simultaneously. Let's call *I* a (necessarily finite) time interval during which process 0 has completed the loop of line 6 but has not yet performed the assignment of line 7. Suppose that, during the time of the interval *I*, `turn` is 1 (this scenario is perfectly possible). In this case, during *I*, process 1 can enter and exit the critical section (*CS*) any number of times without waiting and, in particular, can be in *CS* at the end of *I*. Under these conditions, at the end of *I*, process 0 performs the assignment of line 7 and the reading of line 5, gaining access to *CS* while process 1 can be in it.

Starvation of one of the processes: Let's suppose that `turn=1` and process 0 is waiting in the loop of line 6. It could happen that, in these circumstances, process 1 enters and exits *CS* indefinitely, and therefore the value of its key c_1 alternates between 0 and 1, but it could happen that it does so in such a way that whenever process 0 reads this key c_1, it finds it with the value 0. If this happens, process 0 is indefinitely postponed, while process 1 advances in the execution of its instructions, entering *CS* an unlimited number of times while process 0 does not manage to exit the busy wait in the loop on line 6. The algorithm violates the liveness property.

Exercise 2.4 There are two concurrent processes that represent two ticket vending machines (they indicate the turn in which the customer is to be served), the ticket numbers are represented by two variables $n1$ and $n2$ that initially have a value of 0. The process with the lowest ticket number is served first. In case of two equal numbers, process number 1 is processed first. Prove that:

(a) The absence of blocking and starvation of processes is verified
(b) The assignments $n1:= 1$ and $n2:= 1$ are both necessary

Shared variables and initial values:

```
var n1: integer:= 0; n2: integer:= 0;
```

Process P1
```
begin
while true do begin
(1) n1:= 1;
(2) n1:= n2+1;
(3) while n2!= 0 and n2 < n1 do begin end;
(4) CS:--critical section
(5) n1:= 0;
(6) RS:--rest of sentences
end
end
```

Process P2
```
begin
while true do begin
(1) n2:= 1;
(2) n2:= n1+1;
(3) while n1!= 0 and n1 <= n2 do begin end;
(4) CS:--critical section
(5) n2:= 0;
(6) RS:--rest of sentences
end
end
```

Solution We will first prove the absence of deadlock and the absence of any process starvation with the conditions of (a), i.e., with the assignments: $n1 := 1$ and $n2 := 1$.

Reachability of the critical section: deadlock is impossible, using the proof by contradiction method. The incorrectness hypothesis consists of assuming that there is an execution that leads to deadlock, i.e., that the two processes remain in their busy waiting loops indefinitely in time. In such a scenario, both conditions of these loops (since the variables do not change value) in line 3 must be true, i.e., the conjunction of both conditions will always hold: $n1 \neq 0$; $n2 \neq 0$ and $n1 < n1$; $n1 \leq n2$. Therefore, it would have to be fulfilled, $n2 < n1$ and $n1 \leq n2$, which is impossible.

Non-starvation of processes: suppose one process is busy waiting (in the loop) during an interval T. Let's check how many times the other one can enter *CS* during T. Suppose that process i is in the loop on line 3 during T, and then in that interval $ni>0$ is satisfied and process j (with $i \neq j$) can enter *CS* once, because if that process tries to enter *CS* a second time, during T, before doing so, it must have executed $nj:=ni+1$ on line 2, which necessarily makes the condition $nj>ni$ true; however, if $ni>0$ is still satisfied, we see that process j cannot enter *CS* again. This result implies that the limit on the number of turns required by the equal progress property of the processes' instruction execution is unity (the best possible).

The demonstration that the assignments $n1:=1$ and $n2:=1$ are both necessary, as requested in (b), will be done in two steps:

1. First, we will see that, without such assignments, mutual exclusion is not fulfilled (by providing a counterexample, i.e., an interleaving sequence that allows both processes to access *CS*).
2. Next, we will show that, with the assignments ($n1:=1$ and $n2:=1$), there cannot be two processes in *CS*.

   (b.1) *The mutual exclusion access property is not satisfied without the assignments*: suppose that neither the $n1:=1$ nor the $n2:=1$ assignments are present, and then the values of both variables are 0 initially and both processes start. Suppose process 2 starts first and reaches *CS* in the time interval between reading and

2.8 Exercises

writing the assignment of line 2; then process 1 may also reach *CS*, while process 2 remains in *CS*. More concretely, the interleaving sequence (from the starting configuration of both processes) would be as follows:

```
1. Process 1 reads 0 in n2 (on line 2).
2. Process 2 reads 0 in n1 (on line 2).
3. Process 2 writes 1 in n2.
4. Process 2 reads 0 in n1.
5. Process 2 sees that condition n1 ≠ 0 is not fulfilled and
   advances to CS.
6. Process 1 writes 1 to n1 (in line 2), at this point, both varia-
   bles are set to 1.
7. Process 1 sees that condition n2<n1 is false and advances
   to CS.
```

From that moment on, both processes are simultaneously in *CS*, thus violating the safety property of the algorithm.

(b.2) *Mutual exclusion in the access to the CS of the processes with the assignments*: we now assume that the assignments ($n1 := 1$ and $n2 := 1$) are performed in line 1 of the code of both processes.

Let us suppose that at an instant t, both processes are in *CS*, and let us consider for each process the last time it accessed the entrance protocol (*EP*), lines 2–3, when it managed to enter *CS*. It is impossible, in such a case, that one of the two processes manages to execute the complete *EP* and verify that it could access *CS*, while the other one was in *RS* during all that time, since in this case the second one would clearly not have been able to enter *CS* afterwards because the assignation in line 2 is unfavourable to it and it would be performing busy waiting in the loop of line 3. Therefore, the processes must necessarily execute the assignments on line 1 before either process concludes that it can enter *CS*.

Let us call q the instant at which the second and last atomic write of line 2 is completed by either process. From instant q onwards, neither of the two variables change. Consequently, it is impossible for both processes to evaluate the condition in line (3) after instant q and both determine that they can enter their respective *CS*s. The reason is that if both readings occurred after q, they would observe the same values of $n1$ and $n2$, both greater than zero. For all such combinations, the condition in line (3) only allows at most one process to proceed.

Therefore, the condition evaluations in line (3) must be separated in time by q. Let i be the process that evaluates the condition before q, and j the one that evaluates it after q. All of the above implies that the sequence of some relevant events, prior to instant t, must necessarily be the following:

1. The last of the two assignments in line 1 is executed. At this point, $n1>0$ and $n2>0$ hold. These values remain positive until instant t, when the supposed simultaneous critical section execution occurs.
2. Process i reaches the busy waiting loop and reads nj on line 3. This read must necessarily happen before process j performs its write on line 2, otherwise both would read

the same values and could not both enter *CS*. Since the assignment of line 1 has already occurred and process j's write to line 2 has not yet occurred, the value read from nj must be 1. For process i to proceed into *CS*, the condition in line (3) must be false, i.e., either $nj=0$ or $nj \geq ni$. Since $nj=1$ and $x=ni$, we must have $x \leq 1$. As $x>0$, we conclude $x=1$. Thus, $ni=nj=1$. In this case, only Process 1 is allowed to enter *CS* (since in process 2's loop, the comparison is $n1 \leq n2$, which would be true for both 1s, but process 2 waits in that case). So process $i=1$.

3. Process j (process 2) writes $n2$ on line 2 (i.e., at time q), increasing it to $z=n1+1$. Since $n1=1$, we get $z=2$, and so $n2=2$.
4. Process 2 evaluates the loop condition in line (3): it reads $n1=1$ and $n2=2$. The condition $n1 \neq 0$ and $n1 \leq n2$ holds, so process 2 cannot proceed into the critical section at that point.

Therefore, in step 4, we conclude that necessarily process 2 could not enter *CS* before time instant t. As this is a contradiction with the starting hypothesis (both processes are in *CS* at t), such a hypothesis of incorrectness cannot occur, i.e., there cannot be any time instant with both processes in *CS*, i.e., mutual exclusion is always fulfilled.

Exercise 2.5 The following program is a solution to the mutual exclusion problem for two processes. Discuss the correctness of this solution: if it is correct, then prove it. If it is not correct, write scenarios that show that the solution is incorrect.

```
var c0: integer:= 1;
    c1: integer:= 1;
```

Shared variables and initial values (Fig. 2.23)

Solution *Mutually exclusive access of both processes to the CS is not fulfilled*: there is a scenario that allows the two processes to access the *CS*. Assume that $c1$ and $c0$ are both 1 (initially this happens) and the two processes access the entrance protocol (*EP*) consti-

```
(1) P0();                            (1) P1();
(2) begin                            (2) begin
(3)   while true do begin            (3)   while true do begin
(4)     repeat                       (4)     repeat
(5)       c0:= 1-c1;                 (5)       c1:= 1-c0;
(6)     until c1!= 0;                (6)     until c0!= 0;
(7)     CS:--critical section        (7)     CS:--critical section
(8)     c0:= 1;                      (8)     c1:= 1;
(9)     RS:--rest of sentences       (9)     RS:--rest of sentences
(10)  end                            (10)  end
(11) end                             (11) end
```

Fig. 2.23 Solution to the problem of mutual exclusion for two processes

2.8 Exercises

tuted by lines 4–6 of the processes' code. Assume a scenario given by the following interleaving sequence:

1. Both processes execute the line 5 assignments and line 6 reads (both processes write and then read the value 0), before either process repeats the line 5 assignments.
2. Line 5 assignments and line 6 reads (both processes write and then read the value 1) are repeated before either process reaches line 8.

Therefore, after the readings in step 2, both processes can access the CS.

Exercise 2.6 With respect to Peterson's algorithm for n processes, would it be possible for two processes to reach stage $n - 2$, 0 processes to reach stage $n - 3$ and, in all previous stages, at least one process to exist?

Stages	0	1	....	$n-3$	$n-2$	$n-1$
No. processes	1	1	1 1	0	2	0

Solution: We assume that the first process to reach stage $n - 2$ has arrived because it precedes all the others (applying *Lemma 1*), since if there are no processes at stage $n - 3$, it means that it was the only one at that stage and cannot advance to the next stage unless there are no processes ahead of it.

For a second process to reach stage $n - 2$, one of the following conditions must be fulfilled (applying *Lemma 2*):

1. Precedes all others: this is not the case, as there is already one process at stage $n - 2$.
2. It is not alone in stage $n - 3$: this is not correct either, as the scenario presented in the statement has 0 processes in stage $n - 3$.

Therefore, we can say that the scenario in the statement is not possible.

Exercise 2.7 Design a busy-waiting based hardware solution to the mutual exclusion problem using the `swap(x,y)` machine instruction (instead of using the instruction that reads and assigns atomically one variable), whose effect is to swap atomically the two logical values stored in the *x* and *y* memory locations.

Solution Use the `swap(x, y)` that atomically exchanges the values of *x* and *y* instruction to solve the problem of mutually exclusive access of *n* processes to a critical section (Fig. 2.24):

```
var cs_free: boolean:= true;  --true only if CS is free
```

```
process P[i: 1.. n];
var -- cs_busy_proc variable not shared: true only if
      --this process occupies the CS
  cs_busy_proc: boolean:= false;
begin
  while true do begin
    repeat
      swap(cs_free, cs_busy_proc);
    until cs_busy_proc;
    CS:--critical section
    swap(cs_free, cs_busy_proc);
    RS:--rest of instructions section
  end
end
```

Fig. 2.24 Solution to the mutual exclusion problem for n processes with the machine instruction $swap(x,y)$

Exercise 2.8 Prove that even if we assume a FIFO semaphore implementation of the monitors, the monitor condition queues, which are implemented in such a semaphore simulation, do not comply with the FIFO property when a process is unblocked by the execution of the $c.signal()$ operation by another process.

Shared variables initialisation
```
sem_cond, s: Semaphore;
Init (sem_cond, 0);
Init (s, 1);
Operation c.wait();                    Operation c.signal();
(1) count_cond:= count_cond +1;        (1) if (count_cond >0)
(2) signal(s); --release monitor       (2) then signal(sem_cond)
(3) wait(sem_cond);                    (3) else signal(s)--release monitor
(4) count_cond:= count_cond - 1;
```

Solution In general, we cannot assume that semaphore queues are scheduled FIFO. Therefore, after executing instruction (2) of the $c.wait$ operation script, the process might not immediately proceed to instruction (3) and blocks as intended.

In response to the question posed in the statement, we will say that the execution of instructions (2) and (3) of the $c.wait$ operation is not performed atomically. A process, after executing instruction (2), might be preempted before executing instruction (3), preventing it from blocking at $wait(sem\_cond)$. Finally, if another process invokes $signal(sem\_cond)$ through the $c.signal()$ operation and then exits the monitor, the preempted process could regain control and re-enter the monitor ahead of any other signalled process in the queue sem_cond.

2.8 Exercises

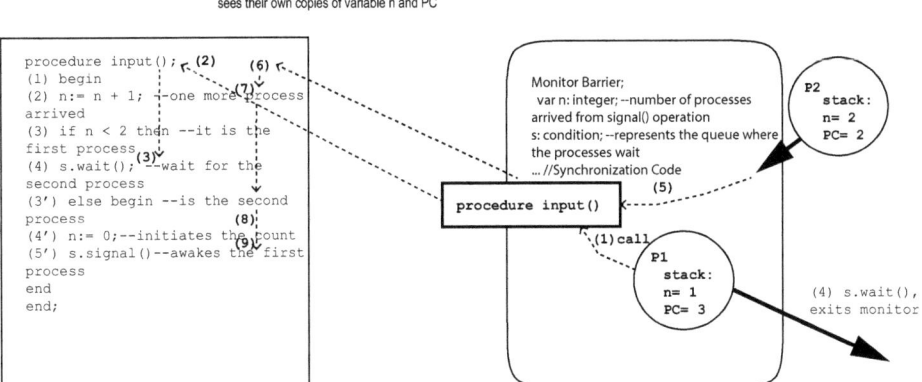

Fig. 2.25 Concurrent execution scenario of a procedure with re-entrant code

Exercise 2.9 Although a monitor guarantees mutual exclusion in accessing its permanent variables, monitor procedures must comply with the re-entrancy property.

Solution Re-entrant code is code that can interrupt its execution and re-execute where it left off without any loss of information. The procedures and functions of today's programming languages all satisfy the property of *re-entrancy* (Fig. 2.25).

Exercise 2.10 Two resources named $r1$ and $r2$ are considered. Of resource $r1$, there are $N1$ copies, and of resource $r2$, there are $N2$ copies. Write a monitor that manages the allocation of the processes' resources, assuming that each of these processes can request: one copy of resource $r1$ and one copy of resource $r2$, respectively. Likewise, any process can request 1 resource of both types. The solution, to be considered correct, must satisfy these two conditions:

(a) A resource shall not be allocated to a process demanding a copy, of $r1$ or $r2$, until at least one copy of the resource of that type is free.
(b) Priority will be given to processes requiring a copy of both resources.

Solution The priority to enter the monitor of processes that are in the input queue is impossible to implement with the semantics of the monitors, which establish by default a FIFO planning of their queues to avoid scenarios of possible starvation of some processes, and it is assumed that all the processes of the program have the same priority. However, it is possible at the program level to assign priority to the condition queues associated with each variable of type `cond`.

In order to prioritise the processes that demand both resources, a condition variable $c3$ is defined in whose queue these processes will be suspended, separately from those suspended in the queues of $c1$ and $c2$ that are waiting to obtain resources of type 1 and 2, respectively. In addition, when a resource, of any type, is released, it is checked if there are processes demanding both resources ($c3.queue()$) to give them access to the monitor in preference to the suspended processes waiting for only one type of resource.

```
Monitor Request_Resource();
 n1,n2: integer;
 c1,c2,c3: cond;
```

Monitor's procedures
```
procedure request_resource1();         procedure request_r1&r2();
 begin                                  begin
  if (n1 = 0) then c1.wait();            if ((n1 = 0) or (n2 = 0))
  n1:=n1-1;--Assigned resource r1         then c3.wait();
 end;                                    n1:= n1-1;
                                         n2:= n2-1;
procedure request_resource2();          end;
  begin
   if (n2=0) then c2.wait();           procedure yield_r2();
   n2:=n2-1;--Assigned resource r2      begin
  end;                                   n2:= n2+1;
                                         if((c3.queue()) and (n1>0))
procedure yield_r1();                      then c3.signal()
  begin                                    else c2.signal();
   n1:= n1+1;                           end;
   if ((c3.queue()) and (n2 >0))
     then c3.signal()
       else c1.signal();
  end;
--Initialisation procedure
begin
 n1:= N1;
 n2:= N2;
end;
```

Exercise 2.11 Program the procedures of a monitor necessary to simulate the abstract synchronisation operation called rendezvous between two processes: the first process ready to synchronise has to wait until the other process is also ready to synchronise.

Solution
```
Monitor Rendezvous;
var c1,c2: cond;
signaled: boolean;
```

Monitor's procedures
```
procedure call_date();                 procedure keeps_date();
 begin                                  begin
  c2.signal ();                          if (not c1.queue)
  if (not signaled)                       then c2.wait();
    then c1.wait();                     signaled:= true;
  signaled:= false;                     c1.signal();
 end;                                  end;

--Initialisation procedure
begin
 signaled:= false;
end;
```

2.8 Exercises

To explain the code of the `Rendezvous` monitor procedures, the following analogy is proposed: suppose that two people arrive at the rendezvous location but are separated by a wall and cannot see each other. One of them shouts when he/she reach the wall, and the other can raise a flag or lean out the other side by climbing a ladder leaning against the wall.

In the procedure `call_date()`, process A calls out (`c2.signal()`) to see if process B has arrived and to make the appointment. If B does not raise the flag (`signalled:=true`), i.e., process B has not yet arrived, then process A waits (`c1.wait()`).

In the procedure `keeps_date()`, process B peeks (`c1.queue()`) to see if process A has already arrived; if it has not yet arrived, it waits (`c2.wait()`). Otherwise, process B raises the flag (`signaled:= true`) to indicate to the other process that the rendezvous can take place.

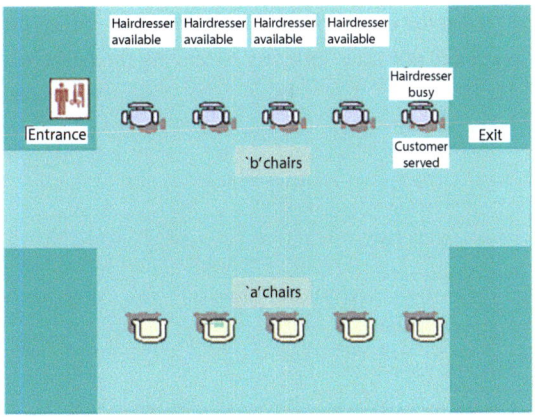

Fig. 2.26 Arrangement of the chairs in the barber shop for a simulation with one monitor of the processes' performance

Exercise 2.12 In a village, there is a small barbershop with one entrance and one exit door. These doors are so narrow that only one person can pass through each time they are used. In the barbershop, there are an indeterminate number of chairs (we assume that there are always free chairs because the barbers do not make the customers wait too long) of two types:

(a) Chairs where customers wait for barbers to come in
(b) Barber chairs where customers wait until their haircut is finished

There is not enough space for more than one person (barber or customer) to move inside the barbershop at any given time. For example, when customers notice that a barber has entered, only one customer may stand up and walk to a type (b) chair. Conversely, the barber cannot approach to cut the customer's hair until the customer has taken a seat.

When a customer enters the barbershop, they can do one of two things:
- They may sit in a type (a) chair and wait for a barber to become available. Once a barber is ready, the customer gets up and moves to a type (b) chair to wait until their haircut is completed.
- Alternatively, if barbers are available, the customer may sit directly in a type (b) chair. A customer does not leave the barber's chair until they are signaled to do so by the barber opening the exit door (Fig. 2.26).

When a barber enters the shop, they waits until there are customers sitting in a chair of type (b) waiting for their haircut. The barber then checks the status of the customers in numerical order (assuming these chairs are numbered), until they find one waiting to be serviced. Upon doing so, the barber starts cutting the customer's hair and becomes busy. Once finished, the barber opens the exit door, waits for the customer to make the payment and then goes outside to freshen up. The barber can not re-enter the barber's shop until they have received payment from the customer they just attended. It is not permissible for a customer to pay a barber other than the one who performed the haircut.

Solution The solution to this simulation problem can be obtained as a generalisation of Exercise 2.11 in which there are now several appointments between barber and client, which occur as the processes (clients and barbers) progress in their execution, and the rendezvous between processes are made one at a time, within the monitor, which represents the barber-shop and the narrowness of the barbershop, which prevents more than one person from changing chairs at a time, entering or leaving the barbershop and paying the barber.

```
Monitor Barbershop();
const num_clients = N0;
var
 chair_a,chair_b,door,awake: cond;
 available,waiting: integer;
 finished: array [num_clients] of boolean;
 paid: array [num_clients] of boolean;
```

Monitor's procedures
```
procedure hair_cut(i:client_number);          function next_client():integer;
begin                                         var
 if (available = 0)                            j: integer = 0;
   then chair_a.wait();                       begin
 waiting:= waiting+1;                          available:= available+1;
 finished[i]:= false;                          if (chair_a.queue())
 awake.signal();                                 then chair_a.signal();
 while (not finished[i]) do                    if (waiting = 0)
  begin                                          then awake.wait(),
    chair_b.signal();                          available:= available-1;
    chair_b.wait();                            repeat
  end;                                           j:= j+1;
 waiting:= waiting-1;                          until not (finished[j] or j > num_clients);
 while (not paid[i]) do                        return j;
  begin                                       end;
    door.signal();
    door.wait();
  end;
end;
--Initialisation procedure
begin                                         procedure get_paid(i:client_number);
 available:=0; waiting:= 0;                   begin
 finished: array [num_clients] of boolean:= true;  finished[i]:= true;
 paid: array [num_clients] of boolean:= true;  chair_b.signal();
end;                                           paid[i]:= true;
                                               door.signal();
                                              end;
```

2.8 Exercises

Exercise 2.13 Demonstrate the correctness of the Producer-Consumer monitor by applying the verification rules for the `c.wait()` and `c.signal()` operations of the monitors with the semantics of preemptive signal semantics, added to the formal Program Logic framework introduced earlier (see Sects. 1.6.4 and 2.7).

Solution To demonstrate the correctness of the code of the monitor procedures, the rules for checking the synchronisation properties of the monitors (see Sect. 2.7.1), for *preemptive* signals, in instructions (4) and (10) of the code of both procedures shall be applied. The unlock condition for the `no_full.wait()` operation of the `insert(...)` procedure is that the *buffer* is not full $(n<MAX)$, which, according to the verification rule for preemptive signals, is verified in the precondition of the `no_full.signal()` of the `remove(...)` procedure. For the operation `no_empty.wait()` of the `remove(...)` procedure, the demonstration is analogous, the unblocking condition in this case being: $n<0$. This condition is verified in the precondition $(n=1)$ of the operation `no_empty.signal()` in (10).

Finally, the postconditions of the if-complete instructions in (7) and (13) include that the monitor invariant is satisfied; therefore, we can conclude that upon completion of both procedures, the monitor invariant is restored, which will also be satisfied at the start of the procedures because the initialisation block (0) will establish the monitor invariant, prior to the execution of any of its procedures.

```
Producer_Consumer Monitor;
  const MAX=M₀ ;
  var n: integer; no_empty, no_full: cond;--permanent variables
                       --Invariant of the Producer_Consumer monitor: I ≡ 0 ≤ n ≤ MAX;
Monitor's procedures
(1) procedure insert(m:message_type);              (1) procedure remove(var x:message_type);
(2) begin                                          (2) begin
      {I} → {0 ≤ n ≤ MAX}                                {I} → {0 ≤ n ≤ MAX}
(3) if n = MAX then                                (3) if n = 0 then
      {I ∧ n = MAX}                                      {n = 0 ∧ I}
(4)   no_full.wait();                              (4)   no_empty.wait();
      {I ∧ n < MAX}                                      {n = 1 ∧ I} → {n > 0 ∧ I}
(5) else                                           (5) else
      {I ∧ n < MAX}                                      {n > 0 ∧ I}
(6)   null;                                        (6)   null;
      {I ∧ n < MAX}                                      {n > 0 ∧ I}
(7) end if;                                        (7) end if;
    {I ∧ n < MAX}                                      {0 < n ∧ I}
(8) n:=n+1;                                        (8) n:= n - 1;
    {0 ≤ n -1∧ n -1< MAX}                              {0 < n + 1 ≤ MAX}→{0 ≤ n ≤ MAX}→{I}
    --Updating buffers and pointers                    --{Updating buffer and pointers}
    {0 ≤ n ≤ MAX} → {I}                                {0 ≤ n ≤ MAX}→{I}
(9) if n=1 then                                    (9) if (n = MAX - 1) then
      {n = 1 ∧ I}                                        {I∧ n = MAX - 1}→{n< MAX ∧ I}
(10)  no_empty.signal();                           (10)  no_full.signal();
      {I}                                                {I}
(11) else                                          (11) else
      {1 < n ∧ I}→ {I}                                   {n ≠ MAX - 1 ∧ I}→{I}
(12)  null;                                        (12)  null;
      {1 < n ∧ I}→ {I}                                   {n ≠ MAX - 1∧ I}→{I}
(13) end if;                                       (13) end if;
     {I}                                                 {I}
(14) end;                                          (14) end;
--Initialisation procedure
begin
(0) n:= 0;
    {n = 0 ∧ I}
end;
```

Exercise 2.14 Propose a solution to the reader-writer problem with monitors by giving priority to writing processes, asumming the preemptive signal semantics of condition variables.

Solution By separating writers and readers into different waiting queues (`writer`, `reader`), it is possible to prioritise either of these processes when the monitor becomes free, which is done in the procedures `end_read()` and `end_write()`; the former unconditionally signals a writer process that might be waiting, because in the absence of `writer_waiting` or `writing`, reader processes can always access; the latter checks that there are no *writers* waiting before giving access to the monitor to a *reader* process. This results in a protocol that prioritises writing processes (that have started the operation and have been suspended) over reading processes. It is not possible to prioritise any process inside one monitor queue.

```
ReadersWriters Monitor;
var
readers,
writer_waiting: integer;
writing: boolean;
writer, reader: cond;

Monitor's procedures
procedure begin_read();                      procedure end_read();
begin                                        begin
  if (writing or writer_waiting > 0) then      readers := readers - 1;
    reader.wait();                             if (readers = 0) then
  readers := readers + 1;                        writer.signal();
  reader.signal();                           end;
end;                                         procedure end_write();
procedure begin_write();                     begin
begin                                          writing := false;
  if (readers > 0 or writing) then             if (writer_waiting > 0) then
    begin                                        begin
      writer_waiting := writer_waiting + 1;        writer_waiting := writer_waiting - 1;
      writer.wait();                               writer.signal();
    end;                                         end
  writing := true;                             else  reader.signal();
end;                                         end;
begin
  -- Variables initialisation
  readers := 0;
  writer_waiting := 0;
  writing := false;
end;
```

Exercise 2.15 For each of the priority schemes in the reader-writer problem, try to think of an application in which the corresponding priority scheme is reasonable.

Solution *Prioritise writers over readers*: in database applications, write operations should be prioritised over read operations so that *reader* processes can obtain the most up-to-date version of the database in question.

Prioritise readers over writers: in applications where sensors are used, we would prioritise the operations of reading the information we capture through the sensor in order to act accordingly and maintain the overall reliability of the system.

2.8 Exercises

Exercise 2.16 For the producer-consumer problem with the improvement of the sleeping barber:

(a) Write a monitor that solves it.
(b) Write the invariant to be checked by the monitor that has been programmed.

The sleeping barber improvement refers to a synchronisation scheme between the producer and consumer processes that avoids sending unnecessary signals. Specifically, it ensures that the operation `no_empty.signal()` is executed only when there is a consumer process blocked and waiting, and alternatively, `no_full.signal()` will be executed when there is a blocked producer. The name of the sleeping barber improvement to the above problem is due to an analogy used to explain the synchronisation behavior and how unnecessary signals can be avoided. Think of the consumer process as a barber and the action of the producer process as the customer in the barbershop. If the barber is constantly alerted with a bell every time a new customer arrives (even while already attending to another customer) it would lead to needless noise and disruption. A more efficient solution is for each new customer to quietly peek into the barbershop: if the barber is sleeping (i.e., not attending to anyone), only then should the customer ring the bell to wake them up.

Solution The difference between this solution, with the *sleeping barber* improvement and that of Exercise 2.13, lies in the placement of the increment operation for the monitor's permanent variable. In this version, the increment is performed earlier, in instruction (7), which changes the unblocking condition for the `no_full.wait()` operation to $\{n \geq N\}$. This condition does not imply that more than N items will be introduced in the *buffer* but rather that there may be $(n - N)$ blocked producers waiting for it not to be full. Thus, it is signalled only if there is already one locked producer. In contrast, the implementation in Exercise 2.13 issued a signal whenever one item was removed from a full *buffer*, as the *unlock condition* was $\{n=MAX-1\}$, even if no producer was actually waiting to insert a new item. The approach is symmetrical for the other synchronisation operation `no_empty.wait()` with the *unblocking condition* $\{n \leq 0\}$. In this case, a signal is sent only if there are $-n$ consumers blocked, as n could take negative values within the `remove(...)` procedure.

```
(1) Monitor Producer_Consumer;
(2) var
(3)   n: integer;
(4)   not_empty,not_full: cond;

Monitor procedures
(5) procedure insert(n);
(6) begin
(7)    n:= n+1;
   --locks if already full
(8)    if (n>N) then not_full.wait();
   --insert buffered data
(9)    if (n≤0) then not_empty.signal();
(10) end;

(11) procedure remove();
(12) begin
(13)   n:= n-1;
   --attempt from an empty buffer
(14)   if (n<0) then not_empty.wait();
   --remove data from buffer}
(15)   if(n-N≥0) then not_full.signal();
(16) end;
```

Exercise 2.17 Cars coming from the north and south intend to cross a bridge over a river (Fig. 2.27). There is only one lane on the bridge. Therefore, at any given time, it can only be crossed simultaneously by one or more cars in the same direction, but cars coming from opposite directions cannot meet on the bridge:

(a) Complete the code for a monitor that solves the bridge access problem assuming a car arrives from the north (south) and crosses the bridge if there is no other car from the south (north) crossing at that time.
(b) Improve the above monitor, so that the direction of traffic across the bridge changes every time 10 cars have crossed the bridge in one direction, while one or more cars were waiting to cross the bridge in the opposite direction.

Solution The solution in (a) does not contemplate a protocol to manage the queue of cars waiting on one side of the river if cars are continuously passing on the other side. Therefore, this solution would meet the concurrent property of safety, but not the property of liveliness.

The solution in (b) tries to avoid the liveliness problems of the previous solution by counting the number of cars that have already entered from x side of the bridge, and when this number is equal to 10, it prevents them from passing, allowing cars from the other side to start crossing when the bridge is free of cars ($x\_passing$=10) (Fig. 2.28).

Fig. 2.27 The mutual exclusion problem for cars with accessing a bridge

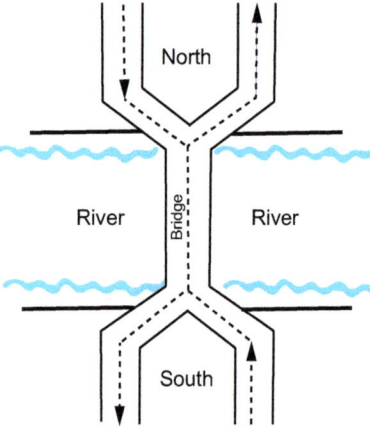

2.8 Exercises

```
Monitor Bridge_Traffic();--solution(a) that does not prevent process starvation
 var
  n_passing, s_passing;
  c1, c2: cond;
```

Monitor procedures
```
 procedure NorthernEnters();              procedure NorthernExits();
  begin                                    begin
   if (s_passing >0)                        n_passing:= n_passing-1;
     then c1.wait();                        if (n_passing = 0)
   n_passing:= n_passing+1;                   then c2.signal();
   if (c1.queue())                         end
     then c1.signal();                    end;
  end;
 procedure SouthernEnters();              procedure SouthernExits();
  begin                                    begin
   if (n_passing >0)                        s_passing:= s_passing-1;
     then c2.wait();                        if (s_passing = 0)
   s_passing:= s_passing+1;                   then c1.signal();
   if (c2.queue())                         end;
     then c2.signal();
  end;
 --Initialisation procedure
 begin
  (n_passing, s_passing):= (0,0);
 end;

Monitor Bridge_Traffic()_Safe;--solution (b) that fulfills the liveness property
 var
  n_passing, s_passing, n_ahead, s_ahead: integer;
  c1, c2: cond;
```

Monitor procedures
```
 procedure NorthernEnters();              procedure NorthernExits();
  begin                                    begin
   if (s_passing >0 or n_ahead = 10)        n_passing:= n_passing-1;
     then c1.wait();                        if (n_passing = 0)
   n_passing:= n_passing+1;                   then begin
   if (c2.queue())                              s_ahead:= 0;
     then n_ahead:= n_ahead+1;                  c2.signal()
   if (n_ahead < 10 and c1.queue())           end
     then c1.signal();                     end;
  end;
 procedure SouthernEnters();              procedure SouthernExits();
  begin                                    begin
   if (n_passing >0 or s_ahead = 10)        s_passing:= s_passing-1;
     then c2.wait();                        if (s_passing = 0)
   s_passing:= s_passing+1;                   then begin
   if (c1.queue())                              n_ahead:= 0;
     then s_ahead:= s_ahead+1;                  c1.signal()
   if (s_ahead < 10 and c2.queue())           end
     then c2.signal();                     end;
  end;
 --Initialisation procedure
 begin
  (n_passing, s_passing, n_ahead, s_ahead):= (0,0,0,0);
 end;
```

Fig. 2.28 Solution to the problem of generalised mutual exclusion of cars with access to a bridge

Exercise 2.18 A tribe of cannibals share a pot that holds M missionaries. When any member of the tribe wants to eat, they serve themselves directly from the pot; unless all the missionaries have been consumed and the pot is empty, then the cannibal wakes the cook and wait until the cook has refilled the pot with another M missionaries. Consider the following skeleton for the processes simulating the cannibals and the cook:

```
Cannibal process              Cook process
begin                         begin
 repeat                        repeat
  serve_1_missionary;           toSleep;
  --eat;                        fill_Pot;
 always;                       always;
                              end;
```

Implement a monitor for the required synchronisation, taking into account that:

(a) The solution must prevent deadlock.
(b) The cannibals may eat as long as there is at least one missionary remaining in the pot.
(c) The cook should only be notified when the pot is empty.

Solution Urgent signal semantics (*SU*) must be assumed so that the procedure `serve_1_missionary` of the `Cannibal` processes executes the operation `wait.wait()`, after interrupting itself when signalling and after the procedure `toSleep()` in the `Cook` has finished but before the procedure `fill_Pot()`, because if the latter is executed before `serve_1_missionary()` is executed again, the signal `wait.signal()` would be lost and could lead to the blocking of the `Cannibal` process.

```
Monitor Tribe;
var
 wait, wake_up: cond;
 pot:integer;
```

Monitor procedures
```
procedure serve_1_missionary();             procedure toSleep();
  begin                                       begin
   if (pot = 0) then                           if (pot > 0)
   begin                                        then wake_up.wait();
     wake_up.signal();                        end;
     wait.wait();
   end;
   pot:= pot-1;
   if (wait.queue() and pot > 0))
     then wait.signal();
  end;

procedure fill_Pot();
 begin
  pot:= M;
  wait.signal();
 end;
Initialisation procedure
begin
  pot:= M;
end;
```

2.8 Exercises

Exercise 2.19 A savings account is shared by several persons (processes). Each person can deposit or withdraw funds from the account. The current balance of the account is the sum of all deposits minus the sum of all withdrawals. The balance can never be negative. We want to use a monitor to solve the problem.

The monitor must have two procedures: `deposit(c)` and `withdraw(c)`. Assume that the arguments of the two operations are always positive and indicate the amounts to deposit or withdraw. The monitor will use the signal and urgent wait (*SU*) semantics. Several versions of the solution must be written, according to the variations of the requirements described below:

(a) Any process may withdraw funds as long as the requested amount c is less than or equal to the available balance in the account at that time. If a process attempts to withdraw an amount c greater than the balance, it must be blocked until the balance increases sufficiently (as a result of other processes depositing funds into the account) for the request to be accepted. Make two versions:

(a.1) Normal FIFO queues without priority
(a.2) With priority queues

(b) Withdrawal of funds to customers is done on a first-come, first-served basis only; if there is more than one customer waiting, only the customer who arrived first can choose to withdraw the amount he/she wants; as long as this is not possible, all customers will wait, regardless of how much the others want to withdraw. For example, suppose the balance is 200 units and a customer is waiting to withdrawal 300 units. If another customer arrives, they must wait, even if they only want to withdraw 200 units. Again, solve this using two versions:

(b.1) Normal (FIFO) queues without priority
(b.2) With priority queues

Solution

(a.1) The first customer with sufficient credit can withdraw, and we assume queues of monitor's condition variables without priority.
Obviously, we have to declare a condition variable in the monitor to make customers who want to withdraw wait. The queue associated with this variable has the standard FIFO scheduling of monitors, but customers cannot resume until there is an available balance equal to or greater than the amount they want to withdraw. Since each time the account is deposited, the stopped processes are signalled, a loop must be programmed in the `withdraw()` procedure to check if there is sufficient balance. If a client cannot withdraw, before returning to the queue again, it has to signal the

next client in the same queue to check if he/she can; this will cause a chain of clients to unblock until either one can withdraw or they are all suspended in the same queue again. A client process, after having withdrawn from its account, has to signal the next one (`queue.signal()`) as there might still be enough left for other clients to withdraw as well.

Monitor module definition (solution, a.1)

```
Monitor Savings_Account_FIFO_Without_Priority;
var
   balance: integer;
   queue: condition;
Monitor procedures
Procedure deposit(amount: positive);        Procedure withdraw(amount: positive);
begin                                        begin
   balance += amount;                           while (amount > balance) do
   queue.signal();                              begin
end;                                               queue.signal();
                                                   queue.wait();
                                                end;
                                             enddo;
                                             balance -= amount;
                                             queue.signal();
                                          end;
```

Initialisation procedure

```
begin
   balance:= M0  --initial amount
end;
```

(a.2) The first customer with sufficient credit can withdraw, and we assume priority queuing.

If we now use *priority condition variables* within the monitor, the problem has a simpler solution than in the previous case. As a priority criterion to order the client processes in the queue we will use the value of the amount that each client wants to withdraw, assuming it is a positive integer. In this way, if the queue contains several processes waiting to withdraw funds, one of those requesting the smallest amount (there may be several requesting the same amount) will always be selected from among the requests. Now, unlike solution (a.1), if the currently selected client cannot withdraw, then no other client behind them in the same queue will be able to withdraw a larger amount. Therefore, unlike the previous solution, it is not necessary for them to notify others before blocking again. However, it is still necessary that, after a client completes a withdrawal, they notify the next waiting process in the queue, as their withdrawal may enable subsequent requests to be fulfilled.

2.8 Exercises

Monitor module definition (solution, a.2)

```
Monitor SavingsAccountQueueWithPriority;
var
  balance: integer;
  queue: condition;
```
Monitor procedures
```
Procedure deposit(amount: positive);      Procedure withdraw(amount: positive);
 begin                                      begin
   balance += amount;                         while (amount > balance) do
   queue.signal();                              queue.wait(amount);
 end;                                         enddo;
                                              balance -= amount;
                                              queue.signal();
                                            end;
```

Initialisation procedure
```
begin
 balance:= M0 --initial amount
end;
```

(b.1) Only the first customer to arrive at the bank can withdraw funds provided there is a sufficient balance, assuming queues are managed without priority.

In this case, the monitor cannot rely on a single non-priorised condition variable queue. If a notified process finds that there is not enough balance to complete its withdrawal, then it returns to the end of queue, thereby losing the priority that it should retain as the longest-waiting process. A simple solution to this problem can be obtained by programming two condition variables to block customers in separate queues while preserving the priority of the earliest arrival by blocking that customer in a dedicated queue.

- A queue where the customer who arrived first at the bank will be suspended, who according to the statement of the exercise must be the first to be able to withdraw when there is sufficient balance. We can name the condition variable associated with this queue: $window$, as it represents the teller's window. This queue will hold at most one client process waiting during the execution of the program.
- The rest of the clients will wait in a different queue, associated with a condition variable named $rest$, such queue will have the standard FIFO scheduling without priority. From this queue, only one process at a time (specifically, the one that has been waiting the longest) will proceed to the window queue when it becomes empty. Obviously, if the $window$ queue does not have any process, then there cannot be any blocked process in the $rest$ queue.

When a customer enters the bank to withdraw, the synchronisation condition ($balance<amount$) is checked directly if the $window$ queue associated to the teller is empty; otherwise, the customer will wait in the queue named $rest$ directly until it is their turn.

Monitor module definition (solution, b.1)

```
Monitor SavingsAccountArriveOrderWithoutPriority;
var balance: integer;
    window, rest: condition;
```
Monitor procedures

```
procedure deposit(amount: positive);          Procedure withdraw(amount: positive);
 begin                                         begin
  balance += amount;                            if (window.queue())
  window.signal();                                then rest.wait();
 end;                                            while (amount > balance) do
                                                   window.wait();
                                                 enddo;
                                                 balance -= amount;
                                                 rest.signal();
                                                end;
```

Initialisation procedure

```
begin
 balance:= M0 --initial amount
end;
```

(b.2) Only the first customer to arrive at the bank can withdraw funds, provided there is a sufficient balance, assuming priority queuing.

It has a similar solution to the previous one with the key difference being that the FIFO order must be respected to withdraw for clients waiting in the secondary `rest` queue. As discussed previously, the FIFO serving order is not guaranteed if the first process in the waiting queue is signalled and there is insufficient balance. In that case, the process would be blocked again at the end of the queue, losing its priority over other customers who were also waiting and arrived later. To achieve a FIFO scheduling of the blocked processes, a single priority queue will be used that will order the processes waiting to withdraw by the smallest value of the local variable `ticket`, in which the turn of the counter variable, permanent of the monitor, is copied when a client tries to withdraw.

Monitor module definition (solution, b.2)

```
Monitor SavingsAccountArriveOrderWithPriority;
var balance, counter: integer;
    queue: condition;
```
Monitor procedures

```
procedure deposit(amount: positive);          Procedure withdraw(amount: positive);
 begin                                         var ticket: integer;
  balance += amount;                           begin
  queue.signal();                               ticket= counter;
 end;                                           counter ++;
                                                if (queue.queue())
                                                  then queue.wait(ticket);
                                                while amount > balance do
                                                   queue.wait(ticket);
                                                 enddo;
                                                 balance -= amount;
                                                 queue.signal();
                                                end;
```

Initialisation procedure

```
begin
 balance:= M0 --initial amount
 counter:= 0
end;
```

2.8 Exercises

Exercise 2.20 Processes $P_1, P_2, \ldots P_n$ share m resources $R_1, R_2, \ldots R_m$, but only one process can use it at a time. A process P_i can start using one resource if it is free; otherwise, the process must wait for the resource to be released by another process. If there are several processes waiting for a resource to become free, the process with the highest priority is granted. The process priority rule is as follows: process P_i has priority i (with $1 \leq i \leq n$), where lower numbers imply higher priority. Design and program a monitor that implements the procedures `request(...)` and `release(...)`.

Solution Let's suppose that we have m resources and that each of the n P_i processes, before using one of the m available resources, calls the `request(id_process):integer` operation function, which will return the number $k:1..m$ of a free resource. In case there is no free resource at the time of calling the operation, then the calling process P_i waits for a resource to become available.

The processes P_i after using a resource call the *release(id_resource: 1..m)* operation, leaving the resource free. If several processes are waiting for a resource, it is granted to the process with the highest priority, i.e., the one with the lowest identifier, of those waiting.

In order to solve this problem with a monitor in an understandable way, we have to propose an invariant of the monitor and the unblocking condition, which has to be fulfilled before a process resumes and continues executing the operation `request()`.

Monitor invariant that ensures safe access of n processes to m resources: we encode in two *arrays* of Boolean variables, the state (*free, busy*) of the resources $(j:1..m)$ and whether a process $(i:1..n)$ has a pending request:

$$\exists j : 1 \leq j \leq m : \text{free}[j] == \textit{true} \rightarrow \forall : 1 \leq i \leq n : \text{request}[i] == \textit{false}$$
$$\wedge \exists i : 1 \leq i \leq n : \text{request}[i] == \textit{true} \rightarrow \forall : 1 \leq j \leq m : \text{free}[i] == \textit{false}$$

Unblocking condition:

$$C[i] : \exists : 1 \leq i \leq n : \text{request}[i] == \textit{true}$$

According to the above invariant and assumptions, the following monitor can be programmed to resolve the concurrent access of n processes to m resources according to a priority order given by the lowest index of each of these processes:

```
Monitor Resources;
var
  free: array[1..m] of boolean;    --true if resource is free
  request: array[1..n] of boolean; --true if process I is waiting
  I:integer;                       --to store index of the released resource
  no_request: condition;
```
Monitor procedures
```
(1) Function request(process_id:1..n):integer;
(2) var k:integer;
(3)   begin
(4)     k:= 1;    --search for a free resource
(5)     while(k<=m) and (not free[k]) do
(6)       k:= k+1;
(7)     if (k > m) then
(8)       begin
(9)         request[process_id]:=true;
(10)        while(request[process_id]) do
(11)          begin
(12)            no_request.signal();   --chain release of waiting processes
(13)            no_request.wait();
(14)          enddo;   -- unblocking condition holds:request[process_id]== true
(15)        return I;
(16)      end
(17)    else
(18)      begin
(19)        free[k]:= false;
(20)        return k;
(21)      end;
(22) end;
(1) Procedure release(resource_id:1..m);
(2) var
(3)   i: integer;
(4) begin
(5)   for i:=1 to n do
(6)     begin
(7)       if request[i] then
(8)         begin
(9)           I:= resource_id;   --give this resource to process i
(10)          request[i]:= false; --wake up process i: unblocking condition holds
(11)          no_request.signal();
(12)          return;
(13)        end
(14)   enddo;
(15)   free[resource_id]:= true;
(16) end;
```
Initialisation procedure
```
(1) begin
(2)   for i := 1 to m do
(3)     free[i] := true;
(4)   for i := 1 to n do
(5)     request[i] := false;
(6)   I:=0;
(7) end;
```

The client processes P_i call the monitor's `request(..)` function, passing its process identifier `i` as a parameter. This function first performs a search (5)–(6), to find the first available resource, checking the status of the resources in order from 1 to *m*. If all resources are occupied, the loop is terminated with the value `k>m`. In this case, it shall execute the direct branch of the conditional of instruction (7), and P_i remains blocked until it is signalled that a resource has become available. As long as process P_i maintains its resource request (`request[i]= true`), it remains in the queue of the conditional variable `no_request`. When another process releases the resource it holds, it does so by calling

2.8 Exercises

the procedure `release(resource_number)`. This triggers a search in the loop (lines 5–14) for the first pending request, which is checked in order from 1 to n. If such a request is found, the resource is assigned to the requesting process i that made the request, thus changing the value of `request[i]` to false and the process is signalled. If, on the other hand, there is no pending request, the instruction (15) is executed, and the returned resource (`resource_id`) is marked as free and, therefore, available to attend the request of a process in the future.

Exercise 2.21 In a system, there are two types of processes: A and B. We want to implement a synchronisation scheme in which the processes are synchronised in groups of exactly of one process of type A and 10 processes of type B. No process can complete its synchronisation operation until a full group has been formed. The synchronisation rules are as follows:

If a process of type A calls the synchronisation operation and there fewer than 10 processes of type B are waiting, the type A process must wait.

If a process of type B calls the synchronisation operation and there are not at least one process of type A and nine other processes of type B already waiting, the type B process must wait.

If a process of type A calls the synchronisation operation and there are at least 10 type B processes waiting, the type A process proceeds, and exactly 10 type B processes are resumed so that the group can synchronize and exit the monitor.

Likewise, if a process of type B calls the synchronisation operation and there is (at least) one process of type A and nine processes of type B already waiting, the type B process proceeds, and exactly one type A and nine type B processes are resumed and exit the monitor.

Processes are not required to be resumed in FIFO order. Design and implement a monitor (assuming *SU* semantics) that provides the required synchronisation between the two types of processes. The monitor can export either a single synchronisation operation for all process types (with one parameter) or a specific operation for type A and a specific operation for type B processes.

Solution To solve this problem, we have to make the following observations:

(a) A process of type A cannot exit the monitor, i.e., finish executing the procedure, if there are not at least 10 processes of type B blocked in the queue of their condition variable and the exit condition is satisfied.
(b) A process of type B cannot leave the monitor if there was not at least one process of type A and nine processes of type B blocked in the two condition variable queues inside the monitor.
(c) As soon as the exit conditions are met, no more processes are allowed to enter the monitor until the process group consisting of one process of type A and 10 processes of type B is exited. To keep things simple, let's just assume that once the group has finished, the system resets and starts taking in new processes to build the next group.
(d) The processes are not required to be unblocked in FIFO order, and we assume SU signal semantics for the operations of the condition variables of this monitor.

(e) The monitor invariant (MI) to be satisfied before any process enters, exits the monitor, or before blocking on a `c.wait()` operation and releasing the monitor is as follows, MI:*num_processesB_inside*<10 or *num_processesA_inside*<1.

The logical synchronisation condition that processes must satisfy in order to reactivate their execution within the monitor and then prepare to simulate the exit of a full group:

$$(C_B : num\_processesB\_inside = 10 \wedge num\_processesA\_inside > 0)$$
$$\vee$$
$$(C_A : num\_processesB\_inside \geq 10 \wedge num\_processesA\_inside = 1)$$

```
Monitor Room;
var
   num_processesB_inside, num_processesA_inside: integer;
   num_processesB_outside, num_processesA_outside: integer;
   insideA, insideB: condition;
```
Monitor procedures
```
(1) procedure enterExitsA();
(2) begin
(3)    num_processesA_inside:= num_processesA_inside+1;
(4)    if (num_processesB_inside < 10)
(5)       then insideA.wait();
          --synchronisation condition CA == true
(6)    num_processesA_outside:=num_processesA_outside +1;
          --synchronisation condition CB == true
(7)    insideB.signal();
(8) end;

(1) procedure enterExitsB();
(2) begin
(3)    num_processesB_inside:= num_processesB_inside +1;
(4)    if (num_processesA_inside=0 or num_processesB_inside<10)
(5)       then insideB.wait();
          --synchronisation condition CB == true
(6)    if (num_processesA_outside = 0)
(7)       then   --synchronisation condition
              --CA == true
(8)           insideA.signal();
(9)    num_processesB_outside:= num_processesB_outside +1;
(10)   if (num_processesB_outside < 10)
(11)      then
              --synchronisation condition CB == true
(12)          insideB.signal();
(13)      else initiate();
(14) end;
```
Initialisation procedure
```
(1) procedure initiate();
(2) begin
(3)    num_processesB_inside:= 0;
(4)    num_processesA_inside:= 0;
(5)    num_processesB_outside:= 0;
(6)    num_processesA_outside:= 0;
(7) end;
```

2.8 Exercises

The `Room` monitor is programmed with two general procedures *(enterExitA* and *enterExitB)* and one procedure for initialising the permanent variables. After instruction (3) which increments the number of processes of each type (*A* and *B*) entering the monitor, it is necessary to check if the conditions C_A or C_B are met for a *full group* formed by 10 *B* processes and one *A* process to leave the monitor. If the condition is satisfied, the processes skip the wait operation on the condition variable queues in the direct branch of the conditional at (5). The instruction (7) of procedure `enterExitA` serves to indicate to a process *B* that it can proceed to instruction (12) and prepare to exit the monitor. The monitor invariant is preserved only if no new process is allowed to enter while a *group* of processes is exiting. This is guaranteed by the semantics of *SU* signals and by maintaining the count of *B* processes ready to exit the monitor (`num_processesB_outside`). The preemptive nature of *SU* signals ensures that no new process can enter while blocked processes of the opposite type are waiting, as the signalling thread yields control to one of them, preventing signal stealing. The *SU* semantics means that the monitor does not become free as long as there are processes that have signalled, in instructions (8) or (12) of `enterExitB` or in instruction (7) of `enterExitA`. As a result the 10th *B* process of the exiting *group* is the only process that calls the procedure `initiate()` before either releasing the monitor or handing it off to the type A process that issued the signal in instruction (7). In this way, it is possible to modify all the variables at once so that no external processes will slip into the monitor while the *exiting group* is leaving, which would lead to race conditions with respect to the assignment of the value of the variables `num_processesX_inside` the monitor and non-compliance with the *MI* invariant.

Exercise 2.22 The following monitor (Barrier2) provides a single procedure named `input ()`, causing the first process to be suspended when called and the second caller to wake up the first, and then both will continue, and so it acts cyclically. Get an implementation of this monitor using semaphores.

```
Monitor Barrier2;
var n: integer;
   -- number of processes that have arrived and tried to complete
       execution after signal()
   s: condition; -- queue where the second process wait

procedure input();
 begin
   n:= n+1; -- one more process has arrived
   if n < 2 then -- if n=1 is the first:
      s.wait() -- wait for second
     else begin -- if it is second
        n:= 0; -- initialise counter
        s.signal() -- wake up the first process
     end
 end;

begin
 n:= 0;
end;
```

Solution The simulation of the `Monitor Barrier2` with semaphores cannot be performed in a fully satisfactory manner because instructions (7) and (8) in the solution's code below are not executed as a single atomic instruction. The execution of instruction (7) releases the mutual exclusion simulating the monitor lock. As a result, at least one additional process may preempt the first process that reached the barrier—before it has executed instruction (8)—and proceed to execute the block of instructions (10)–(14). Which would increment the semaphore value s, even though the first process has not yet blocked on `sem_wait(s)` (instruction 8). Such behavior deviates from the intended semantics of the operation being implemented and may lead to violations of the *liveness* property.

Shared global variables

```
Monitor Barrier2;
var n: integer;
  s: Semaphore;
  mutex: Semaphore;
```

Monitor procedure
```
(1) procedure input();
(2) begin
(3)   sem_wait(mutex);
(4)   n ++;
(5)   if (n < 2)
(6)     then begin
(7)       sem_signal(mutex);--(7)and(8) must be executed as
(8)       sem_wait(s);      --one atomic instruction
(8)     end
(10)    else begin
(11)      n= 0;
(12)      sem_signal(s);
(13)      sem_signal(mutex);
(14)    end
(15) end;
```
Initialisation procedure
```
begin
 n:= 0;
 init(s,0);
 init(mutex,1);
end;
```

If, on the other hand, we assume the existence of a low-level mechanism that guarantees the execution of instructions (7) and (8) in a non-interruptible way, then the implementation above could be considered fully correct, since the hypothetical scenario in which a process starves, which never reaches the instruction (8), because it is preempted by other processes that arrive later at the barrier would be impossible.

Exercise 2.23 This is a classic example often used to illustrate the problem of deadlock and appears in the literature as the Dining Philosophers problem. It can be described as follows: seated around a table are five philosophers and each philosopher alternates endlessly between thinking and eating; between every two philosophers, there is a fork, and in order to eat, a philosopher must acquire both the fork on their right and the one on their left.

2.8 Exercises

Five concurrent processes have been defined, each representing the activity of a philosopher. The processes interact through a monitor, called `MonFilo`. Before eating, each philosopher must acquire his right and left fork. After eating, the philosopher releases both forks. Philosopher `i` refers to their right fork as number `i` and their left fork as number `i + 1 mod 5`. The `MonFilo` monitor provides two procedures, `take_fork(num_fork, num_process)` and `release_fork(num_fork)`, which indicate that one of the philosopher processes wants to take a particular fork. The following code outlines the program logic, excluding the monitor implementation:

```
Monitor MonFilo;
....
 procedure take_fork(num_fork, num_proc: integer);
....
 procedure release_fork(num_fork: integer);
....
 begin
.... --initialisation of permanent variables
 end;
process Philosopher[ i: 0..4 ];
begin
 while true do begin
  MonFilo.take_fork(i,i);      -- argument 1=fork code
  MonFilo.take_fork(i+1 mod 5,i);--argument 2=process_number
  eat();
  MonFilo.release_fork(i);
  MonFilo.release_fork(i+1 mod 5);
  think();
 end
end;
```

Given this monitor interface, respond to the following questions:

(a) Design a solution for the `MonFilo` monitor.
(b) Describe the potential deadlock situation that could occur with the initial solution.
(c) Propose an improved solution that prevents the deadlock by ensuring that no more than four philosophers attempt to pick up their first fork at the same time.

Solution The problem is to solve a mutual exclusion problem in the access to five resources that are shared by the *philosopher* processes; each of these resources (*forks*) is shared by two philosophers that are located in adjacent seats of a circular table. Therefore, the invariant (MI) to be fulfilled before taking and when releasing a *fork* resource by the protocol processes: $0 \leq num\_forks\_occupied \leq 5$. Thus, each unblocking condition $C[i]$, which will allow a `philosopher-i` process to continue its execution, can be expressed as:

$$\forall i : 0 \leq i \leq 4 : C[i] : (num\_occupied\_forks < 5)$$
$$\wedge \left(fork\_busy[i] = false \vee fork\_busy[i + \bmod 5] = false \right)$$

Since the processes progress by acquiring and releasing resources one at a time, the conditions above ensure that at least one of the two forks needed by each *philosopher* to eat is not already in use.

However, a potential deadlock scenario (death by starvation of philosophers) could occur if philosophers acquire only one fork and then indefinitely wait for the second. This possibility must be addressed and cannot be ignored.

Monitor module definition. Solution to (a)

```
Monitor PhilosophersNotSafe;
var
  fork_occupied: array[0..4] of boolean;
  fork: array[0..4] of condition;
```
Monitor procedures
```
procedure take_fork(num_fork, num_proc: integer);
 begin
  if fork_occupied[num_fork]
    then fork[num_fork].wait();
    --C[num_fil] == true, fork relased
  fork_occupied [num_fork]= true;
 end;

procedure release_fork (num_fork: integer);
 begin
 fork_occupied [num_fork]= false;
 --C[num_fork] = true ∨ C[num_fork-1 mod 5] = true
 fork[num_fork].signal();--changes the status of the
                         -- philosophers: i and (i+1)mod 5
 end;
```

Initialisation procedure
```
begin
  fork_occupied:= {false,false,false,false,false};
 end;
```

One possible response is to describe the following execution scenario: a situation is reached during the execution of the program where each philosopher takes one fork and is always missing the other. Since no `philosopher` will release the fork until they have eaten, a situation arises in which all philosophers are waiting indefinitely. This leads to a deadlock where none can proceed, resulting in *starvation* of all `philosophers`, which is a violation of the concurrent safety property of the protocol.

To avoid the scenario of process deadlock scenario described in solution (a), we introduce a new condition: a coordinator (e.g., a butler) is responsible for seating the `philosophers` and ensures that no more than four are allowed at the table simultaneously. Now, to the synchronisation conditions of the processes, we would have to add:

$C_{previous}$= num_philosophers_seated < 4.

2.8 Exercises

Monitor module definition. Solution to (c)

```
Monitor PhilosophersNotSafe;
var
  fork_occupied: array[0..4] of boolean;
  fork: array[0..4] of condition;
  previous: condition;
  num_f12: integer --number of philosophers with only 1 fork
```
Monitor procedures
```
(1)  procedure take_fork(num_fork, num_proc: integer);
(2)  begin
(3)    if (num_fork = num_proc)
(4)      then begin
(5)        if num_f12 = 4
(6)          then previous.wait()
(7)          --C_previous == true, prepared to be seated at the table
(8)      end;
(9)    if fork_occupied [num_fork]
(10)     then fork[num_fork].wait();
         --C[num_phil] == true, fork released
(11)   fork_occupied[num_fork] := true;
(12)   if (num_fork == num_proc)
(13)     then num_f12 := num_f12+1;
(14)     else begin
(15)       num_f12 := num_f12-1;
(16)       if num_f12 < 4 then --C_previous == true
(17)         previous.signal();
(18)     end
(19)  end;
(20) procedure release_fork(num_fork:integer);
(21) begin
(22)   fork_occupied[num_fork] := false;
(23)     --C[num_fork] = true ∨ C[num_fork -1 mod 5]=true, fork released
(24)   fork[num_fork].signal();
(25) end;
```

Initialisation procedure
```
--anonymous procedure of initialisation
(1) begin
(2)   num_f12 := 0; --number of philosophers with 1st and without 2nd fork
(3)   for i = 0 to 4 do
(4)     fork_occupied[i]= false; --all forks are free initially
(5)   enddo;
(6) end;
```

The verification of the $C_{previous}$ is carried out by using a new *precondition* variable in the monitor to make the fifth philosopher wait if there are already four *philosophers* who have already taken the first fork and do not yet have the second one, since this is the state prior to the deadlock situation. By executing instructions (12)–(13), the number of *philosophers* with only one fork is counted. When a *philosopher* gets his second fork, the count is decremented in instruction (15) and signals (17) to the next one who might be waiting to sit him at the table to try to acquire the forks he needs to eat.

Exercise 2.24 Indicate with which type (or types) of monitor signals (*SC*, *SW* or *SU*) the code of the procedures of the following monitors trying to implement a FIFO semaphore would be correct. Modify the code of the procedures so that they could be correct with any of the above signal types.

```
Monitor Semaphore_1;         Monitor Semaphore_2;         Monitor Semaphore_3;
var                          var                          var
   s: integer;                  s: integer;                  s: integer;
   c: condition;                c: condition;                c: condition;
procedure P();               procedure P();               procedure P();
begin                        begin                        begin
   if (s = 0)                   while (s = 0) do             if (s = 0)
      then c.wait();               c.wait();                    then c.wait();
      --{s > 0}                    --{s ≥ 0}                    --{s ≥ 0}
   s:= s-1;                     enddo;                       else s:= s - 1;
   --{I.M.: s ≥ 0}              --{s > 0}                    --{s ≥ 0}
end;                            s:= s - 1;                  --{I.M.: s ≥ 0}
                                --{I.M.: s ≥ 0}           end;
                             end;

procedure V();               procedure V();               procedure V();
begin                        begin                        begin
   s:= s+1;                     notifyAll();                 if (c.queue())
   --{s > 0}                    s: = s+1;                       then--{s =0}
   c.signal();                  --{s > 0}                       c.signal();
   --{I.M.: s ≥ 0}              --{I.M.: s ≥ 0}              else s:= s+1;
end;                         end;                            --{s > 0}
                                                             --{I.M.: s ≥ 0}
                                                          end;

begin
   s:= 0;
   --{I.M.: s ≥ 0}
end;
```

Solution The Semaphore_1 monitor may fail to maintain the invariant $s \geq 0$ if *SC* (signal-and-continue) semantics is assumed. According to the verification rule for `c.wait()` under SC semantics (see Sect. 2.7.2), only the monitor invariant $s \geq 0$ can be safely assumed after the wait. However, a scenario involving signal stealing, where another process enters the monitor after a signal is issued but before the signaled process resumes, can cause this invariant to be violated. Specifically, if process A calls `V()` while other processes are waiting on condition c, s is incremented to 1. But the process B signaled by `c.signal()` might not immediately acquire the monitor. A third process C could enter the monitor instead and call `P()`, decrementing s back to 0. When the previously signaled process B finally resumes, it executes `s:=s-1`, resulting in $s=-1$, which violates the monitor invariant.

Therefore, the Semaphore_1 monitor is only correct when preemptive signal semantics (*SW* or *SU*) is used, which ensure that the signaled process resumes execution immediately and cannot be overtaken by other processes, like process C.

2.8 Exercises

The $Semaphore\_2$ monitor does not ensure the safety property under preemptive semantics. It assumes that `s` will be incremented before any waiting process resumes, which is not guaranteed with preemptive signals. In the `V()` operation, if `c.signal()` wakes up a process but the increment `s:=s+1` occurs after that process begins execution, and `s = 0`, the waiting process will re-evaluate the condition in the `while (s=0)` sentence and block again. As a result, the `V()` call would not have the intended effect of unblocking a waiting process, potentially violating liveness.

The $Semaphore\_3$ monitor, by contrast, is correct regardless of whether signal semantics are preemptive (*SW*, *SU*) or non-preemptive (*SC*). Its `P()` procedure ensures the invariant $s \geq 0$ is preserved by only decrementing `s` when it is strictly greater than zero (`else s:=s-1`). Moreover, this decrement is guarded by a conditional statement that is not followed by a `wait`, as in $Semaphore\_1$, thereby avoiding signal stealing and *SC* race conditions if *SC* semantics is assumed. The `V()` operation checks whether there are any processes waiting in `c.queue()`; if so, it issues a `c.signal()`, otherwise, it increments `s`. This structure ensures that the value of `s` is never reduced below zero, and that the signaling logic is sound regardless of whether the signaled process resumes immediately (as in preemptive semantics) or later (as in SC semantics).

From a formal perspective, in $Semaphore\_3$ monitor; the `P()` procedure's postcondition under `c.wait()` satisfies the expected invariant, and the sequencing of `V()` ensures that signaling and state updates are performed safely. Even in cases of signal stealing under *SC* semantics, the signaled process will block again if necessary, without reducing `s` below 0.

Exercise 2.25 Assume an unknown number of message consuming and message producing processes of a very simple communication network. Messages are sent by the producers by calling the operation *broadcast(m)*, *m* is assumed to be an integer, to send a copy of message *m* to the consumer threads that have previously requested to receive it, which are blocked waiting. Another producer thread cannot send the next message until all consumer threads receive the previously sent message. To receive a copy of a sent message, the consumer threads call the `fetch():integer` operation. As long as a message is being transmitted over the communications network, any new consumer threads that request to receive it will do so immediately, without waiting. The producer thread, which sent the message to the network, will remain blocked until all requesting consumer threads have actually received it. Design and program a monitor that includes among its methods the operations: `broadcast(m)`, `fetch():integer`, assuming urgent signal semantics (*SU*).

Solution

```
Monitor Messages
 Const m0;
var
  message, cons_to_serve: integer;
  message_present: boolean;
  producers, consumers, transmitting: condition;
Monitor procedures
procedure broadcast(m: integer);               function fetch():integer;
 begin                                          var
   while (message_present) do                     m: integer;
     producers.wait();                          begin
   enddo;                                         cons_to_serve:= cons_to_serve+1;
   message_present:= true;                        if (not message_present)
   message:= m;                                     then consumers.wait();
   if (consumers.queue())                         m:= message;
     then begin                                   cons_to_serve:= cons_to_serve-1;
       consumers.signalAll();                     if (cons_to_serve= 0)
       producers.wait();                            then begin
     end                                              message_present:= false;
     else message_present:= false;                    producers.signal();
   if (producers.queue())                           end;
     then producers.signal();                     return m;
 end;                                           end;
Initialisation procedure
begin
  message:= m0;
  cons_to_serve:= 0; message_present:= false;
end;
```

Exercise 2.26 Assume a basic operating system memory page allocation system that provides two operations, `acquire(n:integer)` and `free(n:integer)`, so that user processes can get the pages they need and then free them for use by others. When processes call the `acquire(n:integer)` operation, if there is no memory available to service the request, the request would remain pending until there is a sufficient number of free pages in memory. By calling operation `free(n:integer)`, a process makes n pages of system memory available. We assume that processes acquire and return pages of the same size to an area of memory with a queue structure and where we assume that the problem known as memory page fragmentation does not exist. We are asked to program a monitor that includes the above operations assuming urgent signal semantics (SU).

Program two monitors according to the following conditions:

(a) Strict FIFO order is used to handle calls to the acquire pages operation by the processes.
(b) Relax the above condition and by resolving it with the calls handled in the following order: pending request with the fewest pages first (SJF).

With a strict FIFO order, assuming there is a pending request for 30 pages and the available memory is 20 pages, if a request for 20 pages arrives later, it will have to wait until there is enough memory to serve the 30-page request first.

2.8 Exercises

Solution

(a) The requested solution would be as follows, for which we assume that the processes will call a `request()` procedure, to ensure strict FIFO ordering of requests, before acquiring the pages they need.

Monitor module definition Solution (a)

```
Monitor MemoryFIFO;
var
  mem_available: integer;
  pending_request: boolean;
  wait, obtain: condition;
```
Monitor procedures
```
procedure request();                         procedure release(n: integer);
begin                                        begin
  if (pending_request or obtain.queue())       mem_available:= mem_available + n;
    then wait.wait();                          if (obtain.queue())
  pending_request:= true;                        then obtain.signal();
end;                                         end;

Procedure acquire(n: integer)
 begin
   while(mem_available < n) do
     obtain.wait(); --obtain-queue is strict FIFO
   enddo;
   mem_available:= mem_available - n;
   pending_request:= false;
   if (wait.queue())
      then wait.signal();
end;
```
Initialisation procedure
```
begin
   mem_available:= M0;
   pending_request:= false;
end;
```

(b) We are asked to replace the FIFO scheduling, by default in the monitor queues, of the processes blocked in the `obtain` queue with a policy that priorises those requesting fewer pages, which is known as *SJF* (shortest job first) scheduling in operating systems. To implement this, we only need to substitute the `acquire()` procedure of the previous monitor and change the `obtain` condition variable to a priority condition variable, passing the number of requested pages as the priority parameter. The `request()` procedure is not needed in this case.

```
procedure acquire(n: integer)
begin         --only one queue "obtain" is necessary this time
 while(mem_available <n) do
    obtain.wait(n);
    --priority condition ensures the signaled
    --thread is the best eligible one
 mem_available: mem_available - n;
 if(obtain.queue())
   then obtain.signal(); --priority conditions enforces correct
                         --request eligibility
end;
```

Exercise 2.27 Design and program a controller monitor for an irrigation system that activates every 72 h. The system serves users as long as the tank, which has a maximum capacity of C_1 liters, contains water. If a user calls the `open_close_valve(amount: positive)` procedure and the tank is empty, the controller process must be signalled, and the thread supporting the user's request will remain blocked until the tank is fully refilled. If the tank is not full but still contains some water—though less than the requested quantity—irrigation proceeds with the available amount. The execution of procedure: `control_on_standby()` keeps the controller process blocked while the tank is not empty. The tank is refilled to full capacity when the controller calls procedure: `control_filling()`. Once the tank reaches full capacity (C_1 liters), the previously blocked user-threads must be signalled so they can complete the pending open/close valve operations.

(a) Program the irrigation monitor with the three operations mentioned above, which assume the semantics of urgent signals (*SU*).
(b) Demonstrate that threads calling the above monitor operations can never enter an undefined deadlock.
(c) Program a monitor solution with *SC* signal semantics.

```
process P[i: 1..N];                     process control;
begin                                   begin
  while true do                           while true do
  begin                                   begin
    Irrigation.open_close_valve(litres);    --The tank is initially full
    --water plants...                       Irrigation.standby_contr (); --Wait for 72 hours
  End                                       Irrigation.control_filling();
  enddo;                                  end;
end;                                      enddo
                                        end;
```

Solution

(a) This is a solution scheme similar to that of Exercise 2.18 in which, to avoid losing the signal of instruction (5) of the `control_filling()` procedure, urgent signal semantics (*SU*) must be assumed.

2.8 Exercises

```
Monitor Irrigation;
 const
    quantity=C1;
 var
    current: integer;
    waiting, user_wait: condition;
```
Monitor procedures
```
(1) procedure open_close_valve(amount: positive);    (1) procedure standby_contr();
(2) begin                                            (2) begin
(3)    if (current=0)                                (3)    if (current <>0)
(4)    then begin                                    (4)    then waiting.wait();
(5)       waiting.signal();                          (5) end;
(6)       user_wait.wait();
(7)    end;
(8)    if current < amount then
(9)       current := 0
(10)   else
(11)      current := current - amount;
(12)   if(user_wait.queue() and current<> 0)
(13)      then user_wait.signal();
(14) end;
(1) procedure control_filling();
(2) begin
(3)    current:= quantity;
(4)    if (user_wait.queue())
(5)       then user_wait.signal();
(6) end;
```

Initialisation procedure
```
begin
   current:= quantity;
 end;
```

When it is verified in (3) that the tank is empty, the process signals the controller that is blocked in the waiting queue, so that it can refill the tank. When signalling, process `P(i)` releases the monitor, and the `controlling` process immediately resumes its execution by entering the monitor, completing the instruction (4) of `control_on_standby` and then exits the monitor (5). At this point, the monitor is free. Thanks to the *SU* semantics of the monitor signals, the next instruction to be executed within the monitor is (6) of `open_close_valve`, and, in this way, thus preventing process `P(i)` from remaining blocked. If other signal semantics were used, then it could happen that the `controlling` process re-enters the monitor by calling `control_filling` before the `open_close_valve` call of process `P(i)` has resumed and completed.

In such a case, the signal from instruction (5) of `control_filling()` would be lost, because the signalling process would not be blocked in the `user_wait` queue, having released the monitor before executing instruction (6) `user_wait.wait()`. This would result in process `P(i)` remaining indefinitely blocked.

(b) We now aim to demonstrate the impossibility of program processes to enter in deadlock situation indefinitely. A process `P(i)` could only potentially remain blocked during the execution of the single wait operation that is programmed in instruction (6) of the `open_close_valve`. However, this scenario is prevented by the urgent (SU) semantics of monitor signals. Under *SU* semantics, the controlling process cannot execute `control_filling` until `open_close_valve` resumes execution (there is at least one signaller in the monitor's urgent queue), and the following instruction (6) forces process `P(i)` to wait for the signal, ensuring that the signal issued in instruction (5) of `control_filling` is never lost.

(c) The requested solution would be as follows:

```
Monitor Irrigation;
 const
  quantity=C1;
 var
  current: integer;
  waiting, signalling: condition;  --suppose SC semantics of the condition
```

Monitor procedures
```
(1)procedure open_close_valve(amount positive);   (1)procedure control_on_standby();
(2) begin                                          (2) begin
(3)   if (current=0)                               (3)   if (current <>0)
(4)     then waiting.signal();                     (4)     then waiting.wait();
(5)   while(current = 0) do                        (5) end;
(6)     signalling.wait();
(7)   enddo;
(8)   if amount >= current then
(9)     current := 0
(10)  else
(11)    current := current - amount
(12)end;
(1)procedure control_filling();
(2) begin
(3)   signalling.signalAll();
(4)   current:= quantity;
(5) end;
```
Initialisation procedure
```
(1)begin
(2)   current:= quantity;
(3) end;
```

2.8.2 Proposed Exercises

Exercise 2.28 Let us assume the mutual exclusion algorithm expressed below. We have the processes: $0,\ldots, n-1$. Each process i has a variable $s[i]$, initialised to 0, which can take the values 0/1. Process i can enter the critical section if the following conditions are satisfied:

$s[i] \ne s[i-1]$ for $i > 0$;
$s[i] = s[n-1]$ for $i = 0$.

After executing its critical section, process i shall enforce this:

$s[i] = s[i-1]$ for $i > 0$; (if $s[i-1] \ne s[i]$, previously)
$s[i] = (s[i] + 1) \bmod 2$ for $i = 0$ (if $s[n-1] = s[0]$, previously).

2.8 Exercises

Exercise 2.29 Some old computers had an instruction called TST (TestAndSet). Suppose there is a global variable c in the system, in memory common to the processors, called condition code. Executing the instruction $TST\,(1)$ for the local variable l the result is the same as the atomic execution of the following two instructions:

$l = c;$
$c = 1.$

(a) Discuss the correctness of the solution to the mutual exclusion problem of the following algorithm written as the following program code in a C-like programming language:

Parallel processes

```
void *p1(void *arg){                   void *p2(void *arg){
  int l;                                 int l;
  do{                                    do{
  --rest of instructions                 --rest of instructions
    do{                                    do{
      TST(1);                                TST(1);
    } while(l==1);                         } while(l==1);
  --critical  section                    --critical  section;
    c=0;                                   c=0;
  } while(true)                          } while(true)
}                                      }
```
Main program
```
int main(int argc, char *argv[]){
  int c= 0;
  cobegin
    p1(); p2()
  coend;
}
```

(b) What would happen to the concurrent properties of the above algorithm if the TST instruction was replaced by the above two instructions and executed non-atomically?

Exercise 2.30 The *EX* instruction swaps the contents of two memory locations. *EX(a,b)* is equivalent to an indivisible execution of the following three instructions:

$temp := a;$
$a := b;$
$b := temp;$

(a) Discuss the correctness of the solution of the following mutual exclusion algorithm written in a concurrent variant of the C language:

Parallel processes

```
void *p1(void *arg){              void *p2(void *arg){
  int l;                            int l;
  do{l=0;                           do{l=0;
  --rest of instructions            --rest of instructions
    do{                               do{
      EX(c,l);                          EX(c,l);
    } while(l !=1);                   } while(l !=1);
  --critical section;               --critical section;
    c=1;                              c=1;
  }while(true)                      }while(true)
}                                 }
```

Main program

```
int main(int argc, char *argv[]){
  int c= 1;
  cobegin
    p1(); p2()
  coend;
}
```

(b) What would happen if the atomic instruction *EX* were replaced by the three instructions above and executed non-atomically?

Exercise 2.31 With respect to the following mutual exclusion algorithm for *N* processes, prove the falsity of the following proposition: if a set of processes is simultaneously trying to pass the first loop (5) and the process that owns the turn is passive, then the process from the set that manages to assign the variable `turn` last will always enter the critical section first (Fig. 2.29).

```
var
  flag: array [0... N-1] of (passive, requesting, inCS);
  flag:= passive; turn:= 0..N-1;
  turn:= 0;

process P[i: integer]; --runs forever
  begin
(1)  --rest of instructions
(2)  repeat
(3)    flag[i]:= requesting;
(4)    while (turn !=i) do
(5)      if (flag[turn] = passive)
(6)        then turn:=i;
(7)      endif;
(8)    enddo;
(9)    flag[i]:= inCS;
(10)   j:= 0; --j is local to the process P[i]
(11)   while (j < N)and ((j = i)or flag[j]!= inCS)do
(12)     j:= j + 1;
(13)   enddo;
(14)  until (j >= N);
(15) --critical section
(16) flag[i]:= passive;
  end;
```

Fig. 2.29 Dijkstra's algorithm for the mutual exclusion problem for *N* processes

2.8 Exercises

Exercise 2.32 If in Knuth's algorithm the instruction (6) is changed to this one, if `flag[turn] != inSC`, and then the algorithm would no longer be correct, explain why by indicating the correction properties that would fail.

Exercise 2.33 Concerning the following algorithm, which solves the mutual exclusion problem for N processes, using N boolean variables, `flag:array[0...N-1]` of (`requesting,inSC,passive`). A variable `turn:0...N-1` and the local variable `j`.

(a) Demonstrate that the algorithm verifies all the properties required of a concurrent program, including the fairness property (Fig. 2.30).
(b) Write a scenario in which two processes make it through the loop of instruction (5), assuming that the *turn* is initially taken by process $P(0)$.

```
var
  N: integer;
  flag: array [0..N-1] of (passive, requesting, inCS);
  turn: 0..N-1;

process P[i: integer];-- runs forever
var
  j: integer;
begin
(1) -- rest of instructions
(2) repeat
(3)    flag[i] := requesting;
(4)    j := turn; -- j is local to P[i]
(5)    while (j != i) do
(6)      if (flag[j] != passive) then
(7)        j := turn -- restart from current turn holder
(8)      else j := (j - 1) mod N;
(9)      endif;
(10)   enddo;
(11)   flag[i] := inCS;
(12)   j := 0;
(13)   while (j < N) and ((j = i) or (flag[j] != inCS)) do
(14)     j := j + 1;
(15)   enddo;
(16) until (j >= N);
(17) -- critical section
(18) j := (turn + 1) mod N;
(19) turn := j;
(20) flag[i] := passive;
end;
--- Initialisation
begin
(1) for i := 0 to N - 1 do
(2)   flag[i] := passive;
end.
```

Fig. 2.30 Knuth algorithm for the mutual exclusion problem for N processes

Exercise 2.34 If the following substitutions are made in Knuth's algorithm (Fig. 2.30):

- The condition of the instruction (16) is replaced by the condition: $(j \geq N)$ and $(turn = i$ or $flag\,[turn]) = passive)$.
- The following loop is inserted at instruction (19):

```
while(j! = turn) and (flag[j] = passive) do
    j: = j + 1:
enddo;
```

(a) Verify the properties of mutual exclusion, reachability of the critical section, liveness and fairness of the algorithm.
(b) Calculate the maximum number of turns that a process requesting to enter its critical section may have to wait under Knuth's original algorithm.

Exercise 2.36 Assume a car wash garage with two zones: a waiting zone and a car wash zone with 100 washing places. One car enters the garage wash area only if there is (at least) one free space; otherwise, it stays in the waiting queue. If a car enters the wash area, it looks for a free space and waits until it is attended by a garage employee. Cars cannot re-enter the garage until they are charged for the service by the attendant. We assume that there are more than 100 employees who wash cars, get paid, leave and re-enter the garage. When an employee enters the garage, he/she checks if there are cars waiting to be serviced, i.e., already located in his/her wash bay; if not, waits for a car to be serviced. If there is at least one car waiting, he/she walks around the wash bay until finds it, then washes it, lets the client know that can leave and, finally, waits to be paid. It may happen that several employees have finished washing their cars and are all waiting for payment for their services, but it is not allowed for an employee to charge a car other than the one he/she has washed. It is also necessary to avoid that when two or more employees enter the washing area, having checked that there are cars waiting, they select the same car to be washed. You are asked to program a simulation of the performance of the cars and the garage employees. The simulation will use a monitor with urgent signals (*SU*). The solution to the problem that uses the fewest number of condition variables will be given the highest score.

Exercise 2.37 Consider the concurrent program shown below. In this program, there are two processes, named P_1 and P_2, which try to alternate accessing the monitor *M*. The intention of the programmer when writing this program was that the process P_1 would wait blocked in the queue of the signal *p*, until the process P_2 called the procedure `follow()` to unblock process P_1; then P_2 would wait until P_1 finished executing `M.stop()`, and after doing some processing, `q.signal()` would be executed to unblock P_2. However, the following program may cause to both processes to deadlock when using such a monitor.

2.8 Exercises

```
Monitor Rendezvous;
 var
   p, q: cond;
```

Monitor procedures

```
procedure stop()                procedure follow()
 begin                           begin
   p.wait();                       p.signal();
   --Other instructions            q.wait();
   q.signal();                   end;
 end;
```
Parallel processes
```
Process P1;                     Process P2;
 begin                           begin
   while (true) do                 while (true) do
     Rendezvous.stop();              Rendezvous.follow();
   enddo;                          enddo;
 end;                            end;.
```

Answer the following questions:

(a) Find a scenario in which the concurrent program that launches the execution of processes P_1 and P_2 becomes deadlocked.
(b) Modify the above monitor so that the behaviour of the above program is as desired and the deadlock is avoided.

Exercise 2.38 Demonstrate the correctness of a monitor that implements the circular buffer access operations for the producer-consumer problem using the following invariant:

$0 \leq n \leq N$; no blocked processes.
$0 > n$; there are *abs(n)* blocked consumers.
$n > N$; there are $(n - N)$ blocked producers.

Design and program a monitor that satisfies the above invariant, and satisfies the following conditions:

(a) The operation `not_empty.signal()` is executed only when there are blocked consumers.
(b) The `not_full.signal()` operation is executed only when there are blocked producers. The *buffer* is assumed to have N positions, and the two signalling operations mentioned above are used. It is not allowed to use the `c.queue()` operation to find out if there are blocked processes in any condition variable queue.

Exercise 2.39 Assume that n processes share m printers. Before using a printer, the process P_i calls the operation `request(integer process_id):integer`, which returns the number of free printers. In case there is no free printer at that time, the above method call causes the process P_i to wait for one printer. Processes after using a printer call the procedure `return(integer process_id)`. When a printer becomes free and there are several processes waiting for it, the process with the highest priority of those waiting will be granted the printer. The priority of a process is given by its process index. So a process with a lower index will have a higher priority. If, when a printer is freed, there is no process waiting, then the printer whose identifier appears in the call to `return(integer id_printer)` will be left as a free printer, i.e., not yet assigned to any process. Program the monitor procedures above assuming preemptive *SU* signal semantics, and also write the invariant of the programmed monitor.

Exercise 2.40 Write code for the `P()` and `V()` procedures of a monitor that implements a general semaphore with the following invariant: $\{s \geq 0\} \wedge \{s=s0+nV-nP\}$ and that is correct for any signal semantics (*SW, SU, SC*). The implementation has to ensure that no signal stealing can ever occur by threads calling the operations of the previous semaphore monitor.

Message Passing Based Systems 3

3.1 Introduction to Distributed Programming

The programs of a classical von Neumann computer assume that instructions are sent from memory to the central unit and are therefore conceived for deterministic execution as a single sequential program whose instructions are executed one after the other (Fig. 3.1) in a central processing unit (CPU). However, the desire for greater execution speed has resulted in the introduction of parallelism in programs and the emergence of multiprocessors and multiprocessing.

The serial execution of instructions on a single CPU, according to the aforementioned architecture, presents several problems that reduce system efficiency, since instruction execution is performed in the same way as operations on data, using a common bus that is shared between both actions. This fact limits computational performance and is known as the *von Neumann bottleneck*[1].

The solution to the above problem necessarily involves the introduction of true parallelism, which implies the simultaneous execution of instructions of a program by several processing units. Figure 3.2 shows how a program can be split into instructions and processed by multiple CPUs. Each block of instructions is sent to different CPUs, which improves processing speed and efficiency. The time labels show how work is distributed over time to the available CPUs, which is how multiprocessing is used to run programs more quickly.

---

[1] The von Neumann architecture refers to stored-program computers in which an instruction fetch and a data operation cannot occur simultaneously.

Fig. 3.1 Instructions executed in one CPU

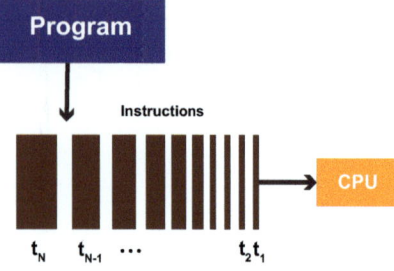

Fig. 3.2 Architecture using multiple computational elements simultaneously

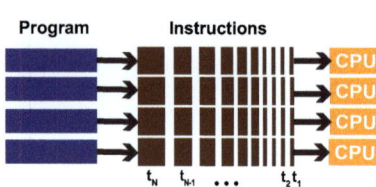

> Problems with *sequential* architectures:
> - More expensive to produce today.
> - Programs need more execution time.
> - Bus speed limitation.

The simultaneous use of multiple computational resources to solve the lack of performance caused by the execution of a sequential instruction stream produces economic benefits, as the system requires less energy, is cheaper to produce and provides better performance because it overcomes the bus bottleneck problem. However, it also has limitations, as it involves learning to program according to a paradigm defined by the new architecture that assumes the advancement of multiple lines of instruction execution, which is very different from the paradigm in which programming is normally learned. In addition, such architectures create new difficulties for debugging programs, since to do so with parallel code, the designer must be able to access each computational unit (each processor core) and its corresponding debugging functions. A multi-core processor must also provide access to the inter-connection network and memory architecture, both at the cache level and at the main memory level, to perform useful code debugging, which greatly increases the complexity of developing tools.

3.1.1 Multiprocessors and Multiprocessing

These are systems that include several computing elements, generically referred to as processors, which share main memory and peripherals in order to execute program instructions simultaneously. Symmetric multiprocessing, also known as SMP, is a common architecture

3.1 Introduction to Distributed Programming

used in modern multiprocessor systems. This is a hardware architecture for a type of multiprocessor in which several identical processors are connected to a single shared main memory, abstracting the individual control of each processor by an instance of the operating system, which interfaces with users and application programs. The SMP architecture (Fig. 3.3a) is hegemonic today, especially for so-called multi-core processors that use it to treat the different cores of a processor as if they were separate processors. In the SMP architecture, processors can be interconnected via buses, crossbar switches, I2 C or mesh-type networks within the chip itself. Notable examples of SMP (Symmetric Multiprocessing) systems, recognized for their widespread adoption, include the following: AMD's Athlon and Opteron processors; Intel's Core i3, i5, i7, and i9 (in select configurations), Xeon, and the now-discontinued Itanium; Sun's legacy UltraSPARC and Oracle's SPARC M7-M8; as well as ARM's v9.2 architecture, featuring the Cortex-X4, A720, and A520 cores.

In order to complete this review, we will refer to the term asymmetric multiprocessing (AMP) (Fig. 3.3b). Historically, during the 1970s, the AMP multiprocessor model was an interim software resource, in order to manage systems with processors of different types, before the appearance of SMP systems. In AMP systems, the CPU is only the arithmetic and logic processor that executes the user applications; it does not have the graphics processing, multithreading, etc. functionality of today's multi-core processors. In addition, all CPUs in an AMP multiprocessor must have the same low-level instruction set for the applications that use them, as a running task could be dynamically reassigned from one CPU to another.

Examples of AMP systems, which were used at the time mentioned above, are the following: IBM (65MP), Burroughs B6800, CDC (6700), DEC (PDP-11 and VAX), Multics and UNIVAC (1108). Today, systems whose CPUs are not all the same often follow other

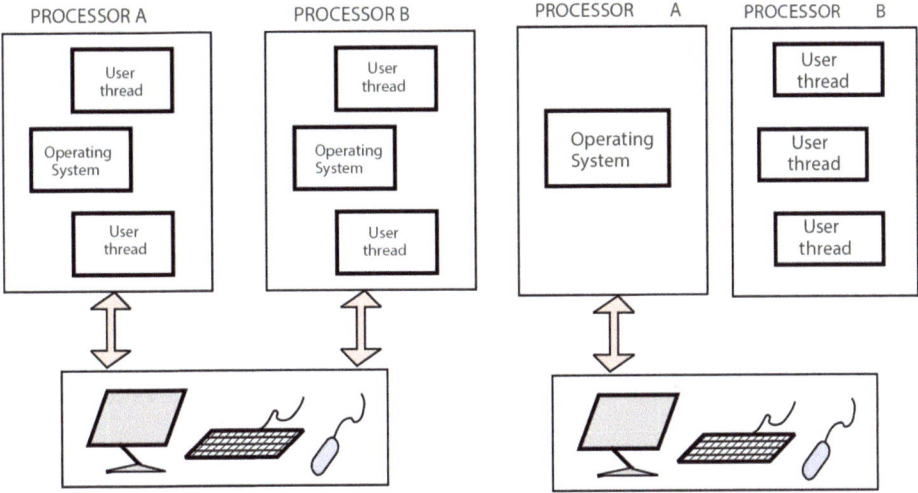

Fig. 3.3 Types of multiprocessor architecture: (**a**) SMP multiprocessor, (**b**) AMP multiprocessor

evolved AMP models, such as non-uniform memory access multiprocessing (NUMA) and clustered multiprocessing.

AMP systems presented a programmability problem, as the operating systems of the time were developed for a single CPU. This issue was not adequately addressed until the advent of SMP systems, in which the operating system and the applications under its control are executed with a finely-grained, synchronized system tick common to all processor clocks, allowing simultaneous execution on all processors.

3.1.1.1 Multiprocessing

Multiprocessing is the use of two or more CPUs in a single multiprocessor system to execute the programs of a single application. The term multiprocessing also refers to a system's ability to manage multiple processors or to be able to reallocate tasks among them during program execution. The term multiprocessing is sometimes used to refer to the execution of multiple concurrent software processes within a system, as opposed to the execution of a single process at any time, which is typical of single-processor systems. However, this concept is more accurately captured by the terms multiprogramming or multitasking, which are commonly used in the context of operating systems. These terms generally refer to the concurrent execution of software code, whereas multiprocessing is a term more appropriate to describe the execution of a program by multiple hardware processors. A system may support both multiprocessing and multiprogramming or only one of these. Computer systems with a single-core processor, and thus lacking both multiprocessing and multiprogramming capabilities, are now exceedingly rare.

From the point of view of the execution model of a program's instructions by a multiprocessor, processors can be utilized to execute either a single sequence or multiple sequences of instructions across various contexts. Michael J. Flynn proposed a classification system (Table 3.1) for types of multiprocessing, which has been maintained to date.

The SIMD model describes multiprocessors that execute a single sequence of instructions in different execution contexts. That is, all processors could be synchronised to execute the same instruction simultaneously, but the result would affect data located in different memory locations. The SIMD type is suitable for vector parallel processing, in which a large amount of data can be divided into parts that are modified independently. In this model, a single sequence of instructions directs the operation of multiple CPUs to perform the same manipulations on the data, even on large amounts of different data at the same time.

Multiprocessors in the MISD model, on the other hand, would execute different instructions, possibly belonging to different execution sequences of the processes in a program but affecting the same memory area. The MISD model mainly offers the advantage of redundancy in computation, as multiple processes perform the same tasks on the same

Table 3.1 Multiprocessing taxonomy

	Unique instruction	Multiple instructions
Unique data	SISD	MISD
Multiple data	SIMD	MIMD

3.1 Introduction to Distributed Programming

data, reducing the chances of incorrect results if one of them should fail. MISD architectures can involve making comparisons between different processors to detect failures.

Apart from the redundancy and security features of this type of multiprocessing, the MISD model has very few advantages and is very expensive to implement. It does not improve program performance. It can be implemented in such a way that the existence of the different processors is transparent to the software. An example of the usefulness of the MISD model is progressive image processing, where each pixel of an image is routed through several hardware processors that perform image transformation steps.

In the MIMD model, the processing of program instruction sequences is divided into multiple threads of program execution, each of which has its own processor state within one or multiple software-defined processes. Since most processors today are multi-core and work with multiple threads waiting to be scheduled, either system threads or user programs, this architecture model is recommended to make good use of the low-level computational resources of today's processors.

The use of multiprocessors following the MIMD model can lead to resource contention problems by processes and even lead to deadlocks, as threads can conflict in an unpredictable way in their access to resources, which is difficult to anticipate and manage efficiently.

3.1.2 Implementation of the Multiprocessing Models

Implementing the MIMD model requires special coding at the operating system level, but does not require substantial changes in applications developed for single-processors systems, unless those applications use multi-threaded programming. That is, the MIMD model is generally transparent to single-threaded programs, provided they do not voluntarily yield control to the operating system during execution[2]. On the other hand, with multiprocessors following the MIMD model, both system software and user programs may need to use software constructs, such as semaphores or locks, to prevent one thread from interfering with another if the two threads intertwine their executions while referencing the same data. Ensuring exclusive access to shared resources during asynchronous thread execution increases code complexity, lowers program performance, and makes code verification essential. Nonetheless, these challenges do not outweigh the advantages of multithreaded execution. Similar conflicts often arise at the hardware level between processors, for example, cache contention and data corruption situations. Usually, such problems must be solved at the hardware level or by a combination of software and hardware using cache-flushing instructions in programs.

There are several possibilities for implementing the MIMD model:

(a) In multiprocessor systems that use shared memory (Fig. 3.4) synchronisation between processes is based on the serialisation of parallel execution of instructions that occurs when several processes try to access the same memory address. This model typically

---

[2] For example, by triggering a call to the operating system.

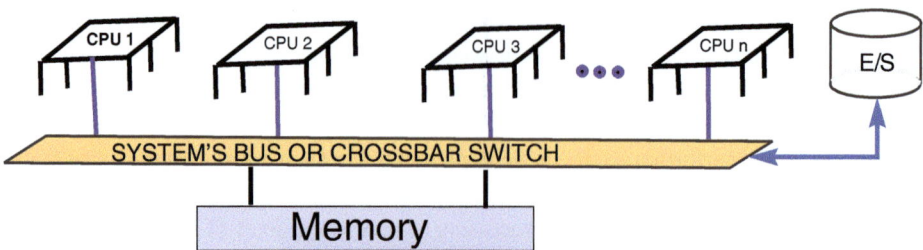

Fig. 3.4 Schematic representation of a multiprocessor with shared memory

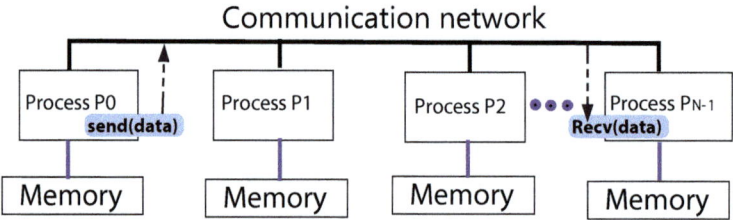

Fig. 3.5 Representation of a multicomputer

relies on concurrent programming based on monitors, semaphores, critical regions, etc. As a result, special hardware mechanisms are needed so that the processors can efficiently access shared memory locations. However, the primary drawback of these architectures is their limited scalability.

(b) In multicomputer systems, shared memory cannot be assumed between CPUs, i.e., all communication and synchronisation has to be carried out through a communication network (Fig. 3.5). This architectural distinction means that, multicomputers have other advantages that make them the most widely used machines today. Additionally, they do not have the scalability problem of memory multiprocessors. To effectively program these systems, a highly flexible programming model is required, which allows to express the different communication modes between processes, as well as to express the non-determinism in communications. The classical concurrent primitives like semaphores, critical regions, monitors, etc. are not well-suited for programming multicomputers.

3.1.2.1 SPMD Structure of a Message-Passing-Based Program

Running a different program in each processor as illustrated in the general model of Fig. 3.5, can be cumbersome in the context of concurrent programming, especially when the goal is for processes to collaborate in solving a common problem or achieving a shared computational objective. Consequently, a distributed programming style called Single Program Multiple Data (SPMD) is often used, in which the code executed by the processes is identical but acting on different data (Fig. 3.6). The SPMD style is a variant of the general MIMD model, and is somewhat similar to SIMD, as all processors execute the same

3.1 Introduction to Distributed Programming

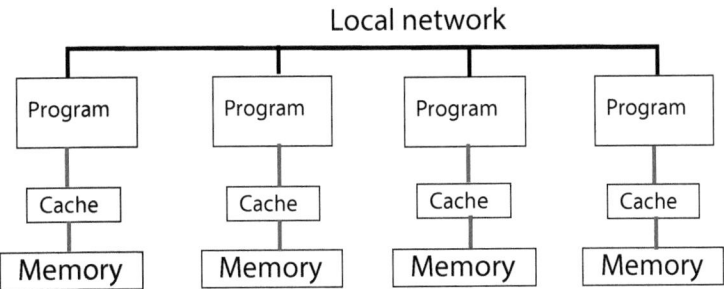

Fig. 3.6 Representation of the SPMD model

program, though on different data. A SPMD program does not have to synchronise in the parallel execution of each individual instruction as would be the case in a SIMD multiprocessor.

Each program includes the internal logic necessary for each process to perform its assigned task according to the value of its identifier, which will be different for each of them and is typically assigned during a distributed configuration stage following compilation.

Example 3.1

As an example of programming, we propose the following code programmed according to an SPMD style for a generic multicomputer.

	Client			Worker 1			Worker 2		
Process defined variables	a	b	e	c	d	f	c	d	f
a:= 3;	3	-	-	-	-	-	-	-	-
b:= 4;	3	4	-	-	-	-	-	-	-
spmd									
c:= rank();	3	4	-	1	-	-	2	-	-
d:= c + a;	3	4	-	1	4	-	2	5	-
end									
e:= a + d{1};	3	4	7	1	4	-	2	5	-
c{2}:= 5;	3	4	7	1	4	-	5	5	-
spmd									
f:= c * b;	3	4	7	1	4	4	5	5	20
end									

Variables a, b and e can be read by all processes but can only be written by the Client. The Worker processes read and write local copies of variables c, d and f. The Client thread can access these variables but distinguishes between them by specifying between braces the processor number returned by the rank() function for each thread.

The Client thread processor executes the common code up to the first spmd block and stops. The processors running the Worker threads have nothing to execute but are aware of the new values of the `a` and `b` variables. All processes synchronise at the `spmd` mark.

In the first `spmd` block, values are assigned to the local variables `c` and `d` of the `Workers`. Each one of them ends the execution of this block with a different value of its variable `c` since each one of them obtains a value from the `rank()` function equal to the identifier of its processor.

In the following program block, the `Client` uses the value of variable `d` local to thread `Worker 1` to assign its variable `e`, and then the value of variable `c` is changed but only in `Worker 2`.

Finally, the processes `Worker 1` and `2` will therefore end up the second `spmd` block with a different value of their local variable `f`: 4 and 20, respectively, since the local value of their variable `c` is different.

3.2 Basic Mechanisms in Message-Passing Systems

Currently, message passing has to be understood as a communication and synchronisation primitive between processes closer to programming languages than to the platform [2] if we understand *computing platform* as the integration of the operating system layer and the network level[3]. If we focus on processor architectures and specifically on *multicomputer* systems, the processes of a concurrent program communicate and synchronise by *message passing*, i.e., we cannot assume the existence of a common memory through which they can communicate or synchronise.

By *communication* we mean that the processes send and receive messages to and from each other, instead of writing or reading access to the shared variables of the program which, in the *multi-computer* model, do not usually exist. *Synchronisation* between processes occurs as a consequence of the fact that the reception of a message is subsequent to the sending of the message and, in general, the execution of the *receive* operation involves waiting for the message to be available on the receiving side. The basic message-passing primitives refer to the sending and receiving of a series of data of a certain type or format between the process sending the message and the receiving process:

```
send(<variables_list>, <destination_identifier>)
receive(<variables_list>, <source_identifier>)
```

Proper programming requires consideration of the specific communication identification scheme used by the programming language or system, as well as the synchronisation mode or semantics of the upstream message passing primitives.

---

[3] Network level, according to ISO standards.

3.2 Basic Mechanisms in Message-Passing Systems

Schemes for Identifying Communicating Processes

The aim is to determine how the message sender and receiver processes identify each other during the execution of a distributed program. In the case of so-called direct naming, process identifiers are used so that the sender can explicitly point to the receiver and vice versa. The main problem with this option is that the process identifiers have to be assigned prior to the execution of the program and this assignment has to be maintained throughout the execution of the application. As a consequence, any change in process identification requires code recompilation. The main advantage of this type of naming is that it does not produce any delay due to the identification of the communicating processes, although it is best suited for 1-to-1 communications, particularly between processes in a distributed application:

```
Process P0;                        Process P1;
  datum                              var
    datum:integer:= 100;               x:integer;
  begin                              begin
    send(&datum,P1);                   receive(&x,P0);
    changes(datum);                    print(x);
  end;                               end;
```

The *identification* scheme between processes that is most flexible, as it allows several communication configurations between groups of processes, is called *indirect naming*. It is based on the use of an intermediate object called a *mailbox* between the communicating processes. In this way, the processes designate the mailbox as the destination or origin of the messages to be exchanged, and therefore, the restriction of the 1-to-1 links implied by the use of direct naming is avoided. There are three types of mailboxes, depending on the relationship established between the processes (Table 3.2).

In message-based communication using ports, the destination is typically a single node within the network or process connection topology, but the origin of the message may be the identifier of one among a set of such processes and need not be specified. Ports thus enable multiplexing, allowing multiple destination points to be addressed on a single node of a connection network. Each process in the programs will receive the remote information through its ports, enabling it to expose multiple services to the network, which could be simultaneously accessed by the remote processes. In networking models, ports are part of the transport layer in the TCP/IP model and of the session layer in the ISO model.

In the case of general mailboxes, the destination of messages sent by a process can be any node in the network, just as any node can be the origin of a message received at the

Table 3.2 Types of messages

Relation	One-to-one	Many-to-one	Many-to-many
Type	channel	port	mailbox

destination. They can be understood as two-sided ports, which multiplex both destination and source points on a single network node. As a consequence, mailboxes are more complicated and inefficient to implement than ports if there is no specialised communication network to support the low-level implementation of their communication operations. In general, sending a message to a mailbox means transmitting it to across the network, and delivering it means notifying all potential recipient processes of its availability.

```
Channel of integer mailbox;      process P₁ ;
process P₀ ;                     x:integer;
 datum:integer;                   begin
 begin                             receive(&x, mailbox);
  produces(data);                  consumes(x);
  send(&datum, mailbox);          end;
 end;
```

On the other hand, channels can be understood as a special type of port that has only one originating node and also as a communication service aimed at establishing connections between software application processes, similar to the concept of a *virtual circuit* between nodes in a communication network. Channels can be used to transmit a continous data stream, so that information is delivered in the order in which it was sent. Unlike packet or frame-based transmission, this approach avoids data fragmentation and prevents reordering during network transmission.

Channels can be implemented using *Transmission Control Protocol* (TCP), by means of a specific protocol that provides virtual circuits on top of the base protocol. Such a virtual circuit can be established by identifying the address pair of the network *sockets*, *receiver* and *sender*, i.e., by providing their *IP* addresses and port numbers. However, this implementation is not suitable for establishing reliable connections between nodes and therefore does not guarantee that the order of data delivery and reception is maintained. On the other hand, the X.25 protocol does provide reliable node-to-node communication and at the same time guarantees quality of service in communications, as this protocol provides virtual channel identifiers (VCI) for deployment and subsequent use in applications.

From the point of view of its implementation in multiprocessors with common memory, if two interacting processes are located on the same processor, the means of message transmission can simply be some *shared* memory to which each processor has access. If, on the other hand, we cannot assume such *shared memory* and there are application processes located on different processors, then the message passing between these processes must necessarily be done through a physical communication medium that connects them and determines the reliability, as well as other properties, of the message passing during transmission.

3.2 Basic Mechanisms in Message-Passing Systems

Semantics of Message-Passing Operations

The meaning or semantics of these operations (`send()`, `receive()`, etc.) may be different, i.e., the result of their execution may vary depending on the level of concurrency adequacy required and the specific communication mode specifically required by a program or application. Therefore, there are different versions of message passing operations, which guarantee or do not guarantee safety compliance in data transmission and offer different communication modes between processes to achieve optimal performance in these operations.

The message passing safety property is fulfilled by a program with the `send()` operation when the execution of this operation ensures that the value received by the destination process is the value of the data just before the call. In the following example, the send operation in process P_0 is considered to have safe semantics, and therefore, process P_1 will always print the value 100 each time this code is executed:

```
Process P₀;                    Process P₁;
  begin                          begin
    data:integer = 100;            x:integer;
    send(&data, P₁);               receive(&x, P₀);
    alters(data);                  print(x);
  end;                           end;
```

A send operation with unsafe semantics could cause the value received by P_1 to be different from `100` if, for example, the `data` value is altered immediately after the call to the `send` operation returns but before the system starts transmitting the value of the `data` variable. Similarly, the `receive` operation with such semantics does not necessarily block the receiving process P_1, and therefore the value of the variable *x* could be altered by other instructions, before the data from the sender process P_0 has been fully transmitted. Normally, systems that offer a non-blocking `receive` operation also have a check operation that indicates at what point the data being received can be altered and thus can achieve semantically safe programming even with a `receive` operation like this.

3.2.1 Blocking Message-Passing Operations

The semantics of this type of message passing operation implies that the `send` operation call returns associated only when the safety property, as defined above, is guaranteed. It is important to note that it will not always be the case that the receiving process will have received the data when the execution of the `send` operation is finished, but rather what needs to be ensured is that any changes to the data during transmission will not violate the safe semantics of the operation.

3.2.1.1 Synchronous Unbuffered Message Passing

In synchronous message passing, communication takes place via a direct link between the participating processes. Suppose that process A sends data to process B. When process A executes the `send` operation, it will wait before continuing its execution until process B executes the `receive` operation of receiving this message. This mode of message passing can be considered as a type of communication analogous to a telephone conversation or a *chat* between two participants.

Before data can be physically transmitted, processes must be ready to participate in the exchange, which requires a *rendezvous* between the sender and receiver (Fig. 3.7), i.e., similar to what happens at the sender, the call to the `receive` operation in the receiving process is suspended until the other process calls the `send` operation and completes the transmission of the data.

The concept of the mechanism called *rendezvous* between communicating processes implies:

(a) Synchronisation between sender and receiver for the exchange to take place.
(b) The sender process could make assertions about the state of the receiver at the synchronisation point, which would allow extending the FLS (Sect. 1.6.2) verification rule system to verify distributed programs with this mode of communication.

Although blocking operations provide application programs with a type of communication that respects message-passing safety semantics, in all cases; however, it is often inefficiently implemented. In Fig. 3.7, it can be seen that the sender or receiver processes suffer idle waiting if the other participant, receiver or sender, has not yet arrived to execute its operation of receiving or sending the message, respectively.

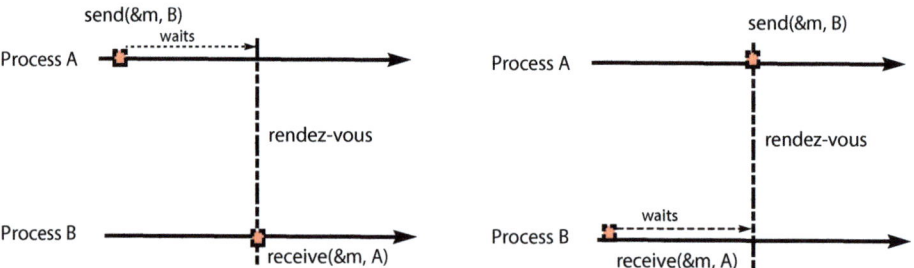

Fig. 3.7 Inter-process rendezvous with synchronous communication operations

3.2 Basic Mechanisms in Message-Passing Systems

Another problem that can compromise the safety properties of message-passing systems is the potential for deadlocks, if the order of execution of `send` and `receive` operations that involve sending two messages sequentially between two processes is not properly coordinated. For example, the following code would result in the indefinite deadlock of both processes P_0 and P_1 if both the `send` and `receive` operations are blocking, as neither process would be ready to receive the message from the other.

```
processP₀ ;                    processP₁ ;
 begin                          begin

  send(&datum₁ , P₁);            send(&datum₂ , P₀);
  receive(&x₂ , P₁);             receive(&x₁ , P₀);
 end;                           end;
```

3.2.1.2 Buffered Message Passing

In this type of message passing, the `receive` operation has the same semantics as the one with synchronous message passing, i.e., it blocks the receiving process until the message is fully received. However, the `send` message passing primitive has different semantics. The communication medium between the processes is now not a direct link between the two processes involved in the communication but rather a message queue. The existence of specialised communication hardware allows process A to continue its execution after calling the `send` operation, because when process A sends the message to process B, it is added to the *buffer* representing the queue of messages to be received. To receive a message, process B executes the `receive` operation, which removes the message at the head of the queue from this *buffer*, and then continues its execution. If at any time during the execution of the application there are no messages to receive, i.e., the *buffer* is empty, then the `receive` communication primitive blocks the receiving process until a sending process places data into the buffer.

3.2.1.3 Low-Level Implementations

Variants of the basic buffered blocking message passing model include enhancements that improve eficiency and flexibility in communication. The first applies to systems that use *channels*, an inter-process communication scheme that was previously introduced as a means of transmitting messages in a 1-to-1 pattern. In some implementations, these systems have a primitive called the `void()` operation, which checks the contents of a given channel and returns `true` if is empty. The practical utility of this would be to prevent blocking of the `receive` operation call when no messages are available. Instead of idle waiting the process can perform some useful alternative work while the message is being transmitted and the channel buffer is no longer empty.

The second variant is that most systems based on blocking message passing use an internal *buffer*[4] (Fig. 3.8a) of fixed length at the receiver. In such systems, the `send` operation only blocks when it attempts to write a message to a occupied channel. When the receiver process starts execution, the system checks whether the message is already available in the *buffer*, and if it is, the system copies the data into the memory area designated for the receiving process.

---

[4] Not to be confused with the user-programmed data structure in programs following the producer-consumer model.

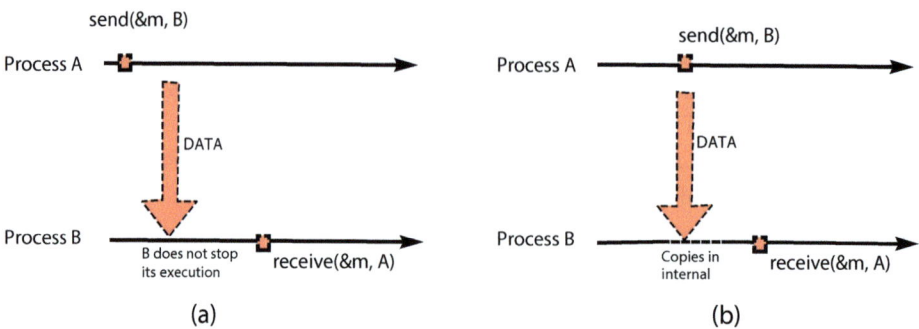

Fig. 3.8 Implementation of buffered blocking message passing: (**a**) without dedicated hardware, (**b**) with dedicated hardware

Table 3.3 Characteristics of blocking operations

Communication mode	Specialised hardware	Synchronisation	Security
Unbuffered	–	Yes (with rendezvous)	Yes
Buffered	Yes	Relaxed	Yes
	No	Yes	Yes

Table 3.4 Causes of inefficiency of blocking message passing without dedicated hardware

Message passing scheme	Reason for inefficiency
Synchronous (rendezvous)	Idle wait of one process
Buffered	Buffer management and possible internal synchronisation overhead

Later, when the receiver invokes the `receive` operation, the system transfers the message from the buffer to the appropriate memory location allocated for reception.

If the platform where it is executed has specialised hardware (Fig. 3.8b), the transfer of the data to the memory of the process will start immediately after it is copied to the internal *buffer*, without interrupting the receiving process at any time; therefore, we say that the synchronisation between the sender and receiver processes will be *relaxed* (see Table 3.3) in this case. If, on the other hand, such specialised hardware is not available, the receiving process will need to interrupt its execution when calling `receive`, participating in the internal transfer of data to the receive. However, this approach allows for faster synchronization compared to a pure rendezvous mechanism.

3.2.2 Non-blocking Message-Passing Operations

Blocking operations ensure semantically *safe* communications with respect to the data being transmitted but suffer from inefficiency when implemented on platforms that do not have specialised communications hardware; the cause of this can be summarised in Table 3.4.

3.2 Basic Mechanisms in Message-Passing Systems

Therefore, instead of relying on blocking operations, we could consider defining non-blocking `send` and `receive` operations, placing the responsibility on the programmer to ensure that the semantics of the message passing they program in their applications is safe. These operations would return control to the program immediately, even before it is safe to modify the data. As a result, the programmer must ensure that no modifications are made to the data during transmission if such changes could lead to errors.

In order to implement this model, the system should provide state-checking mechanisms that indicate whether at any given time the data can be altered without causing the semantics to become unsafe. This approach allows the program to proceed with computations that are independent of the message-passing operation and defer synchronization checks until it is necessary to confirm that the operation has completed.

3.2.2.1 Unbuffered Message Passing

The execution of a `send` operation with non-blocking operations informs the system that a message is pending, but the sending process continues its execution after having sent it. In this way, other computations, not necessarily related to communication, can be initiated by the program while the message is in transmission. The actual data transmission begins only when the receiving process acknowledges the corresponding receive operation. At that point, physical communication between the sender and receiver in the absence of specialised hardware support (Fig. 3.9a) starts, the receiving process must suspend itself from the moment it calls the `receive` operation, until the transmission is complete, so that the safe semantics of the message passing operations can be guaranteed in this case.

If the platform has specialised hardware support for this type of message passing, then the execution of the `receive` operation returns immediately (the receiving process will not be suspended), even if the message has not yet been fully transmitted (Fig. 3.9b). There is a check operation that would indicate when it is safe to access the data being transmitted on the receiving side.

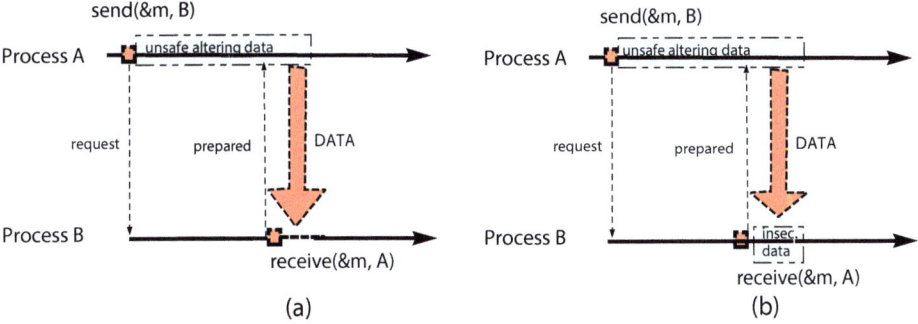

Fig. 3.9 Implementation of non-blocking message passing without buffering: (**a**) without specialised hardware, (**b**) with specialised hardware

3.2.2.2 Buffered Message Passing

The fundamental difference with the previously discussed *unbuffered* mode is that in this case, when the `receive` operation is called, the system immediately begins transferring the message data from an internal receive buffer to the memory location expected by the receiving without suspending the process. As a consequence, the waiting time in the receiving process is reduced, although an access to such data is insecure during this time.

3.3 Distributed Programming Models and Languages

In the following, we focus on multi-computers and the programming models and languages suitable for these computing platforms. To enable the programming of server-type processes, languages introduce a new construct known as a *guarded command*. The semantics of this order stems from the idea, proposed by Dijkstra [17], of considering the selection between several alternatives in a *non-deterministic* way as a *mental aid*, in the development of distributed programs, rather than a drawback. Prior to Dijkstra's article, computer scientists thought of non-deterministic structures as *something to be eliminated* in programs, since these structures were considered as a source of possible errors in the subsequent maintenance phase of the software. As a result, the conventional practice was to eliminate such structures entirely (or at least partially) during the coding phase, by attempting to predict which specific alternative the program would follow at runtime. However, having non-deterministic statements in programming languages can make sense in order to facilitate the implementation of certain types of systems that react to stimuli from their environment.

Consider, for example, the implementation of a controller that counts the number of people entering a museum through two separate doors (see Fig. 3.10). The presence detection sensors at either door can send a signal to the controller that a new person has entered. However, the order in which these signals are received by the controller cannot be predicted; in fact, they might even arrive simultaneously at the controller's receiving process, as illustrated in the figure. A deterministic controller implementation, such as the one shown in Fig. 3.11, is to be considered as totally wrong. Assuming synchronous message passing, the process P_3, which represents the controller, could block if there are no inputs from gate 1, for example, even if people enter through gate 2. The process P_3 that implements the controller is a *server*-type process and, therefore, does not know in advance the

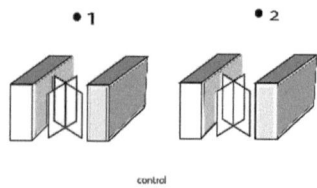

Fig. 3.10 Hardware control model for people entering a museum

3.3 Distributed Programming Models and Languages

```
Process P(i:1..2);                Process P3 ;--controller
begin                             var temp, cont: integer;
  for i:=1 to max_per_day do      begin
    signal:= 1;                     for i:= 1 to max_per_day do
    send(&signal,P3 );              begin
    --pass 1 person                   receive(&temp,P1 );--blocks
  enddo;                              cont:= cont + temp;
end;                                  receive(&temp,P2 );--blocks
                                      cont:= cont + temp;
                                    end;
                                  enddo;
                                  print("No. people:", cont);
                                  end;
```

Fig. 3.11 Inadequate implementation of a controller to detect inputs

client process that is going to communicate with it at any given moment. This inherent uncertainty requires a non-deterministic approach to correctly handle simultaneous or unpredictable input from multiple sources.

3.3.1 Selective Wait with Guarded Commands

A server is a type of process that has to be ready to receive a message from any of its clients, without the order of such communications being predetermined. Furthermore, depending on the state of the data on the server, in each iteration of such a process, it may only permit communication from a subset of its clients. Consider a server process that implements a circular queue, i.e., the buffer of the producer-consumer paradigm, with the classical operations of insertion for the producer processes and deletion for the consumers. When the buffer is full, no further messages from the producers are accepted until at least one consumer communicates with the server process and removes an item from the buffer. Similarly, when the buffer becomes empty, no further communication with consumers shall be accepted until a producer sends a new item to the buffer. When the buffer is in a state other than the above two, communications may be accepted from producer and consumer processes in an order not determined in advance. To prevent the server process from becoming temporarily blocked by attempting to initiate synchronous communication with a stopped consumer or producer process, which could temporarily block it, the server employs guarded commands. These guarded commands ensure that synchronous communication with a client only begins when the conditions necessary to complete the corresponding operation are already satisfied.

Edsger Dijkstra proposed in 1975 new constructs, which he called *guarded commands*, to be included in imperative programming languages that have subsequently been widely used. Guarded commands are used in distributed languages with synchronous communication operations to implement a non-deterministic statement in these programming languages that prevent the blocking of server processes, as described earlier, in systems with synchronous message passing.

Table 3.5 Non-deterministic structured commands for languages with synchronous communication operations

Construction	Purpose
Guarded command	Enable conditional communication with a client process
Selective waiting	Non-determinism in the choice of an alternative, programmed as a guarded command

The aforementioned guarded commands become the basic component statements of the programming notations most suitable for distributed systems with blocking communication operations. Specifically, languages such as Ada, CSP, Occam and SR include a variant of the so-called *selective wait* statement (see Table 3.5). This construct, common across such languages, enables the selection of a guarded command from a set of commands that are ready to be executed:

```
<selective.wait>::= select<guarded.commands.set>end select
<guarded.command.set>::= < guarded.command > {or < guarded.command >}
< guarded.command >::= <guard> -> <sentence.list>.
<guard>::=<boolean.expression>|<boolean.expression>;receive(<arguments>)|receive(<arguments>)
```

A guarded command is said to be *ready* for execution if the boolean expression (or condition) preceding the `receive` operation evaluates to true and also the `receive` operation itself is ready to receive the message to which this particular command refers to.

It is the server process itself that schedules the *selective wait* command. However, the actual selection of which specific guarded command to execute (among those whose guards are currently *ready*) is decided non-deterministically, based on the behavior of the surrounding environment. In each execution of the select statement, only one guarded command is chosen from the subset that is ready to be executed. Therefore, the `select` command can be included inside a loop, so that in each iteration of the loop, a new instance of the `select` command would be executed and, therefore, one new guarded command would be selected.

Example 3.2 A correct implementation, with guarded commands and a selective wait construct can be seen in Fig. 3.12, illustrating the example of the controller that handles human entry through the two doors of the museum.

As can be seen in the code of the aforementioned figure, the `select` command in the `Control` process chooses one of the guarded commands that are ready to be executed (up to two in this case). It will be *ready* the guarded command that within its *guard* has received before the signal sent by a *Gate* process when detecting the entry of a new person. If there are persons in the two doors, then it chooses to receive 1 message from one of them non-deterministically, i.e., we cannot know which door will be chosen by the `Control` process. This selective command continues to execute in a loop until both Gate processes have completed. At that point, the loop exits automatically, and the Control process terminates after printing the total number of visitors who entered the museum during the day.

3.3 Distributed Programming Models and Languages

```
Process Gate [i:1..2];
  var s: integer:=0;
     end: boolean:= false;
  begin
    while (not end) do
      select
        (s<closing.hour and person_present())  ->
          send(s(), Control());
          delay.until (s+1);    --new tick of the clock
          s:=s+1;
      or (s < closing.hour and not person_present())->
          delay.until(s+1);     --new tick of the clock
          s:=s+1;
      or (s >= closing.hour) ->   --default guarded command
          end:= true;
      end select;
    enddo;
    --it is the museum closing hour;
    --wait for 16hrs
    delay.until(time()+16*3600);
    send(start(), Control());
  end;
Process Control();
  var
    cont:= 0;
  begin
      --start the controller
      receive(start(),Gate[1]);
      receive(start(),Gate[2]);

    while(true) do--controller running
      select --the controller process ends automatically when
          receive(s(), Gate[1])->   --both Gate[i] processes do
          cont:= cont+1;
      or receive(s(), Gate[2])->
          cont:= cont+1];
      end select;
    enddo;
    writeln("Total number of persons",cont));
  end;
```

Main Program
```
Input_contol_program;
  begin
      cobegin
        Gate[1]; Gate[2]; Control()
      coend;
  end;
```

Fig. 3.12 Successful implementation of a selective command controller to detect people entering the museum through two gates

In the case of the `Gate(i)` process, the command shall be *ready* when its condition is evaluated and the result is `true`. The first guarded command checks if the closing time of the museum has not yet arrived and if it detects the entry of a person, in which case its *guard* condition is true. The second guarded command is complementary to the previous one in the sense that its guard will be true if no person is detected at this instant, so its component statement is simply to increment the counter `s` which simulates the *tick* of the local clock of the door detection device. The third guarded command of the `select` acts as a default clause of the previous two, and therefore, if the closing time has already arrived, it will suspend each `Gate` process for 16 h, before sending a new start message to the `Control` process.

Therefore, guarded commands allow the implementation of non-deterministic selections in imperative programs, i.e., the alternative chosen to be executed, and even the final state of the program after the command, do depend only on the initial state of the program prior to executing the `select` and the corresponding guarded command.

> Summary of the semantics of the `select` command:
> The subset of *guarded commands* that are ready is determined only once at the start, at the beginning of the command's execution.
> To re-determine which guarded commands are ready, the selective command must be re-executed.
> If no client process sends a message that matches one of the guarded commands whose condition evaluates to true, the server process will be temporarily suspended, as no guarded commands are currently ready.
> Some languages allow programming the selective command with priority alternatives, but in these cases, the selection is no longer non-deterministic.

3.3.2 The CSP Model of Distributed Programming

The programming notation that we are about to describe is based on CSP (*Communicating Sequential Process*) developed by C. A. R. Hoare [24], and its fundamental characteristics include the use of Dijkstra's guarded commands as the fundamental structure of sequential control in programs and considers that they must be the fundamental construction to express non-determinism in the code of the communicating processes of distributed applications. A command with semantics similar to `cobegin-coend` is defined by that notation. The CSP programming notation states that the component parallel processes communicate exclusively through messages since global variables are not allowed. The control state of certain application processes is maintained through generic processes that simulate a state of the network, with transitions triggered by receiving specific types of messages.

CSP defines special commands to perform input/output in processes exclusively through *unbuffered*, i.e., blocking, synchronous message-passing operations:

```
        Process Pi();              Process Pj() ;
          Pj ! expression            Pi ? variable
```

3.3 Distributed Programming Models and Languages

Communication between the two processes takes place when program control reaches process P_i executing P_j !expression, naming process P_j as the destination of its output, and process P_j names process P_i as the source of its input by executing P_i ? x. Furthermore, no logical buffering is assumed in the transmission system; that is, the programming model does not guarantee storage for messages pending reception. A process is blocked from executing an input *(?)* or output *(!)* command until the corresponding process is ready to engage in the rendezvous and complete the communication.

Message passing between processes enforces strict type control, i.e., a message can only be received if its type matches the type declared for the receiving variable. The declaration of types and variables maintains the simple syntax of the Pascal language and are defined within the processes.

The programming notation we will use is static, which translates into the following conditions: the program code determines the maximum number of processes that will exist, and this number remains fixed throughout execution, i.e., no processes are created or destroyed at runtime. There will be no recursive calls to procedures or functions in the process code.

CSP maintains a minimal syntax, so that language instructions that are not related to inter-process communication follow the structured programming syntax of the Pascal programming language. In this way, the CSP programming notation can lead to languages that can be implemented on conventional computers as well as on multiprocessors or multi-computers. However, specific code optimisations will be needed to run the code on each type of architecture.

3.3.2.1 CSP Commands

The notation to be introduced is based on commands. A command specifies the behaviour of the device executing it and may either *succeed* or *fail*. If the execution of a simple command succeeds, then it may have an effect on the internal state of the executing device (e.g., an assignment command ':='), the environment of the containing process (an output command: '!') or both the sending and receiving processes (an input command: '?'). The execution of a structured command in CSP implies either executing one its component commands (in the case of an *alternative* command) or executing all of this component commands (in the case of *parallel* or process-creating order), depending on the type of command. The BNF syntax for the fundamental commands of this notation is presented below.

```
<order>::=<simple.order>|<structured.order>|<list.order>
<simple.order>::=<null.order>|<assignment.order>|<input.order>|<output.order>
<structured.order>::=<alternative.order>|<repetitive.order>|<parallel.order>|<guarded.command>
<null.order>::=SKIP
<list.order>::=<declaration>;|<order>;{<order>}*
```

The *SKIP* command has no effect on the program and never fails. A command list specifies the sequential execution of its constituent commands, following the order in which they appear. Each declaration introduces a *fresh* variable whose scope extends from its point of its declaration to the end of the command list.

3.3.2.2 Assignment Command

An assignment command $x:=e$ specifies the evaluation of the expression on the right-hand side and its assignment to the value denoted by the target variable on the left-hand side:

```
<assignment.order>::=<target.variable>:=<expression>
<expression>::=<simple.expression>|<structured.expression>
<target.variable>::=<simple.variable>|<structured.target>
```

The order of evaluation of the elements in this command is crucial for understanding its behavior. The value of the target variable is determined after a successful assignment and matches the value of the expression evaluated before the assignment. Therefore, if the evaluation of the expression fails, the entire command fails, ensuring that no partial assignment occurs. As a result, the device cannot recover from this failure, and the system will detect it as a failed component during execution.

Lists of expressions that can be assigned all at once to a structured target variable:

```
<structured.expression>::=<constructor>(<expression.list>)
<structured.target>::= <constructor>(<target.variable.list>)
<constructor>::=<identifier>|<empty>
<expression.list>::=<empty>|<expression>;{<expression>}*
<target.variable.list>::=<empty>|<target.variable>;{<target.variable>}*
```

An assignment may fail for the following reasons:

- The value of the expression is undefined, e.g., some of its component operations cannot be evaluated and are undefined.
- The value of the expression does not match the declared value of the target variable.

Consider that two expressions will match if: the identifiers of the constructors match, the length of the list of components of the target variable has to be the same as the list of components of the expression, and the individual types involved in the assignment have to match element by element. You can see the following assignment commands and the consequence of their evaluation by the interpreter in the following codes:

```
x: = cons(left,right)                   --a structured value is
                                        --constructed and assigned to x
Q::[x:char; x := '7'; cons(left,right):=x] --this command fails
insert(n) := has(n)                     --fails because of
                                        --mismatched constructors
```

3.3 Distributed Programming Models and Languages

A structured expression with the empty expression list '()' is the way to define a signal[5]. The same, in the target variable, is used to indicate that only that type of signal will be allowed to be received. For example, the expression: $c := P()$, assigns to the variable c a signal with constructor P and no components; therefore, the command: $P() := c$ will fail if the value of c is not identical to $P()$; and if it is $c = P()$, it has no effect, since it will be interpreted as an idempotent assignment.

3.3.2.3 I/O Orders

Input/output orders specify communication between two processes using *unbuffered* synchronous message-passing. Syntactically, they have to fulfil the following conditions:

- An input order issued by process P_a must specify the name of the other process P_b as the source.
- An output order issued by process P_b must specify process P_a as the destination.
- The target variable of the input order must match[6] the value denoted by the expression evaluated in the corresponding output order.

If the above conditions are met, input and output commands are said to *match*. Matching orders are executed simultaneously if they do not fail and their combined effect is to transfer the value from the output expression to the input target variable. This behaviour is often interpreted as a form of *remote assignment* between two distributed processes.

The synchronisation requirement deriving from the synchronous (unbuffered) communication mode between the processes, including the input and output orders discussed here, implies that the process which becomes ready for communication first must be delayed. In any case, such a delay will end when at least one of these two conditions is met:

(a) the corresponding order in the other process is also ready, or
(b) the other process terminates, in which case the order in the waiting process fails.

3.3.2.4 Failure Conditions

An input command fails if the process representing the origin of the message has terminated.

$[P_1 :: P_2 ?x \| P_2 :: x := 7]$. In this case, process P_2 terminates immediately, and process P_1 will therefore fail.

---

[5] In this context, we interpret the concept of a signal as a synchronous event that changes the state of a process (usually the receiver) but does not contain information (data) that is transmitted.

[6] Order *matching* occurs when there is a variable declared in the target for each data sent from the source, and the data types of both are identical.

Similarly, an exit command fails, if the process representing its destination has terminated or if the expression is undefined.

3.3.2.5 Deadlocks

When a group of processes is trying to communicate, but none of their orders match, then a deadlock situation is said to occur. For a deadlock to exist, the I/O commands of the processes involved must not fail:

$[P_1::P_2!x \| P_2::\ P_1!y]$. There is deadlock because the two commands are output in both processes P_1 and P_2; therefore, these commands do not match, and there is mutual interlocking or deadlock.

Furthermore, if it is the case that the target variable does not declare variables whose type is compatible with that of the output command, then there is also deadlock: $[P_1\ ::x:char;\ P_2?x \| P_2::P_1!(3,5)]$. Deadlock is reached in this case because the process P_1, which issues the input command, declares a variable of type `char` and the process P_2, with issues the output command, attempts to send a list of integers.

3.3.2.6 Parallel Order

A *parallel order* specifies the concurrent execution of its constituent processes. All processes start simultaneously, and the parallel order terminates successfully only when all of them have finished. The relative speed at which these processes execute is arbitrary, and it is unpredictable which processes will terminate first.

```
<parallel.order>::= [<process>{‖<process>}]
<process>::= <process.label>::<order.list>
<process.label>::= <empty>|<identifier>|<identifier>(<subscript>{;<subscript>}*)::
<subscript>::= <integer.constant>|<range>
<integer.constant>::= <number>|<bounded.variable>
<bounded.variable>::= <identifier>
<range>::= <bounded.variable>:<lower.bound>...<upper.bound>
<upper.bound>::= <integer.constant>
<lower.bound>::= <integer.constant>
```

In a parallel order, no process may use a variable as a target if that variable is a target in another process within the same parallel command, as CSP does not allow shared variables.

A process label without subscripts, or with only constant subscripts, simply names the subsequent list of orders. However, a process label with subscript ranges defines a series of processes, each sharing the same label and command list but instantiated with different combinations of values substituted the *bound variables*[7]. In the example below, variable i would be a bound variable:

$X(i:1..n)::CL_i$
--expands to :
$X(1)::CL_1 \| X(2)::CL_2 \| ... \| X(n)::CL_n$

---

[7] Bound variable is a variable whose values can only be taken within a range (usually an integer interval) that is specified in the text of the program or process, in this case.

3.3 Distributed Programming Models and Languages

3.3.2.7 Guarded Commands

Guards serve to prevent the execution of communication operations between processes, when the appropriate conditions for their execution are not met (e.g., inserting data into a full buffer or removing data from an empty buffer). Guarded commands have the following syntax in CSP, given by the BNF description below:

```
<guarded.command>::=<guard>→<order.list>|(<range>{,<range>}) <guard>→<order.list>
<guard>::=<guard.list>|<guard.list>;<input.order>|<input.order>
<guard.list>::=<guard.element>{;<guard.element>}*
<guard.element>::=<boolean.expression>|<variable.declaration>
```

A guarded command is executed if and only the evaluation of its guard does not fail; therefore, the execution of a guarded command shall result in one of the following behaviours of the device on which it is scheduled:

- Success: Boolean expression true and message passing order without delay.
- Failure: Boolean expression evaluates to false. This will also occur if the source process of the input command appearing at the end of the guard has already terminated when evaluating $[P_1::[P_2?x->SKIP] \parallel P_2::SKIP]$, P_1 fails.
- Wait: the Boolean condition of the guard evaluates to true, but the input command is delayed because the sender process has not yet started the communication.

3.3.2.8 Order of Execution of the Guards: Absence of Side Effects

It should be noted for the purposes of tracking process execution that guards are executed from left to right and their evaluation cannot produce any change in state. Consequently, the result of evaluating the boolean expression of a guard has no effect on the values of the local process variables (process state). A possible implementation of the execution of CSP guarded commands could check the failure of a guard by simply trying to execute it and suspending the execution at the moment of failure, since such an evaluation would never affect the state. This would be a correct implementation of guard evaluation, as suspending execution in this way has no effect on the state of the process. The input command appearing at the end of a guard is executed only if the corresponding output command is also ready to be executed at that time.

3.3.2.9 Alternative Order

Alternative order allows processes to non-deterministically select and execute one of several guarded commands. Among the commands whose guards have been successfully evaluated, one is non-deterministically selected and then executed. After its execution, the alternative command is terminated.

At the process level, non-determinism can be understood as the freedom of choice that processes have to choose between several possible communications. This choice is made internally by the process and cannot be controlled externally by its environment, i.e., there is no way that other processes running in parallel with it could influence the choice of one of the alternative and ready-to-run guards.

3.3.2.10 Syntax of Alternative Commands

The execution of an alternative order consists of the execution of only one of its component guarded commands.

```
<alternative.order>::=[<guarded.command>{□ <guarded.command>}*]
```

3.3.2.11 Lack of Fairness in the Execution of Guarded Commands

Fairness in the execution of guarded commands included in an alternative command is generally not guaranteed, even in the case where there are continuously processes prepared to communicate with the input commands of the guards. This is because non-determinism does not mean *randomness*. Instead, the correct interpretation of the meaning of non-determinism is that the desired behavior of a program (its correctness) must be invariant regardless of the specific choices made during execution. Therefore, if a non-deterministic process is observed, it is not possible to predict which alternative will be chosen each time the process evaluates an alternative construct, such as: $P_1::[(P_2?a->S_1(a))\square(P_3?b->S_2(b))]$.

Process P_1 has a choice: it can either receive in the variable *a* the value sent from P_2 and then behave like the process S_1 *(a)* or receive the value *b* and then behave like the process S_2 *(b)* . In the event that both alternatives were available to be executed, with both P_2 and P_3 having sent data, P_1 would make a non-deterministic choice that is neither controlled by P_2 nor P_3, and remains entirely internal to P_1.

What is the result of this CSP order on the device where it is executed?

```
[(i:0..N-1)x:positive;contains(i)=-1;in(x)?x->contains(i):=x]
```

Assuming that all the processes `in(i)` are ready to send data to the device that programmed the alternative construct above, and that the *array* `contains` is initially empty (all values are set to −1); the result of executing this command is the insertion of a new element *x* in to the array. However, it is not possible to predict which value will be inserted, because it depends on which guarded command is non-deterministically selected during the execution of the alternative construct. Those guarded commands that represent elements of the *array* already inserted are not taken into account, in successive executions of this alternative command.

3.3.2.12 Failure Condition of an Alternative Order

If all guards fail, then the alternative order itself fails. Each guard is evaluated only once for each execution of the order, and a failed guard is disregarded for that execution.

Conversely, if one or more guarded commands are delayed, since their boolean expressions were evaluated as true but they are still waiting for the communication required by their input commands, then the complete alternative order is delayed until one of the communications can proceed.

$$[(i:0..N-1)\ x:integer;\ in(i)?x\text{->}out!(i,x)]$$

Note that if all the processes $in(0)$, ..., $in(N-1)$ of the guards were terminated, then executing the above alternative command will fail.

3.3.2.13 Repetitive Order

The repetitive order is used to specify as many iterations as possible of its constituent alternative order, according to the following syntax:

$$\text{<repetitive.order>::= *<alternative.order>}.$$

In other words, executions of the component alternative order continue until it fails, i.e., until all of its guarded commands meet their failure conditions.

3.3.2.14 Delay in the Execution of the Repetitive Order

If a repetitive construct contains only successful guards that each lead to a delay-producing input operation, then the execution of the construct becomes suspended until one of the following occurs:

- There is an output order in the matching processes ready to send, corresponding to one of the incoming orders.
- All source processes named in the input orders of the guards have terminated, so the repetitive order terminates.
- Deadlock exists if none of the above conditions are met.

3.3.2.15 Termination Condition

When all the guarded commands of its constituent alternative command fail, then the repetitive command terminates without causing any effect on the processes in its environment. If, on the other hand, at least one guarded command succeed, the alternative construct continues executing without interruption.

Another possible case of termination is that all processes named in the input orders of the guards have been terminated.

$$[i:=0;*[i<tam;content(i)\neq n\text{->}i:=i+1]]$$

As with the process in the previous example, the elements of the `content` array will be scanned, for $i: 0, 1, 2, \ldots$, until either $i \geq tam$ or a value equal to n is found. In the latter case, the guarded command fails, causing the repetitive construct to terminate. Therefore, this construct will find the value n in the array if it exists.

Example 3.3 A possible termination of the following example would occur if each of the processes `in(0), ..., in(N-1)` included in `mux` had sent data, i.e., if after executing all alternatives of the command, all elements of the array `continue()` are evaluated as *FALSE*.

```
mux::*[(i:0..N-1)continue(i);x:integer;in(i)?x-> out!(i,x);continue(i):= FALSE]
```

3.3.2.16 Conditions for Mutual Interlocks Between Processes

For a set of processes, and each programming repetitive construct, to eventually reach a deadlock situation, none of the following conditions must be satisfied:

1. A pair of I/O orders between processes in the set is successfully matched.
2. All processes named in the input orders of the guards have already been terminated, and as a consequence, the repetitive orders terminate.
3. All guards in the repetitive commands fail.

Example 3.4 *Determination of Deadlock*

- $[P_1::*[P_2?x \rightarrow S] \| P_2::P_1?y]$, none of the three previous conditions is met, and therefore, there is a deadlock between processes P_1 and P_2 of the program.
- $[P_1::*[P_2?x \rightarrow S] \| P_2::P_1!y]$, condition (1) is satisfied, since the input order of process P_1 corresponds to the output order of process P_2, and therefore, there is no deadlock of processes P_1 and P_2 in this case.
- $[P_1::*[FALSE;P_2?x \rightarrow S] \| P_2::P_1?y]$, condition (3) above is satisfied, because the only guarded command in the repetitive order of process P_1 fails, and therefore the process will terminate; process P_2 will also terminate because its corresponding process has terminated. The two processes then terminate, and there is no deadlock.
- $[P_1::[FALSE;P_2?x \rightarrow S] \| P_2::P_1?y]$, in this case, there is a deadlock of both processes, because the order of process P_1 is not a repetitive order but an alternative one (it is not repeated); therefore, P_1 does not terminate and neither will P_2, which is waiting for a communication from process P_1 that never takes place.

Example 3.5

1. A CSP term to determine the greater of two numbers:

$$[(x \geq y \rightarrow m:=x) \square (y \geq x \rightarrow m:=y)]$$

3.3 Distributed Programming Models and Languages

If $x \geq y$, then m is assigned the value x; otherwise, if $x \leq y$, m is assigned the value of y. If both are possible, because $x=y$, either assignment can be executed non-deterministically.

2. A CSP model for the museum's people counters and controller:

```
[P(j: 1..2)::PERSON ‖ P(3)]

PERSON::                              P(3)::
*[i < max_per_day;P(3) ! 1 → i:= i + 1]   cont: = 0;
                                      *[(j: 1..2)P(j) ? temp-> cont: = cont + temp)];
                                      writeln("number of persons", cont);
```

If the variable i reaches the value max_per_day in both P_1 and P_2, then P_3 also terminates, as all processes referenced in the input operations of its guarded commands will terminate too.

3. Implement a CSP server process for binary semaphore and general semaphore operations.

   (a) Binary semaphore:

   $$*[User.proc?P()->User.proc?V()]$$

   (b) General semaphore:

   $$*[User.proc?V()->s:=s+1 \; [] \; s>0;User.proc'?P()->s:=s-1]$$

   The construct terminates when $User.proc$ and $User.proc'$ have terminated or when $Proc.user$ has terminated and $s = 0$.

4. The producer/consumer programmed as three CSP terms: $buffer$, $producer$ and $consumer$ (three communicating processes in parallel):

```
Buffer::                              Producer::
b:array[0..N-1];                       *[TRUE→generate.data;
                                         Buffer!datum]
in,out:0.N-1;
                                      Consumer::
size:0..N-1;                           *[TRUE→Buffer!s()
                                         Buffer?x;consum(x)]
(in,out,size):= (0,0,0);

*[size<N;Producer?b[in]→size:= size+1;
    in:=(in+1)MOD N;
 [] size>0;Consumer?s()→Consumer!b[out];
    size:=size-1;
    out:=(out+1)MOD N]
```

$$[Buffer \| Producer \| Consumer]$$

5. Program a solution in CSP to the philosophers' dinner problem and control that no philosophers' deadlock occurs:

```
fork::                                      Philosopher::
                                            *[TRUE→think();
  *[philosopher(i)?take()→                     room!enter();
      philosopher(i)?release()                 fork(i)!take();
                                               fork(i+1 MOD 5)!take();
   ☐ philosopher((i-1)MOD 5)?take()→           eat();
      philosopher((i-1)MOD 5))?release()]      fork(i)!release();
                                               fork(i+1 MOD 5)!release();
room::                                         room!exit()]
  occupancy:integer;
  occupancy:=0;
*[(i:0..4)occupancy<4;Philosopher(i)?enter()→
    occupancy := occupancy + 1;
  (i:0..4)Philosopher(i)?exit()→
    occupancy := occupancy - 1]
```

$$[phil(i:0..4)::Philosopher \| f(i:0..4):fork \| room]$$

6. Program with CSP a terminal server that receives user commands from 10 consoles and terminates automatically:

```
*[(i:1..10)continue(i); console(i)?c ->
    mux!(i, c);console(i)!ack();
    continue(i):=(c ≠ signal.terminate())]
```

The command receives from any of the 10 consoles, given that the corresponding element of the `continue` boolean *array* is true. The bound variable `i` identifies the console originating the message. The identifier `ack` represents an acknowledgement signal that is returned to the console sending the message. If the `signal.terminate()` character is received, `continue(i)` is set to `false`, thus preventing further receiving from this console. The repetitive command terminates when the values of all the elements of the array `continue` are false.

3.4 Verification of Distributed Programs with Communicating Processes

In this section, we introduce an axiomatic semantics for bufferless synchronous message passing, which will extend the FLS of Hoare's Logic (Sect. 1.6) with new axioms and derivation rules. This extension will allow for the formal proof of correctness of distributed programs using this message passing mode.

3.4 Verification of Distributed Programs with Communicating Processes

To construct a correctness proof for a program using message passing the following, three steps or phases must be completed:

- Build a sequential demonstration for each of the program's individual processes.
- Demonstrate that the proofs obtained in the previous step do not interfere with each other (Sect. 1.6.2).
- Verify that all assumptions made about communication between program processes are satisfied.

Non-interference demonstrations are necessary only if processes have used auxiliary variables[8] in the verification, as ordinary program variables cannot suffer interference because processes in CSP programming notation only modify the values of their own local variables[9].

The semantics of a programming language with synchronous message passing is simpler than that of the asynchronous case, and therefore, making the corresponding proofs is simpler as well. Specifically, if a predicate holds in the precondition of a message-sending statement, it will also hold as the postcondition of the corresponding message-receiving statement, provided that the communication can occur[10], meaning there is no possible deadlock among the program's processes.

3.4.1 Axioms, Interference Rules and Satisfiability Proofs

If the `in` statements, which represent for the purposes of formal demonstration the message receiving operations in a process, and the `out` statements corresponding to the message sending operations *match properly* (Sect. 3.3.2) and are selected by the underlying running system to be executed at some point in the execution of a program, then their combined execution results in the assignment of the evaluated expressions $e_1, e_2, ..., e_n$, to the variables $x_1, x_2, ..., x_n$. We introduced this concept under the name of *remote assignment* in the section mentioned above.

The `channel` entity, a syntactic construct used to declare in the text of the processes, the data type for information transmitted via the message passing instructions will also be defined:

[out::destination!channel($e_1,e_2,...,e_n$) ∥ in::origin?channel($x_1,x_2,...,x_n$)]

---

[8] Auxiliary variables are used to relate the states of two or more program processes; they are only used for proof of correctness demonstration. They are not program variables.

[9] According to CSP semantics, no process can modify the value of a variable of another process.

[10] Of course, it must be assumed that the predicate referred to cannot be interfered, by the execution of other processes, while the communication is taking place.

If the previously mentioned statements do not correspond to each other, nor do any of them correspond with another communication sentence of a different process, then the processes containing the `in` and `out` sentences will block during the execution. This could lead to a situation of mutual blocking or even a complete deadlock of the program. The consequence of this in our FLS for program verification would be that the postcondition of the affected statements cannot collide with any other predicate.

3.4.2 Communication Axioms

In the new rules of the *LP* system of program demonstration that we are going to introduce, the axioms of the communication sentences allow any assertion to be made after the complete execution of each of them:

```
Send sentence:    {P}out::destination!channel(e1,e2,...,en){U}
Receive sentence: {Q}in::source?channel(x1,x2,...,xn){V}
```

In more technical terms, the above axioms allow any predicate to serve as a precondition or postcondition for a communication construct formed by two matching communication sentences `in(receive)` and `out(send)` operations. However, it is necessary to introduce an additional rule, known as the *satisfaction* rule, to guarantee that the effect of executing two matching communication statements (located in different processes of a distributed program) is equivalent to jointly assigning to each of the *target* variables, x_1, x_2, ..., x_n, the result of each of the expressions, e_1, e_2, ..., e_n, that match the first ones, evaluated in the source process. Thus, demonstrating the correctness of a distributed program using these axioms is equivalent to verifying the correctness of a remote assignment of a set of variables. For the purposes of the demonstration this makes it transparent, that the two processes of the program do not share variables and are located in separate machines.

3.4.3 Satisfaction Rule for the Synchronous Communication Between the Processes

To understand the need to establish a satisfaction rule in our FLS, consider the meaning of executing a pair of matching communication statements, such simultaneous execution of both statements is equivalent to executing a single assignment statement that makes the program to evolve into a state in which the postcondition $\{U \wedge V\}$ is satisfied. Therefore, before the combined execution of these statements, the program has to be in a state

3.4 Verification of Distributed Programs with Communicating Processes

satisfying $\{P \wedge Q\}$[11] or in the most general possible state that serves as a valid precondition of the triple: $\{P \wedge Q\} x_1, x_2, \ldots, x_n := e_1, e_2, \ldots, e_n \{U \wedge V\}$[12].

$$\underline{\textit{Satisfaction rule}}: \{P \wedge Q\} \Rightarrow \{U \wedge V\}_{e_1, e_2, \ldots e_n}^{x_1, x_2, \ldots x_n}$$

The interpretation of the above rule is as follows: let `in` be a message receiving statement of a process with precondition $\{P\}$ and postcondition $\{U\}$ and let `out` be a message sending statement, corresponding to the previous receiving statement, located in another process, with precondition $\{Q\}$ and postcondition $\{V\}$; then these matching communication statements, `in`, `out`, cooperate if and only if the satisfaction rule can be proved as a *theorem*[13] of our FLS.

Consequently, any pair of matching communication statements in a distributed program must satisfy the above satisfaction rule. However, it may be the case that two matching statements are never executed due to the internal logic of the algorithm implementing the program. This case can also be included in the proof, which can be formally indicated using the *satisfiability* rule by making the preconditions of both statements *restrictive* enough to ensure that the antecedent of the rule, $\{P \wedge Q\}$, is always false. In this way, what would be demonstrated is that both communication sentences that, although statically match, i.e., are accepted by the compiler, nevertheless, during the execution of the program can never reach a state in which the processes involved actually perform the communication implied by both sentences.

Example 3.6 Consider a program in which process M sends the maximum of two values to process A, the demonstration of both processes is valid, considered individually, and it is also shown that both cooperate by communicating, so that the final value of the variable `m` is the maximum of the initial values $\{I, J\}$, which coincides with the expected result of the program.

```
M::                                              A::
    var i,j:integer;                                 var m: integer;
                                                     {V}
    {i=I ∧ j=J}                                      M?m
    *[i≥j → {i=I ∧ j=J ∧ i≥j}A!i{V}                  {m = max (I,J)}
     ▯ j≥i → {i=I ∧ j=J ∧ j≥i}A!j{V}]
```

The proof of each of the processes, M, A, follows directly from the semantics of the alternative order and from the application of the axioms of communication. In addition to

---

[11] Where $\{P\}$ is the precondition of the input order in the receiving process and $\{Q\}$ is the precondition of the matching out order in the sending process.

[12] Using the weakest precondition operator: $\{P \wedge Q\} \Rightarrow wp(x_1, x_2, \ldots, x_n := e_1, e_2, \ldots, e_n \{U \wedge V\})$.

[13] That is, the demonstration represents a true triple of the program demonstration FLS.

this, the *satisfaction* rule has to be applied to prove that the postcondition of process A is valid after the communication between processes M and A has taken place:

$$(i = I \wedge j = J \wedge i \geq j) \Rightarrow \{m = \max(I,J)\}_i^m$$
$$(i = I \wedge j = J \wedge j \geq i) \Rightarrow \{m = \max(I,J)\}_j^m$$

The above two triples are trivially true.

3.4.4 Communication Orders with Guarded Commands

As communication sentences can appear in guarded commands, such as in *alternative* and *repetitive* structures, similar to those already studied in CSP programming notation, new demonstration rules must be introduced.

With respect to changes in the state of a process that includes guarded commands, it follows that a communication command within a guard $B;\texttt{<communication.command>} \rightarrow S$ has the same effect as moving B and $\texttt{<communication.command>}$ to the list of commands to the left of the '$\rightarrow$' symbol, as illustrated by the following code:

```
M::
    var i,j:integer;
    {i=I ∧ j=J}
    *[i≥j;{i=I ∧ j=J ∧ i≥j}A!i{V}→SKIP{V}
     ▯ j≥I;{i=I ∧ j=J ∧ j≥i}A!j{V}→SKIP{V}]
```

This code is equivalent to the previous example, except that the message passing commands have been moved inside the guards. It produces the same effect, in terms of changing the state variables of the process, as the M process introduced in the previous example.

The fundamental difference between the behaviour of a guarded command where the output communication operation appears in its body and one where the communication operation is part of the guard is that the former one is more prone to deadlock. Even if the guard condition B evaluates to true, the $\texttt{<communication.command>}$ located after the "$\rightarrow$" might not correspond to any communication statement from another process in the program. As a result, the subsequent S statement would never be executed. This scenario could lead to a program deadlock situation if similar conditions occur in multiple processes. However, if we were to consider the command:

$B_1;\ \texttt{<communication.command>} \rightarrow S\ \square\ B_2;\ \texttt{<communication.command>} \rightarrow S'$

Then even if B_1 evaluates to true but the communication command does not match any operation from another process, a deadlock would not necessarily occur. The alternative, with guard B_2, might be still succeed if its communication matches with another process, allowing the command to complete and avoid deadlock.

3.4 Verification of Distributed Programs with Communicating Processes

Since the demonstration rules we are introducing address the prevention of deadlocks between processes during program execution, we can therefore transform guarded commands containing communication operations within their guards into commands with purely boolean guards. This is because the axioms and rules of our demonstration system are not capable of distinguishing between both types of commands with respect to the exclusion of process deadlocks.

3.4.4.1 Alternative Order Inference Rule

We assume that the assertions $\{B_i\}$ of the following inference rule are boolean expressions and the $\{C_i\}$ are communication sentences.

$$\frac{\{P \wedge \neg (B_1 \vee B_2 \vee \cdots \vee B_n) \Rightarrow Q\}, \{P \wedge B_i\} \, C_i; S_i \{Q\}, \, 1 \leq i \leq n}{\{P\} [B_1; C_1 \rightarrow S_1 \square B_2; C_2 \rightarrow S_2 \square \cdots \square B_n; C_n \rightarrow S_n] \{Q\}}$$

The first condition of the rule states that if all guards fail[14], then the program terminates and the postcondition $\{Q\}$ of the alternative order is satisfied. If a different semantics were desired, for example, where the order itself blocks if all guards fail, then the first premise of the rule would need to be replaced with the following assertion: $\{P \wedge \neg (B_1 \vee B_2 \ldots \vee B_n)\} \Rightarrow \{F\}$. The second condition of the rule states that each component guarded command must be verified independently as a separate triple, where the guard B_i must appear as part of the precondition of each demonstration and each of the demonstrations must ensure that $\{Q\}$ holds in the postcondition.

3.4.4.2 Iterative Order Inference Rule

If the invariance of the loop $\{I\}$ is proven after the execution of each of its component guarded commands, assuming that both the invariant $\{I\}$ and the guard's boolean expression $\{B_i\}$ are included in the precondition of the triples $\{I \wedge B_i\} C_i ; S_i \{I\}$, which partially establish the correctness of each command, then we can conclude that the truth of $\{I\}$ is preserved in the postcondition after the execution of the entire repetitive construct:

Termination of the repetitive order can be demonstrated by showing that, after an unknown number of iterations all guard conditions $\{B_i\}$ eventually fail (i.e., not $\{\neg B_1 \wedge \neg B_2 \wedge \ldots \wedge \neg B_n\}$ holds).

$$\frac{(\{I \wedge B_i\} \, C_i; S_i \{I\}, \, 1 \leq i \leq n)}{\{I\} * [B_1; C_1 \rightarrow S_1 \square B_2; C_2 \rightarrow S_2 \square \ldots \square B_n; C_n \rightarrow S_n] \{I \wedge \neg B_1 \wedge \neg B_2 \wedge \ldots \wedge \neg B_n\}}$$

---

[14] That is, all Boolean expressions B_i are evaluated as false.

3.4.5 Demonstration of Non-interference

If the processes of a program refer only to disjoint sets of variables, it would not be necessary to perform a proof of *non-interference* between the individual demonstrations of the processes[15]. However, if auxiliary variables are used in the proofs, a non-interference demonstration becomes necessary whenever the assertions used to establish cooperation between processes share such auxiliary variables. For example, as when applying the satisfiability rule. Interference between assertions involving auxiliary variables and the statements of program processes can arise due to two causes:

1. An assignment action in one process falsifies an assertion in the demonstration of another process.
2. During the execution of a communication statement between two processes, an input command is executed that assigns a variable whose change affects an auxiliary variable in the receiving process, thereby falsifying an assertion used in the demonstration.

Since the auxiliary variables are introduced into the process code solely to facilitate formal proofs, they must not influence the behaviour of the program in which they are included because if they do, they would invalidate such demonstration. For this condition to be met, the following restrictions must be imposed on the use of auxiliary variables:

1. Auxiliary variables may be assigned values or appear on the right-hand side of an assignment statement, provided that the target variable to which they are assigned is also an auxiliary variable.
2. They may be used in assertions associated with receiving messages (input commands) or in expressions for sending messages (output commands), provided that the variables updated as a result of communication are also auxiliary. Additionally, the execution of the corresponding communication operations must not alter the observable state of the program

3.4.5.1 Demonstration of Non-interference Between Corresponding Communication Orders and One Critical Assertion

The execution of a pair of matching communication statements results in a *remote assignment* transferring the evaluated expressions from the output command to the variables specified in the corresponding input command of another process. The result of the execution of this operation must not influence the evaluation of any assertion $\{C\}$ of the demonstration of a third program process running concurrently with the two processes containing the matching pair of communication sentences. That is, given the pair of commands that include the following corresponding communication sentences:

```
In:: Source ? channel(x₁,x₂,...,xn)  ‖  Out:: Target ! channel(e₁,e₂,...,e)
```

---

[15] In fact, the semantics of the CSP *parallel order* imposes such a condition.

3.4 Verification of Distributed Programs with Communicating Processes

then the following triple must be a valid theorem for any assertion *{C}* included in the demonstration of a process running in parallel with the two processes containing the above communication commands:

$$NI_{sinc}(in, out, C) \equiv \{pre(in) \wedge pre(out) \wedge C\} C_{e_1,e_2,\ldots,e_n}^{x_1,x_2,\ldots,x_n} \Rightarrow \{post(in) \wedge post(out) \wedge C\}$$

The verbal interpretation of the above theorem can be stated as follows: if a program with multiple processes can be inferred to be about to send and receive data through the imminent execution of matching `in`, `out` communication statements, then the theorem must hold (the above triple is true). Specifically, if the assertion *{C}* of a third process is true in the current state of the program, and the next state is reached after executing the communication `in` and `out`, then *{C}* must still hold, i.e., there must be no interference between the truth of *{C}* and the realisation of the communication between processes `in` and `out`.

3.4.5.2 Non-interference Inference Rule for Synchronous Communication Commands

Theorems $\{P_i\} S_i \{Q_i\}, 1 \leq i \leq n$ are interference-free if the following conditions are satisfied:

For every assignment action `a` in the proof of $S_i : 1 \leq i \leq n$ and every critical assertion *{C}* in processes, which run concurrently to the process containing action `a`, it must be ensured that *NI(a, C)* is a valid theorem.

For every input statement `in` in the demonstration of $S_i : 1 \leq i \leq n$, every output statement `out` in the demonstration of $S_j : 1 \leq j \leq n$ $i \neq j$ and every critical assertion *{C}* in processes running concurrently with the execution of `in` and `out`, it must be ensured that NI_{sinc} *(in, out, C)* is a valid theorem (provided that the commands `in` and `out` belong to two matching communicating processes).

Example 3.7

Let *C[1..n]* be a set of processes, each containing critical sections in their code. These processes act as clients of a server process that implements a binary semaphore, which alternately receives a *P()* signal and then a *V()* signal from the same client process.

To demonstrate that the following program correctly solves the problem, we need to introduce auxiliary variables that track whether each client process *c[i]* is currently outside or inside its critical section.

```
CLIENT::*[TRUE → Semaphore!P();                 Semaphore::*[(i:1..n) C(i)?P()→
         Critical-Section;                                    C(i)?V()]
         Semaphore!V(); Rest-Instructions]
                    [C(1..n)::CLIENT ‖ Semaphore]
```

Let *in(1...n)* be an array of auxiliary variables, where *in(i)* holds the value 1 when process *C(i)* is executing within the critical section and 0 otherwise. Consequently, the solution to the mutual exclusion problem must satisfy the following predicate as a global invariant of the program MUTEX:

$$\{(\forall i : 1 \le i \le n : 0 \le in(i) \le 1) \land (in(1) + \ldots + in(n) \le 1)\}$$

The assignment of auxiliary variables must occur within the communication statements of the processes, ensuring that these updates are atomic. This guarantee that they capture critical control points with the purpose of carrying out the demonstration.

```
var in: array(1..n) of integer:= 0;
{MUTEX}
CLIENT::*[TRUE → {MUTEX ∧ in(i)=0}        Semaphore::
Semaphore!P(1);                            {MUTEX∧(in(1)+in(2)+…in(n)=0)}
{MUTEX ∧ in(i)=1}                          *[(i:1..n) C(i)?P(in(i))→
Critical-Section;                          {MUTEX∧(in(1)+in(2)+…in(n)=1)
Semaphore!V(0);                            C(i)?V(in(i)))
{MUTEX ∧ in(i)=0}                          {MUTEX∧(in(1)+in(2)+…in(n)=0)}
Non-Critical Section]                      ]
                   [C(1..n)::CLIENT ∥ Semaphore]
```

The predicate *{MUTEX}* serves as a global invariant included in all assertions throughout the demonstration. Additional predicates associated with each client specify the value of each auxiliary variable `in(i)`. If all values of the auxiliary variables `in(i)` are 0, then the critical section is free; otherwise, at most one of these auxiliary variables can have the value 1, indicating that the corresponding process `C(i)` is currently executing code within the critical section.

The individual process demonstrations are valid, considered in isolation, since the only statements that modify values of program variables are the `in ('?')` and `out ('!')` communication operations, and the axioms governing these operations state that the pre- and postconditions can be any predicate. Therefore, the overall validity of the proof for this example, depends on verifying the satisfaction rule NI_{sinc} (`in, out, MUTEX`) and proving the theorems.

In the program above, there are two pairs of corresponding communication statements, those that use the `P()` channel to communicate and those that use the `V()` channel. For the former, the satisfaction rule requires proving the following assertion:

$$(MUTEX \land in(i) = 0 \land (in(1) + \ldots + in(n)) = 0) \Rightarrow$$
$$(MUTEX \land in(i) = 1 \land (in(1) + \ldots + in(n)) = 1)_1^{in(i)}$$

which is a trivially valid theorem. Similarly, for communication sentences using the `V()` channel, one would have to prove:

$$(MUTEX \wedge in(i) = 1 \wedge (in(1) + \ldots + in(n)) = 1) \Rightarrow$$
$$(MUTEX \wedge in(i) = 1 \wedge (in(1) + \ldots + in(n)) = 1)_0^{in(i)}$$

Finally, it remains to prove the absence of interference between the demonstrations of any the two processes in the protocol. As there are no assignment actions, the only possible source of interference would be between the communication statements of the two processes and a critical assertion of a third process. In this program, all communications are established from the client processes to the semaphore process. Therefore, we must prove non-interference between two communication statements, one between a client and the semaphore, and the assertions of a third client process `C[j]`, which, for example, might be executing a communication statement over the `P()` channel. This requirement translates into proving the validity of the following condition:

$$\{MUTEX \wedge in(1) + \ldots + in(n) = 0 \wedge in(i) = 0 \wedge in(j) = 0\} \Rightarrow (MUTEX \wedge in(j) = 1)_1^{in(j)}$$

which is a valid theorem whenever `i` ≠ `j`. The other non-interference theorems can be proved in a similar manner.

3.5 Message-Passing Libraries

Currently, MPI (*Message-Passing Interface*) is a highly valuable tool for developing parallel applications based on message passing [42]. The parallel and distributed programming model typically implemented with MPI is the Single Program Multiple Data (SPMD) model (see Table 3.1). In the SPMD model, all processes execute the same program, although not necessarily the same instruction simultaneously as is required in SIMD.

As its name suggests, MPI is an interface, which means that the standard does not require a specific implementation. Its primary purpose is to provide developers with a collection of functions to design applications without requiring detailed knowledge of the specific hardware on which it will run or the way in which the functions to be used in his program have been internally implemented. The development of the MPI interface and its implementations is the main work of the *MPI Forum*, a group of researchers from universities, laboratories and companies involved in parallel computing, also known as *High Performance Parallel* Computing (HPPC). Essentially, MPI seeks to define a unified programming environment that guarantees full portability of parallel applications, based on a single interface and without specifically prescribing how the platform-dependent implementation should be handled. MPI also offers users and programmers public domain implementations of such an environment that ensures a high level of quality with the aim of promoting the widespread adoption of the standard.

The core elements of MPI include the definition of a language-independent programming interface, along with a collection of implementations of that interface, which are technically known as *bindings*, for the most widespread programming languages in the parallel computing community, i.e., the programming languages, Ada, C and FORTRAN. Anyone looking to develop software using MPI must work with an MPI implementation that includes at least the following elements:

- A function library for C, along with the header file `mpi.h`, with the definitions of those functions and also includes a collection of constants and macros.
- A function library for FORTRAN, along with the header file `mpif.h`
- Commands for compilation, such as `mpicc` and `mpif77`, which are adapted versions of standard compilation commands (`cc`, `f77`) that automatically include the necessary MPI libraries.
- A specific command for executing parallel applications, usually called `mpirun`.
- Tools for monitoring and debugging parallel programs.

MPI is obviously not the only environment available for the development of parallel applications, as there are many other alternatives, such as:

- Using proprietary programming libraries specific to parallel computing, e.g., NX on Intel Paragon, MPL on IBM SP2, etc.
- Choosing PVM (*Parallel Virtual Machine*), which has characteristics similar to MPI, and its core computing model seeks to make a network of workstations operate as a multicomputer.
- Using parallel programming languages or programming languages that incorporate specific instructions for multicore or multicomputer systems, such as Unified Parallel C, Occam, or Go.

As previously mentioned, MPI is primarily designed for the development of SPMD applications. In this model, N copies of the same program are launched in parallel, each executed by an asynchronous process. The necessary instructions to synchronise correctly these processes must be programmed within their code. Since MPI processes operate in separate memory spaces, the exchange of information, as well as the synchronisation between them, has to be done exclusively by message passing. Consequently, MPI provides both blocking and non-blocking message-passing operations. Blocking operations simplify programming and enhance safety, while non-blocking operations allow developers to optimize the performance of distributed applications by hiding communication and transmission overhead. In MPI, point-to-point operations are available for two communicating processes, as well as collective functions or operations to involve a group of processes. Processes can therefore be grouped into *communicators*, which define the scope of collective message passing operations and support a modular design of applications.

3.5 Message-Passing Libraries

Below is an example of a program that uses the MPI *binding* for the C programming language:

```
#include "mpi.h"
#include <iostream>
using namespace std;
main (int argc, char **argv) {
  int nproc; --Number of processes
  int me; --My address: 0<=me<=(nproc-1)
  MPI_Init(&argc, &argv);
  MPI_Comm_size(MPI_COMM_WORLD, &nproc);
  MPI_Comm_rank(MPI_COMM_WORLD, &me);
  --Program body
  cout<<"I am the process " <<me<<" of "<<nproc<<endl;
  MPI_Finalize();
}
```

If we use MPI to develop our parallel programs, then we have to keep in mind that all function names have to start with the prefix MPI; the first letter following the underscore is always uppercase, and the rest are lowercase. Most MPI functions return an integer, which must be interpreted as a *diagnostic* if the operation is executed erroneously. If, on the other hand, the value returned is given by the constant $MPI\_SUCCESS$, the function has been executed successfully.

The keyword MPI_COMM_WORLD refers to the universal communicator, i.e., a communicator predefined by MPI, which includes, by default, all processes in our program.

3.5.1 Functions of MPI

In MPI, *point-to-point* communication functions are available for interactions between two processes, as well as functions and operations that involve a group of processes in a collective communication. Processes can be grouped and form *communicators*, which define the scope of collective communication operations within a program. The MPI standard provides functions to perform the following operations related to the communication of concurrent and distributed processes:

(a) Basic functions
(b) Point-to-point communications
(c) Collective communications
(d) Process groups
(e) Process topologies
(f) Management and interrogation of the environment

3.5.1.1 Basic Functions

MPI defines a set of functions for initialising the execution environment of application processes and other administrative operations for programs that use MPI to produce parallel code. Among the most commonly used functions are the following:

- `MPI_Init()`: to start parallel execution of application processes.
- `MPI_Comm_size()`: to determine the number of processes participating in the application.
- `MPI_Comm_rank()`: for each process to obtain its identifier within the collection of processes that make up the application.
- `MPI_Finalize()`: to terminate program execution.

3.5.1.2 Communicators

A communicator is an organisational element of MPI that defines a group of processes that are allowed to communicate with each other (Fig. 3.13). All MPI communication functions require as an argument a variable prefixed with the type `MPI_Comm`, hereafter simply called *communicator*. Every MPI message must specify a communicator by including its name as an explicit parameter within the argument list of any MPI function. For communication to occur, the communicator specified in the calls to the send and receive operations of two communicating processes must match.

There can be multiple communicators, and a single process can belong to more than one communicator (For example, in Fig. 3.13, the processes P_3 and P_8 belong to two communicators). Within each communicator, processes are assigned consecutive numbers known as *ranks*. A process's rank identifies it uniquely within the communicator and is used to specify the source and destination in calls to send and receive message operations. If a process belongs to more than 1 communicator, then its *rank* will be different in each of them.

MPI automatically provides a default communicator called `MPI_COMM_WORLD`, which is the universal communicator comprising all processors that could communicate in any application. Using `MPI_COMM_WORLD`, any process can communicate with any other process. Additional communicators can be defined that consist of subsets of the available processes. The context of a communicator is referred to as the scope in which message passing occurs, i.e., messages belonging to different communicators are completely isolated from one another. Consequently, a message sent in the context of a particular communicator can only be received in that context. Moreover, the processes participating in a

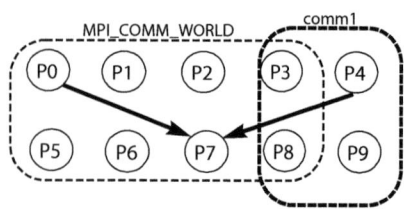

Fig. 3.13 Graphical representation of an MPI communicator

3.5 Message-Passing Libraries

communicator are uniquely identified within it, ensuring safe and predictable communication. Therefore, the following conditions will be fulfilled:

(a) A process can belong to different communicators.
(b) Each process has one identifier, assigned as an integer from 0 to $n-1$, where n is the number of processes of that communicator.
(c) Messages intended for different contexts never interfere with each other.

3.5.1.3 Getting the Information from the Communicator

A process can determine its *rank* within a communicator by calling MPI_Comm_rank. When using *ranks* in programs, we must remember that their values are consecutive and start at 0, whether we program with the MPI *binding* for C or for Fortran. Additionally, a process may have different ranks in the different communicators to which it belongs. In Fig. 3.14, we can see that the processes within communicator 1 *(comm1)* have different *ranks* compared to their ranks in the communicator MPI_COMM_WORLD.

The following C function prototype demonstrates how to retrieve a process's rank:

```
int MPI_Comm_rank (MPI_Comm commun, int*rank);
```

The `commun` argument is a variable of type MPI_Comm, i.e., a communicator. The universal communicator MPI_COMM_WORLD could be used instead, or any other user-defined communicator. The second argument is a pointer to an integer variable *rank*, which the MPI execution system will set to the process's unique identifier within the specified communicator.

3.5.1.4 Dynamic Sizing of the Communicator

A process, within a context, can also determine the size of the communicator to which it belongs, i.e., the number of processes associated with that communicator, with a function call that returns the value of the constant MPI_COMM_SIZE. The following C *binding* function call retrieves the number of processes:

```
int MPI_Comm_size(MPI_Comm commun, int *size);
```

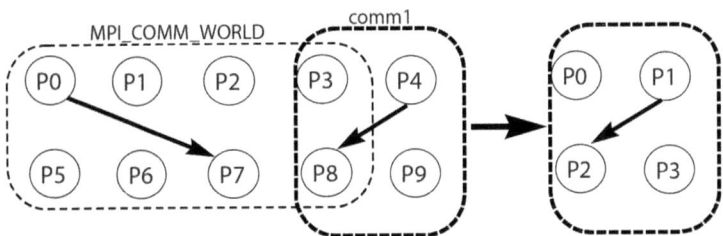

Fig. 3.14 Communication between processes in different contexts

In this function, `commun` is a variable of type `MPI_Comm` representing the communicator. The second argument is a pointer to an integer variable `size` where the communicator's size will be stored. If the communicator were the universal communicator: `MPI_COMM_WORLD`, the value returned corresponds to the total number of processes specified at program launch. For example, if the program is executed with the command:

$mpirun -n 4 a.out,

The `MPI_Comm_size()` function would return the value 4. However, if a communicator other than the universal one is used, it may return a lower number.

Alternatively, the size of the communicator can be determined by the system-dependent environment variable `MPI_PROCS`. However, it is important to note that if a value is specified through the `mpirun` command, it will override the value set by the `MPI_PROCS` variable.

3.5.1.5 Point-to-Point Communications

This refers to *one-to-one* communications that are established between a single pair of processes (see Fig. 3.15). It is the fundamental communication operation in direct communication between two processes, where one process sends data and the other receives them. Since this mode of communication has two *communicating sides*, two operations will be needed, one on each end of the communication, which must be explicitly programmed in the code of the processes involved. Consequently, data transfer does not occur unless both participating processes actively perform their respective operations on their processors.

A message, containing a block of data transferred between processes, consists of a *wrapper* indicating the source and destination processes and a message *body* containing the actual data to be transmitted. The fields composing the message wrapper and the message body can be found in the parameters of the MPI send *(MPI_Send())* and receive *(MPI_Recv())* functions.

The MPI message *wrapper* has four parts: *source, destination, communicator* and *tag*. The source refers to the identifier of the process sending the message, and the destination indicates the identifier of the receiving process, while the communicator specifies a process group to which the source and destination processes belong. The tag field is used to classify processes and is mandatory, but its concrete use is left to the program logic. A pair of communicating processes may use different tag values to distinguish between different types of messages, e.g., one tag value could be used for data messages, while another could be used for status updates from the sending process.

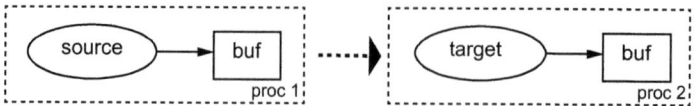

Fig. 3.15 Basic message sending instructions

3.5 Message-Passing Libraries

Basic send and receive message operations in MPI:

```
int MPI_Send(void*buffer,int count, MPI_Datatype data_type,
  int target,int tag, MPI_Comm communicator)
```

```
int MPI_Recv(void*buffer,int count, MPI_Datatype data_type,
  int source,int tag, MPI_Comm communicator, MPI_Status*state)
```

The following three information fields are used in the *body* of the MPI message: first is the *buffer*, which corresponds to the initial memory location where the data used by the `MPI_Send()` operation can be found or where the received data in the case of an `MPI_Recv()` operation will be stored. The argument `count` is next, which refers to the number of `data_type` elements to be sent. The third argument, `data_type`, specifies the type of the data to be sent or received, which in the simplest cases is a primitive data type, such as `REAL`, `INTEGER`, etc., but in more advanced applications, it can refer to user-defined data types constructed from primitive types. In the latter case, user-defined types can be thought of as similar to `structures` in the C programming language and allow the grouping of data that may not necessarily reside in contiguous memory locations. This capability provides great flexibility in defining the content of MPI messages, enabling more complex and efficient communication patterns.

3.5.1.6 Blocking Operations

The `MPI_Send()` and `MPI_Recv()` operations block the calling process until the communication operation *is completed*. This situation occurs when either the message is copied to an internal MPI *buffer* or the processes sending and receiving data synchronise on the message.

In the `MPI_Send()` operation, the message body contains the data to be sent, i.e., a number of elements equal to `count` of type `MPI_Datatatype`. The message wrapper indicates where the data is to be sent. In addition, the call to this function may return an error code.

In the call to the `MPI_Recv()` operation, the arguments that belong to the message wrapper determine the messages that can be received when such a call occurs. The arguments of the call: *source*, *tag* and the *communicator* must match or coincide (the last two) with those of the call to the `MPI_Send()` operation by the sending process, so that the pending message can be received. Only messages sent from the *source* process that have the *tag* indicated in the argument of the referred operation are received, although *wildcard* arguments can also be used, such as `MPI_ANY_SOURCE` and `MPI_ANY_TAG`. There are no wildcards for the *communicator* argument.

The message body arguments specify where the data arriving at the receiving process should be stored, what data type is assumed and the maximum amount of data the receiving process is prepared to accept. If the received message contains more data than expected, an error occurs, and the program will abort. In general, it is the responsibility of the sender and receiver to agree on the data type of the message. If the sender and receiver use incompatible data types in the messages, the results of the execution of the program will be undefined. The *status* argument returns information about the received message. Specifically, it provides the origin and tag (label) of the message, which is particularly important when wildcards are used in message-passing operations. The actual count of the received data elements and a code indicating the outcome of the operation are also made available.

With blocking communication operations, no operation call returns until it completes. The concept of *completion* is simple and intuitive for the `MPI_Recv()` operation, which will indicate that a matching message has arrived and the data has been copied into the variables specified in the call. Afterwards, the received data is immediately available for use.

For the `MPI_Send()` operation, the meaning of *completion* is also simple but less intuitive. A call to this operation completes when the message specified in the call has been delivered to the MPI system. At that point, the variables used in the *send* operation can safely be modified or reused. However, recall that one of two scenarios may occur: (a) MPI copies the message to an internal buffer for asynchronous delivery, allowing the `MPI_Send()` call to complete even if the message has not yet been transmitted to the receiver; or (b) MPI waits for the destination process to post a matching receive before allowing the `MPI_Send()` call to complete. If a message passed to `MPI_Send()` is larger than the size of the available internal buffer, the sending process must block until either the destination process begins receiving the message or additional buffer space becomes available. In general, messages that are copied to the MPI internal buffer will occupy that space until the destination process starts to receive them.

A call to `MPI_Recv()` matches a pending message if the source, tag, and communicator parameters correspond. Additionally, the data type of the received message must match the data type expected by the receiving process for the operation to execute correctly. However, MPI typically does not enforce strict type checking at runtime. Therefore, it is the obligation of the programmer to ensure that the data types match in message passing operations; otherwise, a mismatch may lead to undefined behaviour or cause the program to abort.

Example 3.9 Assume three pairs of processes P_i that send and then receive a message from their neighbour P_{i+1} using synchronous message passing operations and they must be free of reaching a deadlock situation between the processes (see Fig. 3.16).

In order to avoid unrecoverable deadlocks in message sending operations between processes, since these are blocking message-passing operations, the execution order of sending and receiving operations is important. We will assume that even-indexed processes

Fig. 3.16 Graphical representation of exchanges

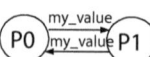
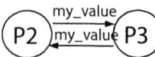
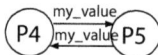

3.5 Message-Passing Libraries

```
int main(int argc, char *argv[]) {
  int rank, size, my_value, value;
  MPI_Status status;
  MPI_Init(&argc, &argv);
  MPI_Comm_rank(MPI_COMM_WORLD, &rank);
  MPI_Comm_size(MPI_COMM_WORLD, &size);
  my_value=rank*(rank+1);
  if (rank %2 == 0) {
    MPI_Ssend(&my_value, 1, MPI_INT, rank+1, 0, MPI_COMM_WORLD);
    MPI_Recv(&value, 1, MPI_INT, rank+1, 0, MPI_COMM_WORLD, &status);}
  else {
    MPI_Recv(&value, 1, MPI_INT, rank-1, 0, MPI_COMM_WORLD, &status);
    MPI_Ssend(&my_value, 1, MPI_INT, rank-1, 0, MPI_COMM_WORLD);}
    cout<< "I am process "<<rank<<" and I have received "<< value <<endl;
    MPI_Finalize();
    return 0;
}
```

Fig. 3.17 Code of two processes exchanging data between pairs of processes in a synchronous and deadlock-free way

will first execute the sending operation and then the receiving one. Odd-indexed processes act just the opposite, first executing the receiving and then the synchronous sending operation. The MPI program code is shown in Fig. 3.17.

3.5.1.7 Synchronous Message Passing

This is an MPI function that produces an *unbuffered*, blocking send on both sides of the communication, i.e., for both the send and receive ends of the message. The synchronous send function `MPI_Ssend()` (see Fig. 3.17) has the same arguments as the *regular* send function: `MPI_Send()`. The send operation terminates only when the corresponding receive operation `MPI_Recv()` is invoked by another process and the the message reception starts. When the call to `MPI_Ssend()` returns, the memory area containing the transmitted data may be reused, and the receiver will then have reached the synchronisation point to receive the corresponding message. The `MPI_Recv()` operation has a synchronous message passing semantics, then the semantics of the two operations involved in synchronous message passing can be understood as equivalent to a rendezvous between both sender and receiver processes, i.e., one of them stops its execution to wait for the other one to execute the corresponding message passing operation.

3.5.1.8 Deadlocks

If we use synchronous message passing operations, it could happen in some program trace that all processes try to receive a message sent by other process, but none of them in the protocol calls the send message operation. If this scenario were to occur, each process would be blocked indefinitely waiting to receive a message that will never be available to be received. In the program in Fig. 3.18, process 0 attempts to exchange messages with process 1. Process 0 cannot continue until process 1 sends a message, nor can process 1 continue until process 0 sends a message. Therefore, such a piece of code is erroneous and leads to a mutual deadlock situation of the two processes.

```
void main (int argc, char **argv) {
  int myrank;
  MPI_Status status;
  double a[100], b[100];
  MPI_Init(&argc, &argv);
  MPI_Comm_rank(MPI_COMM_WORLD, &myrank);
  if(myrank == 0) {
     MPI_Recv(b, 100, MPI_DOUBLE, 1, 19, MPI_COMM_WORLD, &status);
     MPI_Send(a, 100, MPI_DOUBLE, 1, 17, MPI_COMM_WORLD);
  }
    else if(myrank == 1) {
       MPI_Recv(b, 100, MPI_DOUBLE, 0, 17, MPI_COMM_WORLD, &status);
       MPI_Send(a, 100, MPI_DOUBLE, 0, 19, MPI_COMM_WORLD);
    }
  MPI_Finalize();
}
```

Fig. 3.18 Code of two processes presenting a deadlock situation

In the above program, no messages will ever be sent by any process, and no messages will ever be received. We can know when an MPI program is in a deadlock situation the same way that we know when we have an infinite loop in a sequential program, because the program will not do any progress in the execution of its instructions.

3.5.1.9 Status Objects

The reference to such an object appears in the last argument of the `MPI_Recv()` operation and can also be obtained by calling the function below:

```
int MPI_Get_count(MPI_Status*status,MPI_Datatype data_type, int*count)
```

This function allows obtaining information about the message received and the size of this message.

3.5.1.10 Non-blocking Communication

In addition to the blocking communication mode between processes, non-blocking message sending and receiving message-passing operations can be used in MPI, as can be seen in the code of Fig. 3.19. A much more flexible distributed programming of applications can be achieved by using non-blocking communication operations in scenarios that could lead to program deadlocks. Deadlocks can arise due to the relative ordering of receive and send operations between processes in synchronous message passing. Deadlocks also occur by sending messages larger than the size of the buffers that are going to store them on the reception. These scenarios are avoided by using non-blocking message passing.

The operations that we are going to study for programming non-blocking message passing between processes are:

- *Message polling* (asynchronous communication)
- Non-buffered non-blocking send-receive

3.5 Message-Passing Libraries

```
int rank, size, flag, buf, src,tag;
    ...
MPI_Comm_rank(MPI_COMM_WORLD, &rank);
MPI_Comm_size(MPI_COMM_WORLD, &size);
if (rank == 0) {
  int counter=0;
  while (counter<10*(size-1)){
    MPI_Iprobe(MPI_ANY_SOURCE,MPI_ANY_TAG,MPI_COMM_WORLD, &flag, &status);
    if (flag>0){
      MPI_Recv(&buf, 1, MPI_INT, MPI_ANY_SOURCE, MPI_ANY_TAG,MPI_COMM_WORLD, &status);
      src=status.MPI_SOURCE; tag=status.MPI_TAG;
      cout<<"Message from "<<src<<" with tag= "<<tag<<endl;
      counter++;}
    }
    cout<< "Total messages received:"<< counter<<endl;
  }
  else
    for (int i=0; i<10; i++)
      MPI_Send(&buf, 1, MPI_INT, 0, i, MPI_COMM_WORLD);
```

Fig. 3.19 Continuous probing of several unknown sending processes in the receiving process

3.5.1.11 Message Polling Operations

These are operations that check if there is a pending message waiting on a channel. There are two versions of this operation, one blocking and the other non-blocking.

1. The *MPI_Iprobe()* function does not block the calling process if the channel is empty:

   int MPI_Iprobe(int source, int tag, MPI_Comm comm, int *flag, MPI_Status *status)

   Therefore, if a message pending to be received is detected when the function returns, then the receiving process has to get it with a call to *MPI_Recv()*. The call to *MPI_Iprobe* function returns with a *flag* parameter value > 0 to indicate that there is a message on the channel that matches the expected values of the arguments *(source, tag, communicator)*. The argument passed to the call as a parameter of type *MPI_Status* allows us to obtain more information about the message to be received.

2. The *MPI_Probe()* function can block the calling process, i.e., calls to this function return only when there is a message matching the arguments *(source, tag, communicator)*:

   int MPI_Probe(int source, int tag, MPI_Comm comm,MPI_Status*status);

   By using wildcards, this operation allows waiting for the arrival of a message without knowing its source, label or size (see Fig. 3.20).

```
int count, *buf, source;
--I am blocked until a message is detected
MPI_Probe (MPI_ANY_SOURCE, 0,comm, &status);
--The size and sending process of the message is ascertained.
MPI_Get_count(status, MPI_INT, &count);
source= status.MPI_SOURCE;
--Memory is reserved to receive the message
buf=malloc(count*sizeof(int));
--The message is actually received
MPI_Recv(buf,count,MPI_INT,source,0,comm,&status);
```

Fig. 3.20 Receiving message with unknown sender process and message size

3.5.1.12 Non-buffered Non-blocking Send-Receive

The four fundamental operations for programming with non-blocking message sending in MPI are:

1. `MPI_Isend()` which, when called, initiates a send of the message but returns before copying anything into the system buffer. The actual transmission may proceed in the background.
2. `MPI_Irecv()` which starts receiving the message when called by the receiving process but returns before it starts receiving data. The actual reception will happen asynchronously.
3. `MPI_Test()` which is used to test whether any of the above non-blocking operations have been completed.
4. `MPI_Wait()` which suspends execution of the invoking process until the blocking operation specified as its parameter has completed.

The call to the `MPI_Isend()` operation initiates a message sending and returns immediately, without making the calling process wait for the corresponding MPI function call to complete, and syntactically has the following definition:

```
int MPI_Isend(void*buf, int c, MPI_Datatype d, int t,
              int tag, MPI_Comm comm, MPI_Request*reqt)
```

The completion of this operation has the same interpretation as the blocking message passing operations in the previous section, but the message being transmitted is copied to an internal MPI buffer, thus freeing processes of synchronising in message passing. It is important to note that variables passed as arguments in a call to `MPI_Isend()` cannot be used in the code of the invoking process, nor should they even be read until the `MPI_Isend()` operation has completed.

With respect to the non-blocking receive, `MPI_Irecv()` has a fully equivalent definition to the send operation above:

```
    int MPI_Irecv(void*buf, int c, MPI_Datatype d, int s,
                int tag, MPI_Comm comm, MPI_Request*reqt)
```

The *request* argument shall provide an identifier to be used by *test* or *wait* operations, which allows consulting the result of another process' call to `MPI_Irecv()` operation whose status is to be queried or expected to be completed. It can be seen that the call to the `MPI_Irecv()` operation does not include the `MPI_Status` argument, as in the case of the message polling operations `MPI_Iprobe()` and `MPI_Probe()`.

With the `MPI_Request_free(MPI_Request *request)` function, the *request* object can be explicitly released. The value of the `MPI_Status` argument can be obtained by calling one of the status check functions: `MPI_Test()` or `MPI_Wait()`. Obviously, a call to one of these check functions or one of their variants is necessary to determine the completion status of message passing operations when programming with the non-blocking communication operations `MPI_Irecv()` and `MPI_Isend()`. An example can be found in Exercise 3.20.

3.6 High-Level Mechanisms for Programming Distributed Systems

In Hoare's CSP model, message passing is characterised by synchronous communication mode and unidirectional message passing, as each communication channel is used to pass information in one direction only, between a single sending process and a single receiving process. As can be seen from the reference work [24] of this programming notation, the message passing primitives are very low level, but with them, any kind of interaction between communicating processes can be implemented.

However, the programming model that supports CSP-based programming languages is not equally flexible for all communication schemes that are commonly found in applications and often requires detailed adaptation work that can be tedious. For example, implementing a client-server communication scheme between distributed processes can lead to a design that feels unnatural within this programming paradigm:

```
Process Client[i:0..n];                Process Server;
 begin                                   begin
  while true do                           while true do
   begin                                   begin
    Send(Server, request());                (i:0..n) condition(i);
    Receive(Server, response);              Receive(Customer[i],request())->
    --Process the response and              perform.service();
    --do the calculations of                Send(Customer[i], result);
    --the task                            end
   end                                   enddo
  enddo                                 end;
end;
```

In addition, the above solution produces unsafe code, especially if the client's service requests must wait for a completion message from the server process or need to receive a result to continue their computations, as this message could be lost and probably cause deadlock.

Similarly, the server may be affected by an untrusted client that fails before receiving the second message with results. Such a situation would cause the server process crashing.

Therefore, the following pair must represent a logical transaction in order to avoid clients deadlock or server processes crashes:

(send(server,request()),receive(server,response))

and it is not appropriate to represent it as two independent *unbuffered* and blocking message passing operations. The *communication channel* between the client process and the server process should support two-way communication and perform the sending of the request and the receiving of the response from the *Server* as an atomic operation.

3.6.1 The Remote Call Operation

It is a model of communication between distributed communicating processes that can be implemented by means of synchronous message passing at low level, but it has many of the characteristics of the procedure or function calls of imperative languages. In addition to being relatively easy to program with it, for a C or Modula programmer, it allows to implement in a flexible way and with the appropriate level of abstraction of an imperative programming language a client-server-type relationship of system's processes.

With the so-called *remote call* model, several processes are allowed to concurrently and remotely call a procedure owned by another process. The latter controls the execution of the calls it receives by providing in a transparent way to the application programmer a many-to-one communication primitive. In addition, the programming primitive that we will call hereafter *remote procedure call* usually involves two-way information passing from the invoking process to the process that owns the procedure and vice versa.

The remotely called procedure encapsulates a series of instructions that are executed on behalf of the calling or *client* process, before any result is returned. The *remote call* model supports several implementations, two of which are discussed below:

1. Remote Procedure Call (RPC).
2. Remote invocation, also known as rendezvous-based communication model between concurrent processes, which run asynchronously until the point of interaction is reached by both of them.

To distinguish the two models, *remote* in the *remote procedure call* model is often said to mean the location on a different processor or computer; however, *remote* for the remote invocation model means on a different process, which could be invoked locally by a different thread of the same program.

3.6.2 Remote Procedure/Method Call

3.6.2.1 Concept of Remote Procedure

It is a mechanism that allows a program, running on a given node, to execute a procedure located on another node of the communication network. Remote procedure or method calls have a similar syntax to a procedure call in imperative programming languages but a completely different invocation semantics.

Since there must be a program running on a remote processor (*server*) to execute the invocation, we can think of the remote procedure as a *global procedure* for all processes of a distributed program, which is called by the client processes.

The remote procedure is executed by a process created for this purpose on the server that executes the body or main block of that procedure and returns a message with the results. Some implementations of this model have proven particularly useful and efficient in distributed systems at the operating system level. This model has been adopted as a low-level communication mechanism in distributed versions of the UNIX operating system.

A general description of the semantics of a remote procedure call is as follows:

- The arguments of the call are sent to the server, either directly or through a process created for this purpose, called `stub`.
- The client process executing the call is suspended, and therefore this process does not waste processor's cycles while the remote call is being handled.
- The arguments[16] of the server-side procedure call are reconstructed, the procedure is executed and the result-arguments are forwarded to the calling client process.
- The server usually binds a symbolic name to the port from which it receives calls to execute a particular remote procedure.
- It is possible to have several instances of the same procedure running concurrently, if each call from a client process to such a remote procedure creates a new process or thread on the server.

In the latter case, the variables of the procedure need to be accessed concurrently by the threads that are created in the server; therefore, mutual exclusion must be ensured in this access.

3.6.2.2 Implementing the Remote Method in Java

The standard technology proposed in the reference work [31] for distributed programming with Java is called *Remote Method Invocation* (RMI). This technology is based on the remote call model and object-oriented programming; hence, the term *remote method*

---

[16] Note that the architecture of the machine hosting the client process may be very different from that of the server, e.g., different memory word size, etc. Therefore, the reconstruction of the arguments on the server requires processing to adapt the parameters of the call.

invocation is now used instead of the classic systems term, *remote procedure call*, studied earlier.

Using RMI and the Java programming language on the server side, a class that implements the methods to be called remotely is needed. Which methods of that class can be called by other processes is not contained within the class but must be included in a sub-interface of *Remote*:

```
public interface Hello extends Remote{
  public String sayHello() throws java.rmi.RemoteException;
}
```

The *Remote* sub-interface allows, at the implementation level, for each server process programmed with RMI, to register the available objects and the names of the methods that can be called remotely.

```
public class HelloImpl extends UnicastRemoteObject implements Hello{
  public HelloImpl() throws RemoteException{
    super();
  }
  public String sayHello() throws RemoteException{
    returns "Hello everybody!";
  }
}
```

A *HelloImpl()* constructor method has to be declared in the class containing the remote method *(sayHello())*, as the clause specifying to throw the exception *(throws RemoteException)* is mandatory.

```
public static void main(String args[]){
 try{
   HelloImpl h = HelloImpl(); Naming.rebind("hello", h);
   System.out.println("The Hello server is ready.");
 }
  catch(RemoteException re){
  ... --treatment of the exception when it occurs
  }
   catch (MalformedURLException e){
     ... --treatment of the exception when it occurs
  }
 }
```

In the *main()* method of the main class, the object returned by the *HelloImpl()* constructor is bound to the symbolic name *"hello"*. This association between a symbolic name and an object is included in the server's name registry and is made accessible to future client processes remotely.

3.6 High-Level Mechanisms for Programming Distributed Systems

Client processes, in order to be able to use the services of a remote method, such as `sayHello()`, need to program something similar to the following code:

```
public static void main (String args[]){
 System.setSecurityManager(new RMISecurityManager());

 try {
   Hello h = (Hello) Naming.lookup("rmi://ockham.ugr.es/hello");
   String message = h.sayHello();
   System.out.println("HelloClient: " + message);
 }
 catch (RemoteException re) {
    //treatment of the exception when it occurs
 }
```

As can be seen in the simulation of `sayHello()` method call behaviour with RMI, depicted in Fig. 3.21, before the server can start accepting calls from client processes, *stubs* and *skeletons* have to be generated.

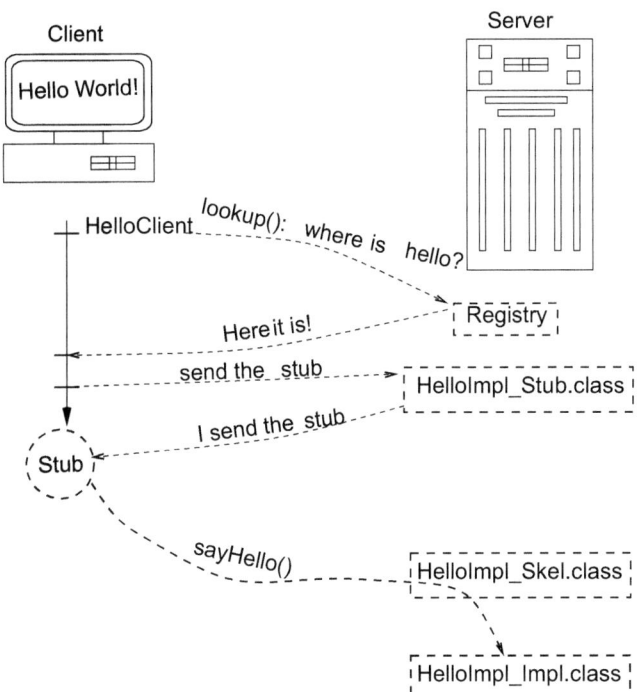

Fig. 3.21 Representation of the execution of `HelloImpl.class`

Each `stub` contains the signature[17] of the methods included in the remote interface. A `skeleton` has a similar function to the `stub`, but on the server side. The `stubs` and `skeletons` are automatically generated on the server, from the source code of the `HelloImpl` class in the previous example. Subsequently, the execution of the name server *(registry)* of the RMI protocol need to be started and then launch the program on the server with the `java` command `HelloImpl&`.

3.6.2.3 Semantics of Parameter Passing in RMI

The Java programming language passes by reference the parameters referring to local objects (not *by copy*) by default, when a method is invoked. If the same parameter passing policy were maintained in remote method calls, the language would be of little use for developing distributed programs, since it would be quite inefficient to pass by reference objects that contain only data, such as *arrays*, records or strings. For example, if an *array* of 100,000 elements is passed by reference to a remote method, 100,000 accesses to a remote machine will be needed to fully complete that array processing in the client machine.

To avoid the serious dysfunction in the Java language that would result from using only parameter passing by reference in remote method calls, the following passing policy has been established when programming with RMI:

1. Actual parameters of primitive types to a call are passed by copy.
2. Object parameters are passed either by reference or by copy, depending on the interface implemented by the object's class:

    (a) `Remote interface`: by reference.
    (b) `Serialisable interface` (but not *Remote*): by copy (i.e., serialized and copied).

Consequently, Java allows the coexistence of two different semantics for calling the methods of the same object-variable. The syntax for invoking methods is the same, regardless of whether the method is included in the interface of a local object or a remote object with respect to the caller. As a consequence of this semantic duality in the calls, the execution of a method can produce different results, depending on whether the call is local or remote, as shown in Fig. 3.22, which shows a program with different outputs depending on whether the `Stack` object is local or remote:

```
stack1=3
stack2=3
```

---

[17] Name, list and type of parameters of a function or method.

3.6 High-Level Mechanisms for Programming Distributed Systems

```
public interface RemoteStack extends
  Serializable{
    public int[] dump() throws RemoteException{
      return cells;
    }
}
public class RMI_test{
  static RemoteStack s1= null;
  static RemoteStack s2= null;
  --stack objects created in different contexts
  s1.insert(3);
  s2.insert(3);
  int[] stack1= s1.dump();
  int[] stack2= s2.dump();
  stack1[0]= 100;
  stack2[0]= 100;
  System.out.println("stack 1:"+s1.top());
  System.out.println("stack 2:"+s2.top());
  }
}
```

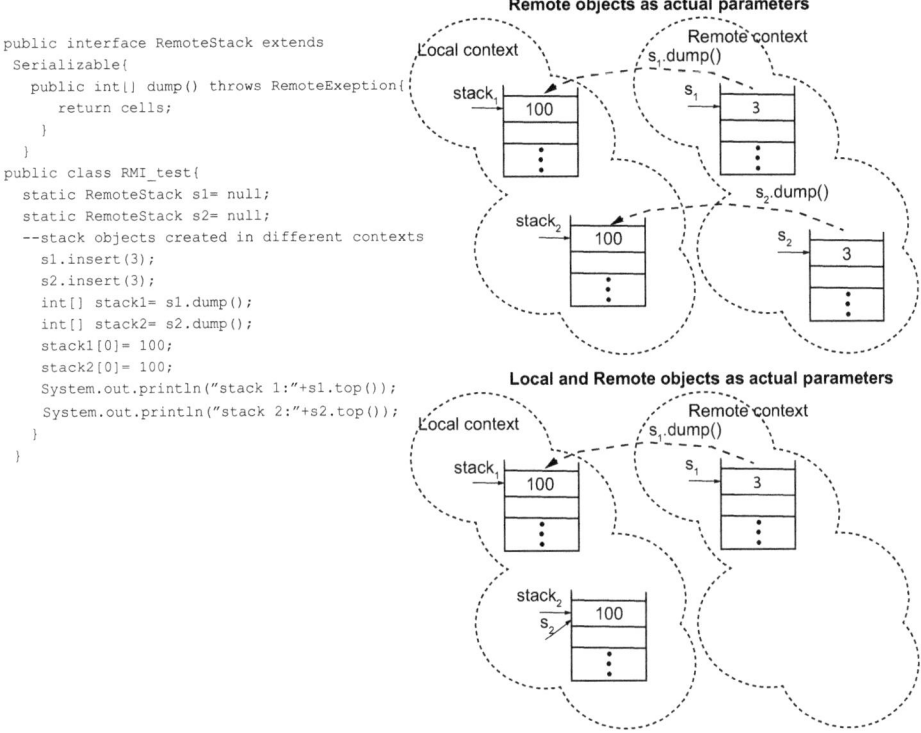

Fig. 3.22 Parameter passing by reference and copying in Java

For the first case that considers the stack objects (s1, s2) as remote. However, if the second object s2 is considered as local, the program would produce a different output:

stack1=3
stack2=100

Since Java allows polymorphism when programming with RMI, there is no way to find out statically, e.g., by following all references to objects in a program, whether an object will be local or remote when its methods are invoked during the execution of the program in which it is used. As a result, it is often difficult to program correct distributed applications, considering only the semantics of parameter passing in remote method invocations, as currently defined in the Java programming language.

3.6.3 Model Based on Synchronisation with Rendezvous

Remote invocations are concurrent programming language statements that allow a process to call a procedure owned and controlled by another process. In this case, the remote procedure is a sequence of one or more instructions that can be located anywhere in the code of a process. Unlike the *remote procedure call* (or RMI) model, the calling process and the process to which the remote procedure belongs can be executed by the same processor.

Each remote invocation is implemented by defining an *entry point* and one or more *acceptance statements* associated with that entry. The Ada programming language [5] follows this model and is the most widely used remote invocation programming language to date.

3.6.3.1 Definition of Entry Points

Within a process, an entry point is defined for each of the procedures that can be called from other processes. Inputs are defined in the context of the process to which they belong. One process making a call has to indicate the entry point and the process that owns it. Unlike the *remote procedure call* based model, entries are not global system names; therefore, they can be repeated in different processes.

While a channel could have at most one process waiting for communication, entry points can have any number of pending calls. Data are communicated between processes through the parameters declared at entry points; so a notation similar to the declaration of parameters in procedures is followed. Since the client processes call the entry points, it is no longer necessary to declare separate channels between each client and the server process. Now, for each entry point, there is a queue that handles calls from the processes on a first-come, first-served basis, implemented as a FIFO queue, to contain the pending calls from the client processes.

In the following code, the circular buffer of `Producer/Consumer` process interaction paradigm is programmed using the following implementation template:

```
Process Buffer;                     Process Producer;              Process Consumer;
  entry deposit(data: data.type);     begin                          begin
  entry take(var x:data.type);          while true do                  while true do
end;                                      begin                          begin
                                            x:=GenerateData();             Buffer.take(data);
                                            Buffer.deposit(x);             ConsumeData(data);
                                          end;                           end;
                                        enddo;                         enddo;
                                      end;                           end;
```

No order of declaration of remote procedures is specified; therefore, processes can make mutual calls from their entry points, even with circularity, as shown below, without deadlocks:

```
              Process A;             Process B;
                entry E;               entry F;
              begin                  begin
                B.F;                   A.E;
              end;                   end;
```

3.6.3.2 Communication by Rendezvous

The code corresponding to the remote invocation call will be executed when the process that has the input defined accepts that call, unlike the remote procedure or method called during an RPC or RMI, respectively, which will be executed immediately, similarly to handling the procedure calls in sequential programming languages.

3.6 High-Level Mechanisms for Programming Distributed Systems

For each entry point, at least one accept statement must be declared in the code the process that owns it. The execution of the accept statement during the execution of the owner process body blocks until the call to the entry point occurs. If at any time during the execution of the process there were several calls waiting in the queue of the entry point, the first of these would be attended to, according to a FIFO order.

Therefore, the accept statement, within the the body of the process that defines the entry point, is executed only when both processes (the one accepting and the one calling the entry point) are ready to hold the communication:

```
Process A;                    Process B;
   entry E(...);                 ...
begin                         begin
   accept E(...);                A.E(...);
end;                          end;
```

The communication established between process *A* and process *B* is called *rendezvous*. This mechanism belongs to a synchronous model of communication between independent concurrent processes. Before and after the *rendezvous* both processes run asynchronously.

The syntax of the accept statement varies if global variables are allowed to be shared between concurrent processes. In this case, the accept statement needs to define a differentiated instruction block which will be executed atomically (similarly to monitor's procedures), i.e., a code area within each *accepting* process that is guaranteed to be a critical section as it may contain expressions that access global variables of the program.

3.6.3.3 Non-deterministic Selection

In the remote invocation model, a process can define multiple entry points, with the execution of different alternatives associated with these entry points managed by an `accept` command similar to a guarded command-protected message reception. Based on this mechanism, we can define a variant of the CSP alternative command, the `select` command that includes a guard (`when` condition) and an atomic block of instructions (`do ... enddo`) for each alternative of the non-deterministic selection.

The introduced non-deterministic selection follows the following syntax given by the BNF description below:

```
<nondeterministic.selection>::=
   select <alternative.select>{ or <alternative.select>}* end select
<alternative.select>::=
   when <guard> do <statement.list> enddo [<block>] | else [<block>]
<guard>::=
   <condition>;<accept.statement> | <condition>;<input.order>| <condition>
```

The semantics of the `select` instruction can be summarised as follows:

- Each block preceded by a `when` clause is called an alternative and can be considered equivalent to a CSP guarded command.

- The section of code text from the reserved words: `when` to `do` is referred to as guard of the alternative, as it may include a logical condition, which must evaluate to true for a rendezvous to occur or for a message to be received by the accepting process.
- Each guard may include a message receive operation (similar to the CSP guarded command) or an `accept` statement (acceptance of a rendezvous).
- The `receive` communication operations reference other processes within the concurrent program ($process_i$), and each of these operations must be associated with a local variable ($variable_i$), where the received value will eventually be stored.

Conditions in the guards are evaluated and state changes in the sending processes occur when the program's control flow reaches a `select` instruction. At that point the guards are evaluated, and one alternative is selected for execution. The determination of the alternative to be executed follows the following protocol:

- If there are executable `guards` (those whose conditions evaluates to true) with an input statement, the alternative corresponding to the earliest started `send` operation in a client process is selected (this behaviour sometimes promotes fairness).
- If there are executable `guards` but none of them has an input statement or an accept command, one of them is selected non-deterministically.
- If there is no executable guards but there are *potentially executable* `guards` (i.e., the condition evaluates to true but the communication is delayed), the `select` command causes the containing process to suspend and wait until one of the processes named in the command initiates a send operation or calls `accept`, at which point the corresponding alternative is selected.
- If there are neither executable nor potentially executable `guards`, no alternative guard can be selected, resulting in an error or the raising of an exception.

Example 3.10 In this example, we present a distributed program for resource allocation based on a Client/Server. To avoid server blocking caused by passive clients, we employ an alternative command structure combined with a set of guarded commands. The following outline can be considered a skeleton to implement a program of a server that allocates resources on demand from client process, adaptable to different programming languages. Each client processes requests a resource from a central *pool* of these, uses it, and then releases it once finished. For this example, we assume the following functions are preprogrammed:

- `get_unit()` and `return_unit()`, which find and return units to some data structure
- `list_insert()`, `list_remove()` and `list_empty()`, which are list management functions

```
Process Server;
--Type of operation = enum (ACQUIRE, RELEASE);
  const int N= 20;
  const int MAXUNITS= 5;
  entry free (enum, int index, int unitid)
  entry request (enum, int unitid);
begin
 int avail= MAXUNITS, index;
 int op_kind, unitid;
 while true do     --some initialisation code
   select          --receives request from process ID= 'index'.
    for index:=1 to N when true;
     accept request(ACQUIRE, index) do
       if (available > 0) --if resources available
          then begin
            avail:= avail - 1;
            unitid = get_unit();            --get resource ID
            send(reply(index, unitid));     --constructs reply
          end;
          else -- (avail == 0)         --if there are no resources left
            list_insert (pending, index);   --save request
     enddo;
or for index:=1 to N) when list_empty (pending));
    accept free(RELEASE, pid, unitid)do   --if pending requests
      avail:= avail+1;                -- returns a resource to the pool
      return_unit (unitid);
    enddo;
or when not list_empty(pending)do     --no requests pending
    index:= list_remove (pending)     --gets PID of the first request
       send(reply(reply(index,unitid));--replies, sending resource
    enddo
  end select;
 end do;
Process Client [i:1..N]
   int unit;
begin
    -- call a resource request
    Server.request(ACQUIRE, i);
    receive(reply(this_i,unit));
     --use the resource
    Server.free(RELEASE, i, unit);   --release if no longer needed
end;
```

3.7 Exercises

This section addresses synchronization and communication challenges encountered in programming distributed algorithms and applications, particularly where parallelism relies on the characteristics of multi-computer systems. Several classic concurrent programming problems are explored, such as "producers and consumers"—with the buffer implemented as a remote server process—"the cigarette smokers problem," "the dining philosophers problem," and "the cannibals problem," all adapted to their distributed versions with non-deterministic message selection based on the order of message arrivals. Some of the proposed problems have been solved using pseudocode based on the MPI message passing interface [42], while others use a notation based on Ada *accept* statements [5] and the non-deterministic selection command proposed by CSP [24] and Ada.

3.7.1 Solved Exercises

Exercise 3.1 In a distributed system, six client processes need to synchronise in a specific way to perform a certain task, such that the task can only proceed when three processes are ready simultaneously. To achieve this, each client sends a request to a controlling process responsible for managing the resource and then waits for a response before proceeding. The controlling process is responsible for ensuring proper synchronisation by receiving and counting incoming requests. The first two requests are not immediately answered, causing the sending processes to suspend while waiting for a response. Upon receiving the third request, the controller simultaneously unblocks all three waiting processes by sending responses. Then, once the three requesting processes are unblocked (after receiving a response), the controller resets its counter and cyclically repeats the same protocol for subsequent requests. The code of the client processes is shown below. Clients use secure synchronous sending to make their request and wait with synchronous receive operations before performing the task collaboratively with the other client processes.

The *Controller* process is to be programmed in pseudocode to correctly implement the synchronisation protocol for the following client processes:

```
(1)  Process client[i : 0..5];
(2)  begin
(3)    while true do
(4)      begin
(5)        send(request, Controller);
(6)        receive(permit, Controller);
(7)        -- Perform_group_task();
(8)      end
(9)  end
```

Solution In this problem, the six *client* processes must synchronize to cyclically perform a group task. Therefore, sending a request to the `Controller` process must block the client process that made the request until it receives permission from the controller to continue. To achieve this, a synchronous message passing `Ssend()` operation must be used in instruction (4) of the client processes. This operation ensures that the send call only returns when the corresponding receive operation is explicitly invoked by the controlling process. Since the task is only to be performed when three `client` processes are ready, the first two client requests are held without response, and the third one will trigger the unblocking of all three waiting client processes, an action that is initiated within the `Controller` loop between lines (11)–(20).

3.7 Exercises

```
(1)  Process Controller;
(2)  begin
(3)    while true do
(4)      select
(5)        for i:= 0 to n-1 do
(6)          when (counter < 3) Receive(request,client[i]) do
(7)            counter:= counter+1;
(8)            received[i]:= true;
(9)        enddo;
(10)     or when counter = 3 do
(11)        for j:= 0 to n-1 do
(12)          if received[j] then
(13)            begin
(14)              Send(permit, client[j]);
(15)              received[j]:= false;
(16)            end;
(17)        counter:= 0;
(18)        enddo;
(19)     end select
(20)   enddo;
(19) end;
```

Exercise 3.2 In a distributed system, three producer processes continuously generate integer values and send them to a buffer process that temporarily stores them in a local array of four integer cells before forwarding them to a consumer process. In turn, the buffer process, serving equally to the rest of the processes, operates as follows:

(a) It sends integers to the consumer process whenever its local *array* contains at least two available elements.
(b) It accepts submissions from producers as long as the *array* is not full but does not accept that any producer can write to the *buffer* twice consecutively.
(c) The code for the producer and consumer processes is provided below, assuming the use of synchronous message-passing operations.

```
Process Producer[i: 0..2];            Process Consumer;
  var datum: integer;                   begin
  begin                                   while true do begin
    while true do begin                     Receive (data, Buffer);
      datum:= Produce();                    Consume(data);
      Send(datum, Buffer);                end
    end                                 enddo
  enddo                               end;
end;
```

Program the behaviour of the *Buffer* process in pseudocode, using a selective wait construct to implement the required synchronisation with the processes that demand or send data.

Solution The Buffer process must ensure that it accepts data from producer processes only if the buffer is not full, but none of the producers will be able to insert data twice in the buffer. To achieve this, the `Buffer` stores the index of the last producer that sent data in the `last` variable. This value is used in the receive operation at instruction (9) to prevent receiving a message from a producer whose index matches the current value of `last`. In the alternative branch of the selective wait at instruction (14), the `Buffer` process sends previously received data (up to four items) to the consumer process as long as there are at least two items left in it.

```
(1)  Process Buffer;
(2)    var tam:integer:=4; data:integer; counter:integer:=0;
(3)        buf: array[0..tam-1] of integer;
(4)        last:integer:= -1;  --last write in the buffer
(5)    begin
(6)      while true do
(7)        select
(8)          for i:= 0 to 2 do
(9)            when (counter < tam and last!= i) Receive(&data,Producer(i)) do
(10)             last:= i;
(11)             buf[counter]:= data;
(12)             counter:= counter+1;
(13)         enddo;
(14)   or    when counter >= 2 do
(15)             counter:= counter - 1;
(16)             Send(&buf[counter], Consumer);
(17)         enddo;
(18)       end select;
(19)    enddo;
(20)  end;
```

Exercise 3.3 Assume a producer process and three consumer processes sharing a buffer of limited size equal to B positions. Each element deposited by the producer process must remain in the buffer until it has been consumed by all three consumers. Each consumer must remove data from the buffer in the same order in which it was deposited, although each may consume data at a different rate. For example, while one consumer has removed elements 1, 2 and 3, another consumer may have removed only element 1. As a result, the fastest consumer can be up to B elements ahead of the slowest one.

Write pseudocode to implement the behaviour of a process implementing the above-mentioned *buffer* process following the described interaction scheme. The solution should use a selective wait to handle synchronization.

Solution The first step is to identify the information that must be represented, followed by addressing the synchronization issues. One possible implementation of the buffer involves maintaining, for each consumer process, an output pointer and a count of the number of elements remaining in the buffer to be consumed (see Fig. 3.23):

3.7 Exercises

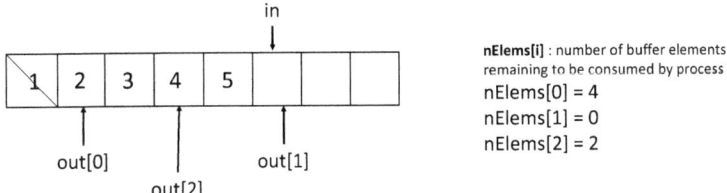

Fig. 3.23 Buffer allowing the removal of each inserted element to three consuming processes

It is important to note that each item inserted by the producer must be consumed by all three consumers before it can be removed from the buffer. For example, in the figure, item 1 in the first position of the *array*, has been removed by all three consumers at that point in execution.

The three consumers, with indexes 0..2, remove the data from the *buffer* in FIFO order, i.e., the order in which the items were deposited in the buffer. In order to implement this, the *array* nElems is used, where each position *(nElems[i])* corresponds to consumer *i* and holds the number of elements in the buffer that consumer *i* has yet to consume. This value can be calculated as the difference between the positions of the producer's insertion pointer *(in)* and the consumer's extraction pointer *(out[i])*.

Because each consumer has its own independent *out[i]* pointer, the fastest consumer may have consumed up to *B* more elements than the slowest one at one point during the execution.

```
(1) Process Buffer;
(2) var B:integer; --buffer capacity
(3)     data: integer; buf: array[0..B-1] of integer;
(4)     in:integer;--insertion pointer in the buffer
(5)     out:array[0..2] of integer:= (0,0,0);--withdraw pointers
(6)     nElems: array[0..2] of integer:= (0,0,0);
(7) begin
(8)   while true do
(9)     select
(10)      for i:= 0 to 2
(11)      when nElems[i] != 0 do
(12)        Send(&buf[out[i]], Consumer[i]);
(13)        out[i]:= (out[i] + 1) mod B;
(14)        nElems[i]:= nElems[i] - 1;
(15)      enddo;
(16)    or when (nElems[0] != B and nElems[1] != B and
(17)        nElems[2] != B) Receive(data, Producer) do
(18)        buf[in]:= data;
(19)        in:= (in + 1) mod B; --circular queue
(20)        for j:= 0 to 2 do
(21)          nElems[j]:= nElems[j] + 1;
(22)      enddo;
(23)    end select
(24)   enddo
(25) end;
```

Exercise 3.4 A group of cannibals share a pot that holds M_0 missionaries. When a cannibal wants to eat, they serve themselves directly from the pot, unless it is empty. If the pot is empty, the cannibal signals the cook and waits until the cook has refilled the pot with M_0 new missionaries. The cannibal and cook processes are to be coordinated using message passing. A pot process will be implemented that includes a selective waiting construct that serves requests from both the cannibals and the cook in order to maintain the required synchronisation, considering the following requirements:

(a) The solution must avoid process deadlock.
(b) Cannibals may eat as long as there are missionaires in the pot.
(c) The cook will only be woken up when the pot is empty.

Solution Unlike Exercise 2.18, in this case, the processes do not share memory, so there is no global variable to track the number of missionaries remaining in the pot. Therefore, the proposed solution is to program a third `Pot` process that maintains the count of remaining missionaries and handles requests from the cannibal processes. The number of cannibal processes can be arbitrary, provided it is defined before compilation, because program must schedule a corresponding number of alternatives, one for each cannibal process. The `Pot` process is also in charge of sending a message to the `Cook` to wake up and refill the pot with missionaries when it becomes empty.

3.7 Exercises

```
Process Cannibal(i:0..2);
 begin
   while true do begin
     Ssend(request,Pot);
     --waiting to serve one missionary
     eat();
     end
   enddo
 end;

Process Cook();
 var
   confirms:bool:=true;
   fill:integer:=0;
 begin
   while true do begin
     --sleep waiting for request to fill in
     Receive(fill,Pot);
     --filling the pot
     fill:= 0;
     Send(confirms,Pot);
    end
   enddo
 end;

Process Pot();
 var
   counter:integer:= M₀;
   fill: integer:=1;
   is_full: bool:= true;
 begin
   while true do
     select for i:=0 to 2
       when counter > 0 Receive(request, Cannibal[i]) do
         counter:=counter-1;
       enddo;
 or    when counter = 0 do
         Send(fill,Cook); is_full:= false;
         Receive(is_full, Cook);
         counter:= M₀;
       enddo
     end select;
   enddo
 end;
```

Exercise 3.5 Consider a set of N processes, $P[i]$ (where $i = 0, \ldots, N-1$), arranged in a ring topology such that each process sends messages to the next one in the ring (with the last sending to the first), forming a unidirectional communication pattern. Each process has a local value stored in its local variable my_value. The goal is to compute the sum of all local values distributed across the processes using the following algorithm: Each process sends the value of its local variable to the next process in the ring and receives a value from the previous one. After performing all iterations, every process will have computed the total sum of the local values originally held by all processes.

Program in pseudocode the distributed processes that compute this sum using the SPMD style and using synchronous send and receive operations, according to the following template:

```
Process P[ i: 0..N-1 ];
  var my_value: integer:=…;--arbitrary value(=i in the figure, for example)
     sum: integer:= my_value; --sum initialised to my_value
  begin
       for j:= 0 to N-1 do begin
          ... enddo
  end;
```

Solution For N processes, the algorithm requires each process to perform a series of iterations to circulate their local values (stored in the variable value) around the ring in a single direction. In the first iteration, each process sends its local value to the next process in the ring and simultaneously receives a value from the previous process. It then updates the sum of its local value by adding the received value. In the following iterations, each process sends the value received in the previous iteration to the next process and, at the same time, receives a new value from the previous process. This newly received value is again added to the local sum. After a total of $N - 1$ iterations, each process will have received and accumulated the local values from all other processes, resulting in every process holding the total sum.

Figure 3.24 shows a case of execution with $N = 4$. In each step processes send their local value to the next one in the ring and receive the local value from the previous. After three steps

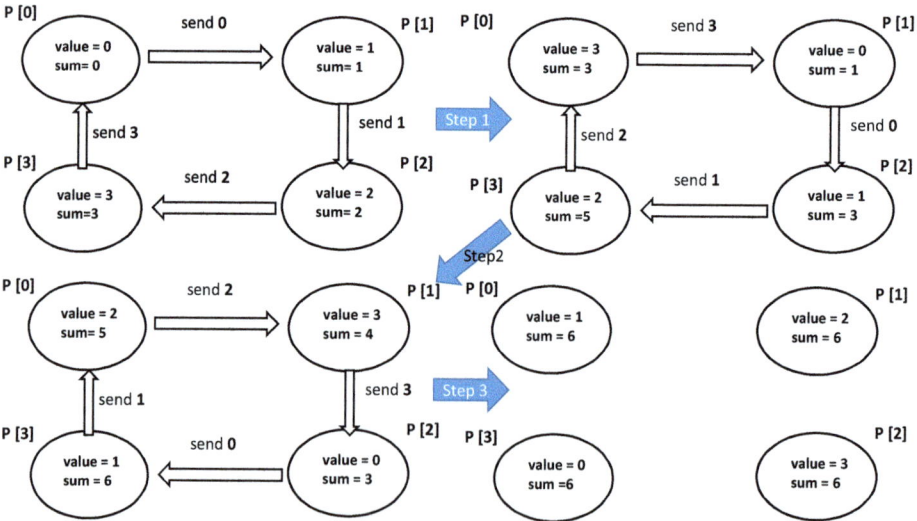

Fig. 3.24 Distributed algorithm for calculating the sum of numbers according to a ring process connection topology

($N-1$), all processes have calculated the same result: $sum = 6$, which corresponds to the total sum of all initial local values. Therefore, the structured code of the processes is as follows:

```
Process P[i:0..N-1];
  var value: integer:=...; -- could be a generated value
                           -- randomly
    sum, temp: integer; sum:= value;

    for j:= 0 to N-2 do
      if (i mod 2) = 0 then
        begin
          Send(value, P[(i + 1) mod N]);
          Receive(value, P[(i - 1) mod N]);
          sum:= sum + value;
        end
      else begin
        temp:= value;
        Receive(value, P[(i - 1) mod N]);
        sum:= sum + value;
        Send(temp, P[(i + 1) mod N]);
      end
    enddo
end;
```

Exercise 3.6 Consider a tobacconist's shop with three smokers and one tobacconist. Each smoker continuously rolls and smokes cigarettes. To roll a cigarette, a smoker needs three ingredients: tobacco, paper and matches. Each smoker has an inexhaustible supply of only one of these ingredients (one has only paper, another only tobacco and the third only matches). The tobacconist, on the other hand, has an unlimited supply of all three ingredients.

In each cycle, the tobacconist randomly places two of the three ingredients needed to roll a cigarette, unblocks the smoker with the third missing ingredient and then waits. The selected smoker can be easily obtained by a function `generates_ingredients()`, which returns the index `0, 1` or `2` of the chosen smoker. The selected smoker picks up the two ingredients from the counter, signals the tobacconist to continue, rolls a cigarette, and smokes for a while. Once notified, the tobacconist, places two random ingredients back on the counter, and the cycle repeats.

Program in pseudocode a distributed solution, which uses asynchronous (reliable) message sending and synchronous message receiving. Implement `Tobacconist` process and three smoking processes: `Smoker(i)` (with $i \in \{0,1,2\}$).

Solution To solve this, we will assume that the smoker processes use synchronous message receiving operations waiting to receive the missing ingredients required to begin smoking. The `Tobacconist` process places two ingredients on the counter by randomly selecting one ingredient to withhold and unblocks the smoker who possesses the third ingredient. After sending the message, it blocks and waits for confirmation from the smoker.

Each smoker process simulates taking the two ingredients from the counter using a `Take()` procedure. The smoker who receives the message (via a synchronous receive operation) unblocks the `Tobacconist`, rolls a cigarette, since they already possess the third ingredient, and smokes.

```
Process Tobacconist;
  var
    ingredient:integer;
    confirmation:boolean:= TRUE;
  begin
   while true do
     begin
       ingredient:=generates_ingredients();
       Ssend(confirmation, Smoker[ingredient]); --i-smoker with i-ingredient
     end
    enddo
  end;

Process Smoker[i:0..2];
  var
    confirmation:boolean;
  begin
   while true do
     begin
       Receive(confirmation, Tobacconist);
       take();
       smoking();
     end
   enddo
  end;
```

Exercise 3.7 In a distributed system, a large number of client processes frequently use a shared resource, and it is desired that as many processes as possible can use it simultaneously. To achieve this, clients send requests to a controlling process to gain access to the resource and wait for a response before proceeding (see the client processes code). When a client finishes using the resource, it sends a release request to the controller and waits for confirmation before exiting. The controlling process ensures proper synchronisation by imposing a special restriction for superstitious reasons: there must never be exactly 13 processes using the resource at the same time.

```
Process Cli[ i: 0....n ];              Process Controller;
  var                                    begin
    req_use: integer:= +1;                while true do
    req_release: integer:= -1;             select
    permission: integer:=....;                      ...—controller commands
  begin                                    end select
   while true do                          enddo
     begin Send(req_use, Controller);    end
      Receive(permission, Controller);
      Use_resource();
      Send(req_release, Controller);
      Receive(permission, Controller);
     end
   enddo;
  end;
```

3.7 Exercises

Program in pseudocode the behaviour of the `Controller` process, using a selective wait construct to implement the required synchronisation between processes. It is possible to use a `select for i:=... to...` statement to define multiple branches of the selective statement that share the same code, depending on the value of the index i.

Solution The solution to the problem involves implementing a selective statement in the `Controller` process to handle client requests for using or releasing the shared resource. Each request will carry a value: (+1 and −1) to request access and release the resource, respectively. The algorithm also uses the value of the variable $pending(-1, 0, +1)$ to indicate whether there is a pending release (−1), a pending use request (+1), or no pending request (0). The variable `customer_e` stores the identifier of the client process that is waiting to use or release the resource.

```
1) Process Cli[i:0..n];
(2)    var req_use: integer:= +1;
(3)        req_release: integer:= -1;
(4)        permission: integer;
(5)    begin
(6)      while true do begin
(7)        Send(req_use, Controller);
(8)        Receive(permission, Controller);
(9)        Use_resource();
(10)       Send(req_release,Controller);
(11)       Receive(permission,Controller);
(12)     end
(13)   enddo
(14) end;
(1) Process Controller;
(2)    var permission, request: integer;
(3)        counter:integer:=0;     --number of clients using the resource
(4)        pending:=0;             --value:1,0,-1
(5)        customer_e:integer;     --number of customer if pending≠ 0
(6)    begin
(7)      while true do
(8)        select for i:=0 to n
(9)          when Receive(request, Cli[i]) do
(10)           if (counter+request+pending=13)
                 then begin
(11)               pending:= request;
(12)               customer_e:= i;
(13)           end
(14)           else begin
(15)             counter:=counter+request+pending;
(16)             Send(permission, Cli[i]);
(17)             if (pending ≠ 0)
(18)               then begin
(19)                 Send(permission,Cli[customer_e]);
(20)                 pending:= 0;
(21)               end
(22)           end
(23)       end select;
(24)     enddo
(25) end;
```

There can never be more than one pending request (*release* or *use*) at any given time, because if a new request arrives while another is still pending, both requests can be processed together within the block of code spanning lines (14)–(21). Notably, if the condition (10): *counter+request+pending=13* holds true, then *pending=0* for sure. A second request (if it has the opposite sign) will cancel out the previous one, or if both have the same sign, the count will skip over the value *13*; therefore, resulting in a *counter* value of either *12* or *14*, thereby respecting the constraint.

Exercise 3.8 Simulate a general semaphore with a synchronous message passing between processes, employing rendezvous-style synchronization.

Solution

```
Operation wait(s)::
  entry semaphore_wait(int s);

 begin
    accept semaphore_wait(s) when (s>0) do
      s:= s-1;
    enddo;
 end;

Operation signal(s)::
  entry semaphore_signal(int s);

 begin
  accept semaphore_signal(s) do
    s:= s+1;
  enddo;
 end;

Process P[i:1..N]::
   var
     int s:=s0 ;
   begin
     semaphore_wait(s)
     --s0 processes can advance this far
     semaphore_signal(s);
   end;
```

The entry point acceptance operation in the implementation of the *semaphore_wait()* operation allows execution of its associated block, i.e., specifically, the decrement of the protected variable s, only when the condition $s > 0$ is satisfied. This ensures that the invariant of the *general semaphore* $(0 \leq s \leq s0)$ is maintained.

Exercise 3.9 Simulate the synchronous message-passing communication mechanism (rendez-vous) using semaphores.

Solution

```
S₁,S₂,mutex;
    inic(S₁ ,0); inic(S₂ ,0); inic(mutex,1);
Process A(i: integer);          Process B(j: integer);
 begin                           begin
   wait(S₁);                       signal(S₁);
   wait(mutex);                    wait(S₂)
   -- instruction block          end;
   -- of the "rendezvous"
   signal(mutex);
   signal(S₂);
 end;
```

If the process that is executed first is $B(j)$, it is suspended when executing the operation $wait(S_2)$ if the value of S_2 value remains equal to "0", as set during its initialisation operation $(inic(S_2,0))$. The only operation that can increment its value is $signal(S_2)$, which is called only after executing $wait(S_1)$, and this, in turn, depends on how many times $signal(S_1)$ has been invoked. Therefore, it must hold that the number of times $signal(S_2)$ has been executed is less than or equal to the number of times $wait(S_1)$ has been executed, and it must also hold that $0 \leq \#wait(S_1) \leq \#signal(S_1)$. This implies that the implementation works correctly only if at most one instance of process $A(i)$ is active assuming the initialisation of the semaphores S_1 and S_2 indicated above. The logic guarantees that only one $A(i)$ process can execute the rendezvous instruction block, and only one process $B(j)$ is unblocked afterwards, and each of them can then execute asynchronously until the next rendezvous. A bidirectional implementation of rendezvous ensures that both processes must reach the synchronization point before either can proceed. Neither process continues until the other is also ready. Once synchronization is achieved, both processes perform their respective actions. The following code demonstrates this behavior:

```
semaphore S1 := 0;    -- Signal from A to B
semaphore S2 := 0;    -- Signal from B to A
Process A;                              Process B;
begin                                   begin
  -- Preparation before rendezvous        -- Preparation before rendezvous
  signal(S1); -- Notify B that A is ready signal(S2); -- Notify A that B is ready
  wait(S2);   -- Wait for B to be ready   wait(S1);   -- Wait for A to be ready
  -- Critical section after rendezvous    -- Critical section after rendezvous
  Perform_Action_A();                     Perform_Action_B();
end;                                    end;
```

Exercise 3.10 A train has N available seats, and passengers board the train one at a time, each occupying a single seat. If all seats become occupied or if no new passengers board within 30 min., then the train departs for a journey, after which N seats become available again. A journey is only made if at least one seat is occupied. If the train has no passengers on board, it remains at the station indefinitely, waiting for someone to board.

Assume the following conditions in order to be able to simulate the operation of the train as a concurrent process *(Train)*, and the passengers as individual processes, the following conditions are assumed. Synchronization between the train and passengers is handled using a rendezvous-style mechanism:

(a) There is an unlimited number of passengers, and each passenger makes only one journey. The `Passenger[i]` process terminates its action after completing the journey it boards.
(b) The train operates continuously on a circular route with only two stations.

You are asked to solve the problem for both the single-train and two-train scenarios. In the two-train case, if a passenger attempts to board train and cannot (due to it being full or unavailable), the passenger waits for one minute, then attempts to board the second train. If boarding is still not possible, they wait another minute and retry the first train, repeating this cyclical behaviour until successfully boarding and completing a journey on one of the two trains.

Solution

```
Process Train[i:1..2];
   const MAX= N0;
   N= free_seats;
   var
      free:=N;
   entry arrives();
   begin
   while(true) do
     select
       when(free>0)accept arrives()do
         free:= free - 1;
       enddo;
     or when free = 0 do
         --Make a trip
         sleep(random%MAX);
         free:= N;
       enddo;
     or when free < N and delay 30*60 do
         --Make a trip
         free:= N;
       enddo;
     end select;
   enddo;
   end;
```

```
Process Passenger[i: 1..N];
   --solved for the case of 1 single train
   begin
   while(true) do
      Train[1].arrives();
   enddo;
   end;


Passenger Process[j: 1..N]

--solved for the case of 2 trains
begin
while(true) do
   select
      Train[1].arrives();
      return;
   or delay 1*60; --wait for 1 minute
   end select;
   select
      Train[2].arrives();
      return;
   or delay 1*60; --wait for 1 minute
   end select;
enddo;
end;
```

In the two-train case, the selective wait statement can also be applied on the side of the process demanding the service, i.e., the process invoking `accept arrives()`. In this case, non-deterministic selection is used as a polling mechanism within the client process, allowing it to check whether the server process is ready to accept the call without requiring the client to remain suspended indefinitely. In addition, a timeout clause `delay T(seconds)` can be programmed in the `select` construct of the client process, specifying a maximum amount of time the client will wait for the acceptance of that call by the server.

Exercise 3.11 There are *N* client processes that interact with the server process that simulates the functioning of a single ATM. Clients withdraw money by invoking the operation `withdraw(num_client,amount)`, which requires the client to identify themselves and specify the amount to withdraw. The ATM responds by dispensing the requested amount if the client has sufficient balance in their account and there is enough cash left in the ATM. Otherwise, the ATM denies the request. To deposit money in the ATM, the operation `deposit(num_customer,amount)` is accepted. For this, the client process simply needs to identify themselves and indicate the amount to deposit. It is assumed that each client number uniquely corresponds to a bank account, meaning each client is associated with exactly one account.

Implement the cashier's functionality as a server process and using selective wait. Assume that each customer initially has a balance of 10 units in their account, and the ATM starts with 1000 units of available cash to fulfill withdrawal requests. When the ATM depletes its units of cash reserve, it will not be able to serve any type of customer request (`withdrawals` or `deposits`) for a period of 1 h. After this delay, the ATM is automatically restocked with another 1000 units of cash. It is important to note that customer deposits do not increase the physical cash reserves held by the ATM, as deposited funds and ATM cash are managed separately within the bank's internal systems.

Solution

```
Process Cashier() ;
  entry withdraw(customer_account_number:integer,var amount:integer);
  entry enter(customer_account_number: integer amount:integer);

  const num_clients= C0;
  var
     cash: integer:=1000;
     account, balance: array[1..num_clients] of integer;
  end;
begin
  while(true) do
   select --N alternatives replicated, 1 for each customer account
    for i:= 1 to N do
     when (cash>0) accept withdraw(account[i], amount) do
      if (cash>=amount and balance[account[i]]>=amount)
        then begin
          cash:= cash - amount;
          balance[account[i]]:= balance[account[i]] - amount;
        end
        else amount:=-1; --failure of the withdrawal order
     enddo; --end of the acceptance order
or   for i:=1 to N do
     when (cash>0) accept enter (account[i], amount) do
        balance[account[i]]:= balance[account[i]]+amount;
     enddo; --end of the acceptance order
or   when (cash=0) do
        delay 60*60;--no service in 1 hour
        cash:=1000;
     enddo
   end select
  enddo;
 end;
```

Exercise 3.12 Program a distributed version of the Dining Philosophers problem, assuming the following components: five fork processes, whose behaviour is that of a binary semaphore, five concurrent philosopher processes, each representing a philosopher's behavior, and a room functioning as a semaphore initialized to a limit on the number of philosophers allowed to enter the dining room at once. This prevents deadlock by ensuring that not all philosophers can simultaneously hold one fork and wait indefinitely for the second. The behaviour of a philosopher process is an indefinite cycle that repeats the following actions: think, enter the room, take his left fork, take his right fork, eat, drop left fork, drop right fork and leave the room.

Solution

```
Process Fork[i: 0..4];
  type
    num_philosopher= 0..4;
    entry take(i:num_ philosopher)
    entry release(i:num_ philosopher)
  begin
    while(true) do
      begin
        accept take(i:num_ philosopher);
        accept release(i:num_ philosopher);
      end
    enddo;
  end;
Process Philosopher[i : num_philosopher];
begin
  while (true) do
    begin
      Room.enter();
      Fork[i].take(i);
      Fork[(i + 1) mod 5].take(i);
      sleep(random() mod MAX_T_EAT);
      Fork[i].release(i);
      Fork[(i + 1) mod 5].release(i);
      Room.exit();
      sleep(random() mod MAX_T_THINK);
    end
  enddo;
end;
```

```
Process Room;
  var
    int occupancy:=0;
    entry enter();
    entry exit();
  begin
    while (true) do
      select
        when occupancy<4 accept enter() do
          occupancy:= occupancy+1;
        enddo;
      or accept exit() do
          occupancy:= occupancy - 1;
        enddo;
      end select;
    enddo;
  end;
```

From the point of view of correctly modelling resource sharing, the *Room* process behaves like a general semaphore initialised to the value '4', with the invariant: $0 \leq \#enter - \#exit \leq maximum.occupancy \land maximum.occupancy = 4$. This allows up to four philosophers to successfully invoke the `enter()` operation before subsequent calls are blocked. As a result, no more than four philosopher processes can simultaneously attempt to take the two fork resources they need to eat. This prevents a scenario leading to a deadlock situation for the philosophers. Each fork process, on the other hand, acts as a binary semaphore, satisfying the invariant: $0 \leq \#take - \#release \leq 1$. This ensures that a fork cannot be acquired more than once without being released first by the philosopher who originally took it.

Exercise 3.13 Assume that a data processing centre has two printers A and B, which are similar, but not identical. There are three types of client processes: those that require printer A, those that require printer B, and those that can use either printer. Each of the

3.7 Exercises

client processes, of any type, will execute a printer request operation followed by a printer release operation. A server process is responsible for managing printer allocation through rendezvous-based synchronization. It is assumed that one client process cannot hold a printer forever, at some point in the future, the client will release the resource.

Solution

```
Process Printer_Server;                                 or accept release(type: printer_type) do
 type printer_type= (A,B);                                 if type=A then
  entry assignA();                                            freeA:=true
  entry assignB();                                         else freeB:=true;
  entry assign(var type: printer_type);                    enddo;
  entry release(type: printer_type);                     end select;
 var                                                    enddo;
  freeA,freeB:boolean:=(true,true);                    end;
 begin
  while(true) do
   select
     when freeA accept assignA() do
       freeA:=false;
     enddo;
   or when freeB accept assignB() do
       freeB:=false;
     enddo;
   or when (freeA or freeB)
         accept assign(var type:printer_type) do
       if(freeA)then
        begin
          freeA:=false; type:=A;
        end
       else begin
          freeB:=false; type:=B;
        end
     enddo;
```

Two additional entry points could have been included in the server process, such as `release_A()` and `release_B()`, to explicitly release printers A and B, respectively, upon acceptance. However, implementing the server in this way would neither improve its efficiency nor enhance the clarity of the client process code. We have chosen to define a single entry point, with a parameter indicating the type of printer being released by the client process.

Exercise 3.14 In a distributed system, three *Producer* processes communicate with a *Printer* process responsible for displaying on-screen a string with the data generated by the producer processes. Each producer process (`Producer[i]` with $i \in \{0, 1, 2\}$) continuously generates its corresponding integer i and sends it to the `Printer` process. The `Printer` process receives data from the producers and prints them to the screen using the `print(integer)` procedure, generating a string of digits as output. However, the processes must be properly synchronised to ensure that the output meets the following constraints: (a) consecutive digits of the same kind (0 or 1) are not allowed, (b) the total number of digits 0 or 1 printed at an instant cannot exceed twice the number of digits 2 printed so far. When a producer sends a digit that violates either of these constraints, the producer will be blocked waiting for the synchronous send `Ssend` to complete. The pseudocode of the producer processes is shown below, assuming non-buffered blocking operations, i.e., synchronous message passing is used.

Solution To ensure that the `Printer` accepts *0* and *1* alternately, a condition is programmed in each corresponding alternative: $last01 \neq 0$ and $last01 \neq 1$, in the two alternatives provided to receive the numbers *0* and *1*, respectively. These conditions prevent two consecutive occurrences of the same digit. The other condition of the first two alternatives ensures the number of 0s and 1s printed so far does not exceed twice the number of 2s printed. The number *2* is received unconditionally in the third alternative because its occurrence is not subject to any constraints relative to the other numbers in the string.

```
Process printing;
 var
   num_01:integer:= 0;
   num_2:integer:= 0;
   last_01:integer:=-1;
   number:integer;
 begin
   while true do
     select
       when=(num_01<2*num_2 or num_2=0) and last_01!=0 Receive(number, Producer[0]) do
         Print(number);
         num_01:= num_01 + 1;
         last_01:= number;
       enddo;
     or when ((num_01 < 2*num_2 or num_2 = 0) and last_01 != 1) Receive(number,Producer[1]) do
         Print(number);
         num_01:= num_01 + 1;
         last_01:= number;
       enddo;
     or when true Receive(number,Producer[2]) do
         Print(number);
         num_2:= num_2 + 1;
         last_01:= -1;
       enddo;
     end select;
   enddo;
 end
```

Exercise 3.15 In a distributed system, there is a vector of *n* identical processes that continously send integer values to a receiver process in an infinite loop, which prints them. The receiver process prints each value it receives. However, if at any point there are no incoming messages, the receiver must block for 10 seconds using `sleep_for(10)`, and then print "no message", before checking again for messages. This behavior simulates energy-saving by processing messages in 10-second intervals. Indicate why this problem cannot be solved using `Receive` or `Ireceive` operations. However, it can be done with selective waiting `(select)` to fulfill the above requirements.

```
Process Sender[i : 1..n]              Process Receiver()
var datum : integer;                   var datum: integer;
begin                                  begin
  while true do                          while true do
    begin                                  ......
      datum := Produce();              end
      send(datum, Receiver);
    end
end
```

3.7 Exercises

Solution This problem cannot be solved by programming the receiver process with a `Receive(...)` or `Irecv(...)` order because neither provides a mechanism to determine whether there are pending messages to receive, and we need to know this to decide whether the receiver should *sleep* for 10 s or execute the receive operation. In the first case, using a `Receive(...)` operation would block the process indefinitively until a message arrives, and that is not what we want, and in the second case, initiates a non-blocking receive and returns immediately, before it starts receiving data, letting it undetermined whether such data has already been sent.

In contrast, the `select` statement supports guards without an input statement, and these guards will only be considered for execution in cases where the executable input command guards have no pending sends to match them, which allows us to know that channels are empty, therefore making the receiver sleep for 10 s.

```
Process Receiver;
  var datum:integer;
begin
   while true do
     select
--If there are messages from the sender, read one out of 1..n
       for i:=1 to n when true Receive(datum, Sender[i])do
          print ("received: ", datum);
       enddo
       else begin
   --will run if no executable guard is immediately available
          print ("no message: I'm sleeping");
          sleep(10);
       end
     end select;
   enddo
end;
```

Exercise 3.16 In a system with *N* sender processes, each sender safely transmits a single message to a receiver process. Each message contains an integer with the sender process number. The receiver process must print the number of the sender process that initiated the sending in the first place. That sender must terminate, while all other sender processes remain blocked.

```
Process Sender[i: 1..N]
  begin
    Ssend(i,Receiver);
  end
Process Receiver;
  var winner: integer;
  begin -- calculate winner
     print "The first submission was made by:....", winner;
  end;
```

For each of the following cases, provide a reasoned explanation of whether or not it is possible to design a solution to this problem. If so, write a possible solution:

(a) The receiving process exclusively uses one or more calls to `Receive`.
(b) The receiving process exclusively uses reception, through one or more `Ireceive` calls.
(c) The receiving process uses only `select`, through one or more guarded command statements.

Solution

(a) When using blocking message reception with `Receive(...)` message operations, the problem cannot be solved because the order in which such messages are sent does not necessarily coincide with the order in which are received. Although each `(Receive(datum, Sender[i]))` targets a specific sender process, the receiver has no way to determine which sender initiated communication first.

(b) This scenario is even worse than (a) because now the order in which messages are received in the receiving process does not necessarily coincide with the order in which calls to the `Ireceive(datum, Sender[i])` operation are executed. As in (a), the order of message reception does not coincide with the order of sending, which is still unknown, so it is not possible to know which process has sent first.

(c) In this case, a solution is possible. The `select` statement allows the receiver to wait for input from multiple sender processes and, when multiple messages are pending, it selects the one whose send operation was initiated first. This makes it feasible to reliably determine which sender was the first to initiate communication and to receive and process its message accordingly.

```
Process Receiver;
  var num, winner: integer;
begin
    select
      for i:=1 to N when true Receive(num, Sender[i]) do
        winner:= i;
      enddo
    end select
    print("The first process that sent is the number: ", winner);
end;
```

Exercise 3.17 Suppose we have N similar concurrent processes:

```
Process P[ i: 1..N ];
   ....
   begin
      ....
      c:= ProduceCharacter();
      Send(c, P[j]);
   end
```

Each process produces $N-1$ characters (through $N-1$ calls to the `ProduceCharacter` function) and sends each character to the other $N-1$ processes. In addition, each process must print all characters received from the other processes (the order of printing is indifferent). The following is requested:

(a) Describe with justification whether or not it is possible to solve this problem using exclusively the `Ssend` operation. If it is possible, provide a solution.
(b) Write a solution using `Send` and `Receive`.

Solution

(a) It is not possible to solve the problem using only the `Ssend()` (synchronous send) operation because all processes would reach a deadlock situation. Each process would be blocked in its first operation (`Ssend()`) call, waiting for another process to receive the message. However, since all processes are simultaneously blocked on sending, none are available to receive, resulting in a deadlock.
(b) In contrast, if non-blocking `Send` and `Receive` operations are used, the solution is simple:

```
Process P[ i: 1..N ];
var c: char;
begin
-- start all sendings
for j:= 1 to N do
  if i != j then begin
    c:= ProduceCharacter();
    Send(c, P[j]);
  end
 enddo;
-- make all receptions
for j:= 1 to N do
  if i != j then begin
    Receive(c, P[j]);
    print(c);
  end
 enddo
end;
```

Exercise 3.18 Write a new solution to Exercise 3.17 in which the order in which characters are printed matches the order in which those characters were sent, using a `select` statement to receive the messages.

Solution Now, unlike in Exercise 3.17, the `select` statement provides a simple solution. It is sufficient to execute the `select` statement $N-1$ times within a loop. In each iteration, ensuring that messages are received, and thus printed, in the same order they were sent, as required by the problem statement.

```
Process P[i : 1..N];
var c : char;
begin
  --Start all sendings
  for j := 1 to N do
  if i != j then
    begin
      c := ProduceCharacter();
      Send(c, P[j]);
    end
  enddo;
    -- Do all receptions
  for j := 1 to N - 1 do
    select
      for k := 1 to N when i != k
        Receive(c, P[k]) do
        print c;
      enddo
    end select
  enddo;
end;
```

Exercise 3.19 Reconsider Exercise 3.17, in which all processes send to all others. Now each data item to be produced and transmitted is a block of bytes with many values (e.g., an image that may be several megabytes in size). The data is represented using the `BlockType` data type. And generated using the `ProduceBlock` procedure. If b is a variable of type `BlockType`, then a call to `ProduceBlock(b)` generates and writes a sequence of bytes into b. Instead of printing the data, it must now be consumed with a call to `ConsumeBlock(b)`.

We assume that each process will run on a separate computer, each with enough memory to hold up to N blocks simultaneously. However, the message passing system (*MPS*) may not have enough memory to hold the $(N-1)^2$ in-transit messages that could exist simultaneously at any time using the original solution. Under these conditions, if the *MPS* runs out of memory, it will delay the execution of the `Send` operations, potentially causing deadlock due to all processes becoming blocked. To avoid this, non-blocking and insecure send operations, `Isend`, should be used instead. Write a solution using `Isend` that guarantees the same order of receiving messages as in Exercise 3.17.

Solution It should be noted that using the operation `Isend` in the sending processes does not guarantee the safety property regarding the integrity of the transmitted data blocks, so the following protocol would not be considered correct:

3.7 Exercises

```
Process P[i: 1..N];
  var block: Block_Type;
  begin
--Start all sendings
  for j:=1 to N do
    if i!= j then begin
       ProduceBlock(block);
       Isend(block, P[j]);
    end;
--All receptions are now done
  for j:= 1 to N do
    if i != j then begin
       Receive(b, P[j]);
       ConsumeBlock(b);
    end
end;
```

This program is flawy because the second call *toProduceBlock()* could overwrite the first block sent, which may still be pending transmission by the *MPS*. Additionally, the process could terminate before the data has been fully sent or received. To prevent this unsafe data delivery, a safer approach is to use an *array* of N blocks, ensuring the array fits within the memory of each process and that the process does not terminate until all the sends have completed.

A second and *safe* version of the solution can be seen in the following code. It uses an array of N blocks and guarantees that no process terminates until all pending sending operations have been initiated (though not necessarily completed):

```
(1)Process P[i: 1..N];
(2) var block: array[1..N] of Block_Type;
...--N-1 blocks shall be used for sending and 1 block for receiving.
(3) status: array[1..N] of Block_Type;
--for controlling when processes end
(4) begin
--Start all sendings
(5)  for j:=1 to N do
(6)    if i!= j then begin
(7)      ProduceBlock(block[j]);
(8)      Isend(block[j], P[j], state[j]);
(9)    end;
     enddo;
(10)for j:= 1 to N-1 do
--All receptions are now made, in the block[i].
(11)  select
(12)    for k:= 1 to N when i!=k do
(13)      Receive(block[i], P[k])
(14)      Consume(block[i]);
(15)    enddo
(16)  end select
     enddo;
--Wait for all sendings to be completed
(17) for k:= 1 to N do
(18)   if i != k then
(19)     Wait_send(state[k]);
(20) enddo;
(21)end;
```

Each array entry holds a block produced in step (7), and the sending in step (8) is started, using non-blocking `Isend()` operations, without waiting for the send to complete. Once sending has started for all of them, the process can start receiving and consuming the block received in each alternative (12)–(16) of the `select` instruction, just as in the previous version of the program.

In the block of instructions (17)–(20), the process `P[i]` waits for all pending send operations, initiated in steps (5)–(9) to complete before terminating. This ensures that all blocks remain in the process's local memory until they are read by the *MPS*. To achieve this, an array of state variables is used with, each of which is associated one of the `Isend` operations from step (8).

Exercise 3.20 In the three previous exercises, each process `P[i]` must wait to receive a data block from each of the other processes `P[j]: (i≠j)`, then consumes that block and proceeds to the next sender (possibly in varying orders). This implies that an already started but pending sending cannot be completed until the receiver has consumed the previous blocks. As a result, the message passing system (*MPS*) could accumulate a large number of in-transit messages, consuming substantial memory due to delayed receptions.

Write a solution in which each process first initiates all its sends and receives, and then only starts consuming the received blocks once all the receives have been completed. In this way, all messages can be transmitted and processed as concurrently as possible. Assume that each process can store at least *2N* blocks in its local memory and that the order in which blocks are received or consumed is indifferent.

Solution In this case, our solution is to use the non-blocking `Ireceive` operation instead of `Receive` or `select` command. Each process uses a `block_rec` array to receive blocks from the other processes, in addition to the `block_env` array used for sending. The code for each process `P[i]` begins by initiating all receive operations to improve the chances that send operations from other processes will immediately find a matching receive. Once all receives have been initiated, the process proceeds to initiate its sends. Consumption of the received blocks occurs when all receives have been completed, ensuring that no block is consumed prematurely. As before, none of the `P[i]` processes can terminate until all sends have been completed.

```
Process P[i: 1..N];
  var block_env: array[1..N] of Block_Type;
      block_rec: array[1..N] of Block_Type;
      env_status: array[1..N] of Guard_Type;
      rec_status: array[1..N] of Guard_Type;
begin
 --Start all receptions
   for j:=1 to N do
     if i!= j then
        Ireceive(block_rec[j], P[j], rec_status[j]);
   --Produce and initiate all the sendings
 for j:= 1 to N do
     if i != j then begin
        Produce_Block(block_env[j]);
        Isend(env_block[j], P[j], env_status[j]);
     end;
   --Wait for all receptions to be finished
 for j:=1 to N do
     if i != j then Wait_recv(rec_status[j]);
       --Consume all blocks
 for j:= 1 to N do
     if i != j then Consume_Block(block_rec[j]);
   --Wait for all the sendings to be completed
 for j:=1 to N do
     if i != j then Wait_send(env_status[j]);
end;
```

Exercise 3.21 To create the sorting algorithm known as pipesort, a process structure is required. This structure consists of a pipeline of parallel processes through which an unordered sequence of elements is passed. The result is a sorted sequence.

Each process can store one element, representing the highest-value character it has received so far. In each process, one character is received, compared with the stored character, and then either sent to the next stage if it is smaller, or retained if it is larger.

In Fig. 3.25 we observe a moment during the execution of the sorting process where the first three stages of the pipeline each have one character stored, while the fourth stage remains empty. If character 'b' is received on the input channel, the first process compares the received value with the stored value, then sends the smaller of the two to its output channel and stores the larger. The second process sends the character 'b' to its output channel and keeps the character 'c' stored in its stage. The third stage sends its stored character, 'a', to its output channel and stores the character it just received, 'b'. The fourth stage stores the character 'a' received from its input channel.

Program the algorithm to sort a string of characters using a pipeline sort. This will require a generic process containing the code of any stage of the pipeline. In addition, to program an input process to read the characters from keyboard and display them on the screen.

Solution The process architecture, with the process inout, to obtain the MPI program is shown in Fig. 3.26.

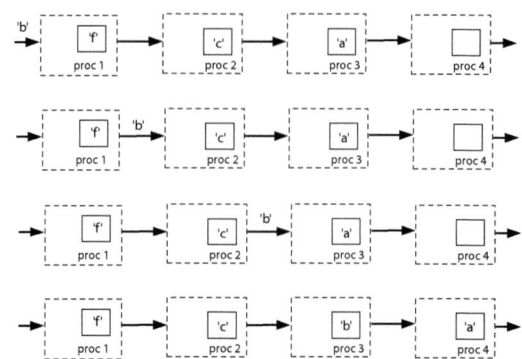

Fig. 3.25 Pipeline sort

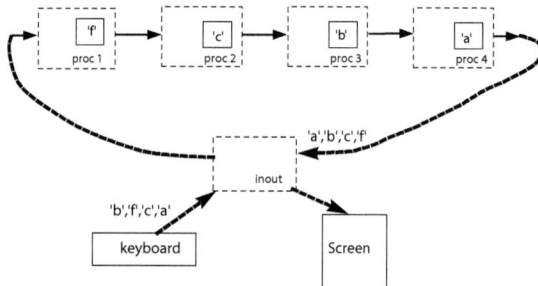

Fig. 3.26 Representation of an instant in the execution of pipeline sorting and the associated input-output process

To ensure the correct termination of the distributed algorithm, i.e., without losing data or blocking processes, we introduce two special integers that serve as "tokens" to change the mode of operation of the program: "99" which signals the (ordered) termination of all processes of the program and "98" which initiates the draining of all stages of the pipeline, moving data towards the last process without immediately displaying it. After sending the token "98", each stage retrieves the initial value ("0"), which must be smaller than any integer intended to be sorted and transmitted during the algorithm's operation. The length of the character string to be sorted must match the number of stages in the pipeline.

3.7 Exercises

The solution code can be seen in Fig. 3.27; instructions (18)–(29) are executed after successfully copying a number equivalent to `"size"` characters from `"line"` buffer into the `"string"` in instruction (15). The `string[i]` elements, converted to integers (20) are sent (23) to the next stage in the pipeline. It is crucial that the last stored character

```
(1) int main(int argc, char *argv[]) {
(2)    int rank, size, value;
(3)    MPI_Status status;
(4)    char* string; char line[128]; bool end = false;
(5)    int x = 0; int aux = 0;int value = 0;int cont = 0; -- New variables
(6)    MPI_Init(&argc, &argv);
(7)    MPI_Comm_rank(MPI_COMM_WORLD, &rank);
(8)    MPI_Comm_size(MPI_COMM_WORLD, &size);
(9)    while (!fin) {
(10)     if (rank == 0) {                           --process with rank=0
(11)       printf("New string>"); fflush(stdout);
(12)       if (fgets(line, sizeof (line), stdin) == NULL)
(13)         fprintf(stderr, "input error");
             --the length of the chain has to coincide with the number of stages
(14)       string = (char*) malloc(sizeof (char) *size);
(15)       if (sscanf(line,"%size[^size]",string) < 1){
(16)         end=true; x= 99;       --Transmit the completion value
                                    --with MPI the adequate message passing function
(17)         MPI_Send(&x,1,MPI_INT,rank + 1,0, MPI_COMM_WORLD); }
(18)       else{              -- 'size' characters have been copied into the chain
(19)         for (int i = 0; i < size; i++) {
(20)           x = (int) (string[i] - 48);
(21)           if (x > value) {
(22)             aux = value; value = x; x = aux;}
(23)           MPI_Send(&x, 1, MPI_INT, rank + 1, 0, MPI_COMM_WORLD);
(24)         }
(25)         MPI_Send(&value, 1, MPI_INT, rank + 1, 0, MPI_COMM_WORLD);
(26)         value = 98;
(27)         MPI_Send(&value, 1, MPI_INT, rank + 1, 0, MPI_COMM_WORLD);
(28)         value = 0;
(29)       }
(30)     else{ --code running processes rank<>0
(31)       MPI_Recv(&x, 1, MPI_INT, rank - 1, 0,MPI_COMM_WORLD, &status);
(32)       if (x == 99 || x == 98) {
(33)         if (x == 99)fin = true;
(34)         else value = 0;
(35)         if (rank < size - 1)
(36)           MPI_Send(&x, 1, MPI_INT, rank + 1, 0, MPI_COMM_WORLD);
(37)       }
(38)       while (!fin) {
(39)         MPI_Recv(&x, 1, MPI_INT, rank - 1, 0, MPI_COMM_WORLD, &status);
(40)         if (x > value) {
(41)           aux = value; value = x;
(42)           x = aux;}
(43)         if (rank < size - 1) {
(44)           MPI_Send(&x, 1, MPI_INT, rank + 1, 0, MPI_COMM_WORLD);}
(45)         else if (x != 99 && x != 98 && x != 0)
(46)           cout << x << endl;
(47)         if (value == 98 || value == 99) {
(48)           if (rank < size - 1)
(49)             MPI_Send(&value, 1, MPI_INT, rank + 1, 0, MPI_COMM_WORLD);
(50)           if (value == 99) fin = true;
(51)           else value = 0;
(52)         }--endif
(53)       }--end while
(54)     }—end else
(55)   }--end while(!fin)
(56) MPI_Finalize();
(57) return 0;
(58) }--end main
```

Fig. 3.27 Pipeline sorting and input/output scheduling programmed with MPI

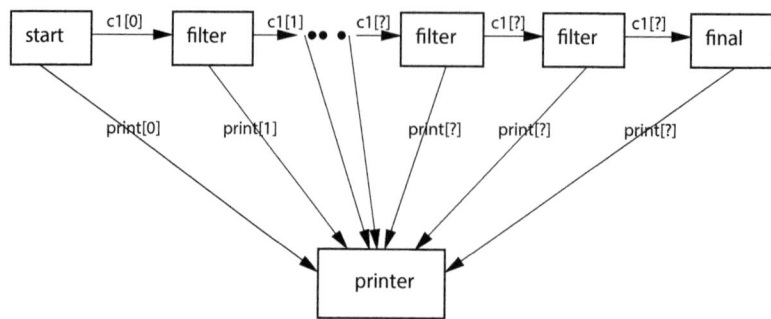

Fig. 3.28 Process pipeline that generates the first *N* prime numbers

is also transmitted (17) because if it is omitted, the program would not work correctly. After sending all characters, the integer *"98"* is sent (27) to trigger the unloading of stages.

The instructions in block (30)–(37) define the code executed by the pipeline processes where `rank<>0`. The first integer is assigned to the variable *x*, specific to the current stage; it must be skipped because it does not belong to the string to be sorted.

The final loop programmed in (38)–(53) is used to filter out all integers representing characters from the string, including the *"98"* end-of-string token, before moving on to process the next string entered from the keyboard. The program terminates when an empty string is entered. As a result, the process with `rank==0` sends (17) the global termination token = *"99"* to all other processes.

Exercise 3.22 The objective now is to program a distributed version of the famous *Erastotenes sieve* method for obtaining the first *N* prime numbers. A pipeline network of concurrent processes, as illustrated in Fig. 3.28, will be used to generate the first *N* prime numbers.

To program this solution, assume that a constant `nLimit` is known and is greater than or equal to the *Nth* prime number. The *start* process generates the first prime number (2) and sends it to the *printer* process, which prints it. The start process generates the next prime (3) and sends it to the first *filter* process, and continues sending subsequent odd numbers (5, 7, 9, and so on).

Solution Each `filter` process begins by receiving an initial value, a *prime* number, from the previous process and then forwarding it to the next process in the pipeline, according to its position. Afterwards, the filter process continuously receives numbers, not necessarily *prime*, from the previous process. If a received number is divisible by the `prime` value initially stored, the filter process discards it. If the number is not divisible, it forwards it for further *filtering*.

3.7 Exercises

```
(1) int main(int argc, char *argv[]) {
(2)    int rank, size, flag, prime, origin;
(3)    MPI_Status status;
(4)    MPI_Request request;                        -- New variables
(5)    int x = 0; int i = 0; int value = 0;int NUM_LIMIT = 100;
       bool fin= false,
(6)    MPI_Init(&argc, &argv);
(7)    MPI_Comm_rank(MPI_COMM_WORLD, &rank);
(8)    MPI_Comm_size(MPI_COMM_WORLD, &size);
(9)    if (rank == 0) {
(10)     x = 2; i=1;                               --first prime number
(11)     MPI_Send(&x,1,MPI_INT,size-1,0,MPI_COMM_WORLD);
(12)     while (!fin) {
(13)       i += 2;
(14)       x=i;
(15)       MPI_Send(&x,1,MPI_INT,rank + 1,0, MPI_COMM_WORLD);
(16)       MPI_Irecv(&x, 1, MPI_INT,size-1, MPI_ANY_TAG, MPI_COMM_WORLD, &request);
           if (x==size-1) fin= true;
(17)     }--end while
(18)   }--end if
(19)   else{                                       -- rank<>0
(20)     if (rank == size - 1) {                   --printer process' code
(21)       while(i<size-1) {
(22)         MPI_Probe(MPI_ANY_SOURCE,0, MPI_COMM_WORLD,&status);
(22)         MPI_Recv(&prime,1,MPI_INT, MPI_ANY_SOURCE, MPI_ANY_TAG,
             MPI_COMM_WORLD, &status);
(23)         origin= status.MPI_SOURCE;
(24)         i++;
(25)         cout << "Prime number " << prime << prime << " received from process "
             << source << endl;
(26)       }--end while
(27)       cout << "The printer process exits" << endl;
(28)       MPI_Bcast(&i, 1, MPI_INT, size-1, MPI_COMM_WORLD);
(29)     }
(30)     else{                                     --filter process' code
(31)     --if rank is size-2 , it is the final process
(32)       MPI_Recv(&value,1,MPI_INT,rank-1,0,MPI_COMM_WORLD,&status);
(33)       MPI_Send(&value,1,MPI_INT,size-1,0,MPI_COMM_WORLD);
(34)       while(!fin){
(35)         MPI_Recv(&x,1,MPI_INT,rank-1,0,MPI_COMM_WORLD,&status);
(36)         if (rank < (size - 2))
(37)           if (x%value!=0) --x is prime number candidate
(38)             MPI_Send(&x,1,MPI_INT,rank+1,MPI_COMM_WORLD);
(39)           MPI_Irecv(&x,1,MPI_INT,size-1,MPI_ANY_TAG,
               MPI_COMM_WORLD,&request);
(40)         if (x==size-1)
(41)           fin= true;
(42)       }—end while
(43)     }—end else
(44)   } -end else
(45)   MPI_Finalize();
(46)   return 0;
(47) }--end main
```

Fig. 3.29 A program that generates the first N prime numbers with MPI

The `final` process in the pipeline receives the last prime number, sends it to the `printer` process and then discards all subsequent numbers it receives, before terminating. The `printer` process must be programmed to continuously receive `prime` numbers from the N processes in the pipeline and display them on the screen as they arrive (Fig. 3.29).

Exercise 3.23 Write in MPI a program consisting of a server process, called `collector()`, and m `generator()` processes. The server process prints sets of up to m integers on different lines of the screen. The integers are randomly generated in a distributed manner by the generator processes, sent to the collector process and printed asynchronously by each generator process. Additionally, the integers must be printed by the collector process in the order in which they were received. The program must also introduce a degree of non-determinism in how numbers are received by the collector. The collector process will perform a number of iterations defined by $N = (min\{n_1, n_2, \ldots, n_m\})$, where n_i, (for $i = 1, \ldots, m$) represents the number of iterations performed independently by each of the m generator processes. Initially, the collector receives the number of iterations each generator will perform and calculates its own number of iterations as the minimum of these values.

In summary, at each iteration, the `collector` waits until a time T to receive a message containing an integer from each `generator` process. It then prints all the numbers received for that iteration. Once the `collector` finishes its N iterations the whole program enters the termination phase, where the collector receives any pending messages from the generators before terminating itself and the entire program.

Solution In the proposed solution, each generator process begins by generating a random integer in the range `1..rangeIter` and send this value to the `collector` process. This number determines the number of iterations to be performed by each of the `generator` process. In each iteration, the generator processes have the following behaviour:

(a) Wait for an arbitrary amount of time (to introduce non-determinism).
(b) Generate a random integer in the range `1..rangeNum`, ensuring that no duplicate values are produced across iterations.
(c) Send the generated number to the collector.
(d) Print the generated number locally, and proceed the next iteration. At the end of its iterations, each generator sends a termination token (`value = "0"`) to the collector to signal completion.

The `collector` process must be programmed with a loop of N iterations, which will correspond to the minimum number of iterations obtained in each of the generator processes at the start of its execution.

At the end of its iterations, the `collector` shall use non-blocking receive operations and `MPI_Irecv()` because the order in which the generators will terminate is not known.

3.7 Exercises

```
(1) int main(int argc, char *argv[]) {
(2)   int rank, size, flag, source, number, iteration;
(3)   MPI_Status status;
(4)   MPI_Request request;                          -- New variables
(5)   char* x; long int alea= 0; bool equal= true;
(6)   int rangeNum = 0;
(7)   int rangeIter = 0;
(8)   int num_generators = 1000;
(9)   int min_iterations = 1000;
(10)  int iter_collector = 1;
(11)  int** number_gen_in_i;
(12)  int* iter_g;
(13)  int* gen_numbers;
(14)  int current_iteration = 0;
(15)  char line[128];
(16)  int nIterations = 0;
(17)  int MAX_SEC = 15;
(18)  int seconds;
(19)  MPI_Init(&argc, &argv);
(20)  MPI_Comm_rank(MPI_COMM_WORLD, &rank);
(21)  MPI_Comm_size(MPI_COMM_WORLD, &size);
(22)  srand(time(NULL));
(23)  if (rank == 0) {                              --collector process code
(24)    cout << "Maximum number of the range [1..rangeNum]-> ";cin >> rangeNum;cout << "\n";
(25)    num_generators = size - 1;cout << "Actual number of generators-> " << num_generators
            << " (1 processor is reserved for the collector).\n";
(26)    for (int i = 1; i <= num_generators; i++) {
(27)      MPI_Send(&rangeNum, 1, MPI_INT, i, 0, MPI_COMM_WORLD);
(28)      MPI_Send(&rangeIter, 1, MPI_INT, i, 0, MPI_COMM_WORLD);
        }                                           --end for
(29)    iter_g = (int*) malloc(sizeof (int)*num_generators);
(30)    number_gen_in_i = (int**) malloc(sizeof (int *)*num_generators);
(31)    cout << "Iterations to be performed received at the collector: ";
(32)    for (int i = 1; i <= num_generators; i++) {
(33)      MPI_Recv(&number, 1, MPI_INT, i, 0, MPI_COMM_WORLD, &status);
(34)      iter_g[i - 1] = number;
(35)      cout<<"g"<< i << "=" << number << " - ";
(36)      number_gen_in_i[i - 1] = (int*) malloc(sizeof (int)*number);
(37)      if (iter_g[i - 1] < min_iterations)
(38)        min_iterations = iter_g[i - 1]; }       --endfor
(36)    iter_collector = min_iterations*num_generators;
(37)    cout << "Receiving data at the collector: ";
(38)    while (current_iteration < iter_collector) {
(39)      MPI_Recv(&number_gen_in_i[current_iteration % num_generators]
             [ current_iteration / num_generators], 1,
               MPI_INT, current_iteration % num_generators + 1, 0,
               MPI_COMM_WORLD, &status);
(40)      cout << "- Receives " <<
               number_gen_in_i[current_iteration % num_generators]
               [current_iteration / num_generators] <<" from the generator "
               << current_iteration % num_generators + 1 << " in its iteration " <<
               current_iteration / num_generators + 1 << endl;
(41)      current_iteration++;
(42)    }-end while
(43)    cout << "Ending collector process: ";
(44)    for (int i = 1; i <= num_generators; i++) {
(45)      MPI_Irecv(&x, 1, MPI_INT, i, 0, MPI_COMM_WORLD, &request);
          cout << "- Generator " << i << " has performed " << iter_g[i -1]
               << " iterations " << " " << "\n";
        }                                           --endfor
(46)  else {                                        --generating process code
(47)    srand(time(NULL));
(48)    MPI_Recv(&rangeNum, 1, MPI_INT, 0, 0, MPI_COMM_WORLD, &status);
(49)    MPI_Recv(&rangeIter, 1, MPI_INT, 0, 0, MPI_COMM_WORLD, &status);
(50)    nIterations = random() % rangeIter + 1;
(51)    gen_numbers = (int*) malloc(sizeof (int)*nIterations);
(52)    MPI_Send(&nIterations, 1, MPI_INT, 0, 0, MPI_COMM_WORLD);
(53)    for (int i=0;i<nIterations;i++) {
(54)      seconds = random() % MAX_SEC + 1;
(55)      sleep(seconds);
(56)      equal=true;
(57)      while (equal){
(58)        number = random() % rangeNum + 1;
(59)        equal = false;
(60)        for (int j = 1; j <= i && !equal; j++)
(61)          if (number == number_gen[j-1]) equals = true;
(62)      }-endwhile
(63)      MPI_Send(&number, 1, MPI_INT, 0, 0, MPI_COMM_WORLD);
(64)      gen_numbers[i] = number;
(65)    }                                           --endfor
(66)    x = 0; --finalise
(67)    MPI_Send(&x, 1, MPI_INT, 0, 0, MPI_COMM_WORLD);
(68)  }                                             --end else
(69)  if (rank == 0) {                              --terminate all processes
(70)    cout << "Terminate the collector" << ".\n";
(71)  } else {
(72)      cout << "End generator number: " << rank << ".\n";
(73)  }
(74)  MPI_Finalize();
(75) return 0;
}
```

The collector is programmed to execute *N* iterations, where *N* is the minimum number of iterations received from all generator processes at startup. In instructions (24)–(25), the user is prompted to input two parameters: the maximum integer value that can be generated *(1..rangeNum)* and the maximum number of iterations for each generator *(1..rangeIter)*. The total number of generator processes is calculated as the value of *MPI_size* minus one, reserving one process for the collector itself. In instruction block (26)–(28), the collector sends this configuration data to all generator processes. Then, in block (29)–(30), it allocates memory for two arrays to store the per-generator values for the maximum number and iteration count.

During each iteration of the collector process, the following steps are performed:

(a) It receives an integer from each *generator* using a blocking *MPI_Recv()* call (line 39).
(b) It prints the data received from each generator (40).

Once the collector completes its predefined number of iterations *(>= iter_collector)*, it switches to using non-blocking receive operations *(MPI_Irecv()* on line 45) to handle any remaining messages and prints the number of iterations completed by each generator process before entering the termination phase (69)–(71) in which each terminated process identifier is printed.

The generator processes are each initialized with a maximum integer value they are allowed to generate, as well as the number of iterations they must perform (48)–(49). In each iteration, the generator operates asynchronously, performing the following steps: waits for a random amount of time (55), generates a random number that must be different from the previously generated values (57)–(62), sends the generated number to the collector (63), saves the generated number and move on to the next one (64)–(65). After completing all its iterations, each generator sends the termination token *(value = "0")* to the collector process *(rank = "0")* to signal completion (line 67).

Exercise 3.24 Write an MPI-based simulation of a card game involving a variable number of players and a single dealer (*croupier*).

The game is divided into a series of hands, which are fixed in number and defined at the start of the program. In each hand, every player draws a card from a shared deck. Each card has a value ranging from 1 to 5 points. After drawing a card, the player reveals it to the croupier and places a bet which includes wagering money and predicting the total sum

3.7 Exercises

of the card values drawn by all players in that hand. Players with a correct sum prediction earn and the winner of the hand collects the money wagered by the other players.

The program must display which hands were won by each player. The following assumptions will guide the implementation:

Players: Each player generates two random integers (1 to 5). The first number represents the card value, while the second is the bet value. The two values must be different. If they are the same, one of them must be re-generated. Once valid values are obtained, the player sends three messages to the croupier:

1. The card value drawn by the player.
2. The player's predicted total sum of all card values drawn in the current hand.
3. A request message asking the croupier whether the player won the hand.

The croupier processes each hand by checking for incoming messages from players containing their card values. Players are only allowed to place bets once all card values for that hand have been received. After collecting the necessary information, the croupier determines which player won the hand. It is essential that the croupier receives card values before processing bets and winner requests.

The program must also generate a table showing which players won each hand.

Solution After performing the initialisation of program variables (1)–(17), the `Croupier` process *(rank= 0)* sends the number of hands to be played to all player processes (21). The *croupier* then executes a loop (33) that runs once for each hand in the game. For each hand, the *croupier* performs the following sequence of actions: it receives the card values drawn by each player (line 38), then receives the bets placed by each player (line 42); next, it calculates the total number of points for the current hand (lines 48–50), determines the winner(s) of the hand (lines 51–58), and finally prints a summary showing which players won the hand (lines 61–71).

```
(1)int main(int argc, char *argv[]) {
(2)    int rank, size, tag, origin;
(3)    MPI_Status status;
(4)    int MAXIMUM_VALUE = 5;
(5)    int MAXIMUM_DELAY = 10;
(6)    int n_hands, n_players, hand_points, seconds, hand, hands;
(7)    int card_points=   -1;
(8)    int bet_points= -1;
(9)    int current_hand= 0;
(10)   int winning= 0;
(11)   int* player_points;
(12)   int* player_bet;
(13)   bool** winners;
(14)   MPI_Init(&argc, &argv);
(15)   MPI_Comm_rank(MPI_COMM_WORLD, &rank);
(16)   MPI_Comm_size(MPI_COMM_WORLD, &size);
(17)   n_players = size - 1;
(18)   if (rank == 0) {                                         --croupier process
(19)     cout << "Number of hands to be played-> ";cin >> n_hands; cout << "\n";
(20)     for (int i = 1; i <= n_players; i++)
(21)        MPI_Send(&n_hands, 1, MPI_INT, i, 0, MPI_COMM_WORLD);
(22)     cout << "Actual number of players-> " << n_players << " (Processor (0) is
                  reserved for the Croupier).\n";
(23)     winners = (bool**)malloc(sizeof (int*) *n_players);
(24)     player_bet = (int*) malloc(sizeof (int) *n_players);
(25)     player_points = (int*) malloc(sizeof (int) *n_players);
(26)     for (int i = 0; i < n_players; i++) {
(27)        player_bet[i] = -1;
(28)        player_points[i] = -1;
(29)        winners[i] = (bool*)malloc(sizeof (bool) * n_hands);
(30)        for (int j = 0; j < n_hands; j++)
(31)           winners[i][j] = false;
(32)     }                                                       --end for
(33)     for (int i = 0; i < n_hand; i++) {
(34)        hand = current_hand;
(35)        cout << "-------------->Hand " << current_hand + 1 << endl;
(36)        while (hand == current_hand) {
(37)           for (int i = 1; i <= n_players; i++) {
(38)             MPI_Recv(&card_points, 1, MPI_INT, i, 0,  MPI_COMM_WORLD, &status);
(39)             player_points[i - 1] = card_points;
(40)           }                                                 --end for
(41)           for (int i = 1; i <= n_players; i++) {
(42)             MPI_Recv(&bet_points, 1, MPI_INT, i, 0, MPI_COMM_WORLD, &status);
(44)             cout << " The player " << i << " wants to bet " << bet_points << endl;
(45)             player_bet[i - 1] = bet_points;
(46)           }                                                 --end for
(47)           hand_points = 0;
(48)           for (int j = 0; j < n_players; j++)
(49)             if (player_points[j] > 0)
(50)                hand_points += player_points[j];
(51)           for (int i = 1; i <= n_players; i++) {
(52)             MPI_Recv(&bet_points, 1, MPI_INT, i, 1, MPI_COMM_WORLD, &status);
(53)             cout << " The player " << i << " wants to know if he won" << endl;
(54)             if (player_bet[i - 1] == hand_points) {
(55)                winning++;
(56)                cout << " Player " << i << " wins hand " << current_hand + 1 << endl;
(57)                winners[i - 1][hand] = true;
(58)             } else {
(59)                    cout << " The player " << i << " loses the hand " << current_hand <<
(60)             }                                               --end else
(61)           }                                                 --end for
(58)           if (hand + 1 != n_hands)
(59)             cout<<"Game goes to hand"<<current_hand+2<<<endl;
(60)        }--endwhile
(61)        if (winning > 0)
(62)          for (int i = 0; i < n_players; i++) {
(63)             cout << " Player " << i + 1 << " wins hands ";
(64)             for (int j = 0; j < n_hands; j++)
(65)                if (winners[i][j])
(66)                   cout << j + 1 << ", ";
(67)                else cout << " 0, "; cout << " ";
(68)          }
(69)        else cout << " No one has won this hand" << endl;
(70)        winning = 0; cout << " ";
(71)     }                                                       --end for
(72)   }                                                         --endif, Croupier process
(73)   else {                                                    --player process code }--players'
(74)   if (rank == 0) {
(75)     cout << "Croupier finished" << ".\n";
(76)   }
(77)   else cout << "Player number is finished:" << rank << ".\n";
(78)   MPI_Finalize();
(79)   return 0;
```

3.7 Exercises

The `player` processes generate the score for the card the player is about to play, calculate the bet, and verify that the bet matches the points (10). The player then sends the card score to the croupier (11), waits a random amount of time, and subsequently sends the bet value to the croupier (14). Afterwards, the player queries (15) if they have won the hand and reduces (16) the number of hands remaining to play.

```
(1)   --processes players
(2)   MPI_Recv(&n_hands,1, MPI_INT,0,0,MPI_COMM_WORLD,&status);
(3)   hands = n_hands;
(4)   seconds= (random()*rank)% MAXIMUM_DELAY+ 1;
(5)   sleep(seconds);
(6)   srand(time(NULL));
(7)   while (hands > 0) {
(8)    do {card_points= random()%MAXIMUM_VALUE + 1;
(9)    bet_points= n_players*abs(random()*rank%MAXIMUM_VALUE+1);
(10)   }while (card_points== bet_points);
(11)   MPI_Send(&card_points,1,MPI_INT,0,0,MPI_COMM_WORLD);
(12)   seconds= random()% MAXIMUM_DELAY +1;
(13)   sleep(seconds);
(14)   MPI_Send(&bet_points,1,MPI_INT,0,0,MPI_COMM_WORLD);
(15)   MPI_Send(&bet_points, 1, MPI_INT, 0, 1, MPI_COMM_WORLD);
(16)   hands--;
(17)  }--endwhile
```

3.7.2 Proposed Exercises

Exercise 3.25 Could the `Send(...)` command be temporarily blocked in non-buffered, non-blocking asynchronous message passing? If so, what could cause such blocking (if you think it could occur)?

Exercise 3.26 Which *MPI* library message passing operations can be used to implement the synchronisation mechanism known as "rendezvous" between two processes?

Exercise 3.27 What issue arises with the following code, which codifies two non-buffered, non-blocking message passing operations, regarding the final values of variables x, y, declared in the program? Additionally, which *MPI* functions would you program to resolve this problem?

```
(1)int main(int argc, char *argv[]) { int rank, size, neighbour, x, y;
(2) MPI_Status status; MPI_Request request_send,request_recv;
(3) MPI_Init(&argc, &argv); MPI_Comm_rank(MPI_COMM_WORLD, &rank);
(4) MPI_Comm_size(MPI_COMM_WORLD, &size);
(5) y=rank*(rank+1);
(6) if (rank mod 2 == 0)
        neighbour=rank+1
      else neighbour=rank-1; -- The following operations can appear in any order
(7) MPI_Irecv(&x,1,MPI_INT,neighbour,0,MPI_COMM_WORLD,&request_recv);
(8) MPI_Isend(&y,1,MPI_INT,neighbour,0,MPI_COMM_WORLD,&request_send);
(9) ...
```

Exercise 3.28 Explain what happens if during the execution of a non-deterministic selection statement all alternatives have conditions that evaluated to true and each one of these is followed by an acceptance statement, but no other process has yet issued the corresponding call required by any of these alternatives.

Exercise 3.29 What would be the result of executing a non-deterministic selection statement if all the conditions in the guards of its alternatives evaluate to false?

Exercise 3.30 Consider the following tasks in a distributed language with remote invocations:

```
Process P1;                     Process P2;
(1) begin                       (1) begin
(2)   while true do begin       (2)   while true do begin
(3)     P2.A;                   (3)     select
(4)     P3.B;                   (4)       accept A do
(5)     P4.G;                   (5)         P3.D;
(6)     P3.E;                   (6)       enddo;
(7)     accept F;               (7)     or accept H do
(8)     P3.C;                   (8)         P3.E;
(9)   end;                      (9)       enddo;
10    enddo;                    (10)    end select;
11 end;                         (11)  end;
                                (12)  enddo;
                                (13) end;

Process P3;                     Process P4;
(1) begin                       (1) begin
(2)   while true do begin       (2)   while true do
(3)     accept D;               (3)     begin
(4)     accept B;               (4)       accept G;
(5)     accept E;               (5)       P2.H;
(6)     P1.F;                   (6)     endo
(7)     accept C;               (7)   end;
(8)   end;
(9)   enddo;
(10)end;
```

Could all the processes become blocked (resulting in a deadlock situation)? If so, explain how this could occur, specifying the line numbers of the instructions involved.

Exercise 3.31 The S_1 process should be programmed with a non-deterministic selection statement that suspends its execution until other processes call its entry point, $E_1()$, within for 10.0 time units. If S_1 does not execute the acceptance command within this time frame, the selective wait will terminate, and the process itself will also terminate.

Exercise 3.32 Why can't delay alternatives and else clauses be combined in a non-deterministic selection statement?

3.7 Exercises

Exercise 3.33 Two types of people enter a room. The room has a narrow door that allows only one person to pass at a time. Their behaviours are as follows:

A type A person cannot leave the room until there are 10 type B people present.

A type B person cannot leave thr room until there is one type A person and nine other type B people present.

The room must always contain fewer than 10 type B people unless no type A person is present. If this condition is violated, a group consisting of one type A and 10 type B people must immediately leave the room. While such a group is exiting, no new people may enter until the entire group has left.

To solve this problem, use the rendezvous mechanism. A server process must be implemented to correctly synchronise the processes representing people entering and exiting the room.

The following skeleton can be used for the code of the people processes. `callA()` and `callB()` notify the server that a type A or type B person wants to synchronize. `waitA()` and `waitB()` block the persons until the required number of both types is present to form a group ready for exit.

```
Process type Person_A;           Process type Person_B;
  begin                            begin
    ...                              ...
    server.callA();                  server.callB();
    server.waitA();                  server.waitB();
  end;                             end;
```

Exercise 3.34 Program a selective wait statement compatible with the `Mutex` process, which implements a binary mutual exclusion semaphore with two entry points. This semaphore is designed to prevent two processes from accessing a critical section simultaneously. One of the two processes must first execute `Mutex(0).post()` to start the protocol correctly.

```
Process Mutex(int i);
  entry wait();
  entry post();

void* p1(void*){                     void* p2(void *){
  Mutex(0).post();                     do { --Outside the CS
  do {   --Outside the CS                Mutex(0).wait();
    Mutex(0).wait();                     --Accessing the CS
    --Accessing the CS                   Mutex(0).post();
    Mutex(0).post();                   }while(true);
  }while(true);                        return NULL;
  return NULL;                       }
}
```

Exercise 3.35 Complete the code of a beverage machine controller, programming a non-deterministic selection within a loop, which is repeated according to the following conditions:

(a) Accept customer requests through: accept `request(num_drink:IN int)`.
(b) When the supply is exhausted, the machine enters a maintenance state for 2 h. After maintenance, all cans are replenished, and the machine resumes service.
(c) Any missing cans are automatically replenished every 24 hours, a process that takes 1 hour.

```
Client Process (int i);                    Process Controller;
  var                                        entry request(num_drink: in int);
  int requests; --5 types of beverages       --Total number of cans
begin                                        int cans:=N;
  request= random()%5;                       while true do
  while true do                              begin
  begin                                        select
    Controller.request(request);                 -- complete
    --sip it before asking for another one    end select;
    delay random()*i mod MAX;                  end;
  end;                                       enddo
  enddo;                                     end; --end Controller
end;
```

Exercise 3.36 Mark each of the following statements about message passing as true or false:

(a) Message passing can only be used in systems without shared memory.
(b) Message passing can be used for communication and synchronization between processes, regardless of whether the platform is distributed or uses centralised memory.
(c) Distributed processes and threads are incompatible. An application using message passing operations can only locate its processes on different computers.
(d) Communication channels between distributed processes can only have one process at each end.

Exercise 3.37 Mark each of the following statements about message passing as true or false:

(a) Synchronous message passing `(Ssend()` and `Recv())` does not produce errors if processes are correctly synchronized.
(b) Unbuffered synchronous receiving operations can block a server process if the corresponding sending process terminates unexpectedly.
(c) A receiving process may modify the received data only after the `Ireceive` operation has completed and a subsequent check confirms its completion.

3.7 Exercises

(d) In an asynchronous (non-blocking and unbuffered) communication, a process must not reuse or modify the data it intends to send until a follow-up operation confirms that the transmission is complete.

Exercise 3.38 Mark each of the following statements about non-deterministic *select* statements in some programming languages as true or false:

(a) The conditions in the guards of a *select* statement's alternatives are evaluated only once.
(b) If a guard condition evaluates to false, the process is blocked.
(c) If all guard conditions of the regular alternatives of the select command are false, a program execution error occurs, in any case.
(d) Always program an else clause to prevent the error.

Exercise 3.39 Mark each of the following statements about the sentence accept as true or false:

(a) When process P_1 calls accept f(in x_1, in/out x_2) in its code the effect is not limited to P_2; rather, it involves a synchronization that affects both P_1 and P_2.
(b) The processes $P_1::P_2.f(a,b)$ and $P_2::$accept f(in x_1, in/out x_2) are synchronised by a rendezvous. Although P2 executes f(in x_1, in/out x_2) locally, the execution reflects changes in the state of P_1 due to parameter passing and result return.
(c) After executing f(in x_1, in/out x_2), P_2 returns the (possibly modified) values of x_1 and x_2 to P_1.
(d) P_2 receives the value x_2 from P_1, operates on it, and the final value is sent back and updated in P_1.

Exercise 3.40 Mark each of the following statements about the options in the sentence as true or false:

```
Process S1();                      Process S2();
 entry E1();                        entry E2();
  select                             select
    when C; accept A do                when C; accept A do
      NULL;                              NULL
    enddo                              enddo;
  or when true delay 10.0 do         or delay 20.0;
      delay 10.0 enddo;              end select;
  end select                        end;
end;
```

(a) S_1 will terminate only if no call to its accept point occurs after 20.0 time units.
(b) If condition C of the select statement of S_1 evaluates to false, then the behaviour of both select statements becomes identical.
(c) The select statement S_1 will wait for 10.0 time units for calls to its accept point.
(d) If no calls to the accept point occur within 20.0 time units, then the behavior of the two select statements is equivalent.

Exercise 3.41 With the Java RMI protocol, a process P_1 calls a remote method o.m(...) of an object or class C, which is implemented on the computer where process P_2 (or servant) runs. For the call of process P_1 to the remote method o.m(...) to be successfully resolved via RMI, one of the following conditions must be satisfied:

(a) The processes P_1 and P_2 must run on the same computer.
(b) The process P_1 only needs access to the remote interface that defines the public methods implemented by the C class.
(c) The process P_2 must always have access to a local *stub* of the remote object o, which can interpret the messages sent to the object o by P_1.
(d) Process P_1 must have access both to the remote interface and to a *stub* object representing the remote instance of the class implementing the referenced method.

Exercise 3.42 In relation to Exercise 3.35, it is now assumed that there are two beverage machines in the building, both with identical operational capabilities. In this case, if a customer attempts to obtain a drink from one machine and is out of service, they will wait for 1 min. before moving to the other end of the building to try the second machine. If the customer is still unable to obtain a beverage, they will wait for a period of 30 min. for the second machine to become operational again. Should they still be unsuccessful, they will return to the first machine and repeat the process. This process will continue until the customer is able to obtain the beverage.

Real-Time Systems 4

4.1 Introduction to Real-Time Systems

Today, the development of real-time systems (RTS) is of great importance, as a wide range of modern applications exhibit real-time characteristics [11]. Notably, 99% of the world's processor production is currently dedicated to embedded systems, whose control software is often built upon a simplified real-time operating system (RTOS) kernel.

An RTS is often confused with systems that are *online*, *interactive* or *simply fast*, a misconception especially common among IT system marketers. The fact that a system is *online* merely implies constant availability, but this does not guarantee that it meets the so-called *responsiveness* property, a key requirement of RTS, defined as the system's ability to respond within a predetermined and bounded time. Moreover, online systems do not necessarily guarantee that a response will occur at all. Similarly, an *interactive* system is one whose response time is perceived as acceptable by a human user. While it is true that RTSs typically operate with high-frequency task cycles for a human (some in the order of hundreds or thousands of times per second), this is not a strict requirement, as a complex system could have a response time of seconds or even days and still operate in real time.

The fundamental condition for a system or application to be considered real-time is that the *response*[1] of a critical task must be completed within a guaranteed time frame, regardless of its duration, while accounting for possible interference from other tasks during execution. Continuous RTSs also require that the time required to process the information in each program cycle be less than the time interval between the start of two consecutive

---

[1] The time elapsed between *activation* (the time when the task is ready to run) and the time when it finishes its work

cycles. Audio processing, video streaming, and Internet telephony are common examples of continuous real-time systems, where timing constraints are essential for correct functionality.

An example of such a system is illustrated in Fig. 4.1. If processing a sound signal requires 1.4 s per second of audio, then the system cannot be considered real-time. However, if the processing takes only 0.9 s, then it is possible to implement it as a real-time system so that the sound can be heard in real time without loss of quality.

There are a number of characteristic elements or properties, which all real-time systems possess and which can help us identify and evaluate them correctly. These include:

- *Reactivity*: RTSs are inherently reactive systems because their operation relies on a continuous interaction with the external environment. This contrasts with transformational systems whose abstract behaviour is similar to that of a mathematical function, which normally responds to the following pattern: *data input, computation* and *output of results*.
- *Determinism*: is a crucial property of real-time systems and consists of the ability to predict, with high confidence, how long it will take for a task to start. This is essential because real-time systems need certainty, and more critical tasks need to be initiated and executed before others. Since most interrupt requests originate from external stimuli, predictable task execution timing is vital to ensure that the system can deliver specific services within defined time limits.
- *Responsiveness*: this property is concerned with the time it takes for a task to begin execution once the interrupt that triggers it has been serviced by the system. The aspects covered by this concept are the amount of time it takes to initiate the execution of the interrupt, the execution time of the corresponding task, and the impact of nested interrupts that may delay execution.

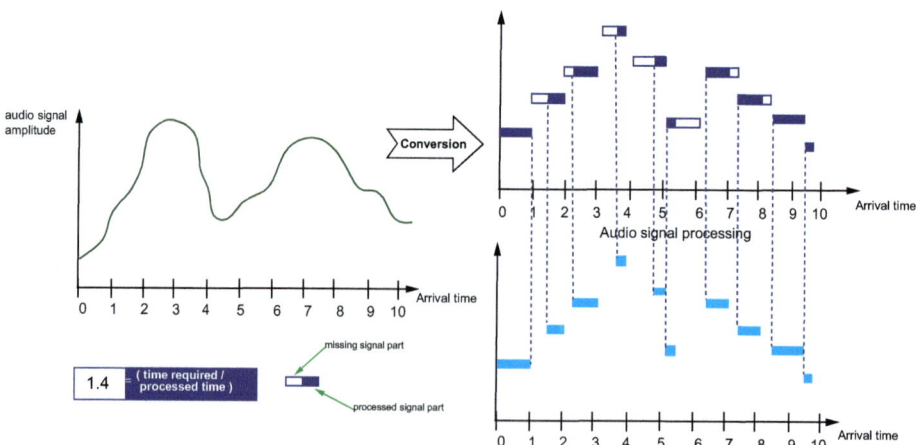

Fig. 4.1 System for continuous processing of audio, video or telephony signals over the Internet

4.1 Introduction to Real-Time Systems

- *Reliability*: a real-time system must not only be fault-free, but also maintain an acceptable quality of service throughout its operation. The system must continue under adverse conditions, such as hardware failures. Normally, a severe degradation of the service provided by an RTS can lead to critical or catastrophic consequences.

The most widely accepted definition of a real-time system is the following: *A real-time system is one in which the correctness of a computation depends not only on its logical accuracy but also on the time at which the result is produced* [11].

In the field of *operating systems*, the POSIX standard defines a real-time operating system as one capable of delivering a required level of service within a pre-specified time limit. In other words, such a system must meet predefined deadlines for all tasks that are classified as real-time.

4.1.1 Classification of RTS

RTSs are classified based on their criticality as either *soft* (permissive) and *hard* (mission-critical or non-permissive). A *mission-critical* system is one in which late delivery of results is unacceptable, as it may lead to system failure or severe consequences. In contrast, a *permissive* system may tolerate some delays, as it would only result in performance losses that, depending on its cost, may be acceptable, even in a deployable version of the final software system.

Consequently, missing a deadline in a mission-critical system results in a total system failure. An example of such a system is the software that controls the docking manoeuvre of spacecraft such as SpaceX's Dragon or Russia's Soyuz at the *International Space Station*, while a video player that occasionally drops a frame provides an example of a permissive real-time system where occasional deadline misses only result in minor performance degradation.

There is a third type of RTS whose behaviour is in the middle of the two previous ones, known as strict or firm real-time systems (see Table 4.1). With this type of system, occasional deadline misses may be tolerated, though they can still degrade the overall quality of service. In contrast to *permissive* RTSs, where there is some gain from late results, in *firm* RTSs, a result delivered after the deadline is considered to have zero utility. RTSs of industrial interest usually contain a mixture of component subsystems from the three classes discussed above.

Table 4.1 Classification of Real-Time Systems (RTS) according to criticality

Designation	Example	Complementary elements
Non-permissive (Hard)	Flight control system in an aircraft	Faul tolerance mechanisms
Permissive (Soft)	Meteorological data acquisition system	Defined upper limits for acceptable reliability loss
Strict (Firm)	Flight reservation control system	Metrics for evaluating response quality

4.1.2 Measurement of Time

The fundamental characteristic of a real-time system (RTS) is its ability to execute instructions within the well-defined time constraints of its tasks. Therefore, in order to properly develop any RTS, it is essential to have adequate mechanisms for time measurement, and tools to control the execution duration of those instructions [13]. Nowadays, it is unthinkable to develop software with real-time features without the support of a high-level programming language and a suitable operating system. Such systems must provide the following features:

- *Real-time clock* for precise time measurement.
- *Mechanisms to activate tasks* at predetermined times.
- *Timeouts*[2] to handle delays or exceptions in execution.
- Programmable real-time schedulers, allowing developers to adapt task scheduling to the specific needs of their application.

Time is a fundamental physical quantity, whose unit in the International System (SI) is the second. In the context of software development, two types of time measurements are generally required:

1. Absolute time: the actual date and time at a given moment.
2. Intervals or relative time: the duration between two events.

4.1.2.1 Absolute Time

To obtain measurements in this case, we need a reference system with an origin which is called the *epoch*. For this, we can use five reference systems:

1. *Local*, this typically corresponds to the time elapsed since the computer system was started.
2. *Astronomical*, for example, the so-called Universal Time (UT0), which is the modern term used for the international measurement of time, using a system based on telescope observations, and which was adopted in 1928 to replace the **GMT** (*Greenwich Mean Time*) system by the International Astronomical Union.
3. *Atomic time*, using atomic clocks distributed around the world, this system is known as International Atomic Time (IAT). It defines one second as a constant duration based on the immutable transition frequency of the caesium atom.

---

[2] A period of time after which an error condition arises if an event has not occurred, an input has not been received, etc. A frequent example is the sending of a message. If the receiver does not acknowledge the message within a preset period of time, it is inferred that a transmission error has occurred, and an exception is raised in the program.

4.1 Introduction to Real-Time Systems

4. *Coordinated Universal Time* (UTC), which is currently the basis for the measurement of time in civilian life, since 1 January 1972. It is derived from IAT but adjusted by adding leap seconds when necessary to stay synchronized with the Earth's rotation.
5. *Satellite Time,* the Global Positioning System (GPS) that also broadcast a global time signal for the entire planet, as well as providing precise timing information and instructions for converting GPS time to UTC.

4.1.2.2 Real-Time Clocks

A *clock*, in the context of this chapter, is a module composed of hardware and software elements that provides the system's real-time value when accessed through a system function. This clock is kept up to date throughout the execution of our system and consists of the following components:

- An *oscillator* circuit that generates electrical pulses.
- A *counter* that accumulates pulses by storing the updated value at a specific memory address.
- A *software* that converts the counter's raw value into time units defined by the International System of Units (SI).

The most important characteristics of a real-time clock are the following:

- *Accuracy*: also referred to as granularity, this defines how frequently a new pulse updates the counter. The value of the smallest *grain of* time the clock can distinguish. The accuracy will depend on the oscillator's frequency and the way it detects and counts pulses.
- *Interval*: the maximum range of time the clock can measure before the counter overflows. This characteristic will depend directly on the accuracy of the clock and the bit-width of the counter. For a fixed counter size, higher accuracy, or smaller the time grain of the clock (1 ns = 10^{-9} s; 1 µs = 10^{-6} s; 1 ms = 10^{-3} s) results in a smaller measurable time interval before overflow.

Accuracy (32-bit word size)	Interval
100 ns	Up to 429.5 s
1 µs	Up to 71.58 min.
100 µs	Up to 119.3 h
1 ms	Up to 49.71 days
1 s	Up to 136.10 years

Since the capacity of the counter is limited, reaching a certain number of accumulated pulses causes the counter to reset to zero. This is known as a real-time clock counter *overflow*. The main effect it has on time measurement in a real-time application is that creates two distinct time scales that must be correctly identified and interpreted:

Fig. 4.2 Representation of a non-monotonic time in real-time clock

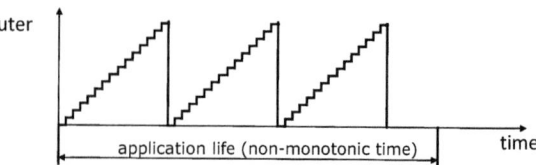

1. *Monotonic time*: this corresponds to the lifetime of the application, which does not exceed the clock's overflow interval. In this case the real-time application completes before the counter overflows.
2. *Non-monotonic time*: in this case, as can be seen in Fig. 4.2, the application runs longer than the counter's overflow period. In such cases, the total elapsed time must be calculated by summing multiple counter cycles, accounting for each overflow event.

The problems with using a *non-monotonic* time scale are the lack of an absolute time reference, i.e., with a single continous time origin, and the inability to directly maintain values such as date and time, since the counter resets multiple times. Additionally, it becomes impractical to measure time intervals that exceed the clock's overflow threshold, as the counter does not track elapsed time beyond that limit in a single, uninterrupted count.

4.1.3 Timers and Delays

A *timer* is a specialised type of clock. Operating systems often use a single *hardware timer* to implement a flexible set of *software timers* that is extensible and therefore adaptable to the needs of various applications. In this scenario, the computer's hardware interrupt service routine (ISR) is responsible for managing all software timers required by user applications. At each expiration of the hardware timer, the system checks whether any scheduled software timer has expired and, if so, initiates its pending actions. Timers are commonly used to control the sequence of actions in a real-time task or external events detected by a real-time application. Their fundamental use in real-time applications is to measure time intervals accurately. To program a software timer, both the *start* and *stop* times must be specified, as shown in Fig. 4.3.

Timers can be classified as either one-shot or periodic. One-shot timers triggers a single interrupt and then stop permanently. Periodic timers generates an interrupt at regular intervals whenever a specified time value is reached. This interrupt is received at regular intervals from the hardware timer. For periodic or continuous timers, expiration times are automatically rescheduled based on their configured activation intervals. One-shot timers, in turn, are either deactivated or removed from the set of active timers after they expire.

Fig. 4.3 Programmable software timer

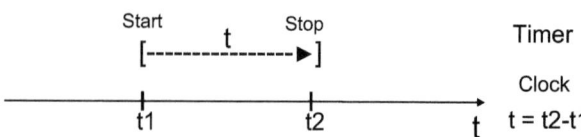

4.1 Introduction to Real-Time Systems

```
periodical task T(periodic_computation_t: milliseconds);
  var
    computation_t: milliseconds;
  begin
   computation_t := periodic_computation_t;
   while true do begin
     --at each cycle produces a delay = 'computation_t' of the task
       delay(computation_t);
     --action to be performed
   end
  enddo
end;
```

Fig. 4.4 Periodic task affected by local drift

The handling of timers seems rather simple; however, certain factors, such as drift or delayed interrupts, can introduce anomalies in expected behavior. These must be minimized during the implementation of software timers, as they can compromise the precision needed to activate time-sensitive application actions or real-time tasks.

Delays are used to control the activation time of real-time tasks in an application and can be programmed, using timers, at the operating system level, or by programming language instructions. The latter approach provides, maximum *portability* and will be achieved[3] for the specified delay duration. A typical syntax might be: `delay<duration>`. For higher temporal precision, such as finer granularity, the function `nanosleep(&(struct timespec){<seconds>, <nanoseconds>}, NULL);` can be used. Its effect is to suspend execution of the task for at least the specified duration from the time the previous instruction is invoked. The execution of the task may be delayed for longer than the specified time due to low precision of the real-time clock, which may not support the required granularity or preemption by higher-priority tasks and the delayed task is postponed in accessing the processor even though the delay time has expired. This effect is known as *drift* of a real-time task and may cause a real-time task to miss its predefined time limits, as is the case with the code in Fig. 4.4.

Since delays that occur in each period of a real-time task due to *local drift* (LD) can be accumulated, leading to *accumulative drift* (AD) over multiple cycles. This gradual change can impact the accuracy of periodic task scheduling, making careful timer handling essential in real-time applications including tasks with delays that are activated periodically.

The elimination of accumulative drift (AD) in periodic task scheduling can be achieved by having the task adjust its delay at each cycle until the next scheduled activation time (Fig. 4.5). This approach ensures that the task's activation remains consistent over time. In this way, each activation of the task may involve a different effective delay duration, since any delays caused by external factors, such as preemption or waiting for processor access, are accounted for and subtracted from the total delay, keeping the task schedulable without missing any deadline.

As can be seen in Fig. 4.6, if in each cycle the periodic task experiences a constant delay or *first approximation*, the AD will gradually increase over time. If, on the contrary,

---

[3] This refers to the *usability* of the same software on different platforms. In order for software to meet this property, the application logic must be abstracted from the interfaces of the system on which the software is deployed.

```
periodical task Fair_T(periodic_computation_t: milliseconds);
  var
    period, next_instant: milliseconds;
  begin
    period:= periodic_computation_t;
    next_instant:= clock_now();      --system's function that returns the current time
    while true do begin
      --action to be carried out periodically by the task
      next_instant += period;
      delay (next_instant - clock_now());
    end
  enddo
  end;
```

Fig. 4.5 Periodical task with accumulative drift removed

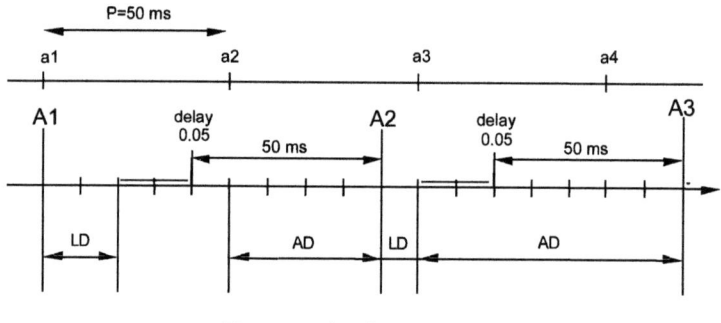

First approximation

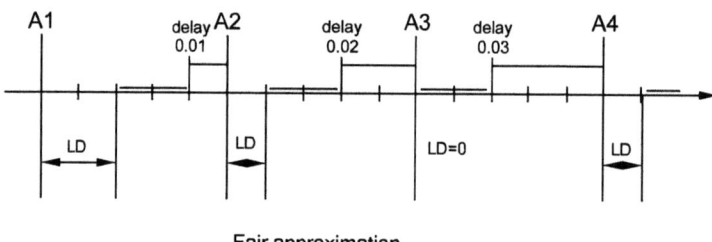

Fair approximation

Fig. 4.6 Drift in tasks with delays. (**a**) First approximation. (**b**) Fair approximation

the delays are adjusted dynamically in each cycle to align with the next scheduled activation time (a_i, i: 1, 2…), then the accumulative drift is eliminated; in this case, we say that we obtain the *fair approximation*.

4.1.4 Waiting Time Limits

Sometimes, it is necessary to limit the time during which a task waits for an event to occur. Tasks can enter various suspended states, for example, when an input/output operation or other operating system service is scheduled to be performed synchronously with the execution of that task. In these cases, if the cooperating task or the device responsible for completing the operation fails, then the suspended task may remain blocked indefinitely. The solution to avoid this situation is to schedule the operation subject to a *timeout*, which would indicate the maximum time during which it will remain suspended. Therefore, if after that time the service is not completed, then the suspended task exits its blocked state, typically triggering an exception that can be used to display a warning message or to return an error code to the user application.

4.2 Simple Real-Time Task Model

To analyze the behavior of a task in a clear and structured way, particularly under worst-case scheduling scenarios, i.e., when a task experiences maximum interference from higher-priority processes, within a real-time program or application, it is necessary to impose certain restrictions to its structure and to the interactions it maintains with the rest of the tasks of the program. Tasks that adhere to these constraints are said to follow the simple task model [12]. Although it is a basic model, the simple task model offers sufficient descriptive power to support the modeling of standard scheduling approaches, such as the one based on static prioritisation of tasks, which remains one of the most widely used strategies in the development and analysis of real-time systems (RTS).

4.2.1 Simple Task Model Characteristics

We consider a real-time program as a fixed set of tasks, i.e., during the execution of the program, tasks are neither created nor destroyed, and they are executed concurrently sharing the time of a single processor. Tasks are assumed to be periodic, with known and fixed periods and independent of each other. There are no semaphores, shared resources, or other synchronization mechanisms that could block a higher-priority task during its execution by a lower-priority task holding a resource it needs.

In this simple model, each task has *a deadline*, which we will consider equal to its period. A task, therefore, must complete the units of execution time assigned to it before the start of its next activation, which will occur when a time equal to its period has elapsed since the beginning of its current activation. Additionally, system overheads such as context switch times and minor delays are ignored in this model.

It is also assumed that no external condition prevents a task from gaining access to the processor if it becomes the highest-priority task at a given moment. Futhermore, events (e.g., clock interruption, signals) are not queued or stored, i.e., they are lost if not handled immediately upon occurrence.

In the simple task model, the maximum computation time required by a task is fixed and known in advance, prior to its execution. This value is denoted by the symbol C, which represents a specific number of time units, and is referred to as the *worst-case execution time* (or WCET). Sporadic tasks, which occur irregularly during the execution of a real-time application and are typically of high urgency when triggered, are not considered within the scope of this model.

4.2.2 Temporal Attributes Associated with a Task

A real-time task τ can be characterised by means of a specific set of temporal attributes. A graphical representation of some of these attributes, which are considered as characteristic elements within a real-time task scheduling scheme, appears in Fig. 4.7. The definition of each of these attributes can be found in Table 4.2.

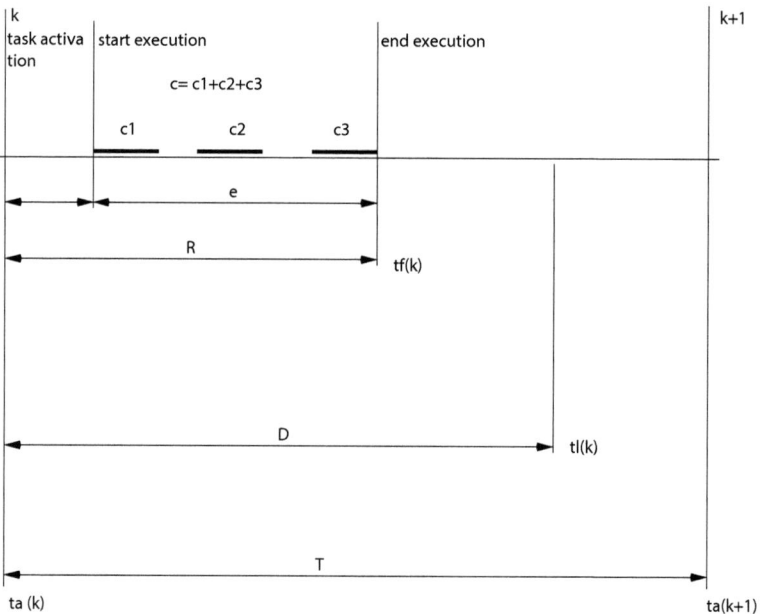

Fig. 4.7 Representation of the temporal attributes of real-time tasks

4.2 Simple Real-Time Task Model

Table 4.2 Definition of the attributes of a real-time task τ.

Notation	Time attribute	Description
P_i	Priority	Priority assigned to the task τ_i (if applicable)
t_a	Time of task activation (arrival time, request time, release time)	The moment a task becomes ready for execution does not necessarily mean that it will start executing at that time.
t_s	Start time (start time)	Time instant at which the task actually starts its execution.
t_f	Finishing time	Time instant at which the task completes its execution.
t_l, d	Absolute deadline	Time limit instant by which the task must complete its execution. It is a fixed value, given by $t_l(k) = t_a(k) + D$(k-th activation).
T	Implementation period	Time interval between two successive activations (k, $k+1$) of a periodic task. It is a fixed value, given by $T = t_a(k+1) - t_a(k)$.
J	Latency	Time interval between the activation of the task and the start of its execution. It is given by $J(k) = t_s(k) - t_a(k)$ and, depending on the system overhead, it can vary between a minimum value J_{min} and a maximum of J_{max}.
c	Computation time	Task execution time.
C	Worst case execution time (WCET)	Task execution time in the worst possible scheduling scenario, when it experiences the maximum possible interference from other tasks.
e	Elapsed execution time	The duration from the start of the task to its completion. It is given by $e(k) = t_f(k) - t_s(k)$
R	Response time	The total time required for the task to complete, measured from activation to completion. It is a variable value, given by $R(k) = J(k) + e(k)$
D	Maximum response time (relative deadline)	Defines the maximum allowable time interval for completing the task's execution.
Φ	Displacement or phase	Time required to activate a periodic task for the first time.
RJ	Relative jitter (release jitter)	Maximum deviation in a task's start time from its activation, measured across two successive activations of the task. It is defined as: RJ = $\max((t_s(k+1) - t_a(k+1)) - (t_s(k) - t_a(k)))$.
AJ	Absolute fluctuation	Maximum deviation in start time across all activations of a task. It is defined by AJ = $J_{max} - J_{min}$.
L	Delay (lateness)	Delay in task completion relative to its deadline for a given activation k of the task. It is defined as: $L(k) = t_f(k) - t_l(k)$. If the task completes before the deadline, the delay value is 0.
E	Excess time	The maximum delay across all task activations. It is defined as: $E(k) = \max(0, L(k))$.
H	Slack (laxity, slack time)	Maximum time a task can be active while still meeting its maximum response time constraint. It is defined as: $H(k) = t_l(k) - t_a(k) - c(k) = D - c(k)$.

4.3 Periodic Task Scheduling with Prioritisation

In general terms, activity or task scheduling can be defined as an area of human knowledge that studies a set of algorithms and integer programming techniques aimed at achieving the optimal allocation of resources and time to activities or tasks, in order to meet specific efficiency objectives. The basic strategy for solving a resource scheduling problem is typically to use a heuristic aimed at maximizing a specific objective function.

In the context of real-time systems, the primary resource to be allocated is usually processor time. In addition, it is often necessary to determine a priori whether all task activations can complete before their respective deadlines, even under the worst-case scheduling scenario.

The determination of the schedulability of a set of real-time tasks is carried out using a process scheduling schema which must contain the following two elements:

1. An algorithm to determine the order in which tasks access system resources.
2. *A mechanism to predict system behavior under worst-case conditions, particularly when maximum interference among tasks occurs.*

There are different types of real-time task scheduling schemes. A static scheduling scheme is one in which the execution order of tasks is determined before runtime and remains fixed throughout execution. On the other hand, a dynamic scheduling scheme allows task priorities to change during execution based on system conditions or task attributes. With a static scheme, we simplify the problem of real-time task scheduling, without losing generality. This task model is currently followed by most real-time applications in very critical systems, such as commercial aircraft flight control systems and in radio-medicine applications.

In more elaborate task models, non-periodic tasks should be considered, which are often triggered by external events and typically represent high-urgency or safety-critical operations. Therefore, according to the simple task model, sporadic or aperiodic tasks will not be addressed. Sporadic tasks are characterized by irregular, event-driven activation patterns with tight timing constraints, while aperiodic tasks lack a periodic activation pattern entirely.

A *preemptive* scheduling scheme is assumed, where a lower-priority task is interrupted when a higher-priority task is activated, as shown in Fig. 4.8, where four tasks share the processing time of two processor *cores*.

To determine whether tasks $\tau_1, \tau_2, \ldots, \tau_n$, with respective periods $T_1, T_2, \ldots, T_n$, can be fully executed within their time constraints, the scheduling timeline should ideally span a duration at least equal to the LCM $(T_1, T_2, \ldots, T_n)$ of the tasks periods. However, it is sufficient to analyse the timeline over the length of the longest task period (T_i) if it is assumed that all the tasks are activated simultaneously, that is, the time offset Φ between any two tasks is 0. This scenario, in which Φ is referred to as the critical instant, as it represents

4.3 Periodic Task Scheduling with Prioritisation

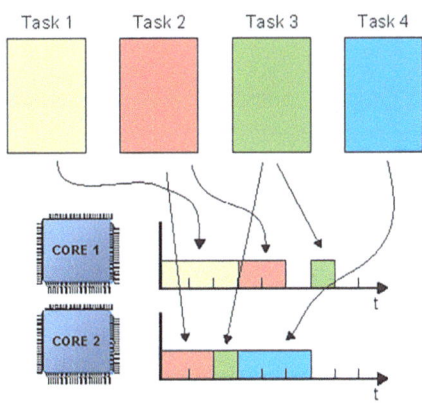

Fig. 4.8 Scheduling 4 tasks on a 2-core processor

the maximum possible load on the processor. From this point forward, tasks are executed in the order given by their priority. When using this scheme, all temporal attributes that influence the scheduling must be statically defined. This includes the maximum execution time of each task and its assigned priority.

Task priority is typically expressed as a positive integer, where lower values correspond to higher priorities. The priority of a task is determined by static attributes such as its period, timeout, or other characteristics that remain constant throughout its execution. This model does not take into account the task's criticality or the consequences to system integrity if a task's execution cycle was not completed within the allocated time frame.

4.3.1 Rate Monotonic Scheduling

Here we will focus on a static scheduling scheme for periodic tasks, in which the priority of a real-time task is determined solely by its period. Specifically, tasks are assigned priorities based on their activation frequency. Tasks with the shorter T_i activation periods (i.e., those activated more frequently) will have the higher P_i priority, regardless of their criticality within the application. Mathematically, this priority assignment is based on a monotonic function of the task period: $T_i < T_j$ means $P_i > P_j$, hence the name of the algorithm. The rate monotonic (RM) algorithm is considered optimal among all static priority assignment strategies, i.e., if a set of periodic tasks is schedulable under any fixed priority assignment scheme, it is also schedulable using rate monotonic scheduling (RMS).

The algorithm, proposed in a seminal paper by Liu and Layland in 1973 [33], is the basis for developing a mathematical theory of real-time task scheduling. This theory is far from being purely theoretical, it incorporates practical constraints arising from real-world applications, thanks to collaborative work between industry and academia. In fact, a large part of the results were obtained as a consequence of collaboration between three institutions: Software Engineering Institute (SEI), IBM and Carnegie Mellon University.

4.3.2 Test of Schedulability

A program composed of a set of periodic tasks is said to be *feasible* if every execution of the program will meet the deadlines of all the tasks. In order to determine, prior to execution, whether an application is feasible using the RM algorithm, it is necessary to have reliable predictive criteria. These feasibility criteria are established based on the processor *utilisation bound* (U) of the set of tasks or by calculating the response time of each task (R_i), which can be computed statically under the assumptions of the simple task model.

Obtaining a feasibility test for a set of tasks with statically assigned priorities has proven to be a non-trivial challenge. In fact, until very recently, no complete set of sufficient and necessary conditions existed for determining the feasibility of arbitrary real-time applications.

We will start by studying some necessary conditions that, intuitively, should be met in order to be able to state feasibility. These conditions are typically derived from static task parameters, such as worst-case execution time, period, and other predefined attributes.

4.3.2.1 Necessary Conditions

The worst-case execution time of any task must to be less than its period: $\forall\ i\colon C_i < T_i$. However, this condition is not sufficient, since one of the other lower-priority tasks may not have completely finished its execution time units when its deadline expires. A task may fail to meet its deadline if it is expected to complete prior to the completion of a higher-priority task. For example, consider the following tasks in Table 4.3.

In the above set of tasks, τ_2 misses its first time limit at $t = 5$. However, even though the condition $C_i < T_i$ is satisfied for all tasks.

Another necessary condition is that the processor utilisation per time unit of all tasks with a lower priority (i.e., higher number values) than *level i* must not exceed the 100%: $\sum_{j=i+1}^{n-1} \frac{C_j}{T_j} \leq 1$. This condition is also not sufficient, because higher-priority tasks may interfere multiple times, potentially preventing task τ_i of priority level *i* from completing on time. Check this for the next set of tasks in Table 4.4.

Table 4.3 Example of two tasks with execution times shorter than the period

Task	Priority	T_i	C_i
τ_1	1	10	8
τ_2	2	5	3

Table 4.4 Example of tasks that interfere several times with another task of lower priority

Task	Priority	T_i	C_i
τ_1	1	6	3
τ_2	1	9	2
τ_3	2	11	2

4.3 Periodic Task Scheduling with Prioritisation

Task τ_3 has one unit of execution pending when its next activation event occurs ($t = 11$). Since its deadline is equal to its period ($D_i = T_i$), it misses its deadline, even though the processor utilization condition is satisfied.

A more refined condition states that the processing of all invocations at priority levels higher than i, i.e., j: 1, 2, ..., $(i-1)$ must be completed at most in time $T_i - C_i$. With reference to the example above, this would imply that all activations of tasks τ_1 and τ_2 that interfere with τ_3 should be completed before $T_3 - C_3 = 9$ time units: $\forall i \sum_{j=1}^{i-1} \left(\frac{T_i}{T_j} \times c_j \right) \leq T_i - C_i$.

Again, this condition is not sufficient, since if a higher-priority task τ_j has a longer period: $T_j > T_i$, then this condition degenerates into the first condition and may still lead to infeasible schedules (task periods and execution times are assumed to be integers, so fractional results in divisions are discarded).

To prevent the cancellation of terms in the summation used in the previous condition, the time window is extended from a single period T_i to a time frame $M_i = \text{LCM} \{T_1, T_2, ..., T_i\}$. This is the least common multiple of the task periods up to τ_i; and it allows precise calculation of the exact number of activations of each task τ_j during this interval: $\left\lfloor \frac{M_i}{T_j} \right\rfloor$.

The new condition, which acquires the name of load ratio, is now expressed as $\forall_i \sum_{j=1}^{i-1} \left(\frac{M_i / T_j}{M_i} \times C_j \right) \leq 1$. However, although it discriminates more than condition 3, it still does not guarantee schedulability. If the computation time of a higher-priority task τ_i (higher priority) exceeds the activation period of a lower-priority task τ_j (where $i < j$), then joint scheduling of both tasks becomes infeasible. This is demonstrated in the task set shown in Table 4.5.

4.3.2.2 Sufficient Conditions

If the priorities are assigned to the real-time tasks τ_i according to the RM algorithm, i.e., based on the highest activation frequency, then the following implication must hold: $T_i < T_j \Rightarrow \text{priority}(\tau_i) > \text{priority}(\tau_j)$. This reflects the principle that tasks with shorter periods (i.e., higher activation frequency) receive higher priority.

4.3.2.3 Liu and Layland Theorems

Liu and Layland Theorem I
In a system of N independent periodic tasks $\{\tau_i\}$ with priorities statically assigned in inverse order of their periods T_i, all task deadlines will be met, regardless of initial offsets if the following inequality is satisfied: $\sum_{i=1}^{N} \left(\frac{C_i}{T_i} \right) < N \cdot \left(2^{1/N} - 1 \right)$.

Table 4.5 Example of tasks with excessive computational time of the highest-priority task

Task	Priority	T_i	C_i
τ_1	1	12	5
τ_2	2	4	2

This inequality is known as the *Rate Monotonic Scheduling* (RMS) *test* or the monotonic rate-based scheduling test. The expression $N \cdot (2^{1/N} - 1)$ represents the utilisation bound *or upper limit* for this test.

If a given task τ_i satisfies the RMS test, it is guaranteed to complete its C_i computational time units before its deadline ($D_i = T_i$) in every activation cycle. Even if the task set fails the RMS test, it may still meet all deadlines. This is because the RMS test provides only a *sufficient*, but not necessary, condition for the feasibility of a set of real-time tasks: $\{\tau_i\}$, $i: 1 \ldots N$.

Even if the RMS inequality is not satisfied, the set of tasks $\{\tau_i\}$ can still be completed. A timeline diagram, commonly known as a Gantt chart, can be constructed, to visualize the execution of all tasks over time. If no task misses its deadline within a time window equal to the LCM$\{T_1, T_2, \ldots, T_i\}$, then the task set can be considered feasible, regardless of whether the RMS bound is exceeded.

However, the problem with creating a Gantt chart becomes impractical for verifying the feasibility of a large set of tasks in complex applications, especially, without access to specialized (and often costly) graphical tools. Table 4.6 shows the upper bounds on processor utilisation for different numbers of tasks. As long as these bounds are not exceeded, the task set is guaranteed to be schedulable under the RM algorithm.

Therefore, as long as the upper limit of processor utilisation (U) of a very large set of real-time tasks, does not exceed 69.3%, the set is considered schedulable under a preemptive scheduling scheme with statically assigned priorities, as defined by the Rate Monotonic (RM) algorithm.

The RMS test is not exact, as it relies on a processor utilisation bound and may fail to confirm the feasibility of certain time-intensive task sets. For this reason, it is said to be a *sufficient but not necessary condition for schedulability*.

For example, the set of tasks illustrated in Fig. 4.9 does not satisfy the RMS test, since its total processor utilisation would be overall: $\sum_{i=1}^{3} \left(\frac{C_i}{T_i} \right) = 0.92857$. The processor utilisation exceeds the bound defined by the test. Specifically, the RMS criterion requires a maximum utilization of $3*(2^{1/3} - 1) = 0.77976$ to ensure that all three tasks are schedulable. However, as shown in Fig. 4.9, all these tasks manage to completely finish their computation within their respective deadlines, demonstrating that the set is, in fact, feasible despite failing the test.

Table 4.6 Lower upper-limit values for different number of tasks

N	Upper limits $(N \cdot (2^{1/N} - 1)) = U_0(N)$ calculation of processor utilisation (%)
1	100
2	82.85
3	78.0
4	75.7
5	74.3
10	71.8
∞	69.3

4.3 Periodic Task Scheduling with Prioritisation

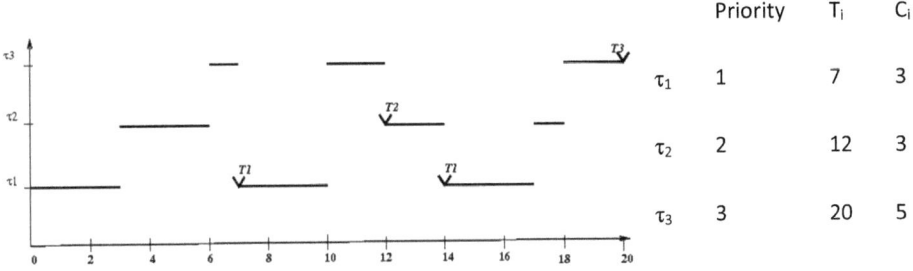

Fig. 4.9 Set of three tasks actually schedulable that do not fulfil the RMS test

The RMS test is not directly applicable, without modification, when considering a more general task model than the *simple task model* we are assuming, especially if the system includes aperiodic tasks or allows priority inversion due to resource sharing between higher- and lower-priority tasks.

Moreover, tests based on processor utilisation limits (U) do not provide information about the actual response times (R) of tasks. Hence, new exact tests have been proposed, i.e., tests that provide necessary and sufficient conditions for schedulability by explicitly calculating the response times for real-time task sets. However, these tests face practical challenges in their numerical implementation, because the calculation of the response times for each task in an arbitrary task set, which can interrupt each other several times during their execution time, does not have, in general, a simple mathematical solution.

Liu and Layland Theorem II

In a system of N independent periodic tasks with static priorities, all deadlines will be met, for any activation of the tasks, if when all tasks are activated simultaneously, each task finishes before the expiration of its maximum response time during the first activation.

Unlike the previous test, this new approach can be applied to task sets for which a maximum processor utilisation limit is defined: $U = \sum_{i=1}^{N} \left(\frac{C_i}{T_i} \right) \leq 1$. However, applying this test to complex task sets is challenging, in particular because it requires that all tasks be activated simultaneously, a condition that is often difficult to satisfy in practice.

> **Advantages of applying the Liu-Layland test II (1973):**
>
> - The upper bound that U can reach is now higher, allowing the test to be applied to a wider range of task sets than the previous RMS test (based on Theorem I), This means that task sets with greater overall processor utilization can still be deemed schedulable under this new criterion.
> - The test is now exact, meaning it provides a necessary and sufficient condition for determining the schedulability of a task set.

4.3.3 Schedulability Tests for EDF Based on Processor Utilisation

Liu and Layland's landmark 1973 paper also introduced a test for a priority assignment scheme based on the proximity of task deadlines $t_l(k) = t_a + D$, where each task is associated with a deadline defined as D. This algorithm is known as Earliest Deadline First (EDF), which at each instant selects the task whose current activation has the closest approaching deadline. EDF provides an exact feasibility test for a set of real-time tasks. The schedulability condition under EDF is given by:

$$\sum_{i=1}^{N}\left(\frac{C_i}{T_i}\right) \leq 1$$

If the total processor utlisation U of the task set is less than or equal to the normalised processing capacity of the processor (i.e., $U \leq 1$), then we can state that, for the simple model of real time tasks, all the deadlines are guaranteed to be met. EDF is considered a dynamic scheduling scheme, because the priority of the tasks changes (will increase) as their deadline approaches during their execution, at each task activation. This contrasts with static priority schemes, where task priorities remain fixed.

For the set of tasks in Table 4.7, all the deadlines are met under EDF, since the processor utilization is: $U_3 = \frac{2}{6} + \frac{2}{8} + \frac{4}{12} \simeq 0.917 < 1.0$. All tasks in this set are schedulable as is shown graphically in the Gantt chart in Exercise 4.4 (see Sect. 4.6).

Although EDF is theoretically superior to static scheduling schemes, since any task set schedulable by a static scheme, is also schedulable by EDF (but not necessarily the reverse). However, in the practice of time-critical system development, static scheduling schemes are preferred, as they are usually simpler to program and, moreover, their implementation is generally more efficient than that of a dynamic prioritisation scheme. With EDF, a higher system overhead would be induced, because task priorities must be recalculated as the execution progresses. Furthermore, dynamic schemes are better suited to systems where some tasks lack well-defined deadlines, which may be difficult or impossible to compute prior to execution.

Table 4.7 Set of tasks that are schedulable with EDF

Task	C_i	D_i	T_i
τ_1	2	5	6
τ_2	2	4	8
τ_3	4	8	12

> **Advantages of static scheduling schemes:**
>
> - A static scheduling scheme is simpler and more efficient to implement.
> - It simplifies the analysis by assuming task sets with predefined, fixed deadlines.
> - It allows for the incorporation of other factors that may influence scheduling when task priority is not only determined by timing constraints.
> - During periods of transient overload, a static scheduling scheme provides more predictable behavior. This is not necessarily the case if a dynamic scheme (such as EDF) is used.

On the other hand, the time limit attribute (t_l) for each task τ_i is usually not the only scheduling parameter to be considered in realistic applications. In many cases, it is more effective to incorporate additional factors, such as task criticality, resource usage, or system state, into the priority assignment, rather than relying solely on deadline calculations, which may be complex or infeasible. Also, during transient overload situations, a static scheduling scheme turns out to be more predictable than dynamic ones like EDF. With static scheduling, tasks with lower initial priority are typically the first to miss their deadlines, preserving the timeliness of higher-priority (and often more critical) tasks. In contrast, if EDF scheme is used, this behaviour is not guaranteed, which could pose a problem if deadline proximity does not align with task criticality.

4.4 General Models of Real-Time Tasks

The simple task model must be extended to accommodate the scheduling requirements of sporadic and aperiodic tasks, as well as to address potential deadlocks that may arise when tasks compete for shared resources that they access under mutual exclusion. The simple model considers tasks as totally independent throughout their execution, which is often too restrictive to be assumed for real applications.

Periodic tasks are typically triggered by local events. In contrast, sporadic tasks are activated by external events, often originating from a remote processor. The period T_s of a sporadic task τ_s is defined as the minimum time interval between two successive activation events. For example, a sporadic task with an activation cycle $T_s = 200$ ms ensures that it will not be triggered more than once every 200 ms. Even if the actual time between two activations ($t_a(k+1) - t_a(k)$) occasionally exceeds 200 ms, the worst case scenario, where activations occur as frequently as allowed, must be assumed in schedulability analysis. Sporadic tasks, when they occur, are usually urgent and have tight response time constraints that are much shorter than their *period*, i.e., $D_i \ll T_i$.

The activation cycle or *period* of an aperiodic task is defined as the average time interval between successive activation events. Unlike sporadic tasks, aperiodic tasks do not have a strictly defined maximum response time requirements. They tend to have permissive deadlines, meaning that occasional deadline misses are acceptable, unlike sporadic tasks, where missing a deadline is not tolerable.

In real-time applications that include sporadic tasks, the RMS test cannot be used directly to determine the feasibility of task execution. This is because using processor utilization alone as the only criterion to solve the schedulability problem, usually leads to a too *pessimistic* result when extended to task sets that include sporadic tasks. As discussed above, for sporadic tasks, a maximum activation rate is defined, typically based on the average inter-arrival time between their triggering events. Considering the maximum rate as a basis for analysis tends to require excessively low processor utilization bounds in order to safely guarantee that all activations, including those of sporadic tasks, are handled without loss. To ensure the schedulability of a mixed task set (including both periodic and sporadic tasks) without risking missed activations, it becomes necessary to impose stricter limits on processor usage. This conservatism can significantly limit system performance if not addressed through more sophisticated analysis methods.

4.4.1 Maximum Response Times Shorter Than the Task Period

When the *maximum response time* (D) of each task coincides with its period, $D_i = T_i$, the RMS provides an optimal prioritization among all static scheduling schemes, i.e., any set of real-time tasks that is schedulable under a static priority assignment scheme is also schedulable if we use RMS.

Similarly, the *Deadline Monotonic Priority Ordering* (DMPO) criterion is considered optimal for task sets where $D_i < T_i$. An example illustrating this scenario can be seen in Table 4.8.

In this example, using RMS based prioritization would not guarantee schedulability, since some tasks may miss their deadlines. However, by assigning priorities according to DMPO, as done in the fifth column of the table, the task set becomes schedulable, and the response times R_i of each task can be computed (sixth column).

The demonstration of the optimality of DMPO in the case that the tasks τ_i satisfy $D_i < T_i$ can be demonstrated through a transformation process that converts any static priority

Table 4.8 Set of tasks that turns out to be schedulable with DMPO

τ_i	T_i	D_i	C_i	Priority	R_i
a	20	5	3	1	3
b	15	7	3	2	6
c	10	10	4	3	10
d	20	20	3	4	20

4.4 General Models of Real-Time Tasks

assignment into the DMPO order. The scheme followed in the proof, though not developed here in full due to its complexity, is outlined below:

1. Begin with any static prioritization of tasks, such as the order determined by the Rate Monotonic algorithm can be used.
2. Iteratively transform the priority ordering, ensuring at each step that the schedulability of the task set is preserved, until the final order aligns with DMPO.
3. Two tasks with adjacent priorities are exchanged.
4. The task that decreases its priority must remain schedulable.
5. The task that increases its priority is now only subject to additional interference from the other, higher-priority tasks.
6. Since the task that retains a lower priority value has a shorter maximum response time, it remains schedulable after the exchange.

At the end of the transformation process described above, an ordering of the tasks according to the priority given by the DMPO is obtained. Since no task becomes unschedulable during the transformation from the initial scheme (RMS) to the final DMPO-based scheme, it can be concluded that any static scheme of prioritisation of tasks is equivalent to DMPO, which can be considered the optimal static priority assignment scheme for task sets where deadlines are less than or equal to their periods.

4.4.2 Interactions Between Real-Time Tasks

The entities constituting a real-time program are not only tasks that execute entirely asynchronously, without interacting with one another. Real-time applications also commonly include *protected objects*, i.e., critical sections, monitors, semaphores, etc., that ensure mutually exclusive access to shared data among the tasks.

The use of protected objects in the development of real-time applications and programs raises the possibility that a task may be blocked not by its normal activation event, but by the need to wait for an external condition to be met. For example, a task may be blocked waiting for another task to issue a `signal()`, on a program's semaphore. A similar situation arises when programming with *monitor* constructs of some concurrent languages, where tasks may be queued on condition variable `c` (e.g., `c.wait()`) and remain blocked until a corresponding `c.signal()` operation is executed within one of the monitor procedures. In languages like Ada, comparable behavior can occur when a task is blocked while waiting to rendezvous with another task or service.

In distributed real-time systems with multiple processors, further blocking scenarios may result from waiting on message reception, bus access, or inter-processor communication. The problem becomes critical when a higher-priority task remains blocked waiting for a lower-priority task to finish executing a critical section of its that cannot be preempted. This violates one of the most important conditions of the simple model: "when a task has sufficient priority to execute, it must be allowed to do so immediately." According to this simple model of real-time task studied above, in no case can it happen that a task can be blocked or delayed if it has the highest priority in the system at that moment, as this would affect the scheduling of all other tasks. Consequently, the schedulability tests studied, such as those based on RMS test, would no longer be safe. Blocking can cause missed deadlines, leading to what is known as a loss of task time limits.

Access to shared resources can lead to blocking of application tasks while they are being used by a specific task, blocking times must be accounted for in the schedulability analysis. If tasks can block during their execution, the schedulability analysis based on the RMS is no longer sufficient unless we also include the blocking time in the computation.

It must be quantified how the left-hand side of the inequality $\sum_{i=1}^{N}\left(\dfrac{C_i}{T_i}\right) \leq U_0(N)$ would be affected if we also consider the eventual blocking of tasks when accessing common and shared resources in mutual exclusion.

The calculation of *blocking time* must be estimated for each set of periodic tasks based on the maximum duration that the shared resources may be held by lower-priority tasks within the same task set.

4.4.2.1 Priority Inversion Phenomenon

It is even possible for the highest-priority task to experience an arbitrarily long delay if lower-priority tasks are continuously executed while it is blocked by a very-low-priority task that maintains access to the resource. This situation is known as priority inversion, and it invalidates any prediction about the schedulability of a set of tasks using the RMS test without appropriate corrections (see Fig. 4.10).

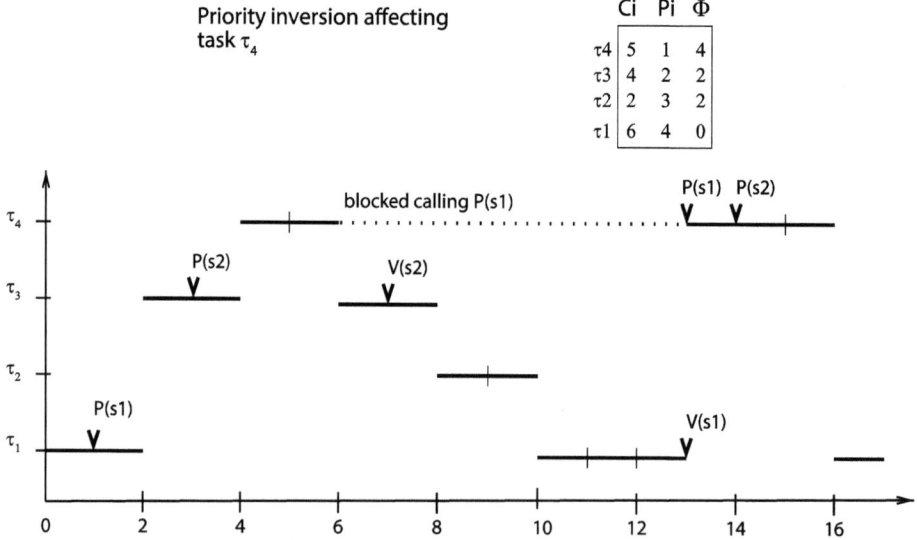

Fig. 4.10 Task priority inversion example

4.4 General Models of Real-Time Tasks

In the figure, note that lower numbers indicate higher priority in the static assignment of priorities to the four tasks τ_i. Priority inversion cannot be completely eliminated if protected objects are used in real-time programs, but the adverse effects on the scheduling of the highest-priority tasks can be minimised by ensuring that blocking is time-bounded and predictable during any given application run.

Priority inversion is arguably a drawback that occurs due to a static prioritisation scheme. In the example in Fig. 4.10 it can be seen how the task τ_4, which is the highest-priority task, suffers a significant delay due to the execution of three lower-priority tasks.

The task τ_1 is started first, after executing one clock *tick*, our unit of execution time, it acquires the semaphore s_1. Then, τ_1 is preempted, when the execution of the task τ_3 starts, which has a higher priority than τ_1. Task τ_3 executes for 1 *tick* and then blocks the semaphore s_2; after executing one additional *tick*, it is preempted by task τ_4, which becomes active at phase $I_4 = 4$. Task τ_4, being the highest priority, begins execution until it attempts to acquire the semaphore s_1, currently held by τ_1, then s_4 becomes blocked. Control returns to τ_3 which resumes execution until it finishes. Afterwards, τ_2 executes its 2 time units. Only after τ_2 completes can, τ_1 resume execution and release semaphore s_1, Once s_1 is released, τ_4 can proceed and run to completion. Finally, the task τ_1 will finish its remaining execution. This sequence clearly illustrates how a low-priority task holding a shared resource can indirectly delay a high-priority task, thereby causing priority inversion. It also shows how the schedulability of the entire system can be jeopardized if blocking behavior is not properly managed.

4.4.3 Non-preemptive Critical Section

It is the simplest protocol that could be imagined to avoid priority inversion in the implementation of a real-time task set that shares resources is to prevent any task from being preempted while it is executing a critical section involving a shared resource. The result of applying this protocol involves that once a task accesses a resource, it retains control of the processor throughout the critical section. Any critical section is executed as if it had a static priority equal to the maximum system priority.

This protocol does not require prior knowledge of the time requirements associated with the use of resources. However, it may induce excessively long blocking of the highest-priority tasks of the application if the duration of the execution time of the critical sections is not bounded or predictable before runtime. Furthermore, the implementation of this protocol may interfere with the execution of all tasks of the application, even if they do not make use of the shared resources by unnecessarily delaying their execution. Figure 4.11 shows an example of the implementation of this protocol.

In the example, τ_1 holds the highest effective priority until it releases the resource, which is signaled by the execution of the operation $V(s_1)$. This will block all tasks in the application until the resource is released, which occurs at $t = 5$. Once released, the highest-priority task τ_4, which was activated at $t = 4$, resumes execution until completion. Then, the

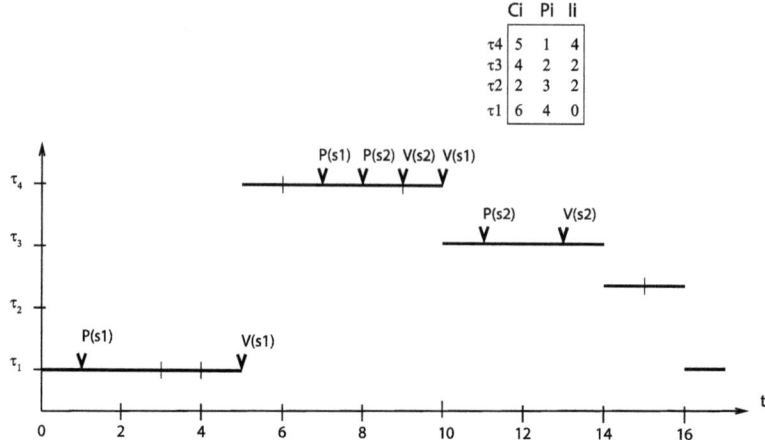

Fig. 4.11 Example of avoiding priority inversion with a non-preemptive critical section

remaining tasks will proceed in ascending priority order: τ_3, τ_2; and, finally, the task τ_1, the lowest-priority task in the application, will execute its remaining unit.

4.4.3.1 Blocking Time Computation

The RMS test can still be used if priority inversion is treated as a constant term within the feasibility inequality. In this case, for each task τ_i, it is necessary to compute the reduction in available processor time due to blocking caused by lower-priority tasks holding resources required by τ_i. This reduction is quantified by the *calculation of the blocking factor B_i* for each task τ_i of the set of tasks in the application. Subsequently, we can apply the RMS test for each task, assuming that the task τ_i will now have a worst-case execution time C_i^*. The worst-case execution time C_i of the task τ_i will be increased by the constant value of the calculated blocking factor: $C_i^* = C_i + B_i$. where C_i is the original worst-case execution time and B_i is the blocking factor. This adjusted execution time accounts for the additional delay τ_i may encounter due to resource contention.

The blocking factor B_i is to be determined by analyzing the worst-case scheduling scenario for the task τ_i, i.e., the maximum time it could be blocked by any lower-priority task τ_j that shares a resource with it.

It should be noted that each protocol that we are going to propose to limit the priority inversion problem provides different values of B_i, as a result of the calculation of the blocking factor for the same task.

Under the non-preemptive critical section protocol, a higher-priority task can be blocked, at most, once by a lower-priority task executing a shared critical section at the time of its activation. Therefore, the calculation of the blocking factor for each τ_i of the complete set of tasks will be given by $B_i = \max_{j>i}(\max_k(D(S_{jk})))$, where S_{jk} represents the k-th critical section executed by task τ_j less prioritised than τ_i and $D(S_{jk})$ is its duration. The inequality ($j > i$), referring to the indices of the identifiers of the tasks τ_i and τ_j reflects the assumed indexing convention where tasks with lower indices have higher priority.

4.4 General Models of Real-Time Tasks

4.4.4 Priority Inheritance Protocol

With this protocol, task priorities are no longer maintained *static* throughout the execution of the program, allowing the system to minimise the effects of priority inversion and optimise processor utilisation in real-time applications.

If the higher-priority task τ_i is blocked waiting for a lower-priority τ_j to release a protected resource (i.e., a mutual exclusion section), then the priority of τ_j is raised to match that of τ_i while τ_j holds the mutual exclusion lock on the resource blocking τ_i. Therefore, during its execution, the effective priority of a task becomes the maximum of: (a) its own base priority (the one used to access the critical section), and (b) the priorities of all higher-priority tasks it is currently blocking. Figure 4.12 shows an execution scenario of four tasks accessing two shared protected objects, represented by the critical sections $\{x, y\}$. The attributes of the tasks shown in the figure are summarised in Table 4.9.

As can be seen in Fig. 4.12, the tasks in Table 4.9 can suffer from two types of deadlocks:

1. *Direct*, Task τ_1 is directly blocked by tasks τ_4 and τ_2 when attempts to access the critical sections represented by the code segments ax and ay, which it shares with these tasks.

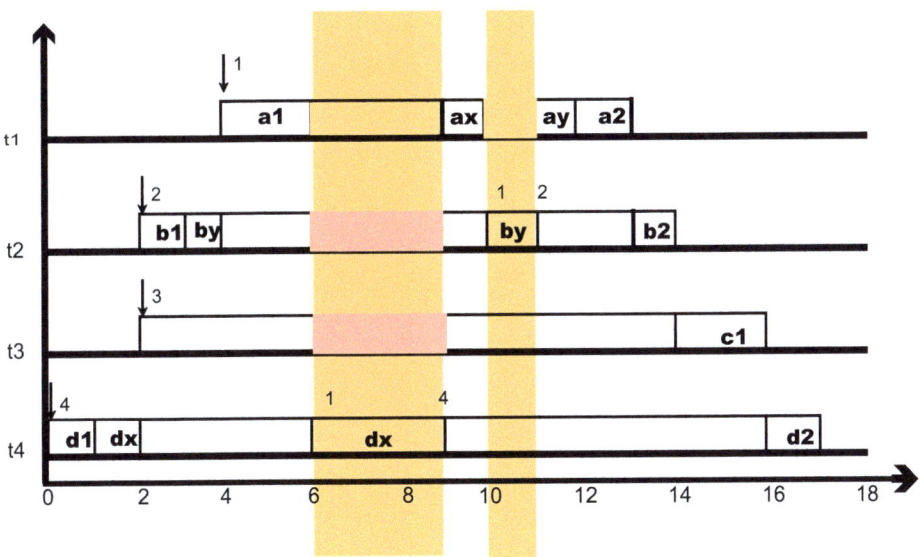

Fig. 4.12 Scenario of four tasks using the priority inheritance protocol

Table 4.9 Set of four tasks accessing critical sections: x and y

Task	Priority	C_i	Actions (time units)
τ_1	1	5	$a1(2); ax(1); ay(1); a2(1)$
τ_2	2	4	$b1(1); by(2); b2(1)$
τ_3	3	2	$c1(2)$
τ_4	4	6	$d1(1); dx(4); d2(1)$

2. *Indirect*, where tasks τ_2 and τ_3 are indirectly blocked by task τ_4 whose priority has been raised to the highest level (priority = 1), or system priority, while it is blocking task τ_1.

Although this protocol effectively reduces the impact of priority inversion, it does not prevent multiple blocking occurrences of a high-priority task during its execution. For this reason, the priorities of lower-priority tasks may change frequently during their execution. Due to this dynamic behaviour, implementing the protocol using a priority-ordered ready queue may be inefficient. In addition, the *priority inheritance* protocol does not prevent either deadlock of tasks subsets in accessing resources, nor does it eliminate the possibility of chained or transitive blocking scenarios.

4.4.4.1 Blocking Time Computation

The fundamental characteristic of this protocol, with respect to its influence on the dynamic behaviour of the program's tasks, is that by applying *priority inheritance*, tasks can only be blocked a limited number of times by lower-priority ones. By temporarily raising the priority of the task holding a protected resource to match that of the highest-priority task it is currently blocking, the protocol prevents preemption by tasks of intermediate priority, effectively mitigating the main cause of priority inversion during the execution of tasks in a real-time application.

We can therefore establish the following facts if the *priority inheritance* protocol is applied:

1. If a high-priority task contains M critical sections, then the maximum number of times it can be blocked during its execution is M times.
2. If there are only N lower-priority tasks (with $N < M$), then the maximum number of deadlocks that the highest priority task may experience is N.

Consequently, to calculate the blocking factor B_i of a task τ_i, it is necessary to identify which critical sections may be in use by lower-priority tasks when τ_i is activated and which of those may block its execution. This includes both direct and indirect blocking, where τ_i might be delayed not due to shared resources but due to temporary priority elevation of other tasks of the protocol.

The blocking factor for this protocol is often difficult to calculate systematically and accurately. Therefore, algorithms for doing so usually provide an estimate of the blocking factor, which consists of providing an upper bound on the blocking time based on the smaller of the two following values:

1. B_i^I : blocking due lower-priority tasks τ_j, which access critical sections, even if they are not shared with task τ_i, as their priority could be raised and indirectly cause blocking of task τ_i:

$$B_i^I = \sum_{j=i+1}^{n} \max_k \left[Duration_{j,k} : Limit(S_k) \geq P_i \right]$$

4.4 General Models of Real-Time Tasks

2. B_i^s: blocking due to all critical sections accessed by the task τ_i:

$$B_i^s = \sum_{k=1}^{m} \max_{j>i} \left[Duration_{j,k} : Limit(S_k) \geq P_i \right]$$

Here $Limit(S_k)$ refers to the ceiling priority, that is, the highest-priority of any task that may access critical section k. In the above protocol, only critical sections S_k that have a priority limit not lower than the priority of the task τ_i are considered. $Duration_{j,k}$ refers to the execution time of critical section k when executed by task τ_j. Finally, the blocking factor for task τ_i is given by:

$$B_i = \min\left(B_i^I, B_i^s\right)$$

4.4.5 Priority Ceiling Protocol

The *priority inheritance* protocol provides an upper bound on the duration a high-priority task of a real-time application may be blocked under the worst-case scheduling scenario for it. However, this upper bound is often an estimate of the blocking factor. It is unacceptably pessimistic in certain scenarios. As previously discussed, the priority inheritance protocol is susceptible to *transitive* priority inversions or deadlock chains that occur, which can significantly inflate blocking time estimates.

To mitigate this limitation, priority-ceiling-based protocols are proposed. These protocols regulate access to shared resources through predefined priority ceilings of the resources, helping prevent unbounded blocking. The most common priority ceiling protocols (PCP) currently in use are the original priority ceiling protocol (OPCP) and the immediate priority ceiling protocol (IPCP). ICPP is designed to provide immediate priority boosting for lower-priority tasks when blocking a resource. OPCP applies priority inheritance when blocking a higher-priority task.

When implemented on a uniprocessor system, priority ceiling protocols offer several important guarantees:

1. A high-priority task can only be blocked at most once during its execution by lower priority tasks.
2. Deadlocks are prevented.
3. Chained transitive blocking is avoided.
4. Mutual exclusion in access to shared resources is guaranteed.

With this type of protocols, task blocking may occur in two situations:

1. When a task attempts to block a resource that is currently held by another task.
2. When a task's access to a resource could lead to multiple higher-priority tasks being blocked.

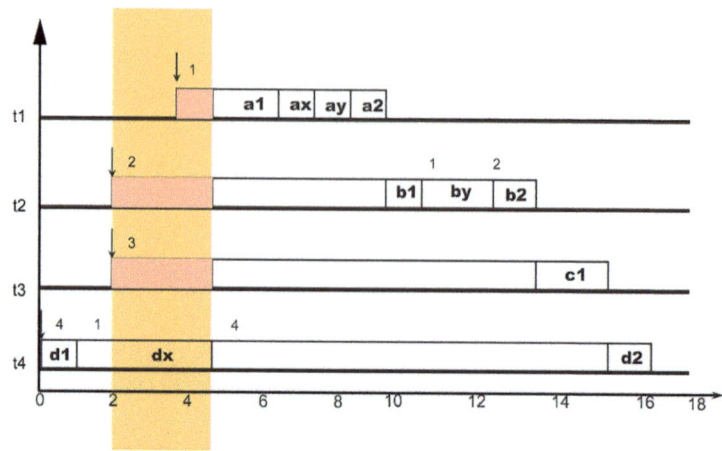

Fig. 4.13 Immediate priority ceiling protocol (IPCP) scheduling for the four tasks in Table 4.9

We will now discuss how the above properties can be met for the IPCP protocol, which part of the POSIX standard for real-time operating systems. First, however, we will define the concept of the *priority ceiling* of a resource as the highest priority of any task that may acquire that resource during program execution.

The *priority ceiling* of a resource effectively represents the highest execution priority that a critical section can have. It is determined across all tasks that could potentially access that resource within the system's execution.

4.4.5.1 Immediate Priority Ceiling Protocol

This protocol is defined in the POSIX standard as *Priority Protected Protocol* (PPP) and is governed by the following rules:

1. Each task is assigned a fixed static priority.
2. Each shared resource has a defined *priority ceiling*, which matches the highest priority of the tasks that use it[4] during the execution of the application.
3. A task has a dynamic priority that is the maximum of its own static priority and the priority ceilings of any resources it currently holds.

In Fig. 4.13 task τ_4 starts executing first. Since resource 'x' is free τ_4 successfully locks it and enters its critical section. Its priority is immediately raised to the maximum level, which corresponds to the *priority ceiling* of that resource (*priority* = 1). While τ_4 holds the resource (for 4 time units, until $t = 5$), no other task can execute.

---

[4]This value is obtained for the resource in question by observing the code of the application tasks before execution begins.

Under this protocol, a task can block only at the start of its execution, because a task may only begin if all the resources it will use are currently unheld. Otherwise, those resources would already have been locked by tasks of equal or higher priority, preventing execution of the task. Consequently, the aforementioned properties such as deadlock prevention, elimination of transitive blocking, and guaranteed mutual exclusion are inherently satisfied by this protocol.

The IPCP protocol is easier to implement than the *original priority ceiling protocol* (OPCP), requiring fewer context switches as blocking of tasks always occurs prior to their execution. On the other hand, the IPCP implementation needs, in general, more priority changes than the original OPCP protocol, since a task's priority is raised each time it locks a resource.

Both ceiling-based protocols (OPCP and IPCP) ensure mutual exclusion in the access to shared resources, without requiring additional synchronisation primitives (semaphores, etc.). Once a task locks a resource, then it inherits the resource's priority ceiling, ensuring it cannot be preempted by any other task that may also use that resource. Therefore, either the task accesses the resource without being interrupted until it completes or the task is blocked before trying to access the resource. In this way, the IPCP protocol inherently guarantees mutual exclusion when accessing shared resources.

4.4.5.2 Blocking Time Computation

Since *priority ceiling* protocols ensure that a high-priority task can only experience a single initial blocking, then the maximum value of the blocking time B_i of a task τ_i is equal to the duration of the longest critical section S_k accessed by lower-priority tasks τ_j, provided those critical sections possess a priority ceiling that is not lower than the priority of task τ_i. Formally:

$$B_i = \forall j : i+1...n, k : 1...m : \\ \left\{ Max_{j,k} Dur_{j,k} \mid prio(\tau_j) < prio(\tau_i), priority\_ceiling(S_k) \geq prio(\tau_i) \right\}$$

It important to note that a task τ_i may experience indirect blocking, i.e., it may be delayed by lower-priority tasks, even if they do not share resources directly with it. Therefore, to calculate the blocking factor under priority ceiling protocols, the duration of all critical sections $\{S_k\}$ accessed by lower-priority tasks $(j : i + 1...n, \{\tau_j\})$ must be considered.

4.5 Scheduling Analysis of Aperiodic and Sporadic Tasks

A straightforward approach to scheduling *non-periodic* tasks in a real-time system would be to assign them a lower priority than non-permissive critical tasks. However, acting in this way, such tasks would run only as background activities, often causing them miss their maximum response times.

To enhance the responsiveness in applications where tasks may occasionally miss a deadline, without compromising the safety of a non-strict or permissive real-time system, an aperiodic request server can be implemented. This server functions as a real or *conceptual* task that preserves the scheduling guarantees of non-permissive periodic tasks, while enabling aperiodic tasks to execute as soon as possible. In this way, strict time constraints are upheld for critical tasks, while more flexible, non-periodic tasks are given improved response times when system resources permit.

4.5.1 Background Server

This solution, which remains compatible with the RMS test, involves allocating dedicated processor time to handle aperiodic task requests. This so-called aperiodic time is periodically replenished, always with the lowest system's priority. It is exclusively reserved for processing pending service requests corresponding to aperiodic tasks that have not yet been activated.

Figure 4.14 illustrates the execution timeline for two periodic tasks, represented by τ_1 and τ_2, along with the server task *BS* processing an aperiodic request at $t = 2.8$, requiring 1.7 time units. The attributes of the tasks shown in the figure are detailed in Table 4.10.

In Fig. 4.14, it can be observed that 0.5 units of the periodic task τ_2, the only active at $t = 0$, are executed first. The task τ_1 has an activation offset of $\Phi = 2$, begins execution at $t = 2$ and runs for 1.5 time units, until $t = 3.5$. At $t = 2.8$, an aperiodic service request of 1.7 units occurred but is not handled until τ_1 completes its execution. This delay occurs because the time allocated for processing aperiodic requests has the lowest system priority and cannot be used while periodic tasks are still pending. As a result, the aperiodic request

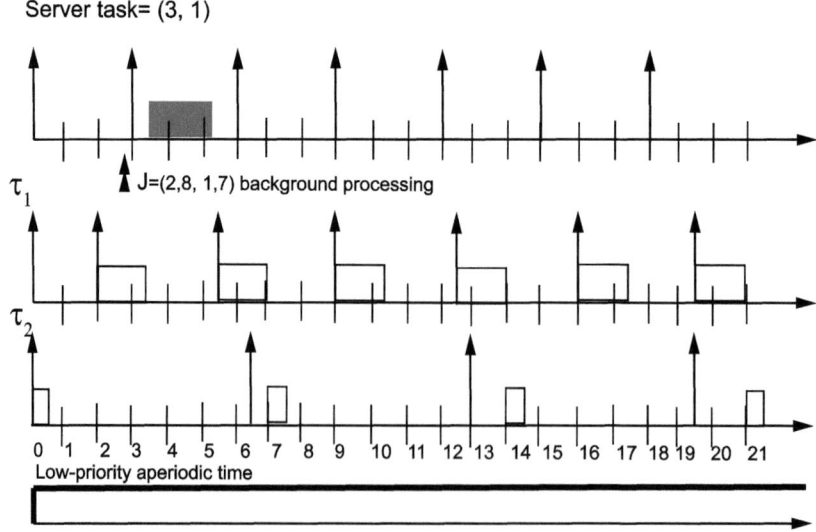

Fig. 4.14 Background (slack stealing) Server Scheduling for Aperiodic Requests

4.5 Scheduling Analysis of Aperiodic and Sporadic Tasks

Table 4.10 Set of two periodic tasks and one aperiodic request server acting as a *conceptual* task

Task	Priority	C_i	T_i	I_i
τ_1	1	1.5	3.5	2
τ_2	2	0.5	6.5	0
BS	3	1.0	3.0	0

is serviced with a response time ending at $t = 5.2$. This technique for scheduling aperiodic requests is known as "Slack Stealing Server" or "Background Server" (*BS*).

Notably, even when there are no pending aperiodic requests, the time reserved for them is not discarded, Instead, it is preserved, though at low priority, for future aperiodic service needs that may occur in the system.

4.5.2 Aperiodic Polling Server

In this case, the aim is to improve the response times of aperiodic tasks in comparison to the Background Server method. An aperiodic service request *polling* task is added to the application tasks, which can be a real or *conceptual* task. This approach avoids the need to create a fully independent task as such in the protocol, instead reserving a block of processor time dedicated to polling and serving aperiodic requests at a lower priority than that of periodic tasks. This is, in fact, time set aside for an additional task that may even be transformed into *periodic* time in the absence of aperiodic requests, i.e., if there are no pending aperiodic requests at the moment of system execution, it will be used to run the active periodic tasks.

Unlike the *BS*, which handles aperiodic requests in the background, a size (C_s) is now reserved, equivalent to the worst-case execution time of an added periodic task. However, unlike regular periodic whose priorities are determined by their period (T_s), the polling task can be assigned a priority based on design needs. This allows obtaining greater flexibility for ensuring responsiveness without affecting the execution of periodic tasks.

Figure 4.15 shows a scenario of execution of two periodic tasks, τ_1 and, along with the handling of an aperiodic request of 1.7 time units which arrives at $t = 2.8$. In this scenario, the system allocates a time C_s (=1 full time unit) of the highest priority to the polling server, with an *activation period* $T_s = 3.0$. As can be seen in the figure, the full reserved time is used at $t = 3.0$ to begin servicing the aperiodic request. The aperiodic request must wait for the second server cycle (at $t = 6$) to complete the remaining 0.7 units. By $t = 6.7$, the server returns its remaining time to the system for servicing periodic tasks, as no further aperiodic requests are pending at that moment.

As with background processing (*BS*), the polling task method, does not guarantee immediate servicing of aperiodic requests. The response depends on both the priority and activation period assigned to the polling task.

Nevertheless, this method ensures the schedulability of periodic tasks under the RMS test, regardless of the number or frequency of incoming aperiodic requests. To achieve this, a maximum time equal to C_s time units is reserved for the polling task in each

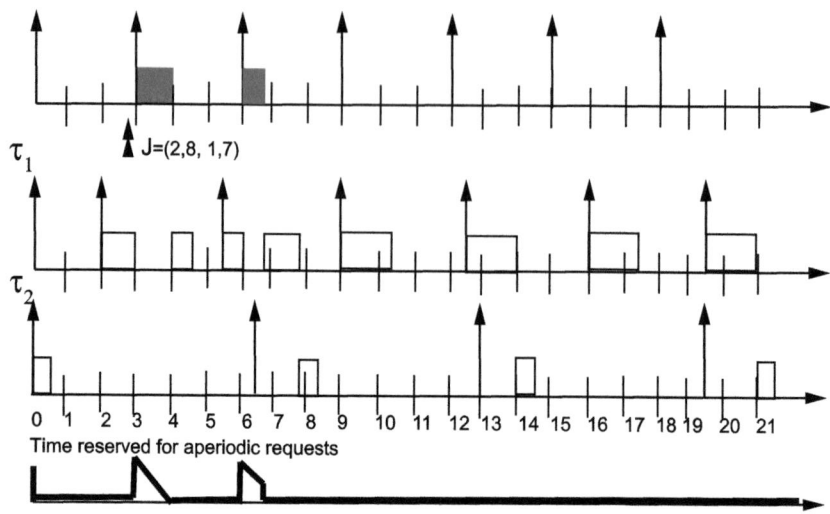

Fig. 4.15 Polling Server scheduling for aperiodic requests using the reserved time ($C = 1.0$)

activation period T_s (or polling cycle). As a consequence, the processor upper limit for the polling task is given by: $U_s = \dfrac{C_s}{T_s}$. Therefore, the combined schedulability of the N periodic tasks (excluding the polling task), using static priority assignment under the RM algorithm, can be guaranteed by satisfying the condition given in Liu and Layland's Theorem-I:

$$\sum_{i=1}^{N} \frac{C_i}{T_i} + \frac{C_s}{T_s} \leq (N+1)\left[2^{\frac{1}{(N+1)}} - 1\right]$$

4.5.3 Deferred Server Approach for Efficient Aperiodic Task Handling

This approach relies on the implementation of a *deferred server* (DS), which preserves the allocated aperiodic time even during periods when no service requests are present, in contrast to the solution based on the polling task where unused time may be lost.

The DS is allocated a maximum capacity C_s, which is used to handle aperiodic requests. This capacity is replenished to its maximum in each cycle (T_s) of the server with a fixed period T_s. To implement the protocol, it is first necessary to perform a schedulability analysis of the real-time application or system in order to determine the appropriate server size. In practice, this corresponds to reserving a portion of processor time for the execution of aperiodic tasks. This reserved time (C_s) is assigned to an aperiodic server task of the highest priority, which is integrated into the system's scheduling along with the remaining periodic tasks, such that: $\sum_{i=1}^{N} \dfrac{C_i}{T_i} + \dfrac{C_s}{T_s} \leq U_0(N+1)$. These C_s and T_s are chosen to ensure

4.5 Scheduling Analysis of Aperiodic and Sporadic Tasks

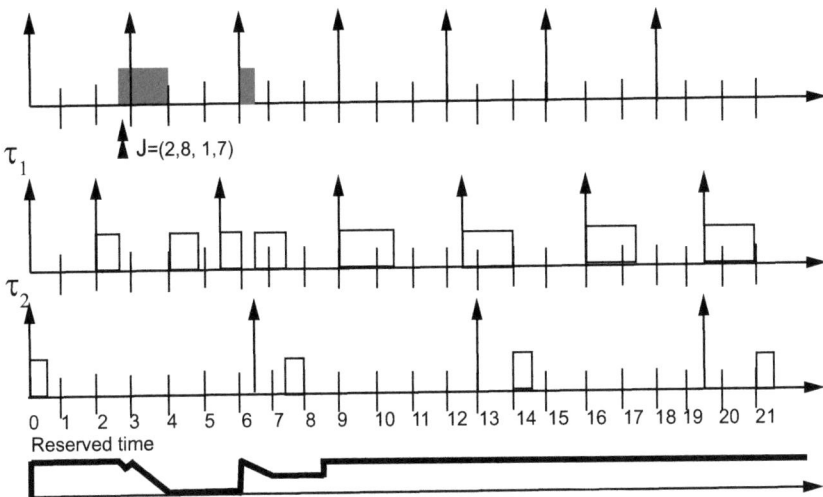

Fig. 4.16 Deferred server scheduling for aperiodic task handling

that all periodic tasks classified as mission-critical in the system always meet their deadlines. This approach guarantees that the execution time dedicated to aperiodic requests remains at a very-high-priority level throughout each defered server cycle, while maintaining compliance with the system's safety requirements. Therefore, when an aperiodic task is released, it is immediately served at the highest priority until the server's capacity is exhausted.

Figure 4.16 shows a scenario of execution of two periodic tasks, τ_1 and τ_2, from Table 4.10, along with the deferred server's processing of a 1.7 time units aperiodic request at time $t = 2.8$. The server capacity C_s is set to 1.0 time and is reset at every cycle of $T_s = 3.0$ units. Unused capacity from previous cycles does not carry over. As illustrated in the diagram, the aperiodic request is served immediately, with the highest priority, preempting task τ_1, and consuming 0.2 units of the time reserved for the deferred server until the server time is replenished at $t = 3.0$. Therefore, at $t = 4.0$, there are still 0.5 units of time remaining to complete the aperiodic request, which is completed once the server time is refilled at $t = 6.0$. Consequently, the aperiodic request has a response time of $R_s = 6.5$, while tasks τ_1 and τ_2 have response times of $(R_1 = 4.7)$ and $(R_2 = 0.5)$, respectively.

4.5.4 Scheduling Analysis

Consider a set of N periodic tasks, $\tau_1 \ldots \tau_N$ along with a *deferred server* D_s that is assigned the highest priority in the system. The worst-case scheduling condition is based on a complex calculation involving the processor utilisation limit U as the sum of two terms:

1. The utilisation (U_s) of the deferred server D_s
2. The combined utilisation of the N periodic tasks

The worst-case scenario for scheduling the periodic task set $\{\tau_i\}$, $i: 1 \ldots N$ occurs when their periods T_i are relatively close and satisfy the bounding relationship: $T_1 < T_2, \ldots, T_N < 2 \cdot T_1$. This situation, which can be seen in the diagram in Fig. 4.17, leads to the highest level of interference between tasks.

In the most general and adverse case, where the most interference occurs between the tasks in the set $\{\tau_i\}$, the deferred server D_s can execute up to three times within the period of the highest-priority task (τ_1). This scenario will occur when D_s delays its service execution, using C_s units of aperiodic time at the end of its period T_s and again at the beginning of the next. In such as situation, as shown in Fig. 4.17, the full utilisation of processor time is achieved, and the worst-case execution parameters (C_s, T_s) of the deferred server D_s, and the corresponding (C_i, T_i) values of the periodic tasks satisfy the following relationships:

$$C_s = T_1 - (T_s + C_s) = \frac{T_1 - T_s}{2}$$

$$C_1 = T_2 - T_1$$

$$C_2 = T_3 - T_2$$

$$\ldots$$

$$C_{N-1} = T_N - T_{N-1}$$

$$C_N = C_s + T_s - 2C_s - \sum_{i=1}^{N-1} C_i = \frac{3T_s + T_1 - 2T_N}{2}$$

since the full processor utilisation factor, which includes that of the periodic and server tasks, is given by the following expression: $U = U_s + \dfrac{C_1}{T_1} + \dfrac{C_2}{T_2} + \cdots + \dfrac{C_N}{T_N}$ and $U_s = \dfrac{C_s}{T_s}$.

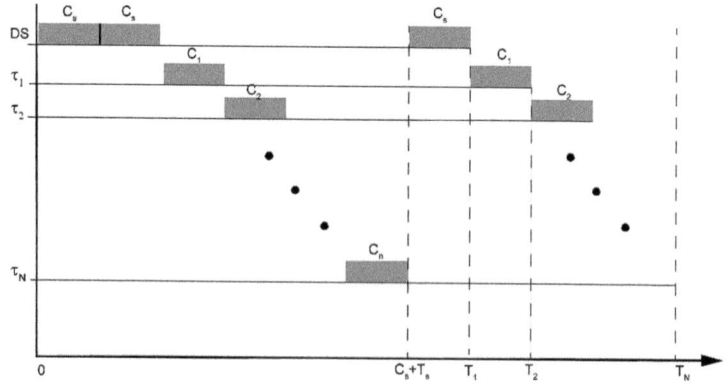

Fig. 4.17 Execution diagram of a set of N periodic tasks and one deferred server to attend aperiodic requests

4.5 Scheduling Analysis of Aperiodic and Sporadic Tasks

Substituting the values of C_i indicated in the previous equations and performing operations on the latter, the total processor utilisation limit U can be written as:

$$U = U_s + \frac{T_2}{T_1} + \cdots + \frac{T_N}{T_{N-1}} + \left(\frac{3T_s}{2T_1} + \frac{1}{2}\right) \cdot \frac{T_1}{T_N} - N \tag{4.1}$$

Considering the previous form (4.1), we can now calculate the minimum value of the function U with respect to the parameter $R_i = \frac{T_{i+1}}{T_i} (i = 1 \ldots N-1)$, which represents the ratio between the period of the next task τ_{i+1} and the current one τ_i, for which we pose the extremum condition of the function $U(R_i)$ cancelling the partial derivative: $\frac{\partial U(R_i)}{\partial R_i} = 0$.
We obtain, then, that the processor utilisation is minimum when all the values of R_i have a value identical to $\sqrt[N]{K}$, where $K = \frac{1}{2}\left(\frac{3T_s}{T_1} + 1\right) = \frac{1}{2}\left(\frac{3}{R_s} + 1\right) = \frac{U_s + 2}{2U_s + 1}$. Then, substituting in Eq. (4.1) R_i by K and $R_s = \frac{T_1}{T_s}$ by $2U_s + 1$, we obtain the *lower* upper-*bound*:

$$U_{mls} = U_s + N \cdot \left(\sqrt[N]{K} - 1\right) \tag{4.2}$$

The lower upper-bound U_{mls}, which is the minimum of the processor utilisation bounds (U) among the sets of tasks that attempt to use all the processor time, has therefore been calculated. After substituting K for its expression as a function of U_s, in Eq. (4.2), we obtain the following canonical expression of U_{mls}:

$$U_{mls} = U_s + N\left[\left(\frac{U_s + 2}{2U_s + 1}\right)^{\frac{1}{N}} - 1\right] \tag{4.3}$$

Taking the limit for $N \to \infty$, we find the *minimum upper limit of* processor time *utilisation* for the D_s, assuming a very large number of periodic tasks:

$$\lim_{N \to \infty} U_{mls} = U_s + \ln\left(\frac{U_s + 2}{2U_s + 1}\right) \tag{4.4}$$

Consequently, given a set of N periodic tasks and a deferred server D_s with utilisation limits U_p and U_s, respectively, the schedulability of the set of periodic tasks is guaranteed with the RMS algorithm if $U_p + U_s \leq U_{mls}$, i.e., if the following inequality is satisfied:

$$U_p \leq \ln\left(\frac{U_s + 2}{2U_s + 1}\right) \tag{4.5}$$

4.6 Exercises

The exercises in this section are framed in real-time task scheduling using the RMS algorithm and Rate Monotonic Analysis (RMA). RMS/RMA [11, 45] comprises a set of techniques that assign fixed priorities to tasks according to their activation frequency. This method provides a mathematically rigorous foundation for the design of highly complex real-time systems.

4.6.1 Solved Exercises

Exercise 4.1

Verify the schedulability, and construct the task execution diagram for the next set of periodic tasks using the Rate Monotonic (RM) algorithm:

	C_i	T_i
τ_1	2	6
τ_2	2	8
τ_3	2	12

Solution The given set of tasks is schedulable according to the RMS test, as the total processor utilization is only 0.75.

The utilization is calculated as: $U = \dfrac{2}{6} + \dfrac{2}{8} + \dfrac{2}{12} = 0.75$. The RMS schedulability bound for three tasks is: $U_0(3) = 3 \times (2^{1/3} - 1) \approx 0.78$ (see Table 4.6). Since $U < U_0(3)$, the task set is schedulable, according to *Liu-Layland Theorem I*.

The schedulability of the given set of tasks can be confirmed graphically using the Gantt chart shown in Fig. 4.18:

Fig. 4.18 Gannt chart for the tasks in Exercise 4.1

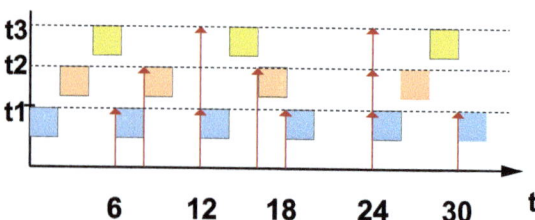

4.6 Exercises

Exercise 4.2

Verify the schedulability of the next task set using the Earliest Deadline First (EDF) scheduling algorithm:

	C_i	T_i
τ_1	1	4
τ_2	2	6
τ_3	3	8

Solution The task set is schedulable under the EDF algorithm if we take, for each task τ_i, the value of the maximum response time D_i equal to its period ($D_i = T_i$). This condition is satisfied, as shown in Fig. 4.19.

It can be seen that the processor utilisation that produces this set of tasks is less than 100%: $U = \frac{1}{4} + \frac{2}{6} + \frac{3}{8} = 0.96$. Therefore, applying *Liu-Layland theorem II*, this set of tasks is schedulable with EDF.

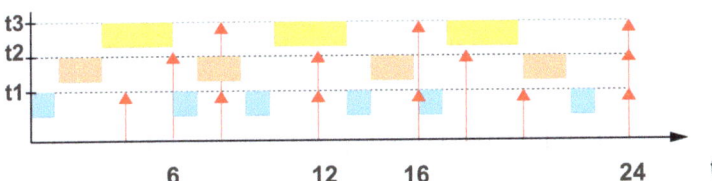

Fig. 4.19 Gantt chart for the tasks in Exercise 4.2

Exercise 4.3

Check the schedulability and construct the task execution diagram using RMS for the next set of periodic tasks:

	C_i	T_i
τ_1	3	5
τ_2	1	8
τ_3	2	10

Solution According to the RMS test, it cannot be guaranteed that this task set is schedulable, as the total processor utilisation: $U = \frac{3}{5} + \frac{1}{8} + \frac{2}{1} = 0.825$ exceeds the upper bound $U_0(3) = 0.78$ assumed by the RMS test.

However, the task execution diagram shown in Fig. 4.20, demonstrates that the tasks are indeed schedulable in practice, despite the RMS test not confirming it analytically.

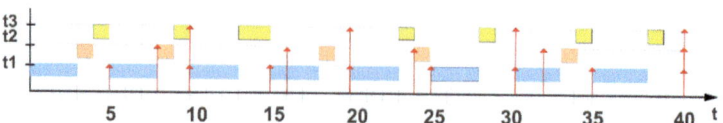

Fig. 4.20 Gantt chart for the tasks in Exercise 4.3

Exercise 4.4

Check the schedulability using the EDF algorithm, and construct the task execution diagram for the following task set:

	C_i	D_i	T_i
τ_1	2	5	6
τ_2	2	4	8
τ_3	4	8	12

Solution This task set is schedulable under the EDF (Earliest Deadline First) scheduling algorithm, since the total processor utilization satisfies the condition: $U = \frac{2}{6} + \frac{2}{8} + \frac{4}{12} \approx 0.917 < 1.0$. As illustrated in Fig. 4.21, the arrows with round heads represent the deadlines D_i for each task, while the others mark the end of each period T_i on the timeline of each task.

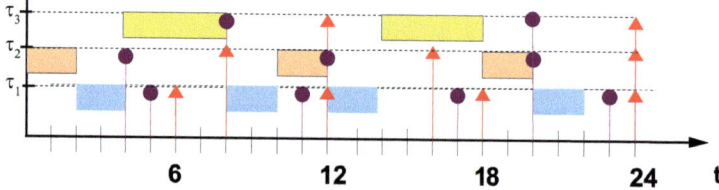

Fig. 4.21 Gantt chart for tasks in Exercise 4.4

4.6 Exercises

Exercise 4.5 Verify the schedulability of the task set from Exercise 4.4, this time using prioritisation based on the maximum response time D_i, also known as Deadline Monotonic (DM).

Solution The task set is not schedulable under the DM algorithm, which assigns static priorities based on the task deadlines D_i. As can be seen in Fig. 4.22, task τ_3 misses its deadline at time $t = \{8, 20, \ldots\}$.

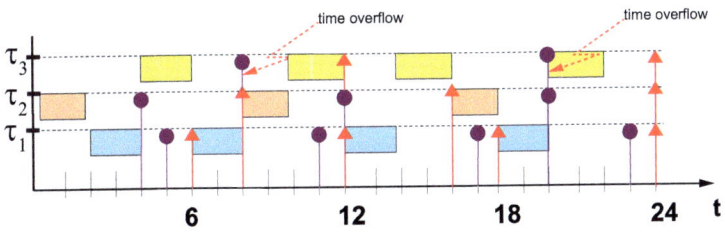

Fig. 4.22 Gantt chart for the tasks in Exercise 4.5

Exercise 4.6

For the periodic tasks $\{\tau_1, \tau_2\}$, the aperiodic service requests $\{J_1, J_2, J_3\}$ and the sporadic request server SS described in the table below, address the following exercises:

(a) Calculate the maximum processor utilisation that can be allocated to the *sporadic server* (SS) to ensure the schedulability of the periodic tasks using the RM algorithm.
(b) Determine the maximum processor utilisation limit that can be assigned to a deferred server (D_s) to preserve the schedulability of the periodic tasks.
(c) Design a feasible task scheduling that accommodates the aperiodic requests J_i, using an D_s implemented as a polling task, which has a maximum utilisation and an intermediate priority between τ_1 and τ_2.

	C_i	T_i
τ_1	1	5
τ_2	2	8
J_1	3	–
J_2	1	–
J_3	1	–
D_s	2	6

Solution

(a) The sporadic server (SS) behaves like a periodic task. In the worst-case scheduling situation, where interference among tasks is maximised, the task set $\{\tau_1, \tau_2\}$ is schedulable under the RM algorithm if the following condition is satisfied:

$$U_p \leq n \times \left(\left(\frac{2}{U_s+1}\right)^{\frac{1}{n}} - 1\right) \Rightarrow U_s \leq 2 \times \left(\frac{n}{U_p+n}\right)^n - 1.$$ This inequality ensures the combined processor utilization from periodic tasks (U_p) and the sporadic server (U_s) does not exceed a safe upper bound for schedulability. The meaning of the variables in the above equation is as follows:

n	Number of periodic tasks
U_p	Use of the processor by periodic tasks
U_s	Processor utilisation by the sporadic server

For $n \to \infty : U_p \leq \ln\left(\frac{2}{U_s+1}\right)$.

Then, for $n = 2 : U_{s_{max}} = 0.33$ if we assume a utilisation limit $U_p = 0.45$. and $U_{s_{max}} = 2 \times \left(\frac{n}{U_p+n}\right)^n - 1$.

(b) The maximum processor utilisation U_s for a deferred server (D_s) that preserves the schedulability of the task set $\{\tau_1, \tau_2 \ldots\}$ is given by the following inequation:

$$U_p \leq n \times \left(\left(\frac{U_s+2}{2 \cdot U_s+1}\right)^{\frac{1}{n}} - 1\right) \Rightarrow U_s \leq \frac{2-K}{2 \cdot K - 1} \text{ where } K = \left(\frac{U_p+n}{n}\right)^n$$

For $n \to \infty : U_p \leq \ln\left(\frac{U_s+2}{U_s+1}\right)$.

We can compute for $n = 2$ that $U_{s_{max}} = 0.25$ if we assume $U_p = 0.45$ and $U_{s_{max}} = \frac{2-K}{2K-1}$.

(c) Given $U_{s_{max}} = 0.25$, we assign the deferred server a period $T_s = 6$ (intermediate priority between $\tau_1 = 5$ and $\tau_2 = 8$) and execution time $C_s = 2$. This satisfies the schedulability condition for $\{\tau_1, \tau_2\}$ and permits aperiodic request handling even with the occurrence of the aperiodic requests, $\{J_1, J_2, J_3\}$, as can be seen in the task execution diagram (Fig. 4.23). The figure shows a scenario of execution of the two periodic tasks, τ_1 and τ_2, of periods 5 and 8 units, respectively. In addition, we have the processing by a polling server task of three aperiodic requests: J_1 of 3 time units, occurring at $t = 2.0$, and J_2 and J_3 of 1 unit, occurring at $t = 7.0$ and $t = 17.0$. In this case, the system assigns a time $C_s = 2$ full units of intermediate priority to the polling task with an activation period $T_s = 6$ time units. As seen in the figure, at $t = 6.0$, all the time allocated to the server is used to partially serve the aperiodic request J_1, which has to wait until the second server cycle (at $t = 12.0$) to complete 1 remaining execution unit. At $t = 13.0$, the second aperiodic request J_2 is served completely. The server time is refilled at $t = 18.0$ to service the last pending aperiodic request (J_3) of 1 unit, and the remaining time is returned to service the periodic tasks, though it is not needed in the deferred server protocol, since at that instant ($t = 19.0$), there are no pending aperiodic requests. The time initially allocated to the server is lost because the first aperiodic request does not occur until $t = 2.0$.

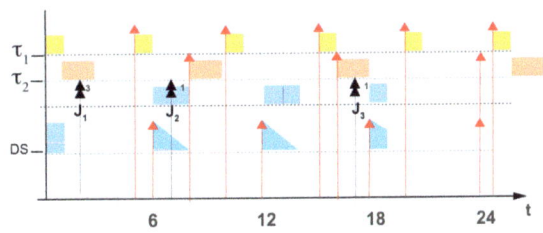

Fig. 4.23 Gantt chart for two periodic tasks and three sporadic requests

4.6.2 Proposed Exercises

Exercise 4.7 The following questions are about general concepts of real-time systems (RTS). Select the correct answer, if applicable:

(a) Real-time programs are characterised by the high execution frequency of their task instructions.
(b) A real-time system is considered *reliable* if its processes never become unresponsive.
(c) A system cannot be classified as real-time if the completion time of all its tasks' first activations cannot be determined.
(d) *Responsiveness* refers to a system's ability to limit the number of nested interrupts affecting any critical task.
(e) A real-time system is defined by having clock frequencies exceeding 10 GHz.

Exercise 4.8 Concepts of time measurement in computer systems. Select the correct answer:

(a) The monotonic time of a computer refers to a time source that never moves backward or runs out and is not affected by changes to the system clock.
(b) The accuracy of a real-time clock is determined by the smallest measurable time interval that is displayed on screen using `gettimeofday(...)` command in Linux.
(c) There are ways to prevent any kind of drift (both local and accumulative) within the time window configured for the start of a real-time task.

(d) In practice, eliminating *drift* would require discounting task-external delays in every cycle.

(e) A computer can support multiple POSIX real-time clocks, depending on how many are implemented and accessible in the operating system.

Exercise 4.9 Concepts of the simple task model of RTSs. Select the correct answer:

(a) The simple task model does not support synchronization between tasks.
(b) In this model, real-time tasks may have different time limits depending on when they are activated.
(c) A task's maximum response time depends solely on when it is activated next.
(d) Assigning priorities based on the shortest response times constitutes a static priority scheme.
(e) Assigning higher priorities to tasks with closer deadlines corresponds to a dynamic priority scheme.

Exercise 4.10

Check the schedulability of the tasks in the following table by calculating the total processor utilisation, and comparing it with the utilisation upper bound (U_3) for RMS. Then, construct the task execution diagram using the Rate Monotonic (RM) scheduling algorithm for the following set of periodic tasks:

	C_i	T_i	Priority
τ_1	3	7	1
τ_2	3	12	1
τ_3	5	20	2

Exercise 4.11

Verify the schedulability of the following set of periodic tasks using the RMS, and draw the corresponding Gantt chart using the RM algorithm for the next set of periodic tasks:

	C_i	T_i
τ_1	1	4
τ_2	2	6
τ_3	3	10

Exercise 4.12 Calculate the response time (R_i) for each of the tasks in Exercise 4.10 and verify that they are 3, 6 and 20 time units, respectively.

4.6 Exercises

Exercise 4.13

Calculate the response time R_i for each task in the following set of periodic tasks:

	C_i	T_i
τ_1	1	4
τ_2	2	6
τ_3	3	8

Exercise 4.14

Calculate the response time R_i for each periodic task in the following table. Note that maximum response times (D_i) are provided to enable the potential application of the Deadline Monotonic scheduling algorithm.

	C_i	T_i	Priority	D_i
τ_1	3	12	1	8
τ_2	6	20	2	10

Exercise 4.15 For the set of tasks in Exercise 4.11 is it possible to find a feasible implementation, i.e., a real-time schedule that ensures all tasks complete each activation before reaching the maximum response times assigned to them in the table. Verifiy that the response times are 1, 3 and 7 times units, respectively.

Exercise 4.16

For task set $\{\tau_1, \tau_2, \tau_3\}$ defined below, complete the following:

(a) Draw the execution timeline diagram, and obtain the response time for each task.
(b) Using the diagram, determine how many times task τ_1 interferes with task τ_3 during the response interval of τ_3.
(c) Repeat the above for the interference of τ_1 and τ_2.
(d) Derive a general expression for the maximum number of times a higher-priority task τ_j can interfere with a lower-priority task τ_i as a function of τ_j's period (T_j) and the response time of τ_i (R_i). Then, discuss whether this can be used to formulate a new exact schedulability test for τ_i based on its timing parameters (T_i, D_i, R_i) and the interference caused by higher-priority tasks.

	C_i	T_i	D_i
τ_1	1	3	2
τ_2	3	6	5
τ_3	2	13	13

Exercise 4.17

Calculate the completion time of the task τ_3 and determine whether all tasks: AS (aperiodic server), SS (sporadic server) and the periodic tasks τ_1, τ_2 and τ_3 are all schedulable, using the parameters provided in the table below.

	T_i	C_i	B_i (Time block access to critical section)	Priority ceiling	Priority
SE	120	5	0	–	1
SA	40	2	0	–	2
τ_1	100	20	20	–	3
τ_2	150	40	20	–	4
τ_3	350	100	0	–	5
S_1	–	–	–	3	–
S_2	–	–	–	3	–

Exercise 4.18

Use a deferred server (D_s) implemented as a polling task with a capacity of $C_s = 2$ and a period of $T_s = 5$, to schedule the following set of tasks:

	C_i	T_i
τ_1	1	4
τ_2	2	6
	a_i	C_i
J_1	2	2
J_2	5	1
J_3	10	2

Exercise 4.19

Given the set of tasks described below, complete the following:

(a) Draw the execution diagram and determine the response time for each task.
(b) Based on the diagram, identify how many times the τ_1 interferes with task τ_3 during the interval defined by τ_3's response time.
(c) Redraw the execution diagram, calculate the response time and indicate the exact time instants when the dynamic priorities of the tasks change. We assume that these tasks are scheduled using the priority inheritance protocol.

	T_i	C_i	I_i	Resources	Priority
τ_1	16	4	5	A, B	4
τ_2	16	4	5	–	3
τ_3	16	5	2	B, A	2
τ_4	18	5	0	A	1

4.6 Exercises

Exercise 4.20 Indicate whether the following statements are true or false:

(a) Assigning priorities based on the shortest time limits results in a dynamic scheduling scheme.
(b) If tasks are scheduled using the Rate Monotonic (RM) algorithm, they are guaranteed to be schedulable if their combined processor utilisation does not exceed the upper bound: $N \times \left(2^{\frac{1}{N}} - 1\right)$.
(c) If tasks are statistically prioritised and always complete before their deadlines, all deadlines will be met.
(d) Static priority scheduling cannot guarantee the schedulability of independent periodic tasks when processor utilisation reaches 100%.
(e) If the system uses a deferred server (D_s) to handle aperiodic requests, and its capacity is exhausted, any new aperiodic requests that arrive before the next replenishment may be lost.
(f) A deferred server implemented as a *polling* task does necessarily have the same priority as the highest-priority periodic task; it is typically assigned an intermediate priority.
(g) Unused deferred server capacity is not cumulative; it is discarded at the end of each replenishment period.
(h) If the D_s has remaining capacity, it may be used to handle pending periodic requests.
(i) An aperiodic request can preempt a periodic task, if the server processing it has a higher priority.
(j) If tasks are scheduled with priority inheritance, a task temporarily assumes a higher priority only when it holds a shared resource required by a higher-priority task.
(k) With the *priority ceiling protocol* (PCP), a task holding a resource cannot be preempted unless the preempting task's priority needs resources currently locked.
(l) Under the immediate priority ceiling protocol (IPCP), a task cannot start if any of the resources it will need during its execution are already locked.

Exercise 4.21 Indicate whether the following statements are true:

(a) When tasks are scheduled using the priority inheritance protocol, the temporary elevation in priority is only maintained as long as the task holds a shared resource required by a higher priority task.
(b) Under the *priority ceiling protocol* (PCP), once a task acquires a resource, it cannot be preempted by tasks that are activated later and that might use resources with the same or lower priority ceiling in the future.
(c) With the *original priority ceiling protocol* (OPCP), a task cannot begin execution until all the resources it will require during its first cycle are available.
(d) If we consider a periodic task that uses the *immediate priority ceiling protocol* (IPCP) to adjust its dynamic priority when accessing resources, then it cannot be interrupted by any task with a lower priority during that time.

(e) With PCP, the highest-priority tasks in the system can be blocked at most once during each execution cycle when accessing resources shared with lower-priority tasks.
(f) The OPCP will always result in lower task response times than those obtained using the priority inheritance algorithm.

Exercise 4.22 With regard to aperiodic and sporadic task servers, select the correct answer:

(a) If the capacity of the deferred server, i.e., the time allocated for serving aperiodic tasks, is exhausted, any aperiodic requests arriving before the next replenishment cycle will be lost.
(b) If the aperiodic request service has exhausted its capacity in the current cycle, the spare time allocated to the periodic tasks can be used to handle pending aperiodic requests.
(c) Unused capacity of the deferred server time is not lost, but it is also not accumulated across cycles.
(d) An aperiodic request will interrupt a periodic task regardless of the latter's criticality.
(e) The aperiodic server is always assigned the highest priority in the system.

Exercise 4.23 Regarding algorithms for solving the priority inversion problem, select the correct answer:

(a) A task retains a boosted priority only while it is holding a shared resource also used by a higher priority task.
(b) With the Immediate Priority Ceiling Protocol (IPCP), a task cannot start executing unless all the resources it will during its first execution phase are free.
(c) A periodic task using IPCP can never be interrupted.
(d) With the Priority Inheritance Protocol, a high-priority task may be blocked by lower-priority tasks, but only once per execution cycle.
(e) IPCP is always more efficient than Original Priority Ceiling Protocol (OPCP).

Bibliography

1. G. Agha, Concurrent object-oriented programming. Commun. ACM **33**(9), 35–36 (1990)
2. G.R. Andrews, *Concurrent Programming: Principles and Practice* (Benjamin Cummings, Redwood City, CA, 1991)
3. G.R. Andrews, *Foundations of Multithreaded, Parallel, and Distributed Programming* (Benjamin Cummings, Redwood City, CA, 1999)
4. K. Arnold, J. Gosling, *The Java Programming Language* (Addison-Wesley, New York, 2005)
5. J. Barnes, *Programming in Ada. Plus an Overview of Ada 9X* (Addison-Wesley, New York, 1994)
6. M. Ben-Ari, *Principles of Concurrent and Distributed Programming*, 2nd edn. (Addison-Wesley, New York, 2006)
7. A. Birrel, B. Nelson, Implementing remote procedure calls. ACM Trans. Comput. Syst. **2**(1), 39–59 (1984)
8. P. Brinch-Hansen, The programming language Concurrent Pascal. IEEE Trans. Softw. Eng. **1**(2), 199–207 (1975)
9. P. Brinch-Hansen, *The Architecture of Concurrent Programs* (Prentice-Hall, Englewood Cliffs, 1977)
10. P. Brinch-Hansen, *The Origin of Concurrent Programming: From Semaphores to Remote Procedures Calls* (Springer, New York, 2002)
11. A. Burns, *Sistemas de Tiempo Real y Lenguajes de Programación* (Addison-Wesley/Pearson Education, Madrid, 2003)
12. G.C. Buttazzo, *Hard Real-Time Computing Systems: Predictable Algorithms and Applications* (Springer, New York, 2005)
13. Manuel I. Capel, *Programación Concurrente y en Tiempo Real* (Ibergarceta Publicaciones, Madrid, Spain 2022)
14. A.M.K. Cheng, *Real-Time Systems: Scheduling, Analysis and Verification* (Wiley, Hoboken, NJ, 2002)
15. O.J. Dahl, B. Myhrhaug, K. Nygaard, *SIMULA: Common Base Language* (Norwegian Computing Center, Oslo, 1970)
16. E.W. Dijkstra, Solution of a problem in concurrent programming control. Commun. ACM **8**(9), 569 (1965)
17. E.W. Dijkstra, Hierarchical ordering of sequential processes. Acta Informatica **1**, 115–138 (1971)
18. E.W. Dijkstra, Guarded commands, nondeterminacy, and formal derivation of programs. Commun. ACM **1**(1), 453–457 (1975)

© The Editor(s) (if applicable) and The Author(s), under exclusive license to Springer Nature Switzerland AG 2026
M. I. Capel, *Concurrent and Real-time Programming*,
https://doi.org/10.1007/978-3-031-85233-6

19. M.A. Eisenberg, M.R. McGuire, Further comments on Dijkstra's concurrent programming control problem. Commun. ACM **15**(11), 999 (1972)
20. N. Gehani, W. Roome, Concurrent C. Softw. Pract. Exp. **16**(9), 821–844 (1986)
21. N. Gehani, W. Roome, Rendezvous facilities: Concurrent C and the Ada language. IEEE Trans. Softw. Eng. **14**(11), 1546–1553 (1988)
22. N. Gehani, Message passing in Concurrent C: synchronous vs. asynchronous. Softw. Pract. Exp. **20**(6), 571–592 (1990)
23. S. Hartley, *Concurrent Programming: The Java Programming Language* (Oxford University Press, Oxford, 1998)
24. C.A.R. Hoare, Monitors: an operating system structuring concept. Commun. ACM **10**(1), 549 (1974)
25. C.A.R. Hoare, *Communicating Sequential Processes* (Prentice-Hall, 1985)
26. R.C. Holt, *Concurrent Euclid, The UNIX System and Tunis* (Addison-Wesley, Reading, MA, 1983)
27. R.C. Holt, P. Matthews, J.A. Roselet, J.R. Cordy, *The Turing Programming Language: Design and Definition* (Prentice-Hall, Englewood Cliffs, 1987)
28. D.E. Knuth, Additional comments on a problem in concurrent programming control. Commun. ACM **9**(5), 321–322 (1966)
29. INMOS Ltd., *Occam Programming Manual* (Prentice-Hall, 1984)
30. L. Lamport, A new solution of Dijkstra's concurrent programming problem. Commun. ACM **17**(8), 453–455 (1974)
31. B.W. Lampson, D.D. Redell, Experience with processes and monitors in Mesa. Commun. ACM **23**(2), 105–117 (1980)
32. D. Lea, *Programación Concurrente en Java: Principios y Patrones de Diseño* (Addison-Wesley/Pearson Education, 2001)
33. A. Lister, The problem of nested monitor calls. Oper. Syst. Rev. **11**(3), 5–7 (1977)
34. C.L. Liu, J.W. Layland, Scheduling algorithms for multiprogramming in a hard real-time environment. J. ACM **20**(1), 46–61 (1973)
35. R. Milner, *A Calculus of Communicating Systems*, Lecture Notes on Computer Science, vol 92(1) (Springer, 1980)
36. G. Nelson, *Systems Programming with Modula-3* (Prentice-Hall, 1991)
37. D. Parnas, The non-problem of nested monitor calls. ACM SIGOPS Oper. Syst. Rev. **12**(1), 12–18 (1978)
38. G.L. Peterson, A new solution to Lamport's concurrent programming problem using small shared variables. Trans. Programm. Lang. Syst. **5**(1), 56–65 (1983)
39. M. Raynal, *Algorithms for Mutual Exclusión* (North-Oxford Academic Publishers, London, 1986)
40. M. Raynal, *Distributed Algorithms and Protocols* (John Wiley, Hoboken, NJ, 1988)
41. N. Santoro, *Design and Analysis of Distributed Algorithms* (John Wiley, Hoboken, NJ, 2006)
42. F. Schneider, G. Andrews, Concepts for concurrent programming, in *Current Trends in Concurrency*, Lecture Notes on Computer Science, vol. 224(1), (Springer, New York, 1986)
43. M. Snir, S. Otto, S. Huss-Lederman, D. Walker, J. Dongarra, *MPI: The Complete Reference* (The MIT Press, Cambridge, MA, 1999)
44. J. Stankovic, Misconceptions about real-time computing: a serious problem for the next generation systems. IEEE Comput. **21**(10), 10–19 (1988)
45. J. Udding, Absence of individual starvation using weak semaphores. Inf. Process. Lett. **23**(3), 159–162 (1986)
46. A. Wellings, *Concurrent and Real-Time Programming in Java* (John Wiley, Hoboken, NJ, 2004)
47. J. Welsh, D.W. Bustard, Pascal-Plus: another language for modular multiprogramming. Softw. Pract. Exp. **9**(1), 947–957 (1979)

48. N. Wirth, *Programming in Modula-2* (Springer, 1985)
49. W. Wulf, Performance monitors for multiprogramming systems, in *2nd ACM Symposium on Operating Systems Principles*, (1969)
50. A. Yonezaba, Analysis of inheritance anomaly in object-oriented concurrent programming languages, in *Research Directions in Concurrent Object-Oriented Programming*, ed. by G. Agha, P. Wegner, A. Yonezawa, (The MIT Press, 1993)

MIX
Papier aus verantwortungsvollen Quellen
Paper from responsible sources
FSC® C105338

If you have any concerns about our products,
you can contact us on
ProductSafety@springernature.com

In case Publisher is established outside the EU,
the EU authorized representative is:
**Springer Nature Customer Service Center GmbH
Europaplatz 3, 69115 Heidelberg, Germany**

Printed by Libri Plureos GmbH
in Hamburg, Germany